Teach Yourself®
the Internet

Teach Yourself®
the Internet

David Crowder and Rhonda Crowder

IDG Books Worldwide, Inc.

An International Data Group Company

Foster City, CA • Chicago, IL • Indianapolis, IN • New York, NY

Teach Yourself® the Internet

Published by
IDG Books Worldwide, Inc.
An International Data Group Company
919 E. Hillsdale Blvd., Suite 400
Foster City, CA 94404
`www.idgbooks.com` (IDG Books Worldwide Web site)

Library of Congress Catalog Card Number: 98-87906

ISBN: 0-7645-7505-8

Printed in the United States of America

10 9 8 7 6 5 4 3

1E/RW/RR/ZY/IN

Distributed in the United States by IDG Books Worldwide, Inc.

Distributed by Macmillan Canada for Canada; by Transworld Publishers Limited in the United Kingdom; by IDG Norge Books for Norway; by IDG Sweden Books for Sweden; by Woodslane Pty. Ltd. for Australia; by Woodslane (NZ) Ltd. for New Zealand; by Addison Wesley Longman Singapore Pte Ltd. for Singapore, Malaysia, Thailand, Indonesia, and Korea; by Norma Comunicaciones S.A. for Colombia; by Intersoft for South Africa; by International Thomson Publishing for Germany, Austria, and Switzerland; by Toppan Company Ltd. for Japan; by Distribuidora Cuspide for Argentina; by Livraria Cultura for Brazil; by Ediciencia S.A. for Ecuador; by Ediciones ZETA S.C.R. Ltda. for Peru; by WS Computer Publishing Corporation, Inc., for the Philippines; by Unalis Corporation for Taiwan; by Contemporanea de Ediciones for Venezuela; by Computer Book & Magazine Store for Puerto Rico; by Express Computer Distributors for the Caribbean and West Indies. Authorized Sales Agent: Anthony Rudkin Associates for the Middle East and North Africa.

For general information on IDG Books Worldwide's books in the U.S., please call our Consumer Customer Service department at 800-762-2974. For reseller information, including discounts and premium sales, please call our Reseller Customer Service department at 800-434-3422.

For information on where to purchase IDG Books Worldwide's books outside the U.S., please contact our International Sales department at 317-596-5530 or fax 317-596-5692.

For consumer information on foreign language translations, please contact our Customer Service department at 800-434-3422, fax 317-596-5692, or e-mail rights@idgbooks.com.

For information on licensing foreign or domestic rights, please phone +1-650-655-3109.

For sales inquiries and special prices for bulk quantities, please contact our Sales department at 650-655-3200 or write to the address above.

For information on using IDG Books Worldwide's books in the classroom or for ordering examination copies, please contact our Educational Sales department at 800-434-2086 or fax 317-596-5499.

For press review copies, author interviews, or other publicity information, please contact our Public Relations department at 650-655-3000 or fax 650-655-3299.

For authorization to photocopy items for corporate, personal, or educational use, please contact Copyright Clearance Center, 222 Rosewood Drive, Danvers, MA 01923, or fax 978-750-4470.

 is a trademark under exclusive license to IDG Books Worldwide, Inc., from International Data Group, Inc.

ABOUT IDG BOOKS WORLDWIDE

Welcome to the world of IDG Books Worldwide.

IDG Books Worldwide, Inc., is a subsidiary of International Data Group, the world's largest publisher of computer-related information and the leading global provider of information services on information technology. IDG was founded more than 30 years ago by Patrick J. McGovern and now employs more than 9,000 people worldwide. IDG publishes more than 290 computer publications in over 75 countries. More than 90 million people read one or more IDG publications each month.

Launched in 1990, IDG Books Worldwide is today the #1 publisher of best-selling computer books in the United States. We are proud to have received eight awards from the Computer Press Association in recognition of editorial excellence and three from Computer Currents' First Annual Readers' Choice Awards. Our best-selling ...For Dummies® series has more than 50 million copies in print with translations in 31 languages. IDG Books Worldwide, through a joint venture with IDG's Hi-Tech Beijing, became the first U.S. publisher to publish a computer book in the People's Republic of China. In record time, IDG Books Worldwide has become the first choice for millions of readers around the world who want to learn how to better manage their businesses.

Our mission is simple: Every one of our books is designed to bring extra value and skill-building instructions to the reader. Our books are written by experts who understand and care about our readers. The knowledge base of our editorial staff comes from years of experience in publishing, education, and journalism — experience we use to produce books to carry us into the new millennium. In short, we care about books, so we attract the best people. We devote special attention to details such as audience, interior design, use of icons, and illustrations. And because we use an efficient process of authoring, editing, and desktop publishing our books electronically, we can spend more time ensuring superior content and less time on the technicalities of making books.

You can count on our commitment to deliver high-quality books at competitive prices on topics you want to read about. At IDG Books Worldwide, we continue in the IDG tradition of delivering quality for more than 30 years. You'll find no better book on a subject than one from IDG Books Worldwide.

John Kilcullen
Chairman and CEO
IDG Books Worldwide, Inc.

Steven Berkowitz
President and Publisher
IDG Books Worldwide, Inc.

WINNER

*Eighth Annual
Computer Press
Awards ≳1992*

WINNER

*Ninth Annual
Computer Press
Awards ≳1993*

WINNER

*Tenth Annual
Computer Press
Awards ≳1994*

WINNER

*Eleventh Annual
Computer Press
Awards ≳1995*

Credits

Acquisitions Editor
Andy Cummings

Development Editors
Philip Wescott, Tracy Brown

Technical Editor
Coletta Witherspoon

Copy Editor
Michael D. Welch

Project Coordinator
Regina Snyder

Book Designers
Daniel Ziegler Design, Cátálin Dulfu,
Kurt Krames

Layout and Graphics
Lou Boudreau, J. Tyler Connor,
Angela F. Hunckler, Brent Savage,
Kate Snell, Michael Sullivan

Proofreaders
Christine Berman, Nancy Price,
Rebecca Senninger, Janet M. Withers

Indexer
Liz Cunningham

About the Authors

David and **Rhonda Crowder** have been selling hypertext systems since the days when you had to explain what hypertext meant. They have been involved in the online community for over a decade, and David was sysop for the FidoNet BBS, Taliesin's Dream. They hypertexted the Dade County (Miami) version of the South Florida Building Code in the wake of Hurricane Andrew as an independent venture and were commissioned to do the Broward County (Fort Lauderdale) version afterward. They run Far Horizons Software, a Web site design firm, and created the LinkFinder and NetWelcome sites. LinkFinder holds a four-star rating from *NetGuide* magazine and NetWelcome is the recipient of several awards, including *NetGuide*'s Gold Site Award. David founded three Internet mailing lists: Delphi Talk (for Borland Delphi programmers), JavaScript Talk (for Web designers), and Java Talk (for Java programmers). The Crowders' book credits include *FrontPage 98 Unleashed*, *HTML 4.0 Unleashed Professional Reference Edition*, and *Dynamic Web Publishing Unleashed*.

To Cougar

Welcome to Teach Yourself

Welcome to Teach Yourself, a series read and trusted by millions for nearly a decade. Although you may have seen the Teach Yourself name on other books, ours is the original. In addition, no Teach Yourself series has ever delivered more on the promise of its name than this series. That's because IDG Books Worldwide recently transformed Teach Yourself into a new cutting-edge format that gives you all the information you need to learn quickly and easily.

Readers told us that they want to learn by doing and that they want to learn as much as they can in as short a time as possible. We listened to you and believe that our new task-by-task format and suite of learning tools deliver the book you need to successfully teach yourself any technology topic. Features such as our Personal Workbook, which helps you practice and reinforce the skills you've just learned, help ensure that you get full value out of the time you invest in your learning. Handy cross-references to related topics and online sites broaden your knowledge and give you control over the kind of information you want, when you want it.

More Answers . . .

In designing the latest incarnation of this series, we started with the premise that people like you, who are beginning to intermediate computer users, want to take control of their own learning. To do this, you need the proper tools to find answers to questions so you can solve problems now.

In designing a series of books that provide such tools, we created a unique and concise visual format. The added bonus: Teach Yourself books actually pack more information into their pages than other books written on the same subjects. Skill for skill, you typically get much more information in a Teach Yourself book. In fact, Teach Yourself books, on average, cover twice the skills covered by other computer books — as many as 125 skills per book — so they're more likely to address your specific needs.

WELCOME TO TEACH YOURSELF

...In Less Time

We know you don't want to spend twice the time to get all this great information, so we provide lots of time-saving features:

▶ A modular task-by-task organization of information: any task you want to perform is easy to find and includes simple-to-follow steps.

▶ A larger size than standard makes the book easy to read and convenient to use at a computer workstation. The large format also enables us to include many more illustrations — 500 screen illustrations show you how to get everything done!

▶ A Personal Workbook at the end of each chapter reinforces learning with extra practice, real-world applications for your learning, and questions and answers to test your knowledge.

▶ Cross-references appearing at the bottom of each task page refer you to related information, providing a path through the book for learning particular aspects of the software thoroughly.

▶ A Find It Online feature offers valuable ideas on where to go on the Internet to get more information or to download useful files.

▶ Take Note sidebars provide added-value information from our expert authors for more in-depth learning.

▶ An attractive, consistent organization of information helps you quickly find and learn the skills you need.

These Teach Yourself features are designed to help you learn the essential skills about a technology in the least amount of time, with the most benefit. We've placed these features consistently throughout the book, so you quickly learn where to go to find just the information you need — whether you work through the book from cover to cover or use it later to solve a new problem.

You will find a Teach Yourself book on almost any technology subject — from the Internet to Windows to Microsoft Office. Take control of your learning today, with IDG Books Worldwide's Teach Yourself series.

Teach Yourself
More Answers in Less Time

Go to this area if you want special tips, cautions, and notes that provide added insight into the current task.

Search through the task headings to find the topic you want right away. To learn a new skill, search the Contents, Chapter Opener, or the extensive index to find what you need. Then find — at a glance — the clear task heading that matches it.

Learn the concepts behind the task at hand and, more important, learn how the task is relevent in the real world. Time-saving suggestions and advice show you how to make the most of each skill.

After you learn the task at hand, you may have more questions, or you may want to read about other tasks related to that topic. Use the cross-references to find different tasks to make your learning more efficient.

Setting Your Home Page

The *home page* is the Web page that displays when you first start your Web browser. You can also return to your home page at any time, regardless of where you are on the Web, by clicking the Home button. Both Netscape Navigator and Microsoft Internet Explorer come preset with a home page for the respective company. *Web Portals*, a fancy name for popular home pages, function as marketing tools for many companies. Both Microsoft and Netscape, as well as other popular sites, think they will be able to get you to their home pages and then bombard you with advertising messages.

Don't worry — you can easily change your home page to anything you want. Some people set the home page to display their own personal Web page, others set it to a favorite site that they routinely visit, and some set it to an Internet search engine. Each approach has its advantages. Almost every personal Web page has a set of links to favorite sites; setting this as your home page lets you have a customized jumping-off point to the parts of the Web you like best. If you are going to be visiting a particular Web site over and over again, it may be advantageous to make it your home page. Making a search engine your home page lets you start off in a place that helps you find whatever you are looking for.

The first two figures on the facing page show you how to set the home page in Navigator and the last

two figures show how to do it in Internet Explorer. Both are very similar, although you'll find minor variations. To set the page you are viewing as your home page, for example, Navigator has a button that is labeled Use Current Page, whereas Internet Explorer has a button that is labeled Use Current.

TAKE NOTE

▶ **SEARCHING FOR LOCAL FILES**

Navigator lets you search your hard drive for a local file to use as your home page, whereas Internet Explorer doesn't have this option. To set a local file as your home page in Internet Explorer, first display it and then click the Use Current button. The last task in this chapter tells you how to display local files.

▶ **USING BLANK PAGES**

Both browsers let you specify a blank page as your home page, although there seems to be no sensible reason why anyone would wish to do so.

▶ **STARTING WITH LAST PAGE VISITED**

Navigator has an option to start up, not with your home page, but with the last Web page you viewed in a previous session. To choose this option, click Last Page Visited under the heading Navigator Starts With (see the top right figure).

CROSS-REFERENCE

See Chapter 3 for more information on search engines.

FIND IT ONLINE

The Excite search engine at http://www.excite.com/ is a very popular home page.

Use the Find It Online element to locate Internet resources that provide more background, take you on interesting side trips, and offer additional tools for mastering and using the skills you need. (Occasionally you'll find a handy shortcut here.)

WELCOME TO TEACH YOURSELF

The current chapter name and number always appear in the top right-hand corner of every task spread, so you always know exactly where you are in the book.

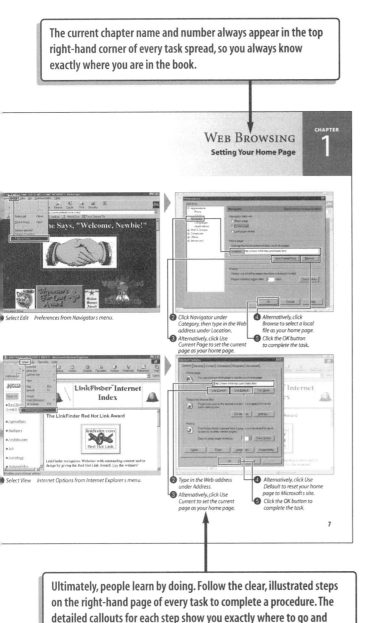

Who This Book Is For

This book is written for you, a beginning to intermediate PC user who isn't afraid to take charge of his or her own learning experience. You don't want a lot of technical jargon; you *do* want to learn as much about PC technology as you can in a limited amount of time. You need a book that is straightforward, easy to follow, and logically organized, so you can find answers to your questions easily. And, you appreciate simple-to-use tools such as handy cross-references and visual step-by-step procedures that help you make the most of your learning. We have created the unique Teach Yourself format specifically to meet your needs.

Ultimately, people learn by doing. Follow the clear, illustrated steps on the right-hand page of every task to complete a procedure. The detailed callouts for each step show you exactly where to go and what to do to complete the task.

Personal Workbook

It's a well-known fact that much of what we learn is lost soon after we learn it if we don't reinforce our newly acquired skills with practice and repetition. That's why each Teach Yourself chapter ends with your own Personal Workbook. Here's where you can get extra practice, test your knowledge, and discover ideas for using what you've learned in the real world. There's even a visual quiz to help you remember your way around the topic's software environment.

Feedback

Please let us know what you think about this book, and whether you have any suggestions for improvements. You can send questions and comments to the Teach Yourself editors on the IDG Books Worldwide Web site at **www.idgbooks.com**.

Personal Workbook

Q&A

1 What does *HTML* stand for?

2 What is a *home page*?

3 What are the three kinds of hyperlinks?

4 What does *session history* mean?

5 What does *URL* stand for?

6 What is the difference between *bookmarks* and *favorites*?

7 What is a collection of Web pages called?

8 What are the two most popular Web browsers?

ANSWERS: PAGE 374

20

After working through the tasks in each chapter, you can test your progress and reinforce your learning by answering the questions in the Q&A. Then check your answers in the Personal Workbook Answers appendix at the back of the book.

Another practical way to reinforce your skills is to do additional exercises on the same skills you just learned without the benefit of the chapter's visual steps. If you struggle with any of these exercises, it's a good idea to refer to the chapter's tasks to be sure you've mastered them.

WEB BROWSING
Personal Workbook

CHAPTER 1

Read the list of Real-World Applications to get ideas on how you can use the skills you've just learned in your everyday life. Understanding a process can be simple; knowing how to use that process to make you more productive is the key to successful learning.

EXTRA PRACTICE

1. Display a History list in Internet Explorer or Navigator.

2. Visit a Web site and set a page on it to be your home page.

3. Go to the **cnn.com** site by typing in the address.

4. Bookmark a site and return to it later from another site.

5. Use the Back and Forward buttons to move between two Web pages.

6. Go to the site at **http://www.vtourist.com/ webmap/usa.htm** and use the image map.

REAL-WORLD APPLICATIONS

If you are watching Geraldo Rivera on TV and he mentions a Web site run by *Salon* magazine, you could go to your computer and type **http:// www.salonmagazine.com/** into your browser, and then go to the site and read the referenced articles.

A friend hands you a floppy disk with a copy of his Web site on it and asks you for your critique. You could open the files and view the Web pages.

You might be researching a term paper and, late at night, find several sites relating to your subject matter. You could bookmark all of them for later perusal.

You might find a new search engine that has a more pleasing interface than the one you've been using as your home page. You could set the new one as your home page.

Visual Quiz

The item on the right side of the screen is a shameless plug. What is the one on the left side? How do you display it? How do you hide it?

Take the Visual Quiz to see how well you're learning your way around the technology. Learning about computers is often as much about how to find a button or menu as it is about memorizing definitions. Our Visual Quiz helps you find your way.

21

Acknowledgments

Thanks to Andy Cummings, Chip Wescott, Michael Welch, and Coletta Witherspoon of IDG Books Worldwide, and to our agent, David Fugate of Waterside Productions. Thanks also to Andrea Burnett and Stephanie Rodriguez of the IDG Books publicity department who made sure everything ran smoothly. No book ever reaches the shelves without a lot of work by a lot of different people, all pooling their unique talents and perspectives over a long period of time. We're thankful that we've been able to work with some of the best. Space doesn't permit us to list everyone who helped make this book a reality, but we thank you all.

Contents

Contents

CONTENTS

CONTENTS

Contents

PART

I

The World Wide Web

This part introduces you to the World Wide Web, how it works, and how to use it. We cover both Netscape's Navigator Web browser that's part of the company's Communicator suite of programs and Microsoft's Internet Explorer, showing you the strengths and weaknesses of both browsers.

In clear language that's easy to understand, this part demystifies topics such as following links from one Web page to another, understanding Web addresses, and bookmarking your favorite sites so you can easily return to them whenever you want.

We also show you how to make copies of Web text and images on both paper and disk, how to download programs from the Web, and how to use the Web for secure transactions.

Next, you'll see how to find what you're looking for on the Internet, from finding a particular phrase on a Web page to searching the entire World Wide Web using different kinds of online search engines and Internet indexes.

Finally, we tell you how to customize your Web browser so it works exactly the way you want it to. You'll see how you can take control of your Web experience by setting colors and text size to your preferences, controlling how your browser prints Web pages, speeding up your Web surfing, modifying your browser's toolbars to suit yourself, and lots more.

CHAPTER 1

MASTER THESE SKILLS

▶ Setting Your Home Page

▶ Using Hyperlinks

▶ Using the Back and Forward Buttons

▶ Using Go and the History Button

▶ Typing In Web Addresses

▶ Bookmarking a Site and Returning to It

▶ Opening Local Files

Web Browsing

The World Wide Web, also called the WWW or just "The Web," is the most versatile and appealing part of the Internet. Just about anything you can imagine can be found somewhere on the Web. If you need information for a term paper on Möbius strips, you'll find it. If you want to check out stock prices, they're there. If you don't have a window view in your office, you can look through your computer screen at live beach shots of Hawaii or Australia.

The Web is composed of millions of parts called *Web sites,* all of which are interconnected to form the largest electronic database in the world. Each Web site is made up of at least one *Web page,* the basic element of the WWW. To say that Web pages are basically collections of text and images is like saying that a Rembrandt is a sheet of canvas with paint on it. The incredible diversity and beauty of design to be found on the Web is so addictive that many people find themselves spending endless hours poking into every nook and cranny of the Web.

Web pages are constructed using *Hypertext Markup Language (HTML).* Despite its intimidating name, HTML is a very simple and well-designed system that most people find very easy to use. Even if you're not going to put up your own Web page, though, you'll find that the Web is a wonderful place to explore.

To get onto the Web, you have to use a program called a *browser* that lets you view Web pages. The two most popular Web browsers today are Netscape Navigator and Microsoft Internet Explorer. Both are very similar in their basic functions, though each has its own unique features as well. Many people keep both programs on their computer. If you're already connected to the Internet, your Internet Service Provider (ISP) has doubtless supplied you with one or both of these browsers. They are also commonly available on CD-ROMs that accompany many computer books or that can be found in most computer stores. If you're a Microsoft Windows user, you probably already have Internet Explorer. The latest versions of browsers can also be downloaded from the companies' Internet sites — **http://www.netscape.com/** for Navigator and **http://www.microsoft.com/** for Internet Explorer. By the time you get this book, both browsers should be in version 5 (or close to it).

Setting Your Home Page

The *home page* is the Web page that displays when you first start your Web browser. You can also return to your home page at any time, regardless of where you are on the Web, by clicking the Home button. Both Netscape Navigator and Microsoft Internet Explorer come preset with a home page for the respective company. *Web Portals*, a fancy name for popular home pages, function as marketing tools for many companies. Both Microsoft and Netscape, as well as other popular sites, think they will be able to get you to their home pages and then bombard you with advertising messages.

Don't worry — you can easily change your home page to anything you want. Some people set the home page to display their own personal Web page, others set it to a favorite site that they routinely visit, and some set it to an Internet search engine. Each approach has its advantages. Almost every personal Web page has a set of links to favorite sites; setting this as your home page lets you have a customized jumping-off point to the parts of the Web you like best. If you are going to be visiting a particular Web site over and over again, it may be advantageous to make it your home page. Making a search engine your home page lets you start off in a place that helps you find whatever you are looking for.

The first two figures on the facing page show you how to set the home page in Navigator and the last two figures show how to do it in Internet Explorer. Both are very similar, although you'll find minor variations. To set the page you are viewing as your home page, for example, Navigator has a button that is labeled Use Current Page, whereas Internet Explorer has a button that is labeled Use Current.

TAKE NOTE

▶ SEARCHING FOR LOCAL FILES

Navigator lets you search your hard drive for a local file to use as your home page, whereas Internet Explorer doesn't have this option. To set a local file as your home page in Internet Explorer, first display it and then click the Use Current button. The last task in this chapter tells you how to display local files.

▶ USING BLANK PAGES

Both browsers let you specify a blank page as your home page, although there seems to be no sensible reason why anyone would wish to do so.

▶ STARTING WITH LAST PAGE VISITED

Navigator has an option to start up, not with your home page, but with the last Web page you viewed in a previous session. To choose this option, click Last Page Visited under the heading Navigator Starts With (see the top right figure).

CROSS-REFERENCE

See Chapter 3 for more information on search engines.

FIND IT ONLINE

The Excite search engine at **http://www.excite.com/** is a very popular home page.

① Select Edit ⇨Preferences from Navigator's menu.

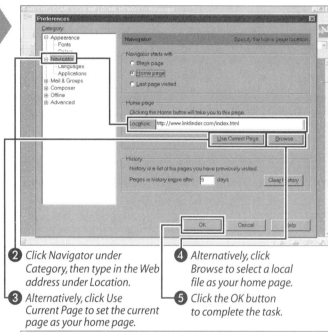

② Click Navigator under Category, then type in the Web address under Location.

③ Alternatively, click Use Current Page to set the current page as your home page.

④ Alternatively, click Browse to select a local file as your home page.

⑤ Click the OK button to complete the task.

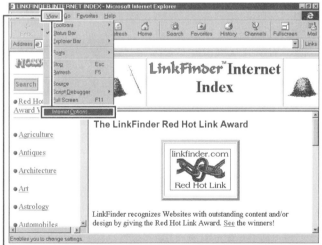

① Select View ⇨ Internet Options from Internet Explorer's menu.

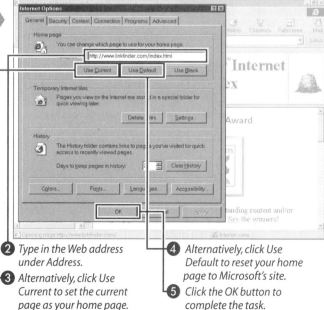

② Type in the Web address under Address.

③ Alternatively, click Use Current to set the current page as your home page.

④ Alternatively, click Use Default to reset your home page to Microsoft's site.

⑤ Click the OK button to complete the task.

Using Hyperlinks

yperlinks (often just called *links*) are the connections between Web pages. Links are the heart of the World Wide Web. Clicking a link takes you from the page you are viewing to another page, or perhaps to an image. Links can also be used to play sounds, movies, or to let you download a file. They are usually text, and are normally displayed as blue, underlined words, as shown in the figure on the top left. The color of a link changes to purple once you have visited it. This color change helps you keep track of which links you have and haven't been to. However, as you surf the Web, you will doubtless run across many variations on the standard approach. Among the most common are *image links* and *image maps*.

Images are any graphic, ranging from photographs to drawings. Regular images just appear, unadorned, on the Web page you are viewing. Image links, though, are outlined in a blue rectangle, thus helping you recognize them as such. The figure on the top right shows an image link. With both text and image links, you simply click the link to go to a new page.

Image maps are not outlined in blue, but are usually recognizable due to the fact that they are composed of a variety of separate images grouped together, with each different image holding an obvious meaning. Many image maps are actual geographical maps, just like you would see in an atlas. You may, for instance, run across an image map of the United States like the one in the figure on the bottom left. Clicking one of the states might take you to information about a company's offices and plants in that state. If you wonder if an image is an image map or not, just run your mouse across it and observe the changes in the status line of your browser. If it is an image map, different Web addresses appear in the status line as you move the mouse pointer across the image map.

It is possible for Web designers to create links that do not look like the normal ones, and you will often find these on Web sites that use a magazine style for their layout, like the one in the figure on the bottom right. A basic rule is, if it looks like a table of contents, it's a set of links. To be certain, just move your pointer over a suspected link and see if a Web address appears in your status line.

TAKE NOTE

▶ COPING WITH NONSTANDARD LINKS

It is possible for Web designers to create links that do not look like normal ones, and you will often find these on Web sites that use a magazine style for their layout, such as the one in the fourth figure. A basic rule: If it looks like a table of contents, it's a set of links. To be certain, just move your pointer over a suspected link and see if a Web address appears in your status line.

CROSS-REFERENCE

For more on links, see Chapter 17.

FIND IT ONLINE

One of the best image map creation tools is CoffeeCup Image Mapper ++ at **http://www.coffecup.com/**.

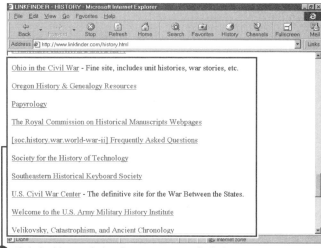

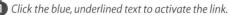

❶ *Click the blue, underlined text to activate the link.*

❷ *Click the blue outlined image to activate the link.*

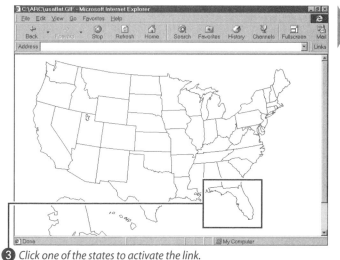

❸ *Click one of the states to activate the link.*

❹ *Click part of the table of contents to activate the link.*

Using the Back and Forward Buttons

Web browsers keep track of where you've been, enabling you to retrace your steps without having to click prepared links. The Back button takes you back along the trail you followed to reach your current Web page, and the Forward button lets you change your mind and go forward again until you reach the last page you visited. For example, say you start at your home page, follow a link to a second site, and then follow a link from there to a third site. If you click the Back button once, it takes you from the third site to the second site; one more click of the Back button returns you to your home page. If you then click the Forward button once, it takes you again to the second page; one more click of the Forward button takes you to the third page.

When you first launch your Web browser, both the Back and Forward buttons are grayed out, indicating that they are not available for use, as shown in the figure on the top left. This is because, at this point, you haven't gone anywhere in this Web-surfing session. There is no site to go back to, nor one to go forward to. The first time you link to another site, however, the Back button becomes active and available, as shown in the figure on the top right, because there is now someplace you can go back to. The Forward button is still unavailable, because there is no site to go forward to. If, however, you use the Back button to return to your home page, the Forward

button becomes available and the Back button grays out again, as shown in the figure on the bottom left. This is because you now have the option of going forward to the site you had visited, but there is no place to go backward to. With only these two sites in the browser's memory, each one is the end of the line at one end or the other.

In a normal Web-surfing session, you will probably go to more than one site, though, and the Back and Forward buttons are both available through every site except the first and last, as shown in the figure on the bottom right.

TAKE NOTE

▶ GETTING OUT OF DEAD ENDS

The humble Back button suddenly becomes a life-saver when you run into a bad link. Web sites come and go all the time, and you will run into the dreaded "404 File Not Found" error sooner or later. Just sigh, hit the Back button, and go on about your way.

▶ LINEAR THINKING

It can sometimes be a bit confusing to keep track of what's "back." If you've just used the Back button, then you reach the previous page you visited by clicking the Forward button.

CROSS-REFERENCE

See the next task on history lists for more information.

FIND IT ONLINE

NetWelcome at **http://www.netwelcome.com/** is a good place to learn about the Web.

① *Both the Back and Forward buttons are grayed out at the start of a session.*

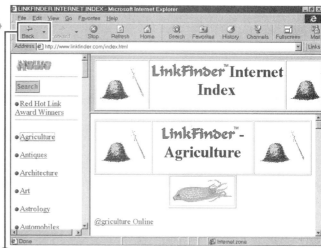

② *Click a link and the Back button becomes available.*

③ *Click the Back button to return to your home page and the Forward button activates.*

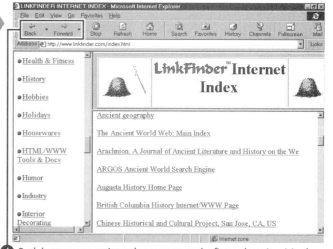

④ *Both buttons are active unless you are at the first or last site visited.*

Using Go and the History Button

You already know, from the section on the Back and Forward buttons, that your Web browser keeps track of where you've visited. What if you want to return to a site that is eight or nine steps back, though? Do you have to hit the Back button again and again, waiting for all those Web pages to display along the way? Fortunately, the answer is no. In Navigator, you just click Go in the menu, and a list of all the pages you've visited in the current session drops down, as shown in the figure on the top left. Simply click the one you want to go to, and you're instantly there without having to go through all the intervening steps.

Internet Explorer has a more involved and sophisticated approach to the session history. Clicking the History button brings up a listing, not only of the current session, but of every place you've been for the last month. To keep things manageable, only the sites from today's surfing are initially displayed. The earlier days in the same week are available for expansion at the click of a mouse button, as are the sites visited during each of the previous weeks. If you've been to lots of sites in the current session, you will have to scroll the listing up and down to view them all. The History listing is built along the lines of file folders, much like those on your hard drive. Each Web site you've been to makes one folder, and the contents of that folder are the individual Web pages you've visited within that Web site.

TAKE NOTE

USING THE OTHER GO

Internet Explorer also has a Go menu, but it does not activate a list of sites you have visited. Instead, it takes you to specific destinations: Forward, Back, and Up one level. You can also use it to go to your designated Home Page, the Channel Guide, or Search the Web. The Go menu can also take you to Mail, News, and My Computer.

UNDERSTANDING SITE ORDER

The session history in Navigator appears in the reverse order in which you visited the sites, with the most recently visited site at the top of the list and the earliest visited at the bottom. In Internet Explorer, the visited sites are listed alphabetically, without regard to the order in which you visited them.

ENCOUNTERING STICKY SCROLLING

Internet Explorer has a minor glitch in the history list. When you scroll the visitation history up and down, the scrolling works smoothly only when you are not at the beginning or end of the history list. When you reach the bottom of the list, the last item shown will be partially covered by a gray bar that disappears when you move your mouse away from the scrolling arrow. The same is true of the reverse situation, when you scroll to the top of the history list and the first item is obscured.

CROSS-REFERENCE

See the preceding task on the Back and Forward buttons for more information.

FIND IT ONLINE

You can find Netscape support at **http://help.netscape. com/products/client/communicator/index.html**.

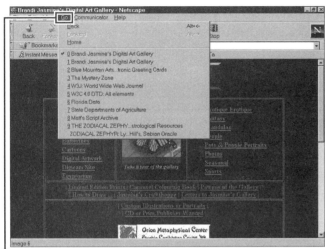

① In Navigator, select Go from the menu, and then click the site to which you want to jump.

① In Internet Explorer, click the History button.

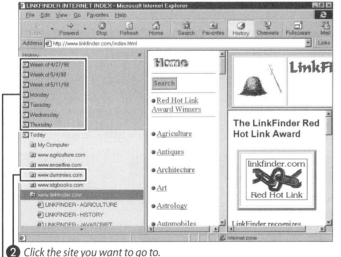

② Click the site you want to go to.

③ To bring up expanded site listings from earlier days and weeks, click the notation for that time.

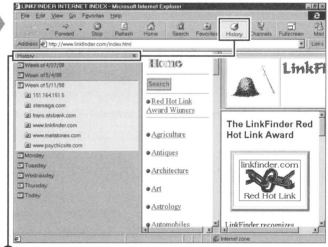

④ To close the history listing, either click the X or click the History button again.

Typing In Web Addresses

Both browsers have a white rectangle under the toolbar where they show the current Web address of the page you are viewing. In Navigator, it's labeled Location and in Internet Explorer, it's labeled Address. Regardless of what it's called, not only can you view the address there, but you can type one in as well. This is very useful if you see a Web address in some non-Internet medium such as a TV ad or a business card and wish to visit the Web site.

A full Web address includes several elements. For instance, the technically proper Web address for idgbooks.com is **http://www.idgbooks.com/**. You don't need to type the whole thing, though. Both Web browsers are smart enough to add the technical details. Just type **idgbooks** and hit the Enter key. The browser adds all the rest for you. The only time this doesn't work is with the relatively small number of Web sites that use an ending other than .com, such as .org, .edu, and so forth.

You also will find that, when typing in Web addresses, the browser will take over at some point and fill in the remaining portion for you. For example, if you visit the Excite search engine site at **http://www.excite.com/** and later begin to type in that address, you'll only get to the "e" in excite before the rest is automatically finished. Of course, if you've recently visited lots of sites that start with "e" or "ex,"

then you might have to type a few more letters before your browser can figure out which one of these you want.

TAKE NOTE

▶ **UNDERSTANING UNIFORM RESOURCE LOCATORS**

A Web address is technically known as a Uniform Resource Locator, or URL for short (some people pronounce it as "earl"). They are also sometimes referred to as Universal Resource Identifiers (URI), Universal Document Identifiers (UDI), and Uniform Resource Names (URN). Each one has a slightly different technical meaning, but are often used interchangeably. Sometimes the names get mixed up, even by professionals, so don't be surprised to hear a Uniform Resource Locator called a Universal Resource Locator or a Universal Resource Identifier called a Uniform Resource Identifier. For practical purposes, just stick with URL and you'll be fine.

▶ **SWITCHING BROWSERS**

If you're using one browser and run across a Web page that uses features only available in the other one, just copy the Web address from the browser you're using, start up the other one, and paste the Web address into the edit box of the second browser. Then just hit the Enter key (or double-click the address). The second browser will jump directly to the Web site you want to view with it.

CROSS-REFERENCE
See Opening Local Files later in this chapter.

FIND IT ONLINE
Technical information on URLs can be found at **http://www.w3.org/TR/WD-html40-970708/htmlweb.html**.

Breaking Out of Frames

When you are visiting a Web site that uses frames and click a link to another Web site, you will normally just go to the second site. Poor Web site design, however, can sometimes cause the second site to be displayed within the frames of the first one. If this happens to you, just click your Back button to return to the page you clicked the link from. Next, click in the Location (or Address) box, then place your mouse pointer over the link to the site you want to visit. The address will appear in your status line. Type it into the Location box and hit the Enter key to go to the new site.

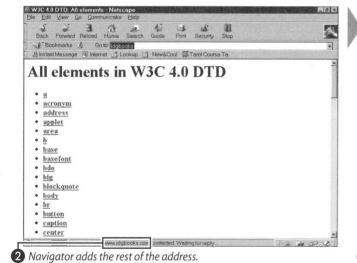

❶ Type in the partial address **idgbooks**.

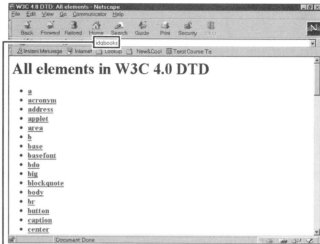

❷ Navigator adds the rest of the address.

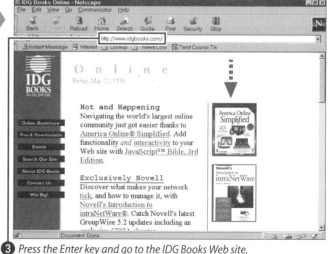

❸ Press the Enter key and go to the IDG Books Web site.

Bookmarking a Site and Returning to It

When you find a Web site you particularly like, you can always get back to it by remembering its Web address and typing it in later. Or you can recall what other sites you visited that led you to it and attempt to follow the trail again, or use a search engine to relocate it. Fortunately for all of us, there's a much easier way to do this — just tell your browser to remember the site. Both Navigator and Internet Explorer keep lists of sites you want to remember.

Navigator uses the "bookmark" metaphor, whereas Internet Explorer calls it a "favorites" list. Either way, it's one of the most useful parts of any Web browser — one you'll find yourself using over and over again. Navigator has a straightforward interface, but Internet Explorer's is a bit confusing. In Navigator, you click the Bookmarks icon, as shown in the first figure on the next page, and then follow the steps listed. Internet Explorer, though, actually has two different Favorites interfaces, one as a button and the other as a menu item. This is not just a routine case of a menu option duplicating a button function. The Favorites button acts exactly like the History button. It brings up a list of your bookmarked sites, but won't let you add a new one. This enables you to conveniently navigate to several of your favorite sites, without having to constantly return to the menu. To close this feature, just click the X in the upper right-hand corner of its pane. To add a new bookmark site, you must use the Favorites menu item instead.

TAKE NOTE

► STICKY SCROLLING AGAIN

Just as with the History listing, the top and bottom items in the Favorites listing (when accessed by the button method) are obscured when scrolling until you move the mouse pointer off them.

► LOOKING AT MORE BOOKMARKS

With Internet Explorer, you simply scroll the listing of bookmarks just like the History list. With Navigator, however, excess bookmarks are accessed by clicking More Bookmarks at the bottom of the bookmark list. The extended listing this action brings up acts a little bit differently from the usual bookmarks. Although you just single-click the regular bookmarks to activate them and go to the bookmarked site, the ones in the extended list require a double-click to activate.

► REVISITING SITE ORDER

The default site order differs between the two browsers. Internet Explorer displays favorites in alphabetical order (in both versions), whereas Navigator displays them in the order they were added.

CROSS-REFERENCE
See the earlier section on the History button.

FIND IT ONLINE
You can find help for Microsoft Internet Explorer at http://support.microsoft.com/support/c.asp?PR=IE&FR=0.

❶ In Navigator, click the Bookmark icon.

❷ To add a site to the listing, click Add Bookmark.

❸ To go to a bookmarked site, click the site's name.

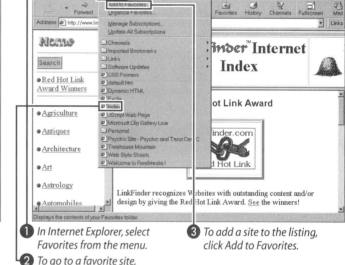

❶ In Internet Explorer, select Favorites from the menu.

❷ To go to a favorite site, click the site's name.

❸ To add a site to the listing, click Add to Favorites.

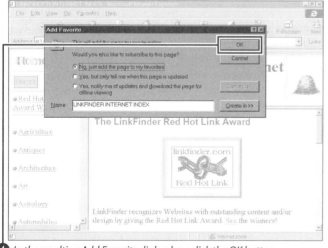

❹ In the resulting Add Favorite dialog box, click the OK button.

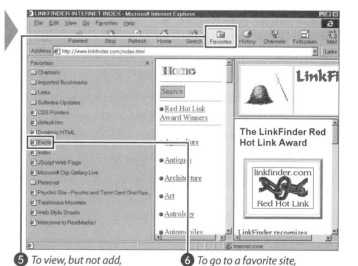

❺ To view, but not add, favorites, click the Favorites button.

❻ To go to a favorite site, click the site's name.

Opening Local Files

Not every Web page is on the World Wide Web. Some of them are on your hard drive or even on a floppy disk. It may be that you have created your own and want to look at it, or perhaps you've downloaded one from someone else's site. It's increasingly common these days for Web pages to be included on a disk or CD-ROM as a type of electronic catalog or brochure.

The addresses for such local files follow a different format than those you find on the Web. Instead of starting with "http" and naming a server, the URL contains the path to the specific file on your computer. Internet Explorer displays the path much like Windows Explorer, with the drive name, a colon, and a backslash preceding the folders and subfolders. Navigator places "file:///" before the full path to indicate that the document you are viewing is a local file rather than a Web page.

The process of opening local files is virtually identical in both Navigator and Internet Explorer. In both programs, it's a three-step process, and only the second step differs slightly. You tell the browser you want to open a file, and then either type in the location of the file or browse your hard drive for it. When you find it, you select it and finish. The only differences between Navigator and Internet Explorer in this case are that Navigator has slightly different phrasing and one extra option that doesn't concern us here, and that Internet Explorer also has a drop-down list of previously opened files that Navigator lacks.

TAKE NOTE

▶ USING DOWNLOADED SITES

Many sites make compressed versions of themselves available for downloading and installation on your local drive. This lets you access a copy of the site without putting extra strain on their Web server resources. The links from page to page within the downloaded site still function normally in most cases. This is because most sites use just the name of the Web page's file as the Web address in links, instead of using the full URL (for instance, "music.html" instead of "http://www.soundoff.edu/music.html"). These types of Web addresses are called *relative URLs* and enable an entire Web site to be moved to a different server without affecting its functionality. In some cases, though, you may find that clicking a link on a local Web page leads you out into the World Wide Web instead of to another page on your own system. It's normal for some to do so, but if you find that every link does this, contact the Webmaster of the site and let them know that they seem to have used absolute URLs instead of relative ones.

▶ MIXING FILES

If you do keep copies of other Web sites on your hard drive, make sure to keep each one in its own distinct folder, or you will end up scrambling them together. For instance, the vast majority of Web sites call their main page *index.html,* and uncompressing two different sites into the same folder could cause a file overwrite.

CROSS-REFERENCE

See Setting Your Home Page in this chapter.

FIND IT ONLINE

An excellent example of a downloadable site can be found at **http://www2.dgsys.com/~bunning/top.htm.**

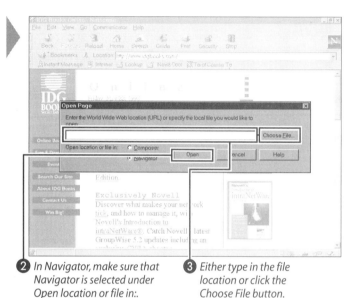

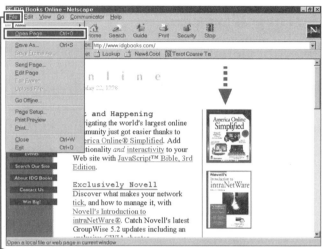

❶ *In Navigator, select File⇨Open Page from the menu.*

▪ *In Internet Explorer, select File⇨Open. See figure below.*

❷ *In Navigator, make sure that Navigator is selected under Open location or file in:.*

❸ *Either type in the file location or click the Choose File button.*

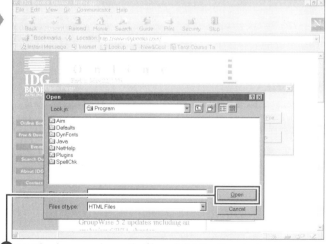

❹ *In Internet Explorer, either type in the file location or click the Browse button.*

❺ *In either browser, choose the file and click the Open button.*

Personal Workbook

Q&A

1 What does *HTML* stand for?

_____

_____

2 What is a *home page*?

_____

_____

_____

_____

3 What are the three kinds of hyperlinks?

_____

_____

_____

4 What does *session history* mean?

_____

_____

_____

_____

5 What does *URL* stand for?

_____

_____

6 What is the difference between *bookmarks* and *favorites*?

_____

_____

_____

_____

_____

_____

7 What is a collection of Web pages called?

_____

_____

8 What are the two most popular Web browsers?

_____

_____

ANSWERS: PAGE 376

EXTRA PRACTICE

1 Display a History list in Internet Explorer or Navigator.

2 Visit a Web site and set a page on it to be your home page.

3 Go to the **cnn.com** site by typing in the address.

4 Bookmark a site and return to it later from another site.

5 Use the Back and Forward buttons to move between two Web pages.

6 Go to the site at **http://www.vtourist.com/webmap/usa.htm** and use the image map.

REAL-WORLD APPLICATIONS

✔ If you are watching Geraldo Rivera on TV and he mentions a Web site run by *Salon* magazine, you could you go to your computer and type **http://www.salonmagazine.com/** into your browser, and then go to the site and read the referenced articles.

✔ A friend hands you a floppy disk with a copy of his Web site on it and asks you for your critique. You could open the files and view the Web pages.

✔ You might be researching a term paper and, late at night, find several sites relating to your subject matter. You could bookmark all of them for later perusal.

✔ You might find a new search engine that has a more pleasing interface than the one you've been using as your home page. You could set the new one as your home page.

Visual Quiz

The item on the right side of the screen is a shameless plug. What is the one on the left side? How do you display it? How do you hide it?

_____

_____

_____

_____

_____

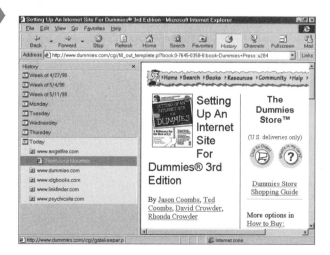

CHAPTER 2

MASTER THESE SKILLS

▶ **Printing Web Pages**

▶ **Copying and Pasting Web Text**

▶ **Saving Web Pages**

▶ **Saving Frames**

▶ **Saving Images**

▶ **Downloading Files**

▶ **Getting Plug-Ins**

▶ **Recognizing Secure Servers**

Advanced Web Browsing

Once you master the basics of moving around the World Wide Web, you'll quickly realize that there's a lot more to Web surfing than just reading and looking at pretty pictures. You'll soon be prompted to do more than simply *look* at what you discover. You can print the Web page, paste part of it into another program such as a word processor or e-mail program, and even save all or part of a Web site to your own hard drive or a floppy disk.

In addition to Web pages, other types of files are available on the World Wide Web, and you can download them at will. There are games and utilities, e-mail and graphics programs, and just about anything else you can name that you can get delivered right to your desktop via the Internet. Most software companies now make bug fixes and upgrades available via download from Internet sites, thus saving everyone lots of money and materials.

To keep up with emerging technology, browsers are designed to accept add-on programs called plug-ins that seamlessly extend their functionality. Popular plug-ins include Adobe Acrobat Reader for displaying documents created in other, non-HTML, formats, Crescendo and RealAudio for playing music clips, and Macromedia Shockwave for interactive multimedia. You can install them ahead of time, or you can just wait until you need them and get them then.

More and more as time goes on, you'll find yourself shopping online, cruising the Web looking for bargains and items you just can't find locally, even in large cities. If you can imagine it, it's somewhere in the world, and the world of today is the world of the Internet. The biggest shopping mall in history is being built today right on top of your desk, and electronic commerce, or *e-commerce*, is going to change the way we live. Secure transactions are essential, and you need to be able to protect yourself by recognizing when you are and aren't on a secure Web server.

Printing Web Pages

L et's say you find a humor page that contains jokes you want to share, or an interesting news item on the CNN site that you want to keep. Both Internet Explorer and Navigator make it easy to print such Web pages. To print a Web page in either Web browser, just hit the Print button. When printing in Navigator, you get a standard Windows Print options dialog box, as shown in the figure on the top right, that lets you change printer settings before you go ahead with the printing. In Internet Explorer, the page just prints right away without displaying any options. To get the Print options dialog box in Internet Explorer, select Print from the File menu.

The Print options dialog box in Internet Explorer, though, has quite a few more options than does the standard one, as shown in the figure on the bottom right. The top half is identical to the standard one, but the bottom half has special options relating to frames and links. The frame options let you print out the screen layout, one particular frame, or each frame separately.

Of the two options at the bottom of the dialog box, the first is dangerous and the second is really of use only to the designer of the Web page. The dangerous one, *Print all linked documents*, can be useful only if you mean to print out an entire Web site that you know well. Otherwise, you'd better have an awful lot of printer paper and a better-than-average

amount of patience, because a Web page may have thousands of links to other pages. If you're not familiar with the one you're printing, don't select this option.

The last option, *Print table of links*, does just that. In addition to printing the Web page, it prints a table that lists both the text of the link and the URL it links to. This provides a really useful tool for diagnostic or hardcopy backup purposes if you're responsible for the Web page in question. Exactly what use it is for a stranger visiting someone else's Web site is an open question.

TAKE NOTE

▶ **PRINTING FRAMES WITH INTERNET EXPLORER**

It's unfortunate that Internet Explorer, with its sophisticated frame printing options, can have problems printing a Web page with a complex frame layout. When you choose the *All frames individually* print option in printing complex layouts, the first couple of frames will be sent to the printer. At that point, and before the actual printing begins, an error message will inform you incorrectly that another program is using the printer and you have to close that program before trying to print this Web page again. Closing the error message box frees up the printer, and the first couple of frames will print, but the rest will not be sent to the printer at all.

CROSS-REFERENCE

See Chapter 4 for more information on printing preferences.

FIND IT ONLINE

You can find a site with frames at
http://www.linkfinder.com/.

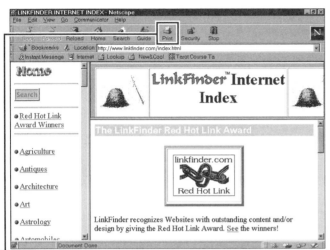

➊ In either browser, click the Print button.

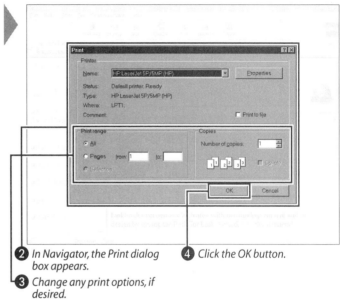

➋ In Navigator, the Print dialog box appears.

➌ Change any print options, if desired.

➍ Click the OK button.

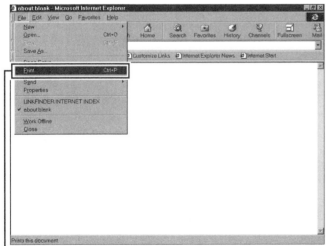

➎ In Internet Explorer, select File ➪ Print from the menu.

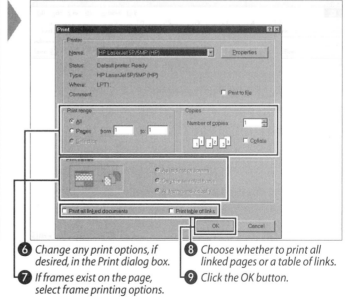

➏ Change any print options, if desired, in the Print dialog box.

➐ If frames exist on the page, select frame printing options.

➑ Choose whether to print all linked pages or a table of links.

➒ Click the OK button.

Copying and Pasting Web Text

I n the course of Web surfing, you may often find some quotation or factoid on a Web page that you want to include in a report. Or perhaps you want to e-mail it to a friend. Whatever your needs, the process is absolutely identical in both Navigator and Internet Explorer.

One thing you might notice is text that you copy and paste from a Web page to another program loses all its formatting along the way. If the words you copy are done up in large, red letters, they still show up as normal text when pasted into a word processor, just as though you had typed them from scratch. This is because the appearance of text on the World Wide Web is controlled by the HTML code that underlies the Web page display. The text itself is all that is transferred.

Some exceptions exist, however. More advanced word processors such as Microsoft Word often retain the HTML formatting, as these applications have been developed to interact with the Web. Regardless, it's best to assume that what you see on a Web page might not translate directly when pasted into other applications.

The same technique can be used to copy Web images. While text can be pasted into virtually every program known, though, images can only go into certain ones, such as graphics and word processing programs.

CROSS-REFERENCE

See Chapter 5 for more information on e-mail.

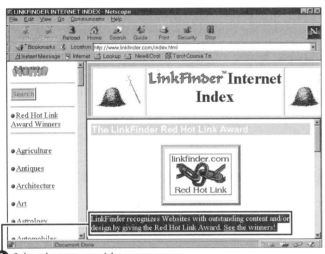

1 *Select the text you wish to copy.*

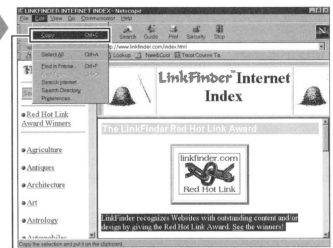

2 *Select Edit ➪ Copy from the menu.*

3 *Open the program you want to paste the text into.*
4 *Place the cursor where you want to insert the text.*

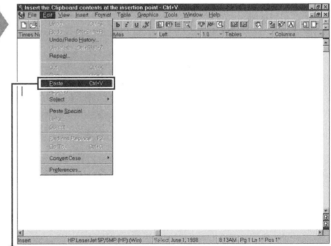

5 *Select Edit ➪ Paste from the menu.*

Saving Web Pages

At times you may need to keep information from a Web site handy so you can refer back to it frequently. To avoid reconnecting to the Internet and running into potential pitfalls such as busy signals and slow traffic, you can save Web pages to your hard drive. This way, you can work offline, but still have the information at your fingertips, complete with links — assuming you also download the pages that are linked to the main document.

If the author of the Web page you downloaded is well-organized, he or she will have implemented relative URLs. This way, as long as all of the pages are located in the same area of your hard drive, you won't get an error. Otherwise, you could end up with a "File Not Found" message in your browser.

In both browsers the menu options for saving files are the same, although the keyboard shortcuts are slightly different. There's no difference if you're using a mouse. Both function in the same manner and offer the same options. The Navigator version is used in the figures on the facing page, but you'll find no difference in the process. If you've ever used Windows before, you're no stranger to the basic method: If you don't want to save the file in the initially displayed folder, just navigate to the folder you want to save it in and click the Save button. The file name of the Web page is already listed, and you can change it if you wish before you save the file.

CROSS-REFERENCE
See Chapter 1 for how to open local HTML files.

FIND IT ONLINE
See **http://techweb.com/speed/tr_tip/tip1112.html** for tips on long file names with DOS and Windows 3.x.

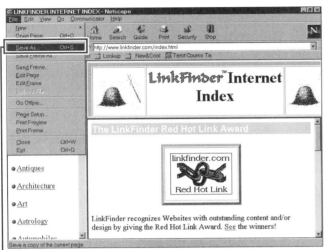

1 Select File ➪ Save As from the menu.

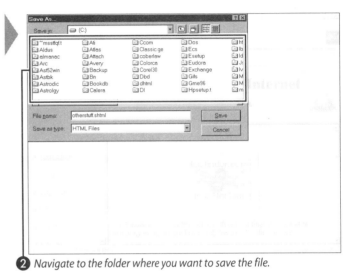

2 Navigate to the folder where you want to save the file.

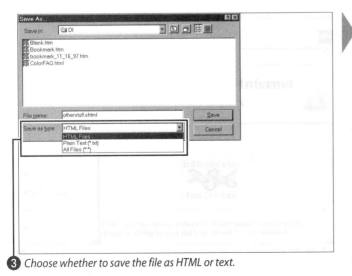

3 Choose whether to save the file as HTML or text.

4 Click the Save button.

Saving Frames

Depending on who you talk to, frames are either a fabulous design option or evidence of the ultimate decline of civilization. Frames are actually several different Web pages that all occupy your screen at the same time. Properly used, they can add great functionality to a Web site. Improperly used, they're nothing more than annoying clutter. Typically, one of the frames is used as a navigational tool that you can use to jump to different sections of the Web site. In effect, it's used as an interactive table of contents. This can be very helpful in organizing all the pages you've downloaded.

Saving Web pages that have frames can be a little more complicated than saving standard Web pages. Some sites are designed specifically with framing in mind, so viewing such pages without the frames might look awkward. You need to save all components of the Web page, not just one.

Both browsers fall flat on their faces when faced with saving a Web page with frames. To save a framed page, you simply need to understand its structure. Remember, it's a series of Web pages, not just a single one. The main, controlling Web page is called the *frameset*. If you want to reconstruct the total look of the Web site, you'll need to save the frameset. If you just want the content of one or more frames, all you need to do is save the frames you're interested in, but it's usually best to save the whole thing.

The problem is, Navigator won't let you save the frameset, and Internet Explorer won't let you save the frames. The good news for users of both browsers is that there's a workaround — a way to do it even though the program isn't designed to do it. One obvious solution is to use both browsers — Internet Explorer to save the frameset and Navigator to save the frames. However, either browser can be made to save all the parts of a framed Web site.

Continued

Continued

TAKE NOTE

▶ SAVE FRAME AS

Navigator has two separate File menu options, Save As and Save Frame As. You can use them interchangeably when saving frames, because they both work exactly the same way.

▶ GETTING HELP FROM TEXT EDITORS

To save the frameset, you have to copy a framed page's source code and paste it into Notepad or another text editor and then save it. Make sure you save the frameset and all of the frames in the same folder, so you can view the page properly.

CROSS-REFERENCE

See Chapter 13 for more information on viewing HTML source code.

FIND IT ONLINE

There's a good discussion of misusing frames at
http://www.webpagesthatsuck.com/.

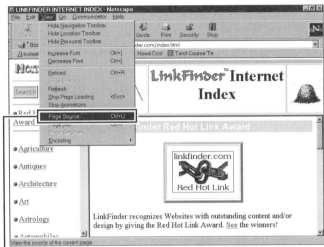

❶ Select View ➪ Page Source from the menu.

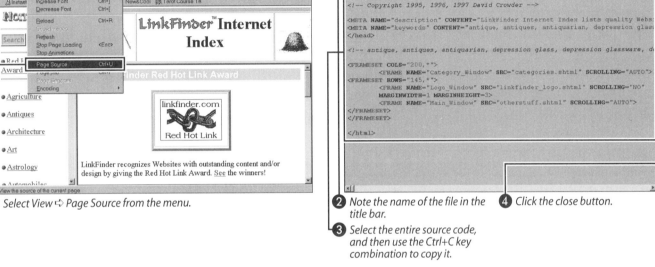

❷ Note the name of the file in the title bar.

❸ Select the entire source code, and then use the Ctrl+C key combination to copy it.

❹ Click the close button.

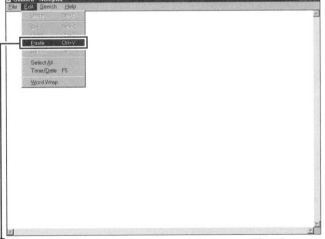

❺ Open Notepad and paste the source code into Notepad by selecting Edit ➪ Paste from the menu or by using the Ctrl+V key combination.

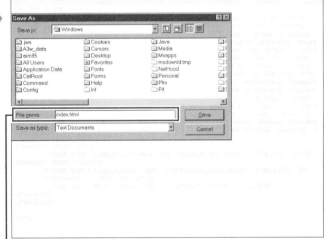

❻ Save the file, using the same file name.

Saving Framed Pages in Internet Explorer

You have the exact reverse of Navigator's problems with Internet Explorer. If you want to save the frameset, there's no problem whatsoever. Just follow the standard procedure for saving Web pages. Because the frameset is all that Internet Explorer recognizes, it'll be the one that's saved. If you want to save the individual frames in the Web site, however, you've got to be prepared to do a little bit of finagling. Just as with Navigator, it's a matter of viewing and saving the HTML source code. With Internet Explorer, though, it's a little bit easier. When you go to view the source code of an HTML page, instead of a built-in view that Navigator has, Internet Explorer launches Windows Notepad automatically, with the source code displayed as a text file. Here's the weird part — even though Internet Explorer refuses to save a frame, the source code that is displayed in Notepad is that of the currently selected frame. All you have to do is right click anywhere in a frame and select View Source from the popup menu that appears (do not select View ⇨ Source from Internet Explorer's menu or you'll get a wrong file name — a bug in Internet Explorer), and Notepad appears with the HTML source displayed. Unlike with Navigator, you don't have to separately launch Notepad, nor do you have to copy and paste; the source code is ready for saving. The file name is already in place; unless you want to

change it (which would defeat the purpose), just click the Save button and you're done. Repeat the procedure for each frame on the page and the entire Web page is saved to your local hard drive.

TAKE NOTE

▶ SAVING IN THE SAME FOLDER

Even though you're saving what appears in your Web browser to be a single Web page, don't forget that you're actually saving a series of interrelated Web pages when you save frames, and that the frameset organizes the frames. If you don't put the frameset and all the frames in the same folder, the frameset won't be able to find the frames when you reload everything from your local hard drive.

▶ UNDERSTANDING FRAME CONTENTS

Technically speaking, the separate Web pages are just that — plain old Web pages. The frames exist because of the frameset, and it's the content of the frames that is defined by the Web pages.

▶ IF YOU REALLY HATE FRAMES . . .

Not everyone loves frames. In fact, Vincent Burton hates frames. That's why he created the Frame Haters Union — because he says it's hard to navigate framed sites on the Web. If you jump to Burton's site (unframed, of course), you can find some interesting articles on the frame debate — and even join his union. Find the site at **http://www.concentric.net/~Vburton/fhu.shtml**.

CROSS-REFERENCE

See the section on saving Web pages earlier in this chapter.

FIND IT ONLINE

Astronomy magazine has helpful instructions for navigating framed sites at **http://www.kalmbach.com/astro/astronomy.html**.

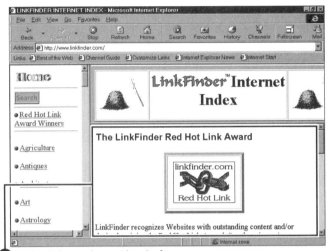

① *Right-click anywhere within the frame you want to save.*

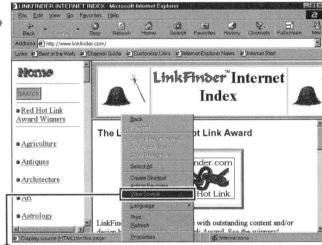

② *Select View Source from the popup menu that appears.*

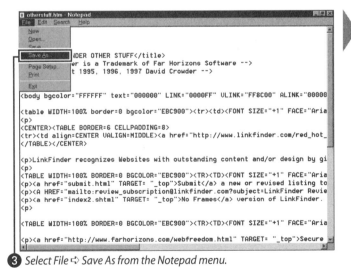

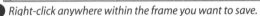

③ *Select File ⇨ Save As from the Notepad menu.*

④ *Choose the folder where you want to save the file.*

⑤ *Click the Save button.*

Saving Images

When you save a Web page on your hard drive, the images you see on it aren't saved along with it. That's because the images are not really a part of the Web page, but separate files that are linked to it. Web browsers make it look like the images are a part of the page. When a Web browser constructs the display on your screen, it reads the HTML file, gets the names and locations of the linked image files, and places them on your screen along with the elements that are actually a part of the Web page. To have a complete copy of a Web page, make sure you save the images on the page as well as the page itself. Another thing to keep in mind is that some pages use actual images for the background, so you need to make sure the background image is also saved — if you want the page to look like it does on the Web.

Animated images that you find on Web pages will still work when they are downloaded and viewed with a browser offline. However, not all "advanced" images will work without some special components. For example, image maps are essentially images that have sensitive areas mapped onto them with HTML code. When you save the image, you only get the image by itself, and not the related code. You must also save the source code for the image map in order to make it effective.

CROSS-REFERENCE

See Chapter 17 for more information on linking images.

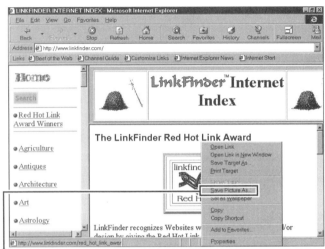

① To save an image in Internet Explorer, right-click it and select Save Picture As from the popup menu (in Navigator, select Save Image As).

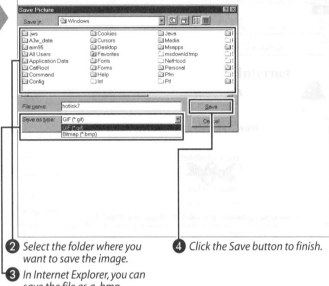

② Select the folder where you want to save the image.

③ In Internet Explorer, you can save the file as a .bmp (Windows bitmap) graphic if you wish.

④ Click the Save button to finish.

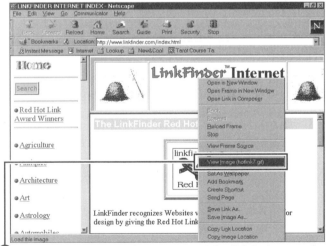

⑤ To view an image separately in Navigator, right-click the image and then select View Image from the popup menu.

⑥ The image will be displayed all by itself. Click the Back button to return to the Web page you were viewing.

Downloading Files

Downloading is the process of getting a file from a remote computer and putting it on your own hard drive. Many Web sites make files available for you to download. The process is virtually identical with both major browsers; only the names of the buttons are a bit different. It starts just like activating any other hypertext link. When you click a link to a downloadable file, your browser recognizes that the file is not a regular HTML file and you'll get a dialog box asking you if you want to save the file to your hard drive or open it on the spot.

If you decide to save a downloaded file to your hard drive, pick a folder that is relatively uncluttered (the Windows directory would be a bad choice) so you can locate the file easily once you're ready to open it. You might want to create a temporary folder that you should remember to delete at a later date. Another idea is to create a folder for "permanent" downloads (files you know you'll want to keep for a long time), to go with your temporary folder. By choosing which folder to download to at the time of download, you can save yourself the trouble of figuring out later if you really need to keep the files. Numerous trips online can cause the downloaded files to accumulate, and a periodic purging of unneeded files will save you time down the road.

TAKE NOTE

▶ USING DOWNLOADED FILES

Most files you download will be one of three types: graphics, executable files, or compressed files. To see the graphics, you'll need to load them into a program that can display them. Usually, this would be a graphics viewing program such as IrfanView (you can also load GIF, JPEG, or PNG images into your Web browser just as you would a local Web page). Executable files are programs that are ready to run. Compressed files need a program such as WinZip to uncompress the files before you can use them.

▶ FREEWARE AND SHAREWARE

Both individual programmers and companies often give away software for a variety of reasons; these programs are known as *freeware*. Small software companies that can't afford to distribute packaged wares on store shelves often use Web sites to put up their programs for downloading. You can download the program and try it to see if you like it. If you don't, you just delete it. If you do like it, you can buy it directly from the manufacturer; this marketing approach is called *shareware*. In some cases, the shareware is fully functional, but often it's limited in some way. For instance, a program might work for only 30 days or 100 uses.

CROSS-REFERENCE

See Chapter 3 for more information on finding files to download.

FIND IT ONLINE

The Web site at **http://www.shareware.com/** has lots of shareware files for download.

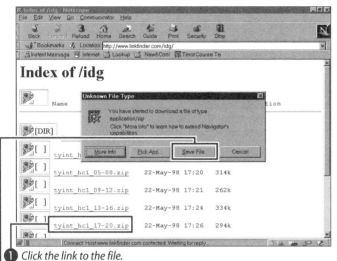

① *Click the link to the file.*

② *In Navigator, click the Save File button.*

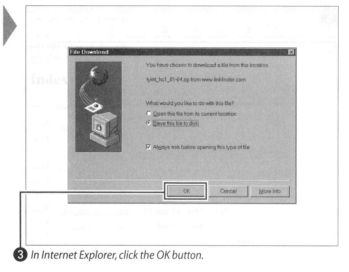

③ *In Internet Explorer, click the OK button.*

④ *In either browser, select the folder where you want to save the file, and then click the Save button.*

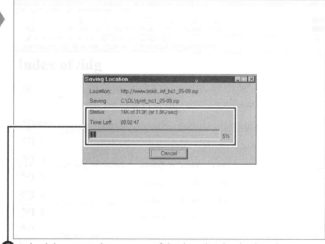

⑤ *In both browsers, the progress of the download is displayed.*

Getting Plug-Ins

Plug-ins are programs that extend the capabilities of Web browsers. They are designed to integrate seamlessly with the browser so that, once installed, you never need to think about them again. You can deliberately add a whole load of plug-ins any time you want by visiting the appropriate Web sites at Netscape and Microsoft, but that's not necessarily the best way to handle it. It's quite likely that you will never need all the available plug-ins, so why bother installing them all? It's better to save your hard drive's resources and just add them as needed.

The purpose of plug-ins is to let Web browsers use nonstandard file formats (that is, file formats that are not a part of the normal HTML-based world of the Web). Plug-ins exist for just about every possible file type. Want to play a .ram sound file? Get the RealPlayer plug-in. Want to read .pdf document files? Get the Adobe Acrobat Reader plug-in. The iChat plug-in turns a Web page into a chat room. Other plug-ins do everything from putting a calendar in your browser to letting you view 3D worlds in real time.

If you're using Navigator and you surf to a Web site that uses files that require a plug-in, your browser will recognize the situation and ask you if you want to add the appropriate plug-in (Internet Explorer doesn't do this — if you're using it, you'll have to just add the plug-ins yourself ahead of time). Depending on the plug-in, Navigator does one of two things. It either takes you to the plug-in maker's home page so you can download it (see the top two figures) or to the Netscape Plug-in Finder Web page, where a list of available plug-ins that handle that file type provides you with links to download the one of your choice (see the bottom two figures).

CROSS-REFERENCE
See Chapter 9 for more information on chat rooms.

FIND IT ONLINE
Netscape plug-ins: **http://home.netscape.com/ comprod/products/navigator/version_2.0/plugins/ index.html**. Microsoft's: **http://www.microsoft.com/ ie/download/** (select Add-ons).

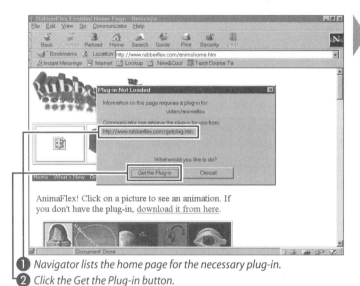

① *Navigator lists the home page for the necessary plug-in.*
② *Click the Get the Plug-in button.*

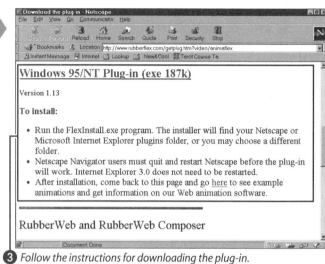

③ *Follow the instructions for downloading the plug-in.*

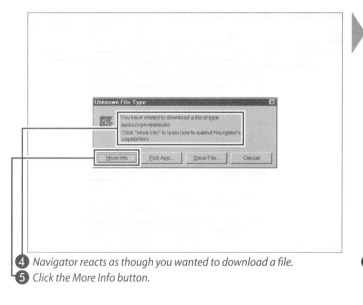

④ *Navigator reacts as though you wanted to download a file.*
⑤ *Click the More Info button.*

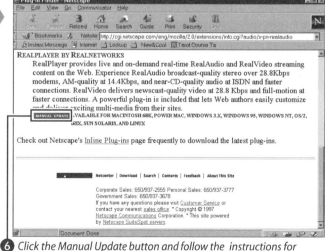

⑥ *Click the Manual Update button and follow the instructions for downloading the plug-in.*

Recognizing Secure Servers

Although much of the supposed security problems with the Internet are more media hype and scare stories than real, it's probably best to be just a bit paranoid and cover yourself as though the rumors were true. Yes, credit card fraud does exist on the Internet, but credit card fraud also happens at your local shopping mall. The same people who write about how unsafe it is to give credit card information on the Net think nothing of handing their credit cards to total strangers in a store, and probably don't worry much about throwing away the receipt when they get back home or to the office, even though it has all the information a trash raider needs to use the credit card.

However, financial information sent over the Internet does pass through several computers on the way to its destination, and unscrupulous people with enough technical knowledge can intercept that information. Thus, it's a really good idea to refuse to place orders with any Web site that isn't secure. Secure Web sites encrypt the information your browser exchanges with them. That way, even if it is intercepted along the way, it cannot be read by a third party.

Secure Web sites are identified by Navigator via a padlock icon. The lock is always present in the status bar. If the Web site you are visiting is not secure, the lock icon is open, as shown in the figure on the upper left. If the site is a secure one, the lock is closed, as shown in the figure on the upper right. Internet Explorer uses a similar approach, but the lock only shows up when you're at a secure site (see the bottom-right figure).

TAKE NOTE

▶ CERTIFICATE AUTHORITIES

Secure Web sites are certified via *digital certificates*, which are coded recognition signals known only to the local network administrator and the officials at a *certificate authority*. Certificate authorities such as VeriSign are organizations that exist for the sole purpose of verifying the identity of people and organizations. You can, if you wish, get your own digital certificate to install in your Web browser, which certifies to the people you deal with that you actually are who you say you are. While this has little use at the present time, it is expected to become the common form of ID on the Internet in the future.

▶ DIGITAL CASH

One interesting twist on the digital certificate is the new concept of digital cash. Companies such as DigiCash and CyberCash issue digital certificates that represent money (much like a piece of green paper in your wallet represents the gold the Federal Reserve has in storage). You can transfer these certificates over the Internet to pay for purchases.

CROSS-REFERENCE
See Chapter 4 for more information on Web security.

FIND IT ONLINE
VeriSign at: **http://www.verisign.com/**;
DigiCash at: **http://www.digicash.com/**;
CyberCash at: **http://www.cybercash.com/**.

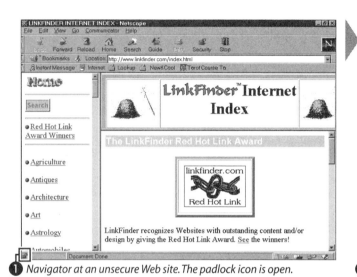

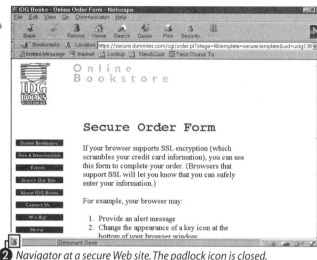

1 *Navigator at an unsecure Web site. The padlock icon is open.*

2 *Navigator at a secure Web site. The padlock icon is closed.*

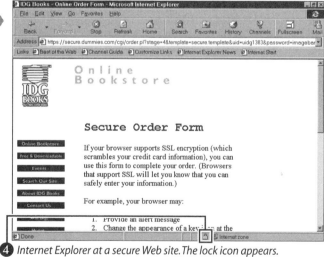

3 *Internet Explorer at an unsecure Web site. No lock icon appears.*

4 *Internet Explorer at a secure Web site. The lock icon appears.*

Personal Workbook

Q&A

1 How do you print a table of a Web page's links in Internet Explorer?

_____

_____

2 How do you get text from a Web page into a word processor?

_____

_____

3 What happens if you save a Web page as plain text?

_____

_____

_____

4 What is a *frameset*?

_____

_____

_____

5 How do you view an image separately from its Web page?

_____

_____

_____

_____

6 What is *shareware*?

_____

_____

_____

7 Why do you need plug-ins?

_____

_____

8 What is a *certificate authority*?

_____

_____

_____

ANSWERS: PAGE 377

EXTRA PRACTICE

1 In Internet Explorer, print just the selected frame.

2 Save a Web page and all its associated images.

3 Save the contents of an individual frame and display them as a separate Web page in your browser.

4 Download a file and install it.

5 Go to the Netscape plug-in page and add a plug-in to your system.

6 Go to the VeriSign site and order a personal digital certificate (there's a free six-month version).

REAL-WORLD APPLICATIONS

✔ You need a copy of an out-of-print novel to complete a collection. Using a search engine, you might find a small bookstore in Japan that has a copy of the book you want, and you place order.

✔ A friend without Net access asks you for help on a research project. You track down all the necessary information and print out the Web pages.

✔ You find a Web site whose features you really like, and you download all its pages and images, and then study the source code to see how the site achieved its look.

✔ You might find a music page that has just the song you want to hear, but they use a sound file format your browser doesn't support. You add the appropriate plug-in and enjoy the music.

Visual Quiz

What is the dialog box in the figure? How do you call it up? What do the options do? Which ones are necessary for normal usage?

_____

_____

_____

_____

_____

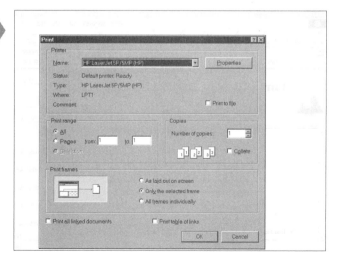

CHAPTER 3

Web Searching

I t's easy enough to find text on a Web page. All you do is use the local Find feature of your Web browser to track down a word or phrase. But what about the Web as a whole? How do you get to the page where you want to begin?

Lots of Web sites have the sole purpose of helping you find exactly what you're looking for. You'll find two basic kinds of search sites. The first type uses a program that surfs the Web nonstop looking for new sites to add to its database. The programs are generically called *robots*, but you will also hear them referred to as *spiders* (because they spend all their time moving around the Web). These robots carefully note every word in the Web pages they visit. We'll be exploring Excite, one of the premier robot-fed search sites.

The other kind of search site is a Web index. Web indexes are created by hand. They use human Web surfers to get their data. The human's job is essentially the same as that of the automated spiders—to go out and find sites. The main difference is in the focus. Spiders gather in absolutely everything they

find, but humans exercise discretion, picking sites for the quality of their content. Although you're likely to find a larger number of listings in a spider-based search site's database, you're more likely to find meaningful and useful listings in a Web index. We'll show you how to use Yahoo!, one of the oldest and best of the Web indexes.

Both types of search sites use input from Web designers to add to their collections. When designers create a Web site, they use a form at the search site to add their site to the listings. In the case of the spider-based search sites, this means that the spider is going to pay a visit to your site and include all the words on your Web pages in its database. In the case of Web indexes, it means that someone will take a look at your site and decide how to classify it.

The idea of search sites inevitably led to the development of the super-search site—a search engine that searches other search engines. You can use these sites to gather information from several different search sites simultaneously. We'll be using SavvySearch to show you how they work.

Using the Local Find Command

Text-heavy Web pages, such as scientific papers or movie scripts, can be difficult to sort through to find a word or phrase that you need. Thankfully, major browsers have tools to help you locate such items. Navigator and Internet Explorer have nearly identical approaches to finding text on a Web page you're viewing. Each one has certain benefits and detriments, and the one you prefer to use for this purpose will depend on your personal tastes and needs. Because Internet Explorer has one extra setting, we'll use it for the illustrations on the facing page.

The Find dialog box is identical in both browsers, except that Internet Explorer has one more checkbox option — *Match whole word only*. Type your search term (called *keywords*) in the box labeled *Find what*. If you want the search to be case-sensitive, click the *Match case* checkbox. If you're using Internet Explorer, tell it whether to match whole words only. If you do select whole words only, then the search term "pitcher" won't find "pitchers." Assuming you're starting at the top of the Web page, leave the Direction setting set to Down, and then click the Find Next button. The find feature locates the first occurrence of the search term and highlights it. If you want to stop there, click the Cancel button. If you want to continue looking for more occurrences, click the Find Next button again. When no more occurrences are left to locate, you will be told so.

CHOOSING YOUR PHRASES WISELY

You will probably see that the Local Find command works best for you when the text on a page seems overwhelming. However, you should make sure that your search phrase is long enough to be specific, because a single word, even if it's unusual, can appear several times in seemingly unrelated areas of a page. You might have to run the search several times, refining the search each time, for this tool to be most useful.

MOVING THAT PESKY DIALOG BOX

The Find dialog box remains on your screen while the search is in progress, and it might block the appearance of the words or phrases you seek. You can move it out of the way if this happens.

SEARCH AGAIN

One thing that Navigator has that Internet Explorer doesn't is the capability to repeat a find command without going through the whole procedure all over again. This is especially useful if you need to look for the same text on different Web pages. You can go to each page and read it, or you can use the find feature on each page after you call it up. With Internet Explorer, this means following the whole four-step process on every page. With Navigator, just hit the F3 function key with each new page (you can also use the Ctrl+G key combination). You get the search performed right away, and you won't have to put up with the Find dialog box covering up the text you're trying to read.

CROSS-REFERENCE

See the section on keywords later in this chapter.

FIND IT ONLINE

For tips on searching, see The Internet Consulting Detective at **http://www.intermediacy.com/ sherlock/index.phtml**.

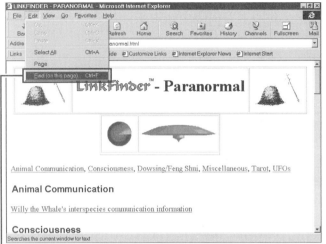

1 Select Edit ⇨ Find (on this page) from the menu. This brings up the Find dialog box.

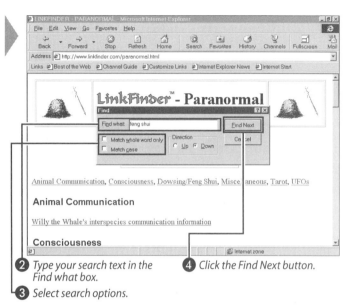

2 Type your search text in the Find what box.

3 Select search options.

4 Click the Find Next button.

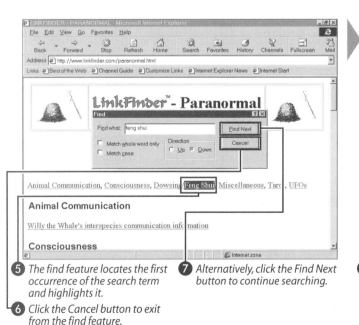

5 The find feature locates the first occurrence of the search term and highlights it.

6 Click the Cancel button to exit from the find feature.

7 Alternatively, click the Find Next button to continue searching.

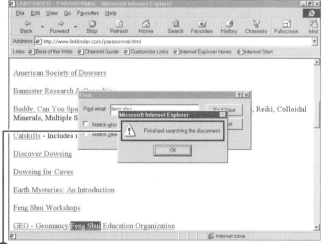

8 The find feature tells you when no more occurrences of the search term exist on the page.

Using the Search Button

The Web's best asset is that is enables the general public to access vast amounts of information from a variety of resources in a very short period of time. To reach the major sites that hold the information you need, you have to search for them. Different search engines turn up different sites, and present them in distinctly different ways. Because the Web has a lot of useless information that still shows when you do a search, it's best to use a combination of search engines.

Both Netscape and Microsoft recognize the importance of search engines to Web surfers, so they include search access right in their browsers. In both browsers, the Search buttons are just to the right of the Home buttons, although they look different. In Navigator, the Search button shows a picture of a flashlight (see the upper-left figure); in Internet Explorer, it has a picture of a magnifying glass over a globe.

If you click the Search button in Navigator, you'll go straight to Netscape's search page (see the figure on the upper right). To initiate your Web search, type your search terms in the box labeled *Search the Web:* and then click the Seek button.

The Search button in Internet Explorer brings up a separate window on the left side of the browser (see the figure on the lower left). This shows, by default, the last search engine you used via the Search button. If this is the first time you've used this feature, you'll be taken to the Microsoft search page right away.

Otherwise, you'll get a drop-down list that shows the ones you've used previously.

TAKE NOTE

▶ MAINTAINING ORDER

The advantage of Internet Explorer's search system is that the search engine resource pane stays constant, so you can keep track of which engines you've used, and which you still need to invoke. You can also adjust the size of the search pane, or close it entirely, to accommodate your needs.

▶ STAYING ON A ROLL

Some search engines list all the results they find, and then give you the option of launching a new search with another engine from its own site. Others, such as Yahoo, automatically enlist another search engine (such as AltaVista) to aid in its own search. Either way, you should be aware of what is happening, so you don't duplicate an engine's efforts later on.

▶ EXTRA FEATURES

At both the Netscape and Microsoft search pages, it's worth scrolling down and taking a good look at what else they have to offer. Both offer more search engine choices than are immediately visible. At Netscape, you can also find links to search tips and reviews by users of the different search engines. At the bottom of the Microsoft search page, you can specify your own choice for a search engine to be included in the search window.

CROSS-REFERENCE

If you want to have custom buttons for your favorite search sites, see Chapter 4 for how to add your own toolbar buttons.

FIND IT ONLINE

See Internet Search Tool Details at **http://sunsite.berkeley.edu/Help/searchdetails.html**.

❶ In either browser, click the Search button.

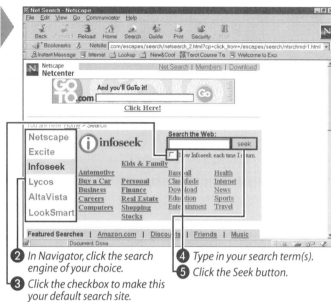

❷ In Navigator, click the search engine of your choice.

❸ Click the checkbox to make this your default search site.

❹ Type in your search term(s).

❺ Click the Seek button.

❻ In Internet Explorer, type in your keywords and click the Search button.

❼ To choose another search engine, click Choose a Search Engine.

❽ Pick a search engine or click List of all Search Engines.

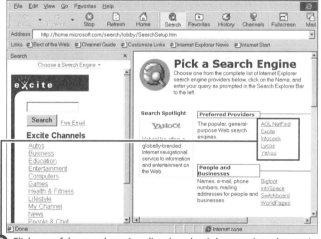

❾ Click one of the search engines listed on the right to replace the one in the search window.

Using Excite

The Excite search engine, located at **http://www.excite.com/** (see the figure on the upper left), is an excellent source of Web links.

Excite tries to anticipate the types of things you'll look for, and groups them under topic headings. It's usually best to start your search by narrowing down the category as much as possible. If you're looking for a new hardware peripheral for your PC, you'll have more success by following the Computers & Internet category down to the Hardware subcategory and entering your criteria there, rather than starting your search from the main Excite page. Besides, while you're on the Hardware page, you might come across sites you wouldn't have thought to investigate, such as a magazine article on the best peripherals to purchase.

In addition, the main Excite page has links to such distractions as current events, stock market quotes, sports scores, weather forecasts, and chat services. You even have the option of customizing the main page to your own needs, so your searching will be more efficient.

Whether you are in the main page or a subcategory, you can access the search engine itself, which lets you enter a combination of words to find what you're looking for. Surrounding the words with quotes forces Excite to look for sites containing the specific phrase, as opposed to sites that contain either of the words. For more tips, see the section on

Boolean Logic on this page. Most searches turn up several pages worth of material.

TAKE NOTE

▶ BOOLEAN LOGIC

George Boole was a 19th-century British mathematician. The author of such works as *An Investigation of the Laws of Thought*, he heavily influenced the computer industry that was to follow in the century after his death, and much of today's circuitry design follows rules he laid down in his discussions on logic. Fortunately, you don't have to understand any math to use Boolean logic in your searches. Just three little words: AND, OR, and NOT. If you have two keywords and you have to find both of them on the same Web page, you put AND between them (soap AND opera). If either term will do, use OR (soap OR opera). Beware, though — you'll get stuff on shampoo and Luciano Pavarotti instead of about General Hospital with this example. If there's a word you want to exclude from your search, use NOT (soap NOT opera). Some search engines use the variations AND NOT or BUT NOT instead of NOT; click the site's help link before using a search site for the first time so you'll know what method they use. The terms have to be capitalized like they are here to work properly.

▶ FREE E-MAIL

Excite also offers free e-mail accounts. Just click the Account: Email link to find out how to get it.

CROSS-REFERENCE

See Chapter 9 for more information on free e-mail.

FIND IT ONLINE

Check out Advanced Searching: Tricks of the Trade at **http://www.onlineinc.com/onlinemag/MayOL/zorn5.html**.

❶ Type in your search term(s).

❷ Click the Search button.

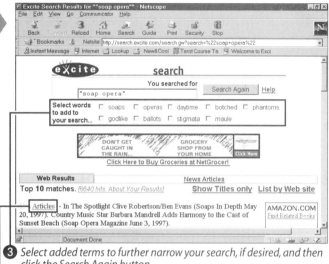

❸ Select added terms to further narrow your search, if desired, and then click the Search Again button.

❹ Click one of the links to go to the associated Web page.

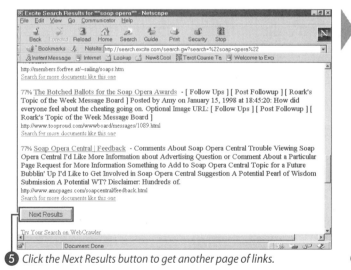

❺ Click the Next Results button to get another page of links.

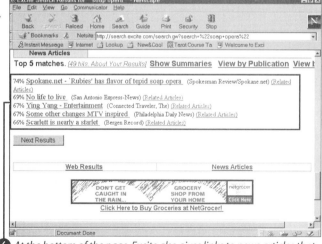

❻ At the bottom of the page, Excite also gives links to news articles that match your keywords.

Using Yahoo!

Yahoo stands for "Yet Another Hierarchical Officious Oracle" and it has a more light-hearted theme than Excite. It's located at **http://www.yahoo.com/**, and it's designed in a manner similar to Excite. Although it, too, boasts a search engine, you can browse through the listings without using it if you've got a lot of time to spare. Just click one of the categories (see the figure on the upper left), and follow a series of links down through lots of subcategories (that's what makes it "hierarchical") until you get to what you want.

If you'd rather do it the easy way, just type in your keywords and click the Search button. The results, as shown in the figure on the upper right, are similar to the ones you get from Excite, but each Web page link is headed by links to the Yahoo! category it was found in. You can view other information in that category by clicking on that link. The entire path for the category appears at the top of the page, and you can follow it back up if you want to find other subcategories you might like to view.

Otherwise, just continue to scroll down the page until you find a likely link. If you reach the bottom of the page without finding what you're looking for, just click the Next 20 Matches button to get more links.

TAKE NOTE

▶ THE YAHOO! SUCCESS STORY

Just in case you thought the day of the entrepreneur was over, Yahoo! was started by a couple of Stanford college students named David Filo and Jerry Yang back in 1994. Today, its stock is traded on NASDAQ (the symbol is YHOO). Filo and Yang each hold the title of "Chief Yahoo" in this major corporation.

▶ YAHOO! INTERNET LIFE

In addition to providing a considerable Web presence, the folks at Yahoo! publish their own magazine. We're talking the made-of-paper, find-it-at- your-local-newsstand kind of magazine, not the newfangled e-zine kind of thing you'll find on the Web. It's called *Yahoo! Internet Life*. If you want to try a trial copy, drop in to **http://www.zdnet.com/zdsubs/yahoo/home.html** and fill out the online request form.

▶ YAHOO! EXTRAS

Yahoo!, like Excite, also offers free e-mail accounts, as well as links to breaking news. Yahoo! also provides similar interfaces with each of its other Yahoo! branches that cover many U.S. cities and several countries throughout the world. One search site, Yahooligans!, is specifically designed for children. Each of these sites makes searching easier and more user-friendly for newcomers.

CROSS-REFERENCE

For more information, see the preceding section on the Excite search engine.

FIND IT ONLINE

You can find another Web index at **http://www.linkfinder.com/**.

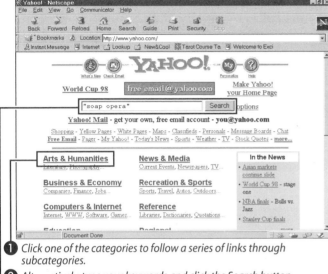

1 *Click one of the categories to follow a series of links through subcategories.*

2 *Alternatively, type your keywords and click the Search button.*

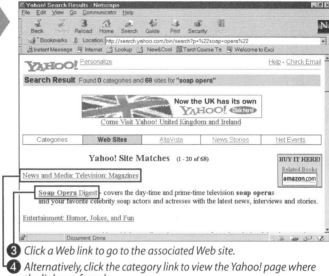

3 *Click a Web link to go to the associated Web site.*

4 *Alternatively, click the category link to view the Yahoo! page where the link was found.*

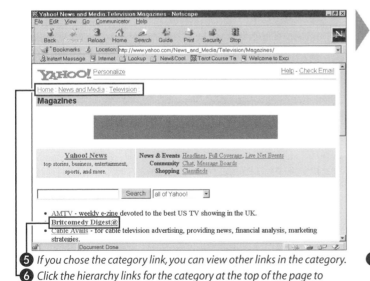

5 *If you chose the category link, you can view other links in the category.*

6 *Click the hierarchy links for the category at the top of the page to follow it back up.*

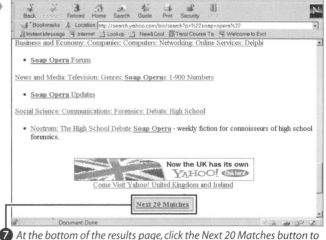

7 *At the bottom of the results page, click the Next 20 Matches button to get more links.*

Using SavvySearch

I f one search engine is good, then a couple of dozen at once is great. SavvySearch, at http://guaraldi.cs.colostate.edu:2000/, takes your search terms and simultaneously submits them to several different search engines, compiles the results for you, and lets you sample from the top responses. The benefit in speed and scope is obvious; the tradeoff is that you don't get all the listings the way you would if you went to each search engine individually.

SavvySearch doesn't take Boolean terms like other search engines, but sets the logical relationship between keywords in the first option. If you click the drop-down list next to *Search for documents containing*, then you'll get the choice of *All query terms*, which is the same as putting AND between them all, *All query terms, as a phrase*, which is just like putting quotation marks around the keywords, or *Any query term*, which is the same as putting OR between them all.

The *Display results* option lets you pick whether you want just the Web page's title (Brief), a title and short description (Normal), or title, description, and URL (Verbose). The next option lets you set how many results you get. You can choose 10, 20, 30, 40, or 50. The final option, *Integrate results*, causes all the search sources to be merged together, eliminating duplicates.

The figure on the lower left shows results listed by source; the one at the lower right shows integrated results.

TAKE NOTE

▶ ASSESSING THE ENGINES

Even with Integrated results, the Web Search engines are listed in parentheses, so you can figure out which engine has rendered the best results, and use that tool for your next search. This might save you time in the future, because you won't need to pore through pages and pages of search results from several different engines. SavvySearch provides links to the other search engines on its results page, so you can perform a new search immediately, if you wish.

▶ RINGSIDE SEAT

Do you ever wonder what other people are searching for when they use a search engine? You can watch the action live by dropping in to the Search Voyeurs. Magellan has one at **http://voyeur. mckinley.com/cgi-bin/voyeur.cgi**. Every 15 seconds, a group of the latest search keywords entered by people using it are displayed. If you want to see the results, you can click any interesting search. There's another one on the Webcrawler site at **http://webcrawler.com/Games/SearchTicker. html**. This one looks like a stock ticker, and you can click the terms as they go by to see the search results (but you gotta be fast!). Neither one violates anybody's privacy, as there's no way for anyone to tell who's typing in the terms. You won't know who's looking, but it's still kind of interesting to watch.

CROSS-REFERENCE

See the sidebar on Boolean logic earlier in this chapter.

FIND IT ONLINE

See Evaluation of Selected Internet Search Tools at **http://www.library.nwu.edu/resources/internet/sea rch/evaluate.html**.

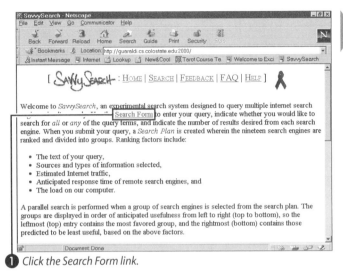

1 Click the Search Form link.

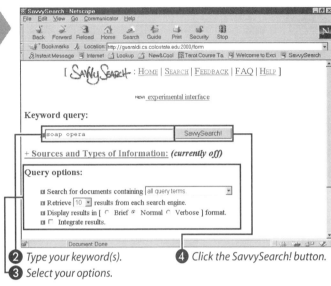

2 Type your keyword(s).

3 Select your options.

4 Click the SavvySearch! button.

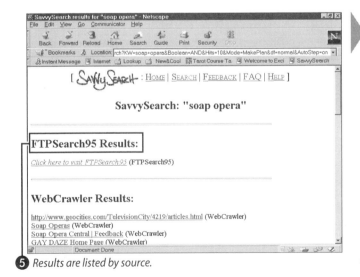

5 Results are listed by source.

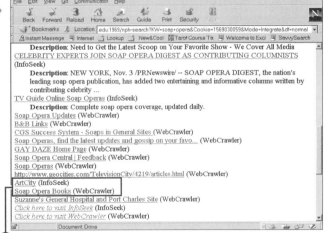

6 If you selected the Integrate Results option, results are merged.

Personal Workbook

Q&A

1 What is a *spider*?

_____

_____

2 What is a *Web index*?

_____

_____

3 How do you find a term on a Web page you're viewing?

_____

_____

_____

_____

4 What is a *keyword*?

_____

_____

5 What is the difference between the Search buttons in Navigator and Internet Explorer?

_____

_____

_____

6 Who was George Boole?

_____

_____

_____

7 What are the three Boolean operators?

_____

_____

_____

8 What does Yahoo stand for?

_____

_____

_____

ANSWERS: 377

EXTRA PRACTICE

1 Go to the SavvySearch site, scroll down on its main page to the listing of search engines, and follow the links to some other ones. Familiarize yourself with at least three of them.

2 Use both Navigator and Internet Explorer to run a search. See which is faster.

3 Using Internet Explorer, perform a case-sensitive Find operation.

4 Visit one of the Search Voyeurs and observe. Click some search terms to see the results.

5 Visit Yahoo! or Excite and sign up for free e-mail.

6 Try the three different display settings at SavvySearch and see which one you like best.

REAL-WORLD APPLICATIONS

✔ You've run a search and found several Web pages that match your keywords. You might want to try using Navigator's F3 key to repeat the Find operation on each page as you visit it to speed your evaluation of each page's contents.

✔ You have a complicated search to perform. You may want to combine Boolean operators to narrow down the search.

✔ You're sure you have good search keywords and can't get the results you want. Consider switching to another search engine and trying the same ones there.

✔ Your new Web site is up and running. If you want to draw more traffic to it, you should list it with the major search engines.

Visual Quiz

How would you get a Web page that looked exactly like this one?

_____

_____

_____

_____

_____

CHAPTER 4

Customizing Web Browsers

Web browsers come all ready to go. All you have to do is install them, launch them, and you're off and running, surfing the World Wide Web. Like most programs, though, they're customizable. You can add your own link buttons to supplement the ones that are already included, and modify some of the technical details to suit yourself.

Actually, you've already had a slight taste of customizing — back in Chapter 1, when you set your own home page instead of the default one. And your bookmark list is a personal touch that won't be found on anyone else's Web browser. Most of the other things you can do to customize your Web browser are just as easy as those tasks.

For starters, you can control how you view Web pages. You don't have to settle for whatever you find. If a site has busy background images that interfere with your reading of the text, just get rid of them. If the colors are a truly hideous blend, you don't have to suffer — just change them. You can make the text larger or smaller, eliminate the images entirely for faster Web surfing, and — if you're using Navigator — set your browser so it prints Web pages exactly the way you want them for easier reading without changing the way you view them onscreen.

If you don't like the placement of the toolbars, both of the major browsers let you change their layout. Move them up and down. Put them next to one another. Add and rearrange buttons to link to favorite sites. You can even eliminate the toolbars entirely if you prefer to use the menu to issue commands.

You can change security settings to make things either more stringent or less annoying, depending on what your personal needs are.

Web browsers keep copies of the pages and images you view as you surf the Web, taking up space on your hard drive. You can decide how much space you want to devote to this aspect of browsing, altering settings to suit yourself and your particular computer system.

If you're using Internet Explorer, you can take advantage of Microsoft's new channel technology to subscribe to special Web sites that tell your browser when they're updated and let Internet Explorer connect to them automatically to retrieve the information.

Customizing Web Page Colors

M ost people assume they are totally at the mercy of the original designers when it comes to viewing a Web page's colors. Actually, both Netscape Navigator and Microsoft Internet Explorer let you set the colors yourself, overriding the designers' choices. Because many Web designers have little training in the application of color to communication, an awful lot of Web pages are nearly unreadable, so this capability is a very good thing for Web surfers. As with many other options, the procedure in both browsers is similar.

Customizing Colors in Navigator

You'll see four color boxes and three checkboxes on the Preferences dialog box. The color boxes let you set the colors you prefer to be displayed on Web pages for text, background, unvisited links, and visited links (the change in color between visited and unvisited links is an aid to helping you find an earlier followed trail or avoid retracing your steps unnecessarily). Clicking any of the color boxes leads you to a Color Preference dialog box where you can choose whatever colors you desire for those four settings. Just click the color you want (or define a custom color), and then click the OK button and you're back in the Preferences dialog box.

Continued

Continued

TAKE NOTE

▶ USELESS WINDOWS COLORS

The Use Windows Colors selection, according to the official Netscape documentation, is used to "set the text and background display to their original settings." In actual usage, however, it has no effect whatsoever unless the Web page you are viewing has no color specifications. In such a case, the colors you have chosen for Windows are used. Selecting this option overrides any text or background color choices you make.

▶ KEEPING UNDERLINED LINKS

Although you can choose to deselect Underlined links, it is not really a good idea to do so, because the underlining helps to readily identify links. In fact, use of underlining for any purpose other than identifying links is officially deprecated by the World Wide Web Consortium (also known as W3C), the official standards body of the Web that develops consensus among different companies on, among other things, HTML.

▶ CUSTOMIZING TAG APPEARANCE

Some browsers handle HTML tags such as <STRONG> and <EM> differently, applying different colors or styles to them, instead of their normal bold and italic attributes, respectively. In addition, those browsers sometimes give you the option of selecting how you would like these tags to affect the marked text. Check your help files to see if your browser has these capabilities.

CROSS-REFERENCE
See the following section for how to override Web page fonts.

FIND IT ONLINE
Find a very good set of links to Netscape color sites at **http://the-light.com/netlinks.html**.

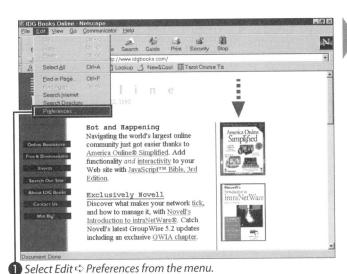

❶ *Select Edit ⇨ Preferences from the menu.*

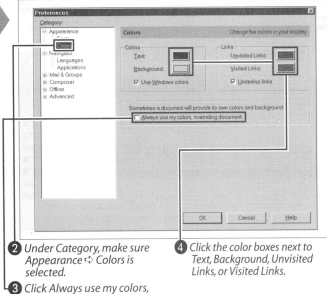

❷ *Under Category, make sure Appearance ⇨ Colors is selected.*

❸ *Click Always use my colors, overriding document.*

❹ *Click the color boxes next to Text, Background, Unvisited Links, or Visited Links.*

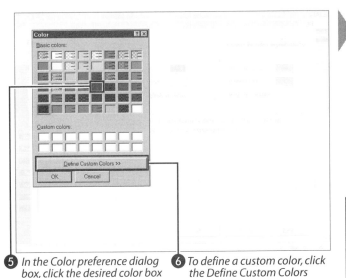

❺ *In the Color preference dialog box, click the desired color box under Basic colors or Custom colors.*

❻ *To define a custom color, click the Define Custom Colors button.*

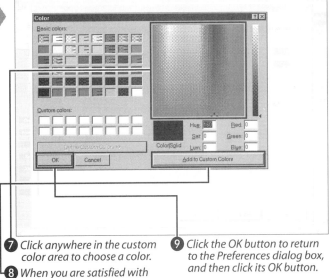

❼ *Click anywhere in the custom color area to choose a color.*

❽ *When you are satisfied with the color, click Add to Custom Colors.*

❾ *Click the OK button to return to the Preferences dialog box, and then click its OK button.*

Customizing Web Page Colors
Continued

Make sure you don't forget to check the box that says Always use my colors, overriding document. Otherwise, the changes you make to the colors will have no effect. Once you do this and click on the OK button, all the Web pages you access will be displayed in the colors you selected, regardless of the designers' choices.

Customizing Colors in Internet Explorer

Unlike Navigator, Internet Explorer makes you go to two different dialog boxes to make your Web color choices. You must first click the Accessibility button (which, despite the misleading name, has nothing to do with handicapped Web accessibility) to bring up the dialog box where you choose to override existing Web page colors. Click the OK button to return to the Internet Options dialog box. Once back in that dialog box, you then click the Colors button.

The Colors dialog box in Internet Explorer is very similar to the one in Navigator, except that the phrasing is slightly different. As with Navigator, you can choose to use your specified Windows colors for displaying Web pages that have no color specified. And, as with Navigator, you can choose to set the colors for text, background, visited links, and unvisited links (of course, you can feel free to set any one color or any combination of colors—you are not required to set all of them). The process for choosing basic or custom colors is identical to that for Navigator.

TAKE NOTE

▶ **HOVER COLOR**

Hover color is a special Internet Explorer setting that changes the color of a link when your mouse pointer is over it ("hovering"). To activate this option, click the Use hover color button, and then click the color box to the right of it. Follow the normal process to choose either a standard or custom color for it.

▶ **CUSTOM COLORS**

Although you have the capability to define practically any color you can imagine — or can develop through the interactive custom color dialog box — unless you have some particularly powerful design consideration that demands a nonstandard color, it is best to stick with the basic colors. The basic colors are carefully chosen to show up more or less the same regardless of the color resolution at which they are viewed. Both of the major Web browsers are programmed to recognize and properly display these colors. Custom colors, on the other hand, may display beautifully at high color settings, but suffer markedly at lower color settings due to a technique called *dithering*, which is used to approximate a color at lower color settings. Thus, a perfect custom color in a truecolor setting on a great monitor, when viewed by a visitor with a 256-color video card and a cheap monitor, may look positively awful. You might want to take a look at your Web pages at different video resolutions to see what they look like.

CROSS-REFERENCE

See Chapter 13 for more information on Web page colors.

FIND IT ONLINE

You can visit the World Wide Web Consortium at http://www.w3.org/.

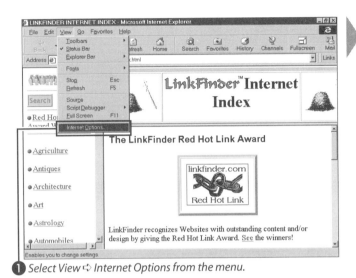

❶ Select View ➪ Internet Options from the menu.

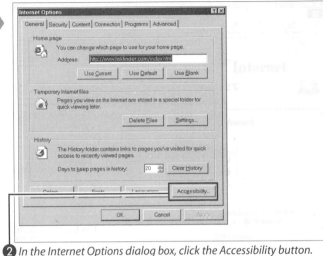

❷ In the Internet Options dialog box, click the Accessibility button.

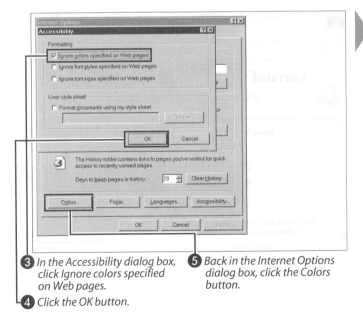

❸ In the Accessibility dialog box, click Ignore colors specified on Web pages.

❹ Click the OK button.

❺ Back in the Internet Options dialog box, click the Colors button.

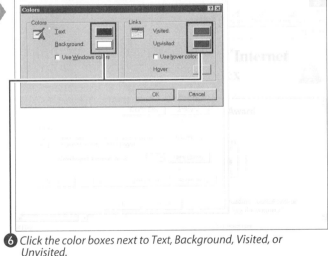

❻ Click the color boxes next to Text, Background, Visited, or Unvisited.

Setting Web Page Fonts

As with Web page colors, you can also choose which fonts will be displayed when you visit Web pages. Once again, Navigator puts all settings in one place while Internet Explorer requires you to go to two different dialog boxes to make your choices.

Setting Fonts in Navigator

If you have a large number of fonts on your system, it takes a few seconds for Navigator to load all the information, so be patient if the dialog box doesn't immediately change when you click the Fonts option in the Preferences dialog box. Although the wait can be a bit annoying, it is in a good cause. Navigator doesn't just display the names of the fonts like Internet Explorer does — Navigator actually shows the name in the font style itself, so you can see exactly what the font looks like.

Navigator gives you three options for handling Web page fonts. One is to totally override the designers' choices and substitute fonts of your own choosing. The other is to accept their font choices except when they specify dynamic fonts (dynamic fonts increase the downloading time of the Web page you are viewing, making for a slower display in exchange for more precise control by the designer). The third is to accept their font choices even when they include dynamic fonts.

Other than that, you simply need to choose which font styles and sizes you want to be used for both variable-width and fixed-width fonts. Most fonts are variable-width (also called *proportional*), so that's the most important setting. A few Web pages use some fixed-width fonts, but it's rare.

Continued

Continued

TAKE NOTE

FONT SIZE ON THE FLY

You can change the font size quickly while viewing a Web page. To make the fonts larger, select View ⇨ Increase Font from the menu. To make them smaller, select View ⇨ Decrease Font from the menu. This is a temporary setting; the next time you start Navigator, sizes will be normal.

CHANGING CHARACTER SETS

Character sets are the alphanumeric characters — letters, numbers, and so forth — that your computer can display. The character set used in North America is very different from the one used in, say, Japan. You don't generally need to concern yourself with this option. Whatever country you bought your computer in, it will have the appropriate character set already installed. Internet Explorer lists only the character sets that are actually installed on your computer, while Navigator lists all the common ones. If you choose a character set in Navigator that is not installed, Navigator reverts back to the default character set.

CROSS-REFERENCE

See the preceding section on customizing Web page colors.

FIND IT ONLINE

Find the Netscape support page for dynamic fonts at **http://home5.netscape.com/comprod/products/communicator/fonts/index.html**.

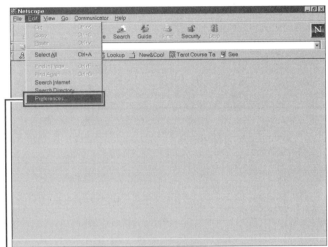

① *Select Edit ⇨ Preferences from the menu.*

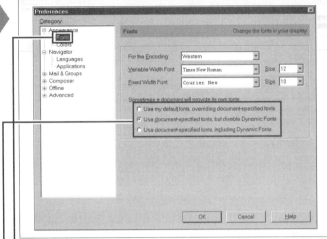

② *Under Category, make sure Appearance ⇨ Fonts is selected.*
③ *Click one of the three font handling options.*

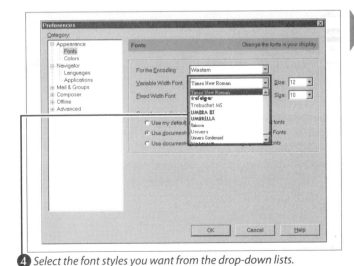

④ *Select the font styles you want from the drop-down lists.*

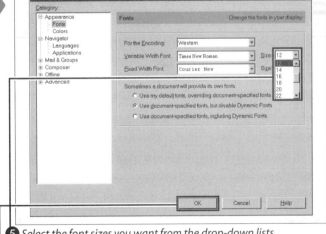

⑤ *Select the font sizes you want from the drop-down lists.*
⑥ *Click the OK button.*

Setting Fonts in Internet Explorer

Internet Explorer only lets you specify whether to ignore the designers' fonts or not, although you are able to choose to ignore font styles or font sizes separately. If you choose only the styles option, then the sizes specified by the Web page designer will be unaffected, but the look of the font will be your choice. If you choose only the size option, then the appearance of the fonts on the Web page will be unaffected, but the fonts will be larger or smaller as you specify. If you choose both, then you have taken control over both the appearance and size of Web page fonts.

Where Navigator lets you choose the specific size in points (a point is $\frac{1}{72}$ of an inch) of the fonts, Internet Explorer has only five options: Smallest, Small, Medium, Larger, and Largest. Although this lacks the precision Navigator provides, if you use it in conjunction with the Ignore font sizes specified on Web pages option and do not choose the Ignore font styles specified on Web pages option, you can alter the proportions of a Web page without otherwise changing its appearance.

Next, click the OK button to return to the Internet Options dialog box, where you then click the Fonts button to bring up the Fonts dialog box. As with Navigator, Internet Explorer lets you choose the font style and size for both variable-width (here called *proportional*) and fixed-width fonts.

TAKE NOTE

▶ **FONT SIZE ON THE FLY, PART TWO**

You can change font sizes temporarily in Internet Explorer while viewing a Web page. To do so, select View ⇨ Fonts from the menu. The Fonts submenu has the same five options as the normal method: Smallest, Small, Medium, Larger, and Largest.

▶ **EASY ON THE EYES**

Those of us who no longer have the keen vision we had in our youth really appreciate the ability to increase the font size at will. Whether you're an aging Baby Boomer or have any kind of vision impairment, this option can greatly improve your enjoyment of the Web.

▶ **FONT SAMPLES**

Unfortunately, Internet Explorer lacks the Navigator bonus of being able to see a sample of the font while choosing it. However, if you have both browsers installed on your system, as many people do, you can make your font choices in Navigator, note them down, and choose the same settings in Explorer.

▶ **SAVING FONTS AS GRAPHICS**

Some Web page designers avoid font issues by saving text in odd fonts as graphics. You can consider this option when designing your own site.

CROSS-REFERENCE

See Chapter 13 for more information on Web page fonts.

FIND IT ONLINE

The Microsoft typography Web site has free fonts at **http://www.microsoft.com/typography/fontpack/default.htm**.

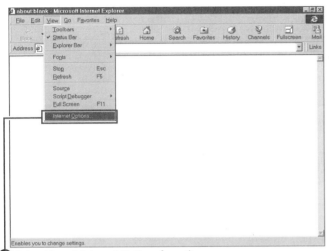

1 Select View ⇨ Internet Options from the menu.

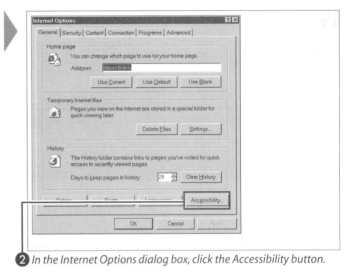

2 In the Internet Options dialog box, click the Accessibility button.

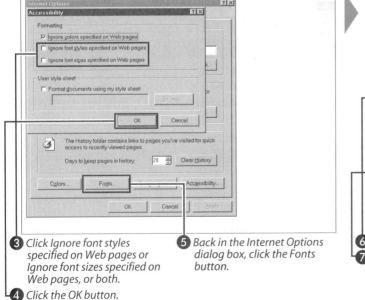

3 Click Ignore font styles specified on Web pages or Ignore font sizes specified on Web pages, or both.

4 Click the OK button.

5 Back in the Internet Options dialog box, click the Fonts button.

6 Select the font styles and sizes you want from the drop-down lists.

7 Click the OK button.

Setting Printing Preferences

Navigator and Internet Explorer are so similar in many of their functions, but here's one where they have an important difference. The page setup dialog box for Internet Explorer is really not much more than a standard print options dialog box. The one in Navigator, though, has a variety of options that can make your Web surfing experience much nicer.

Page Setup in Navigator

Navigator's page setup is both simple and useful, enabling you to choose how the printed page will look without regard to the appearance of the onscreen Web page. The first thing you find on it is a set of five checkboxes. The first, Beveled Lines, lets you set whether horizontal rules on the Web page will print as outlines or solid, filled-in lines (technically, the "outline" or 3D version is actually supposed to look like it's embedded when viewed on a Web page, while the "solid" version looks like it's painted on). The next two options, Black Text and Black Lines, cause text and lines to print black regardless of their color on the Web page. Last Page First does just what it says; if your printer paper comes out face up instead of face down, then use this option to have the printed pages stack in proper front-to-back order. The Print backgrounds option causes any background image on the page to be printed as well as the foreground material.

What these options mean in practical terms is that, if you are looking at a page with a purple background and yellow lettering with light green lines, and you want to print out a readable version on paper, you can select Black Text and Black Lines, deselect Print backgrounds, and print a nice, black-on-white version of the page. The third and fourth figures illustrate the difference in appearance between the screen version and the printed version.

The center section lets you set the page margins, and the bottom section lets you select which standard header (top of page) and footer (bottom of page) data is printed on the page.

Continued

TAKE NOTE

▶ BLANK PAGES

One thing to keep in mind with the Navigator page setup options is that you really need to be careful with the Print backgrounds option. If you leave it off and don't select Black Text, then white or light colored text will not show up on the printed page; you'll have a blank white page. If you leave it on and do select Black Text, then any page with a dark background will likewise be unreadable when printed; this time, you'll have a totally black page. Make sure to deselect Print backgrounds and select Black Text, just to play it safe.

CROSS-REFERENCE

See Chapter 2 for how to print Web pages.

FIND IT ONLINE

NetWelcome's site at **http://www.netwelcome.com/** has a dark background and light lettering.

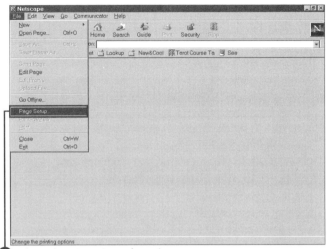

① Select File ⇨ Page Setup from the menu.

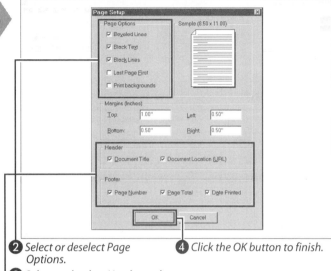

② Select or deselect Page Options.

③ Select or deselect Header and Footer options.

④ Click the OK button to finish.

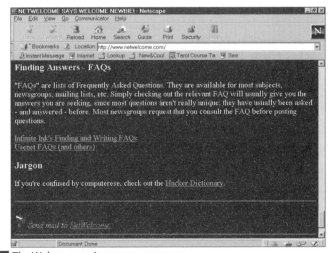

■ The Web page as it appears onscreen.

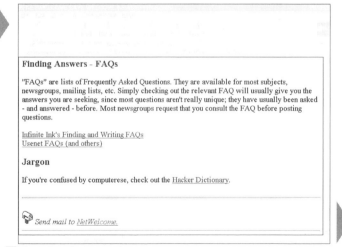

■ The printed page version.

Setting Printing Preferences

Continued

Page Setup in Internet Explorer

The figure on the top right shows the Internet Explorer Page Setup dialog box. The bulk of the options are just the standard printer choices you will likely leave alone, such as paper size, source (which tray in your printer the paper is drawn from), whether it's printed in normal vertical (portrait) position or sideways (landscape), and the margin width. The Printer button lets you access a dialog box where you can choose which printer you will use, if you have more than one printer connected to your system.

The only options of real interest related to printing Web pages are the Header and Footer. By default, the top of the printed page (header) shows the title of the Web page, the page number, and total page count (such as "Page 2 of 7"). The bottom of the printed page (footer) shows the URL of the Web page and the date the page was printed (Navigator prints both the date and the time by default). You can change the default settings to suit yourself, using the official codes shown in the sidebar on the facing page (for instance, you can add the time along with the date like Navigator does). You can also use your own text in the headers and footers. For example, if you want to have your company name show up on the bottom left, just type it in as the first thing under Footer. If you want to print your name as the header and you

want it flush right, just put **&b&bYour Name** in under Header, inserting your name instead of "Your Name" of course.

TAKE NOTE

▶ MENU KEYBOARD SHORTCUTS

Although the menu choices for getting to the Page Setup dialog box are identical in Navigator and Internet Explorer, you'll find a slight difference in the keyboard shortcuts. In Navigator, you press Alt-F for File and then G for Page Setup. In Internet Explorer, you press Alt-F for File but then U for Page Setup. So, if you don't want to use your mouse, you hit the G key in Navigator or the U key in Internet Explorer after you select the File menu with the Alt-F key combination.

▶ MARGINAL DIFFERENCES

Internet Explorer has a 0.75-inch default margin, while Navigator has a 0.50-inch default. Because a printed Web page is usually a bit different than the one you see onscreen, this means that more of the Web page will fit on a page printed from Navigator than on a page printed from Internet Explorer.

▶ PRINTER SETTINGS

Feel free to monkey with any of the printer settings in the Page Setup dialog box. Any changes you make will affect only Internet Explorer; they do not carry over to other programs. It's a really, really, really, good idea to note down the original settings before you make any changes, though.

CROSS-REFERENCE

See Chapter 2 for how to print Web pages.

FIND IT ONLINE

Good tips on using printers with Windows lurk at http://www.winmag.com/tips/hwprint1.htm.

Internet Explorer Header and Footer Codes

Internet Explorer's Header and Footer codes implement formatting with the ampersand sign.

▶ An ampersand character (&&)

▶ Center or right-align text (&b or &b&b)

▶ Short or long format Date (&d or &D)

▶ Regular or military time (&t or &T)

▶ Total pages or current page number (&P or &p)

▶ URL or Title of the Web page (&u or &w)

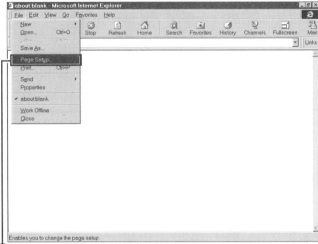

① Select File ➪ Page Setup from the menu.

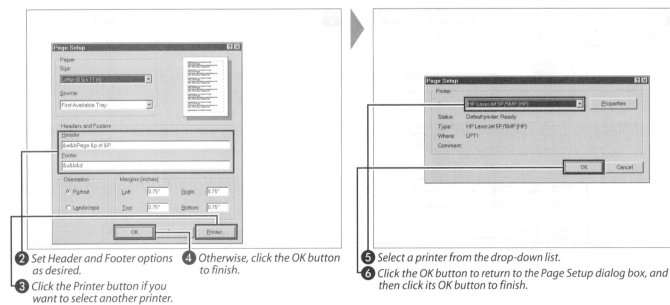

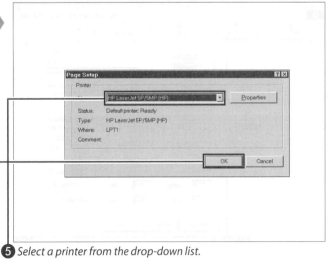

② Set Header and Footer options as desired.

③ Click the Printer button if you want to select another printer.

④ Otherwise, click the OK button to finish.

⑤ Select a printer from the drop-down list.

⑥ Click the OK button to return to the Page Setup dialog box, and then click its OK button to finish.

71

Setting Text-Only Web Pages

The variety and beauty of its graphics is one of the main reasons people enjoy the World Wide Web so much. If you're in a hurry, though, the graphics quickly become one of the Web's greatest annoyances. Images greatly slow down the display of Web pages. The more images a page has, the slower it will display due to the increased download time caused by large graphics files. Both of the major browsers include images by default, but let you choose to leave them out.

In Navigator, you only have a single choice to make, as shown in the second figure. In Internet Explorer, though, you must make three choices (see the fourth figure). This is because Internet Explorer supports some nonstandard features not found on most Web pages. These features (animation and video) will only become an issue when you access a Web page where the designer specifically included them, knowing they would only work on Internet Explorer.

All of these nonstandard features are also available to users of Navigator, but they are not built in to the browser, which is why you don't have to change any settings for them. In Navigator, they are supplied by plug-in modules that add optional capabilities to Web browsers, which are explained in Chapter 2. Plug-ins work with both Navigator and Internet Explorer.

TAKE NOTE

► FILES AND DOWNLOAD TIME

When you follow a link to a Web page, you're actually asking a remote computer to supply your Web browser with a collection of related files. In most cases, the text is a single file, but most Web pages have several image files linked to them. Your browser's job is to get all these different files and patch them together to create the Web page as you see it on your screen. Because text files are very small and image files are usually much larger, the addition of images vastly increases the download time (the time required for the remote computer to send the files to your computer).

► SOUNDS

Internet Explorer also has another nonstandard feature — background sound. While you're disabling the image components, you might also want to disable the Play sounds function, because many sound files also take a long time to download.

► JAVA

Java is a programming language popular on the Web; Java programs, or *applets*, can be added to Web pages. A page using Java also loads more slowly than a conventional page. You can disable Java while you're disabling the image loading. In Navigator, deselect Enable Java, which is under the image loading option. In Internet Explorer, scroll down a bit from Multimedia until you find Java VM and deselect Java JIT compiler enabled.

CROSS-REFERENCE

See Chapter 2 for more information on plug-ins.

FIND IT ONLINE

Java's home on the Web is located at http://192.9.9.100/java/.

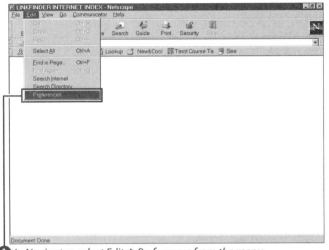

1 In Navigator, select Edit ⇨ Preferences from the menu.

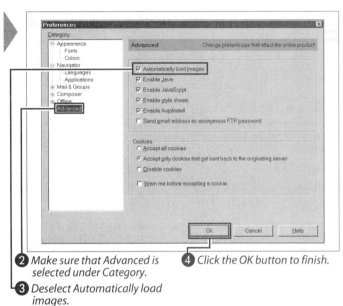

2 Make sure that Advanced is selected under Category.

3 Deselect Automatically load images.

4 Click the OK button to finish.

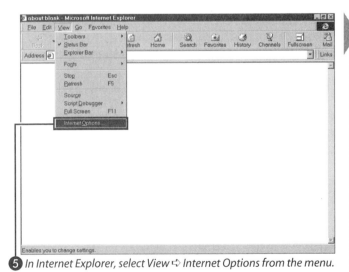

5 In Internet Explorer, select View ⇨ Internet Options from the menu.

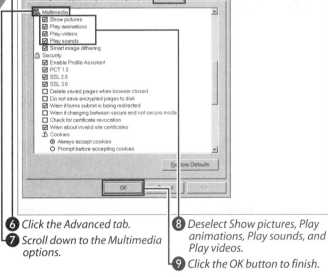

6 Click the Advanced tab.

7 Scroll down to the Multimedia options.

8 Deselect Show pictures, Play animations, Play sounds, and Play videos.

9 Click the OK button to finish.

Customizing Toolbars

Toolbars were created in applications to make tasks easier for a user to accomplish. You can invoke virtually any procedure with the mere click of a button. The problem is that a lot of toolbars that an application (such as a Web browser) supplies by default might not have exactly the tools you need, so you attach several toolbars to the top of your window. This can be a problem as well, limiting the full view of a Web page, and cluttering up the top of the browser with way too many icons. Thanks to some foresight on the part of the browser designers, however, you have the ability to add or subtract from toolbars, move toolbars around, and even move the buttons around within the toolbars.

Both Navigator and Internet Explorer let you add your own buttons to the toolbar so you can go directly to a favorite site without going through the bookmark/favorite procedure. The choice to add a toolbar button rather than adding a link to the bookmark/favorite list should depend on how often you wish to go to that Web site. In effect, this lets you create multiple home pages, because you can go to the Web pages you have toolbar buttons for as easily as when you click the Home button to go to your home page. The process of adding your own link buttons is easy and almost identical in both browsers, but the procedure for removing them is another matter. It's pretty clumsy in Navigator and really easy in Internet Explorer.

Continued

TAKE NOTE

▶ THE LOCATION ICON

The Location icon is located between the words Bookmarks and Location on the middle toolbar (which is, appropriately enough, named the Location toolbar). It shows a floating help message that says "Drag this to create a link to this page" when you place your mouse pointer over it.

▶ REARRANGING BUTTONS

You can change the order and position of your custom buttons on the Personal Toolbar by dragging them from their current position and dropping them where you want them. This is also true of the buttons that are already there when you install it, except for the Lookup and New&Cool buttons. These two buttons are different from the rest, because they trigger menus instead of links when you click them.

▶ UPDATING THE LINKS

Even though you create a button linked to a particular site, the site might move to a new location, or disappear completely. If this happens, you have to go to the new site and place a new icon in the Links bar. The button does not update the link automatically.

CROSS-REFERENCE

See Chapter 1 for more information on bookmarks.

FIND IT ONLINE

Find the Communicator/Navigator FAQ at **http://help.netscape.com/faqs/commctr4x.html**.

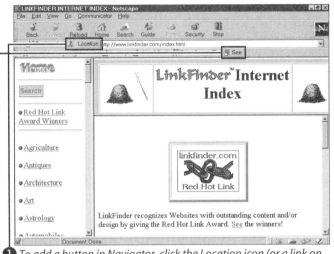

① To add a button in Navigator, click the Location icon (or a link on a Web page).

② Drag it to the Personal Toolbar and drop it there. The button is added.

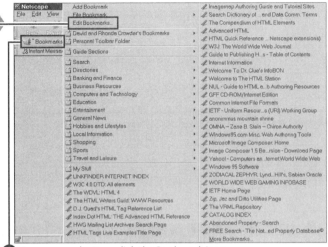

③ To remove a button, click the Bookmark icon.

④ Select Edit Bookmarks from the popup menu.

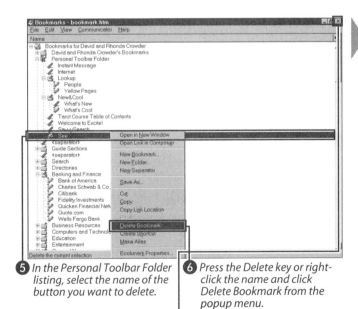

⑤ In the Personal Toolbar Folder listing, select the name of the button you want to delete.

⑥ Press the Delete key or right-click the name and click Delete Bookmark from the popup menu.

⑦ Click the Close Window button to finish.

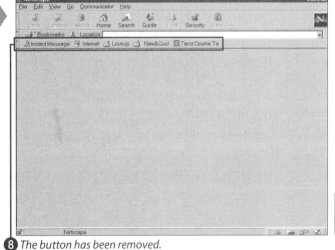

⑧ The button has been removed.

Customizing Toolbars

Continued

Toolbar Buttons in Navigator

Most of the toolbars in Navigator can't be customized — they can be removed or moved, but you can't add any buttons to them. The exception to this is the lowest toolbar, which is called the Personal Toolbar. All you have to do to add a button to it is, drag a line to that toolbar. To delete a button, you must go to the Personal Toolbar Folder and delete the link from the list that appears.

Toolbar Buttons in Internet Explorer

Internet Explorer's version of the Personal Toolbar in Navigator is called the Links bar. You've probably never seen it, because for reasons known only to Microsoft, it's tucked out of sight off the right side of the browser. Find the word "Links" to the right of the Address bar, click it and, without releasing the mouse button, pull down. The Links bar will appear, and you can release the mouse button. From now on, it'll stay there unless you put it back.

TAKE NOTE

▶ **HOLDING THAT BUTTON DOWN**

When you click a link you find on a Web page, intending to drag it to the Links bar, make sure you don't release the mouse button until you're ready to drop it on the Links bar. Otherwise, you'll activate the link and go to another Web page instead of creating your custom link button.

▶ **DEFAULT LINK BUTTONS**

You don't have to keep the buttons that came on the Links bar. If you don't want them, delete them. The process is exactly the same as for your own custom buttons.

▶ **REARRANGING LINK BUTTONS**

You can change the order of the link buttons simply by dragging them to where you want them on the Links bar and dropping them there. This is true for the default buttons as well as your custom ones. If you have so many link buttons that they're not all visible, you can scroll to see the hidden ones by clicking the little arrows to each side of the Links bar.

▶ **RECYCLING**

Don't forget to empty your Recycle Bin every now and then. The files in it still take up space on your hard drive, even if they don't show up anywhere else.

CROSS-REFERENCE

See the next section for more information on toolbars.

FIND IT ONLINE

Read recycle bin instructions at **http://wwwp.wfu/ edu/Computer-information/Support-Center/ Win95Help/recycle.htm**.

1 To add a button in Internet Explorer, click the Explorer icon in the Address bar (or a link on a Web page).

2 Drag it to the Links bar and drop it there.

3 The button is added.

4 To remove a button, right-click it.

5 Click Delete from the popup menu.

6 You need to confirm the deletion. Click the Yes button and the link button will be removed.

Rearranging Toolbars

The toolbars in your Web browser don't have to stay in the positions they came in. If, for some reason, you'd prefer to see the Location or Address toolbar on the bottom instead of in the middle, that's up to you. In either Navigator or Internet Explorer, just drag the toolbars into the position where you want them and drop them there. The other toolbars will move out of the way to make room for them, dropping down if you're moving a toolbar up or moving up if you're moving a toolbar down, as shown in the figure on the top left. You can even put two toolbars in the same level, and one will shrink to let the other one fit in.

You can also make the toolbars just plain disappear, leaving only the menu. Why would anyone want to do this? Well, it's true that most people prefer to use the icons and buttons rather than the menu, but toolbars take up a lot of space. Minimizing the toolbars frees up screen space that can show more of the Web page you're looking at. The figure on the upper right shows Navigator with one of its toolbars minimized.

You can do the same thing in Internet Explorer, but the process is a bit different and requires a few more steps. The bottom figures illustrate the difference.

CROSS-REFERENCE
See Chapter 1 for more information on typing in URLs.

FIND IT ONLINE
Find Internet Explorer's FAQ at **http://support. microsoft.com/support.c.asp?PR-IE&FR=0.**

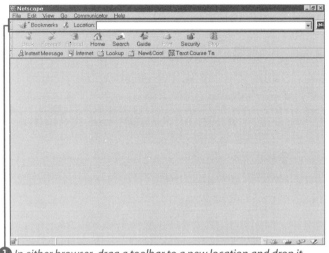

① *In either browser, drag a toolbar to a new location and drop it there.*

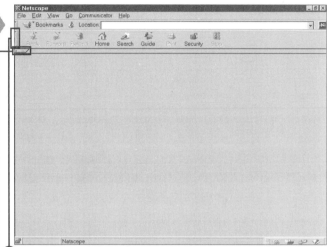

② *In Navigator, click the downward arrow to minimize the toolbar.*

③ *Click the rightward arrow to restore the toolbar.*

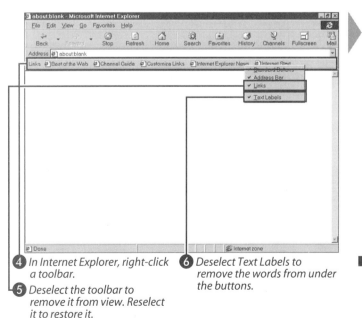

④ *In Internet Explorer, right-click a toolbar.*

⑤ *Deselect the toolbar to remove it from view. Reselect it to restore it.*

⑥ *Deselect Text Labels to remove the words from under the buttons.*

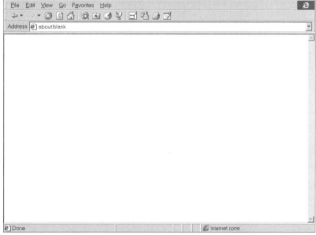

■ *Internet Explorer with Links bar and Text Labels deselected.*

Changing Security Settings

The security settings that Navigator and Internet Explorer come with are usually all you're likely to need. It's probably best to be just a bit paranoid and change these settings as little as possible. In particular, make sure you don't change the settings that enable SSL 2.0 and SSL 3.0. SSL stands for *Secure Sockets Layer,* the premier method for conducting secure transactions on the World Wide Web. SSL lets your browser and the remote computer exchange information that is encrypted so it can't be read in transit by third parties. If you disable the option to use SSL, you won't be able to use secure Web servers.

One setting you might wish to change is the one that alerts you whenever you enter or leave a secure Web site. This setting is not really needed. As detailed in Chapter 2, secure Web sites are already identified by both browsers via their lock icons. Because the lock icon in either browser already clues you in about the security status of a Web site, having an alert box pop up every time you enter or leave a secure site gets to be annoying very quickly. In Internet Explorer, this setting is *Warn if changing between secure and not secure mode.* Navigator actually has two separate settings: *Entering an encrypted site* and *Leaving an encrypted site.* The single setting in Internet Explorer doesn't leave much room for flexibility, but

Navigator's separation of the two situations — entering and leaving a secure site — gives you a reasonable third option. Even though it is annoying to have to cancel an alert box to enter a secure site, it's good to know if you suddenly leave one unexpectedly. It's very easy for a sloppy Web designer to create a secure site in which the actual order form is unsecure. If you're using Navigator, you can keep the *Leaving an encrypted site* warning active to protect you against this eventuality, but you can still lessen your aggravation by disabling the *Entering an encrypted site* alert.

TAKE NOTE

▶ THE SECURITY TAB

Internet Explorer has a Security tab in the Internet Options dialog box. This lets you assign low and high security settings to particular sites. It's best to just leave these alone (if you need to assign a high security setting to a site, don't visit it). If you want to get a look at how the default options are set, select Custom and click the Settings tab. Unless you're an expert, don't change these settings. The settings you need to actually concern yourself with appear under the Advanced tab, as shown in the figure on the lower right.

CROSS-REFERENCE

See Chapter 2 for information on making online purchases.

FIND IT ONLINE

You'll find a good site on Web security at **http://www. -ns.rutgers.edu/www-security/index.html**.

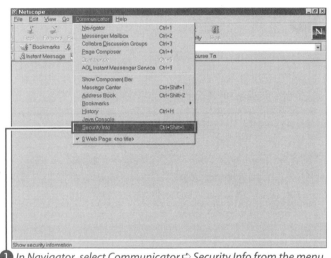

❶ *In Navigator, select Communicator ⇨ Security Info from the menu.*

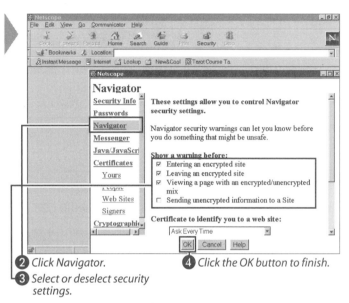

❷ *Click Navigator.*

❸ *Select or deselect security settings.*

❹ *Click the OK button to finish.*

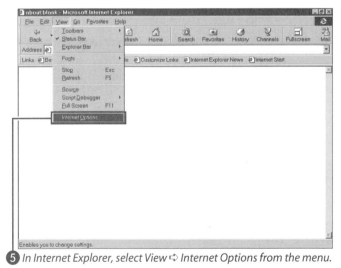

❺ *In Internet Explorer, select View ⇨ Internet Options from the menu.*

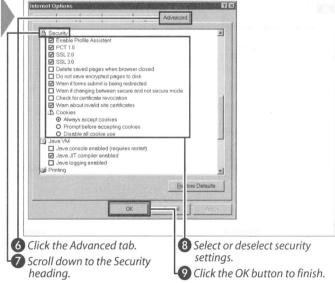

❻ *Click the Advanced tab.*

❼ *Scroll down to the Security heading.*

❽ *Select or deselect security settings.*

❾ *Click the OK button to finish.*

Setting Cache Size

Web browsers keep a copy of files of Web pages, images, and so forth on your hard drive. The reason for this is that, if you go back and forth among the same Web sites several times (as is likely when Web surfing), the experience would be very time-consuming if your browser had to get the same files over and over again from a remote computer. By keeping a local copy, a Web page is displayed much more quickly. You pay a price for this, though. Hard disk space is precious; it seems like file size always manages to stay a jump ahead of hard-drive size. You can increase or decrease the size of the cache on your hard drive. If you desperately need space, you can even flush the cache entirely. If, for some reason, you don't want to use the default folder for the cache, you can change that, too.

You can also set how picky the browser is about comparing the cached version of a Web page with the online version. Because the vast majority of Web pages change from time to time, you should never use the "Never" setting for this, or you'll never get an updated version. On the other hand, checking with every single access defeats the whole idea of a cache. The only time to set your browser to check every single time is when you are dealing with time-critical changes, as with a stock ticker.

TAKE NOTE

▶ DIFFERENT METHODS

Navigator actually has two caches, one in RAM and one on disk. Internet Explorer has only the one on disk. In Navigator, as shown in the figure on the upper right, you can specify the exact size of both caches. In Explorer, shown in the figure on the lower right, you can only specify a percentage of your hard drive. Even at the lowest setting of 1%, this can be a huge chunk of space on a multi-gigabyte hard drive.

▶ VIEWING CACHE FILES

In Internet Explorer, you can look at the list of files in the cache while you set the size. Click the View Files button to bring up the listing. Although Navigator doesn't have this button, the process in it is actually easier, because you can do it at any time. Just type the words **about:cache** in the address box and hit your Enter key.

▶ AUTOMATIC FLUSHES

When the cache is full and new pages need to be added to it, the browser automatically dumps the oldest files. If your browser seems to be hanging briefly for no apparent reason, look at the status line and see if it says it's deleting old files from the cache during those pauses.

CROSS-REFERENCE

See Chapter 2 for information on saving Web pages.

FIND IT ONLINE

NBC Europe has a good cache adjustment page at **http://www.ncbeurope.com/browser.htm**.

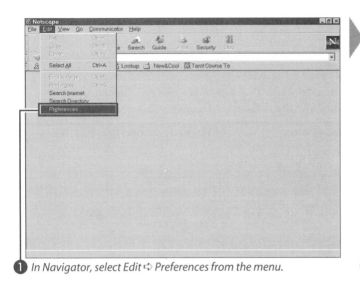

1 In Navigator, select Edit ⇨ Preferences from the menu.

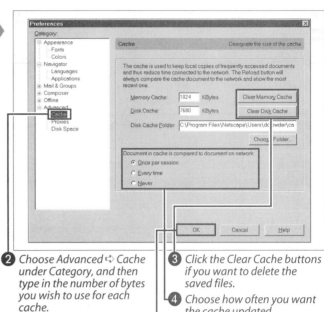

2 Choose Advanced ⇨ Cache under Category, and then type in the number of bytes you wish to use for each cache.

3 Click the Clear Cache buttons if you want to delete the saved files.

4 Choose how often you want the cache updated.

5 Click the OK button to finish.

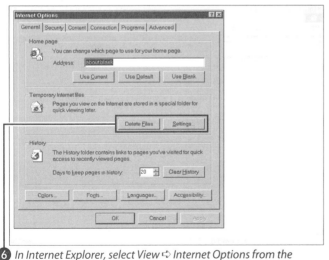

6 In Internet Explorer, select View ⇨ Internet Options from the menu. Click Delete Files to clear the cache or Settings to change settings.

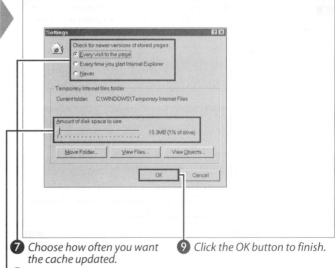

7 Choose how often you want the cache updated.

8 Use the slider bar to change the amount of disk space used by the cache.

9 Click the OK button to finish.

Adding Channels via the Active Desktop

This task is a Microsoft-specific option available only in Internet Explorer. Channels are automatic updates of Web pages that are, in theory, delivered to your desktop automatically. However, despite the TV-sounding term, channels aren't what you'd think — they are not actually broadcast to you. The actual process is exactly the same as if you surfed to the site and downloaded the pages. What happens is that Internet Explorer keeps a list of sites you want to be updated on and a schedule of how often to update them. At the appointed times, it goes and gets the updates for you without you having to do it manually. It's not really broadcast technology, but it's still a pretty nice feature.

Perhaps the most interesting aspect of this channel feature is that it doesn't have to show up in Internet Explorer. Through the Windows Active Desktop, the information can also show up right on your desktop, along with the icons for your programs. Microsoft has several channels available to which you can subscribe, and many Web sites have added their own channels you can subscribe to at the click of a button.

The Microsoft channels Web site lets you preview various channels (they currently showcase over 3,000 channels). The Channels window enables you to access channels by category. If you want to see the whole Web page without scrolling, click the Channels button again to make the Channels window go away. To preview a channel, click its icon. A sample of the channel loads in Internet Explorer. Once you find a channel you want to add, you can choose to just add the channel to the Channel bar; subscribe, but not download (getting only notifications that the channel has been updated); or download the whole channel.

TAKE NOTE

▶ SCHEDULING

The schedule for updates can vary from moments in the case of a stock ticker to monthly in the case of an online magazine.

▶ SKIPPING THE CHANNEL GUIDE

Several channels are already listed in Internet Explorer that you can check out by going directly to them instead of going through the Microsoft channels site. Some of them, such as the Disney channel, are standalone buttons in the Channels window, while others are listings under major categories such as Sports, Business, or Entertainment. Clicking a standalone button connects you to the channel, while clicking a category shows you the listing under it.

CROSS-REFERENCE

See Chapter 1 for information on downloading Web pages.

FIND IT ONLINE

Read about "IE4 Channel Subscription Tips" at http://www.iehelp.com/user/nr971116.asp.

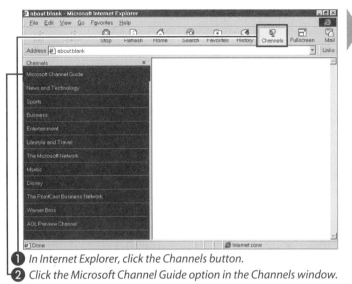

❶ *In Internet Explorer, click the Channels button.*

❷ *Click the Microsoft Channel Guide option in the Channels window.*

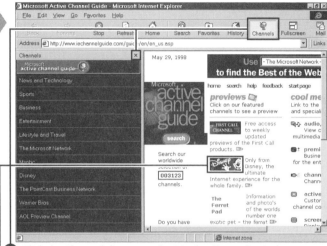

❸ *Click the Channels button or the X in the Channels window to close the Channels window.*

❹ *Click a channel icon to see a preview.*

❺ *Click Add Active Channel to add the channel.*

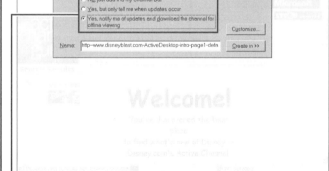

❻ *Select your subscription options.*

❼ *Click the OK button. The channel will be added.*

85

Personal Workbook

Q&A

1 What is a *hover color*?

_____

_____

_____

2 Why should you refrain from using custom colors?

_____

_____

_____

3 What are *dynamic fonts*?

_____

_____

_____

4 How do you speed up download time?

_____

_____

_____

5 How do you add a custom link button?

_____

_____

_____

6 How do you move a toolbar?

_____

_____

_____

7 What is a secure Web site?

_____

_____

_____

8 Why do browsers use disk caches?

_____

_____

_____

ANSWERS: PAGE 378

EXTRA PRACTICE

1 Set the background color to red in Navigator or Internet Explorer.

2 Put your name in the header of a printed page using Internet Explorer.

3 Add a link button for the Web page at **http://www.idgbooks.com/** to your toolbar.

4 Move the link button you just added to the far left of the toolbar.

5 Move your Location or Address bar to the bottom of the toolbars.

6 Increase your cache size, and then return it to its original size.

REAL-WORLD APPLICATIONS

✔ You may need to find some information fast. You can set your browser so it won't display images; this way you can rapidly move through several Web sites, gathering the data you need without looking at the pretty pictures.

✔ Your elderly aunt pays you a visit and wants to surf the Web. You might reset the fonts so they are larger and she can see them better.

✔ Your hard drive might be short on space. You empty the cache to get more room.

✔ Your boss complains about having to dig through all those bookmarks to find his favorite sites. You quickly add the ones he wants to his toolbar and get a large raise.

Visual Quiz

What is this? How do you get to it? What do you do there?

_____

_____

_____

_____

_____

_____

Communicating on the Net

In this part, we show you how to use the different methods of talking to other people on the Internet. Keeping with the basic approach of this book, all the programs we cover are free. These programs also share two qualities: Each is simple to use yet offers advanced capabilities. This way, you can get going right away, but the programs will still be useful to you as you grow in experience and begin to explore all the different things Internet communication has to offer.

We cover what e-mail is, how to send and receive messages, how they're relayed across the Internet to the correct address, how to check spelling, sending the same message to two or more people, saving and printing messages, building an address book, message encryption for privacy, the etiquette of e-mail, and how to avoid being deluged by junk mail.

Next, we dive into the fascinating world of newsgroups, the topical discussions that are relayed around the world. You'll see how to find the newsgroups you're interested in and how to participate in them.

We also introduce you to the live, instant online communication known as Internet Relay Chat where people gather in virtual rooms to meet, talk, and party. Then you'll find out about online communities, where people with similar interests join together in cyberspace.

Finally, we tell you how to use Internet telephony to make free long-distance phone calls.

CHAPTER 5

E-mail Basics

If you've never used e-mail before, trust us — you're going to love it! E-mail is vastly superior to sticking a piece of paper in an envelope, putting a stamp on it, licking it and dropping it in a mailbox, and then waiting to see how many days it takes for your letter to arrive and how many more days it takes to get a reply. Regular mail is laughingly called *snail mail* by e-mail users because of the amount of time it takes to move paper from one building to another via trucks and planes. And let's not even think about international mail delays.

With e-mail, you type your message, hit the send button, and it's winging its way to the recipient at the speed of light. Well, okay, it's a little bit slower than light, but for all practical purposes, it's instantaneous. Transit times of 1 or 2 minutes are not unusual. That's about 1,500 times as fast as a really swift snail mail delivery. International delivery is just as fast, because the Internet has no borders. You can send a message from Chicago to Tokyo just as easily as you can from New York to L.A — or from Minneapolis to St. Paul.

All it takes is an e-mail address. You got one when you signed up with your ISP. Usually, it's some variation on your own name added to the name of your ISP. For instance, if you're named Jane Smith and your ISP is something.net, your e-mail address might be janes@something.net or jsmith@something.net. When someone wants to send you e-mail, they just send it to that address. The message is relayed along the Internet to something.net, which sends it on along to its user, jsmith. If you're not on a permanent Internet connection, something.net holds on to your messages until you link up and ask for them, and then the ISP sends them to your local computer via your e-mail program.

Many people have multiple e-mail accounts, and you can have them from more than one provider. Some are paid, while others are offered free from various sources such as Juno, Excite, Netscape, and various online communities (discussed in Chapter 9).

Lots of different e-mail programs are available, with a variety of features and costs. In this chapter, we'll be using Pegasus Mail, which is a free, but full-featured e-mail program.

Configuring E-mail

Part of the fun of e-mail is customizing it to reflect your personality. The nice thing about using a POP client such as Pegasus Mail is that you have easy access to the Personal Name that appears on your messages, as well as signature files that appear at the bottom of each message you send. If other people in your household will be using Pegasus to check their mail, you can even serve as the Administrator, granting levels of access to other users.

When you first start up Pegasus Mail, you'll need to provide it with some information so it'll know who you are and what to do with your e-mail. The level of responsibility you take starts when you set up the mailboxes. You have a choice of just setting yourself up on Pegasus Mail (which you can still do in a multiuser environment, if the other users prefer to use a program such as Microsoft Outlook), or sharing the application with others. Regardless of whether you're in charge of a network or only one computer, you should be the one with Administrator privileges, so you can add or delete users as necessary.

You don't have to worry about previous administration experience when setting up Pegasus for other users. Much of this application is intuitive, and various components will guide you along. The Internet Setup Wizard is one tool that makes your job easy. Using this wizard is covered in the next task.

TAKE NOTE

▶ **SORTING E-MAIL**

To avoid a mess, you should make sure each user's e-mail goes into a separate folder. You can establish such a system from the beginning, when you add new users to Pegasus.

▶ **KEEPING SECURE E-MAIL**

Because Pegasus Mail is a POP client that stores messages on your hard drive, it's easy to access other people's mail on the same computer. Unless you've installed Windows NT (which enables multiple users to maintain separate, secure files), you might have to come up with an alternate solution.

▶ **UNDERSTANDING CLIENTS AND SERVERS**

The Internet works as a system composed of two kinds of computers — those computers that provide services and the computers that use those services. The computers that provide services are known, appropriately enough, as *servers*. The ones that use the services are known as *clients*. Both the computers themselves and the programs that perform the tasks can be known by these names. Thus, your e-mail program is an e-mail client that accesses an e-mail server to pick up and send its messages. Along the same lines, your Web browser is the client that accesses the Web server that provides it with the Web pages it displays.

CROSS-REFERENCE

See Chapter 6 for advanced e-mail techniques.

FIND IT ONLINE

You can find lots of Windows e-mail clients at
http://www.sharewarejunkies.com/winemail.htm.

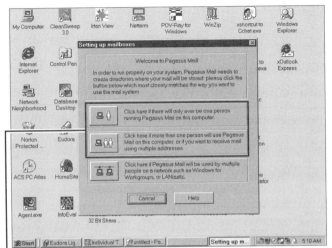

1 *Click the top button if you're the only user. For multiple users, click the middle button.*

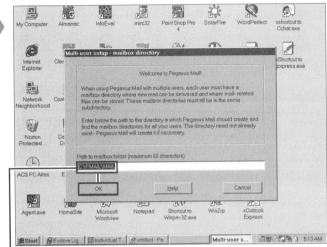

2 *Either change the folder path or just click the OK button to continue.*

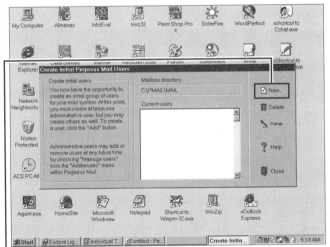

3 *Click the New button to add new users.*

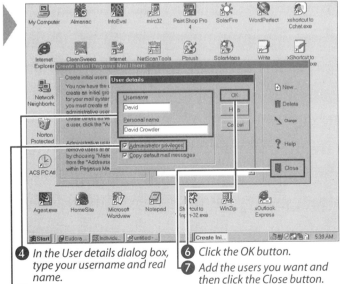

4 *In the User details dialog box, type your username and real name.*

5 *To add and delete users, check the Administrator Privileges checkbox.*

6 *Click the OK button.*

7 *Add the users you want and then click the Close button.*

E-mail Internet Setup Wizard

In most cases, your ISP will provide you with all of the information you need when you are setting up your mail client. Other than your username, the most important pieces of information you need for e-mail are the names of your ISP's POP3 server and SMTP server. The POP3 server is just the server at your ISP that handles your incoming mail for you and holds it for you until you log on and download it to your e-mail client. The SMTP server is the server that sends your e-mail messages out to other people. Chances are that the addresses for these servers follow the convention of "pop" (or "smtp"), followed by a period, and your ISP's address (for example, "pop.yourisp.net" and "smtp.yourisp.net"). It is possible, however, that your ISP provided you with the IP address (four sets of numbers separated by dots) for the servers. Either way, the addresses should still be valid.

When you launch the Internet Setup Wizard, it asks for your username and password. It's important to note that your username and password might not be the same as the ones you entered for Pegasus Mail; they're the ones your ISP acknowledged when you signed on with them. In most cases, you should maintain continuity and use the same username and password. It's easier to remember one set of login information than it is to remember two.

Continued

TAKE NOTE

▶ GETTING THE DATA FIRST

Before you start with the Internet Setup Wizard, you should have on hand the following information from your ISP. They should have provided you with these items when you signed up. If you don't know the data already, call them up and ask them for it.
- ▶ Your e-mail address.
- ▶ Your e-mail username as assigned by your ISP.
- ▶ Your password for logging on to your ISP.
- ▶ Your POP3 (incoming mail) server address.
- ▶ Your SMTP (outgoing mail) server address.

▶ CHANGING YOUR MIND

The Internet Setup Wizard makes it easy for you to change settings any time before you're done with it. If you want to abort the setup procedure, you can just click the Cancel button at any time to stop things. If you realize you put something in wrong and you've already moved on to other screens, you can hit the Back button to return to previous screens and retype your responses.

▶ THE @ SYMBOL

E-mail addresses consist of three parts. The first part is your username. The middle part is the @ symbol, which is spoken aloud as "at," and the last part is the organization that hosts your e-mail account — thus, if your e-mail address is ralph@xyz.com, you're "Ralph at xyz dot com."

CROSS-REFERENCE

See the section on picking up e-mail messages later in this chapter.

FIND IT ONLINE

Read about Internet standards, including POP3, at **http://www.byte.com/art/9702/sec6/art3.htm**.

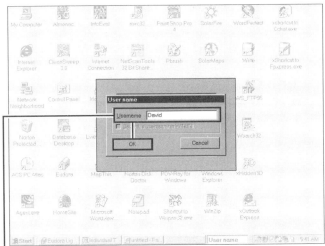

1 Enter your username and click the OK button.

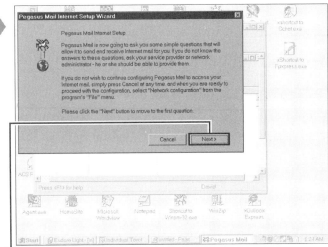

2 Click the Next button to proceed.

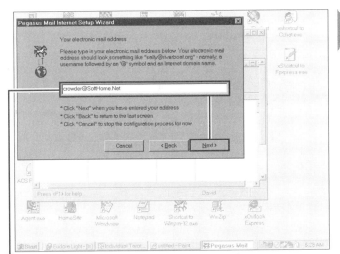

3 Type in your e-mail address and click the Next button.

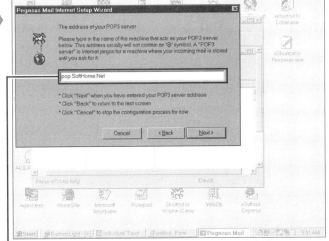

4 Enter the address of your POP3 server, and then click the Next button.

The password will not show up the way you type it. Instead, it appears as a line of asterisks (like *******) as you type it in. This is a security measure; most programs use it so someone looking over your shoulder can't read your password.

In order to know how to coordinate the pickup and delivery of your mail, Pegasus also needs to know whether or not you have a permanent connection to the Internet. Unless you have a dedicated line (such as ISDN or a T1 line), you will need to select the Dialup option. When using a modem to dial up and get your e-mail from your ISP, you have the option of staying connected for only the time necessary to upload outgoing messages or download incoming messages. The rest of the time, you can work in "offline" mode, where you can take your time composing messages, and not incur any additional charges from staying connected to a server. Messages you compose in this mode are placed in a queue, to be sent out the next time you log on to the mail server. See the task later in this chapter that deals with queued messages.

TAKE NOTE

▶ E-MAIL SERVERS AND ALPHABET SOUP

The incoming mail server is called POP3. This stands for Post Office Protocol, Version 3. The outgoing mail server is called SMTP. This stands for Simple Mail Transfer Protocol.

▶ TYPING PASSWORDS

When you type in the password, you need to be careful to get it right. Because it displays as a series of asterisks, you don't get the normal feedback you get when you type other things. And don't forget that your password is case-sensitive — don't type capitals where you used lower case or vice versa.

▶ WAITING TO GET THROUGH

If you try to connect to your ISP and access your e-mail after you set up Pegasus Mail, but can't get through, don't panic. Heavy traffic on the Internet might prevent you from making an easy connection. You might have to wait and retry it. Usually, you will hear a busy signal and a dialog box will pop up, indicating that the line is busy. If your modem makes noises that sound like you have made a connection, but you still can't get through, make sure you entered your information correctly. If you have, contact your ISP's help line.

CROSS-REFERENCE

See the section on sending e-mail messages later in this chapter.

FIND IT ONLINE

There's a plain language explanation of SMTP at **http://www.busn.ucok.edu/tips/INFO_INT/smtp.htm**.

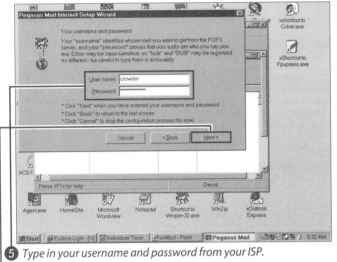

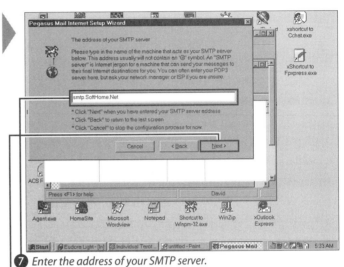

5 *Type in your username and password from your ISP.*
6 *Click the Next button to proceed.*

7 *Enter the address of your SMTP server.*
8 *Click the Next button to proceed.*

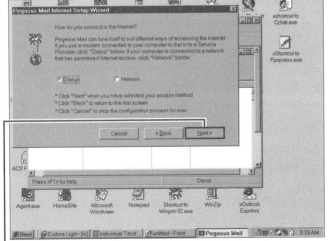

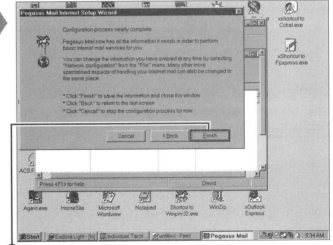

9 *If you connect via a dialup connection, click the Next button to move on.*

10 *Click the Finish button.*

Sending New Messages

Your first order of business might be to send a message to your friends and colleagues, announcing your e-mail address. At the very least, you should probably send a test message to someone you know, to see if you can reach others without problems.

You need two things to send a message to someone via e-mail: the person's e-mail address and something to say. While the latter part is up to you, we'll show you the rest of the process in Pegasus Mail.

By default, Pegasus has a two-part procedure for sending messages. After typing your message, you must click the Send button and then, when you return to the main screen, you have to click the Send Queued Mail button. This serves two purposes: If you are not connected to the Internet, you don't have to connect for every message you send; you can save them up and send them all at once. The other benefit of this queued format is that you can delete or modify a message before it's sent out, if you change your mind. It's sort of a safeguard. If you don't think you'll need this setup, you can read the following task, which explains how to get rid of the queued message step.

When sending messages, it's a good idea to keep a copy, so you can refer to it later. In most e-mail applications, as in Pegasus, you can either write your own address in the cc: field (see the task later in this chapter on using the carbon copy feature), or tell the application to save a copy of all outgoing messages.

TAKE NOTE

▶ FINDING E-MAIL ADDRESSES OF WEBMASTERS

If you're on a Web page, you can usually find the e-mail address of the Webmaster at the bottom of the page in the form of a "mailto" link (the *Webmaster* is the person in charge of the Web site — sometimes, the e-mail link is to the owner of the page instead). Generally, all you have to do is click the link and send a message from the Web browser, but you can also note down the address for later reference and send a message from your regular e-mail client.

▶ MODEM SHORTHAND

Modems today run at speeds of up to 57,344 bps (bits per second) and they're getting faster all the time. Way back in the days when modems ran at 300 bps, it took a lot longer to transmit messages. Thus, messages tended to be short and to the point, much like telegrams. Modem users found that it was necessary to find shortcuts for common expressions. Even though things run so much faster now, the old abbreviations still hang on. That's why you'll often see such signoffs as TTFN ("Ta ta for now"), TIA ("Thanks in advance"), or TTYL ("Talk to ya later"). Other common abbreviations and their variations work their way into the main body of messages, too, such as IMO ("In my opinion"), IMHO ("In my humble opinion"), and IMNSHO ("In my not-so-humble opinion"). Check the link under Find It Online below for a full listing.

CROSS-REFERENCE

See the section on sending to multiple recipients later in this chapter.

FIND IT ONLINE

You'll find popular e-mail abbreviations listed at **http://www.usyd.edu.su/netting/news/extra/nacronyms.html.**

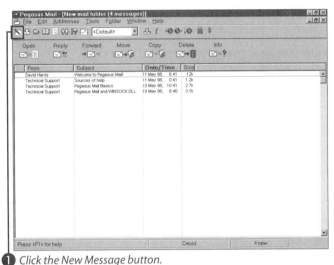

1 Click the New Message button.

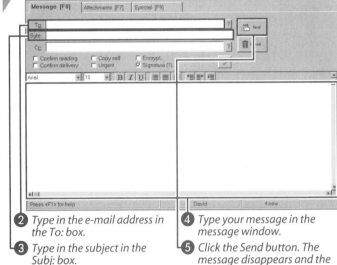

2 Type in the e-mail address in the To: box.

3 Type in the subject in the Subj: box.

4 Type your message in the message window.

5 Click the Send button. The message disappears and the main screen reappears.

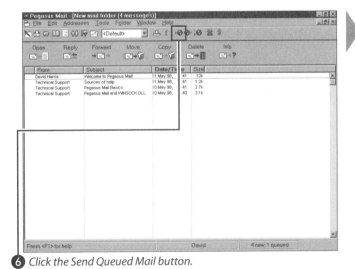

6 Click the Send Queued Mail button.

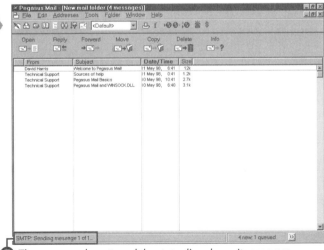

7 The message departs and the status line shows its progress.

Eliminating the Queue

If you think it's silly to have to tell Pegasus Mail to send a message twice, you're not alone. While it's set up by default to put messages in a queue and wait for you to tell it to send all the queued messages later, you don't have to leave it that way. You can set things so that your message is sent the instant you first tell the program to send it, right after you write it. No lines, no waiting, no reservations required. All you have to do is navigate to the *Advanced network configuration options*, and select the checkbox labeled *Send mail at once without placing in queue*. From then on, whenever you hit the Send button after you write a message, the message gets sent right away.

If you don't have a permanent connection to the Internet, you should strongly consider keeping the queue system. As mentioned in the last task, you can modify the messages at the last minute, and you can keep from having to reconnect for every message you send out. This can considerably affect the use of your phone line and make your time online more efficient. If you have a series of sizeable files to send, then the time to log on, type a message, attach a file, send a message, and then type a new message will add up. However, if you type out your messages, attach files, and send them to the queue all before you log on, you will have kept the phone lines open for important incoming calls. When it comes time to log on and send the messages in the queue, you can leave your computer and complete other activities.

TAKE NOTE

▶ THAT OTHER BUTTON

If you decide you like the queue and want to stick with it, then you might want to be aware of the other toolbar button that affects sending queued e-mail messages. You already know about the first "globe" button from the previous section, and you'll remember that there are three of them. The second globe button is for picking up e-mail messages from your POP server, and its functions are discussed in the section on picking up messages. The third globe button is a combination of the two — it both picks up all incoming messages and sends all queued messages. It can't do both at once, of course, although you can treat it as though it does do so for all practical purposes. First, it makes a connection with the POP server, and then, when it is done downloading any incoming e-mail, it breaks that connection, connects with the SMTP server, and sends out all of your waiting messages, after which it breaks the outgoing connection. If you're going to stick with queued messages, it's a real labor-saving device — one-stop shopping.

CROSS-REFERENCE
See the preceding section on sending new messages.

FIND IT ONLINE
The IETF (Internet Engineering Task Force), at **http://www.ietf.org/**, keeps track of technical standards.

1 Select Tools ⇨ Options from the menu.

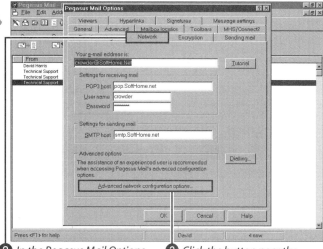

2 In the Pegasus Mail Options dialog box, click the Network tab.

3 Click the button near the bottom labeled Advanced network configuration options.

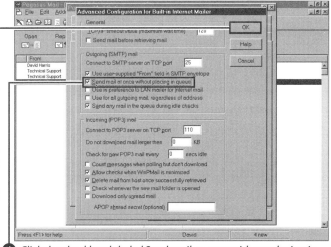

4 Click the checkbox labeled Send mail at once without placing in queue.

5 Click the OK button. This returns you to the Pegasus Mail Options dialog box.

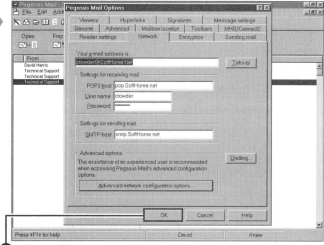

6 Click the OK button to complete the task.

Using the Spell Checker

Unless you're an English composition major, odds are that you need a little help with spelling now and then. Even we professional writers slip up from time to time, and the final step before submitting a chapter to our editors is to run a spelling check on it.

Make sure the checkbox labeled *Skip quoted (">")* *lines* is checked if you are replying to a message. Otherwise, the spelling checker checks the parts you quoted from the message you're replying to; you'll just end up having to correct someone else's spelling errors, and there's not much point in that. The ">" part, by the way, is because quoted lines start with the greater-than character to distinguish them from your own prose.

The spelling checker looks in its dictionary and comes up with a list of words that are close to it in spelling. Generally speaking, it's very likely that one of the suggested words will be the correct one, and in this case, it is indeed in the list of suggested replacements. The simple solution is to select the correct word and click the Change button. The incorrectly spelled word is automatically replaced by the right one and the spelling checker moves on, checking the rest of the message.

Continued

TAKE NOTE

▶ WHEN DOES IT MATTER?

If you're just dropping a line to a friend, precision isn't that important. In more formal contexts such as business communications, though, poor spelling can leave a lasting bad impression. Your basic rule here is, if the message is important, take the time to check the spelling.

▶ USING TWO DICTIONARIES

Some strange variations differentiate the two dictionaries. You'd expect to find such variations as "color" in the U.S. one and "colour" in the U.K. one, of course. But in our example message, "Olga" is in the U.S. dictionary, but not in the U.K. one and "Dave" is in the U.K. one, but not in the U.S. one. Both correctly identify the misspelling of "chickn," though.

▶ GETTING A FOREIGN VERSION

Pegasus is available in a variety of languages, such as Dutch, French, German, Polish, Spanish, and a few others. If you communicate frequently with someone in one of these languages, you can download other versions at **http://www.pegasus.usa.com/lang**. This way, you don't have to worry about an English spelling checker marking everything incorrectly.

CROSS-REFERENCE

See the section on replying to messages later in this chapter.

FIND IT ONLINE

Check out Common Errors in English at **http://www.wsu.edu:8080/~brians/errors/errors.html**.

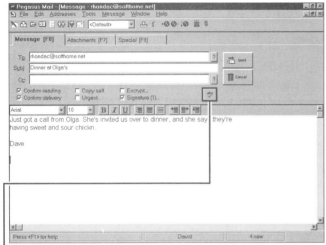

① When your message is complete, click the Spelling Check button.

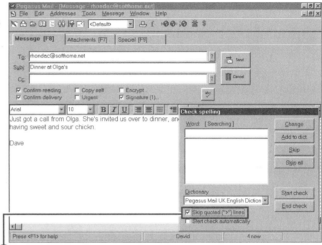

② Make sure the checkbox labeled Skip quoted (">") lines is checked if you are replying to a message.

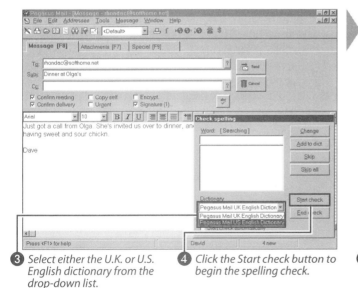

③ Select either the U.K. or U.S. English dictionary from the drop-down list.

④ Click the Start check button to begin the spelling check.

⑤ If your cursor is not at the beginning of the message, the spelling checker asks if it should start at the beginning. Click the Yes button.

Using the Spell Checker

Continued

When the spelling checker highlights a correctly spelled word that is not in its dictionary, it suggests several possible replacements, but because the word is not misspelled, that's not a solution. You have three different options for dealing with this situation. If you want to make sure you never have to deal with this again, you can add this word to the dictionary. This way, the next time the spelling checker encounters the word, it'll know it's spelled correctly. Just click the Add to dict. button and you're safe forever more.

The second possibility is to just tell the spelling checker to ignore the word and move on. If you click the Skip button, the spelling checker passes right over the word, but if it runs into it again in the same message, it stops again and you'll have to hit the Skip button every time this happens.

If you don't want to add the word to the dictionary, and you don't want to have to choose Skip at every occurrence of the word all through the message, then click the Skip all button. This way, when the spelling checker encounters the term again in this message, it'll still ignore it. This option doesn't have any effect on future spelling checks of other messages, though. Both versions of the Skip command are temporary measures.

TAKE NOTE

► CHECKING THE LINGO

If you have a particularly long message that you plan to send to friends or family, and you use a lot of nicknames and "special lingo," you might want to avoid the spelling checker altogether, or you'll spend most of your time telling Pegasus to skip the "misspelled" words.

► CUTTING OUT EARLY

If you want to stop checking the spelling before the entire process is completed, you can click the End check button to abort the process.

► USING OTHER EDITING TECHNIQUES

If you tend to run short on time, you can define certain abbreviations to stand for familiar phrases, and then expand them with a quick keystroke. All you have to do is access the Glossary dialog box by selecting Edit ➪ Glossary ➪ Edit/create. You'll find several abbreviations already entered. You can modify these, or create new ones by clicking Add. To expand an abbreviation in your message, just type it in, then press Ctrl+/ or Ctrl+E.

CROSS-REFERENCE

See Chapter 7 for information on participating in mailing lists.

FIND IT ONLINE

Don't miss Mama's Hot 100 Grammar Goofs at http://www.unl.edu/mama/grammar/college.htm.

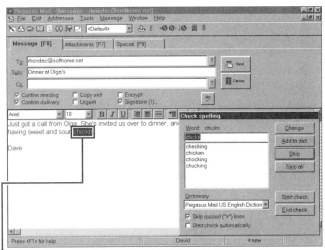

6 The spelling checker highlights a misspelled word and suggests replacements.

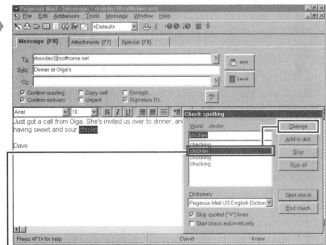

7 Select the correct spelling and click the Change button.

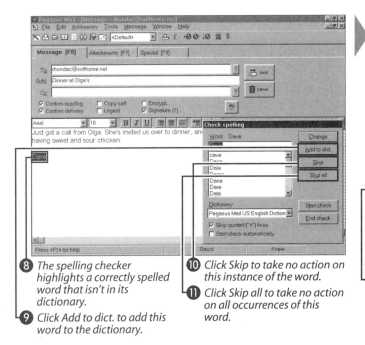

8 The spelling checker highlights a correctly spelled word that isn't in its dictionary.

9 Click Add to dict. to add this word to the dictionary.

10 Click Skip to take no action on this instance of the word.

11 Click Skip all to take no action on all occurrences of this word.

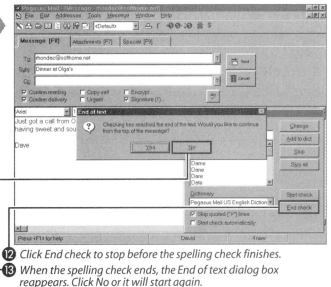

12 Click End check to stop before the spelling check finishes.

13 When the spelling check ends, the End of text dialog box reappears. Click No or it will start again.

Using Carbon Copy

If you're old enough to remember typewriters that didn't have any memory (we confess to using ones that didn't even use electricity), then you'll remember carbon paper. If you wanted to have more than one copy of a letter, you'd take two or three sheets of typing paper and put carbon paper between them. Then, when you typed the letter, the carbon on the interleaved sheets would print on the extra sheets of paper (and your fingers) and make a less-than-perfect but readable copy of the original. Although one of the purposes behind this was to have a copy for your files, another was to have a copy to send to someone other than the person the letter was addressed to. The first copy was just called a "carbon copy" and it was abbreviated "cc." If you wanted to send a copy to someone on the sly without listing them, though, that was called the "blind carbon copy" or "bcc." The names of these options, "cc" and "bcc," appear in e-mail as relics of the past.

To add a second recipient to your e-mail message, type in the address in the space labeled "Cc:," as shown in the figure on the upper left. You can also click the "?" to the right of the Cc box, which brings up the Recently-used addresses box. The blind carbon copy procedure is, appropriately enough, hidden from normal view. To send a blind carbon copy, you have to click the Special tab to get to the Blind CC box.

CROSS-REFERENCE
See Chapter 6 for more information on mail filtering.

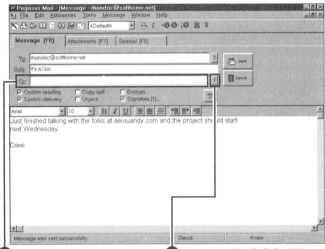

① To add another recipient, type in their address in the space labeled "Cc:."

② Alternatively, click the "?" to the right of the Cc box, which brings up the Recently-used addresses box.

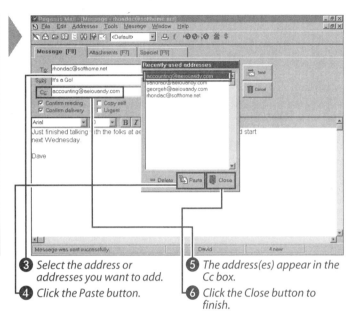

③ Select the address or addresses you want to add.

④ Click the Paste button.

⑤ The address(es) appear in the Cc box.

⑥ Click the Close button to finish.

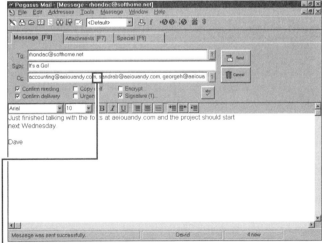

⑦ Commas separate multiple addresses.

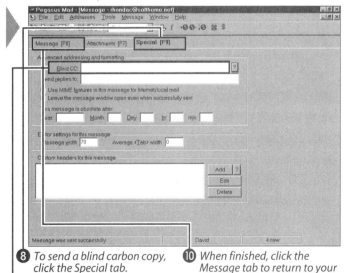

⑧ To send a blind carbon copy, click the Special tab.

⑨ The Blind CC box works exactly like the Cc box. Just follow Steps 1–6.

⑩ When finished, click the Message tab to return to your message.

Sending to Multiple Recipients

If you routinely need to send messages to the same group of recipients and you don't want to have to carbon copy all of their addresses manually every time you send a message to them, there's a quicker way to do it called *distribution lists*. A distribution list is a file of e-mail addresses that you use in place of a single address. You just feed Pegasus Mail the name of the distribution list and it takes care of seeing that every person on that list gets a copy of your message e-mailed to them.

Netiquette and Spam

Netiquette is a combination of the words *Internet* and *etiquette*. There's no official set of rules, but it boils down to the golden rule: If you wouldn't want it done to you, don't do it to someone else. One of the grossest violations of netiquette is called *spamming* — sending vast amounts of unsolicited e-mail. Although the folks who make the lunch meat aren't happy about the term, it's here to stay and has become a part of the Net's own language.

You may wonder how such a strange connotation came about. Monty Python. The old British comedy troupe had a skit in which a restaurant served nothing but spam. When the first mass e-mail abusers struck, it seemed like there was nothing in anybody's

mailboxes but their get-rich-quick schemes. Nothing but spam. Today, most ISPs won't tolerate spamming, either incoming or outgoing, and Pegasus Mail's license specifically forbids using it for spamming. Unfortunately, there's no way to totally end it. Sensing a good market, there are even some ISPs that openly welcome spammer business.

What can you do about it if you're inundated with spam? One simple solution is to use mail filtering (see Chapter 6) to automatically delete the junk mail as it comes in. Another is to note the ISP the spam is being sent from. Let's say it's coming from the e-mail address garbagemail@alkdjf.com. You can send a message to abuse@alkdjf.com or postmaster@alkdjf.com along with a copy of the unwanted junk mail. If it's a responsible ISP, they'll look into the problem and will probably cancel the spammer's e-mail account. For other solutions, visit the link under Find It Online below.

In the Distribution Lists dialog box, click the Edit button. This brings up the distribution list's own dialog box, with the name of the new distribution list already filled in. The dialog box itself is titled the same as the new distribution list. You'll need to type in an entry for the To field unless you want every message going out to the distribution list to have every single recipient separately listed at the top.

Continued

CROSS-REFERENCE

See the preceding section on using carbon copies in this chapter.

FIND IT ONLINE

You'll find a lot of information on fighting spam at http://spam.abuse.net/spam/.

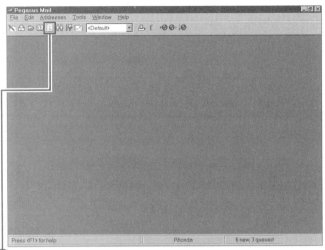

1 Click the Distribution List button.

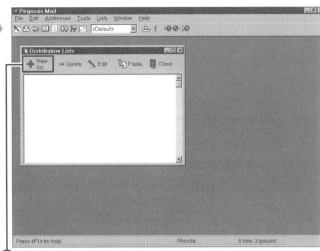

2 In the Distribution Lists dialog box, click the New list button.

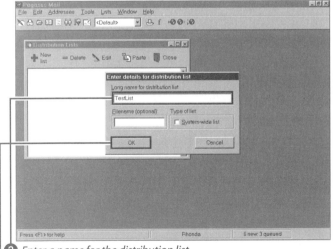

3 Enter a name for the distribution list.

4 Click the OK button.

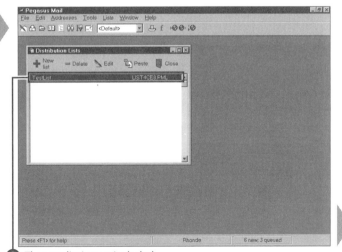

5 The new list is now included.

The entry should have a name for the group, and the format of this is very important; if you don't get it exactly right, the distribution list won't work. The group name must be enclosed in quotation marks, and it must be followed by your e-mail address enclosed in angle brackets. In the example shown in the figure on the lower left, we've used "Test List Members" for the group name, followed by an e-mail address. This means that, when the messages sent to the group are received, instead of a list of every member at the top, the messages will just say To: Test List Members.

Next, you'll have to enter e-mail addresses of everyone who's going to be a list member. Yes, it's a tedious task, but you only have to do it once, and think of all the time it'll save you in the future. Make sure you hit Enter at the end of each address, because each different e-mail address has to be on its own line. When you've got them all entered, click the Save button.

In your initial message to the group, you should inform the recipients that they've been added to your list. You might also want to request confirmation that the recipient's actually got your message.

TAKE NOTE

REPLY TO

If you put in an e-mail address in the Reply to box, then it overrides any Reply to address specified in any messages you send to the distribution group.

OTHER OPTIONS

The options represented by the checkboxes in the figure on the lower left are the same as those in normal messages. As with the Reply to option, they take precedence over any settings in individual messages sent to the distribution group. Be cautious when setting global options that override individual message options. Locking yourself in like that is only occasionally beneficial. For instance, if you were to set all messages to the group at an urgent priority, they would soon be taken, like the boy who cried wolf, as just ordinary messages without anything urgent about them.

MAINTAINING DIFFERENT GROUPS

Establishing distribution lists enables you to send particular messages out to people with specific interests. For example, you might set up one distribution list for a group that is working on a project at your place of employment, one for a group of friends, and one for family members. Be careful not to confuse the groups, however. You probably wouldn't want the people at work getting odd messages about your social activities on weekends.

CROSS-REFERENCE

See the section on sending e-mail messages earlier in this chapter.

FIND IT ONLINE

Another great antispam site is **http://eddie.cis. uoguelphca/~tburgess/local/spam.html**.

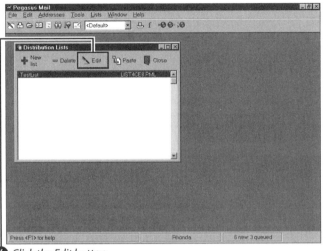

6 Click the Edit button.

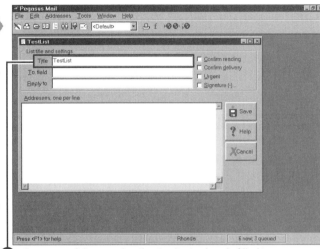

7 The name of the new distribution list is already filled in.

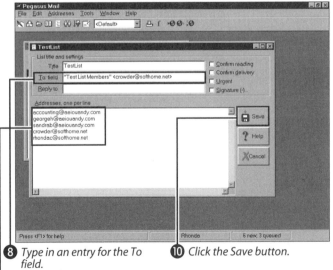

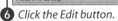

8 Type in an entry for the To field.

9 Enter e-mail addresses of list members.

10 Click the Save button.

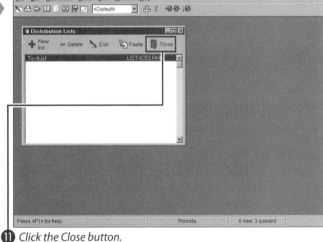

11 Click the Close button.

Sending a Message to the Distribution List

Sending a message to a distribution list in considerably easier than setting up the list. When the blank message window opens, click the Distribution List button. Select the distribution list you want to send the message to, and then click the Paste button. You won't see anything happen, so resist the temptation to click it again. Click the Close button to return to your message.

Back in the message blank, the To field has been filled in with a strange bit of gibberish. Actually, it's two things that are special to Pegasus Mail. The first part is the @ symbol. In this case, it tells Pegasus Mail that the bit that follows is the file name for the distribution list, which was entered automatically when you hit the Paste button back in the Distribution Lists dialog box (the "PML" file extension stands for Pegasus Mailing List). All that remains for you to do is to type a subject and the body of your message, and then click the Send button, and the message will go out to all the distribution list members.

You can take advantage of the distribution list function to start sending out your own newsletter, like many of the subscription lists you'll find on the Internet. Using the filtering techniques in the next chapter, you could even have new subscribers send you mail to have their names added to your list.

TAKE NOTE

▶ DO-IT-YOURSELF PML FILES

If you already have a similar list of e-mail addresses, you can create your own PML files from them with only slight modifications. The actual content of the file LIST4CE8.PML used in the example is as follows:

```
\TITLE TestList
\SENDER "Test List Members" <crowder@
softhome.net>
\NOSIG Y
accounting@aeiouandy.com
georgeh@aeiouandy.com
sandrab@aeiouandy.com
crowder@softhome.net
rhondac@softhome.net
```

As you can see, it's nothing more than a list of e-mail addresses, each on its own line, and some basic header information. The \TITLE header states the name of the distribution list, the \SENDER header shows the To field that will be put in the message, and the \NOSIG Y just means that there's no global signature file for these messages. Make sure you save the file as a plain-vanilla ASCII text file, though, or it won't work.

▶ FINDING EXAMPLES

You can do searches on the Web to find examples of distribution lists. Subscribe to one, and see how it works. Just go to a search site and enter the words "distribution lists."

CROSS-REFERENCE

See Chapter 6 for information on signature files.

FIND IT ONLINE

Find one more antispam site at **http://www.interhack. net/people/cmcurtin/rants/spam.html**.

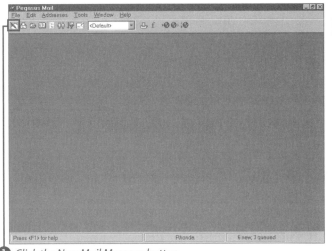

1 Click the New Mail Message button.

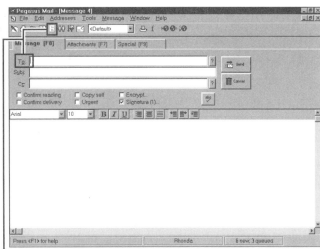

2 With the cursor in the To field, click the Distribution List button.

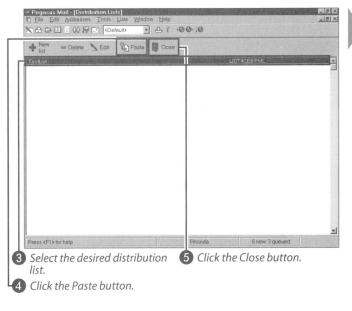

3 Select the desired distribution list.

4 Click the Paste button.

5 Click the Close button.

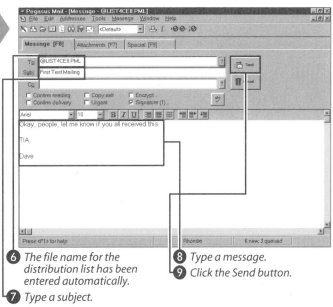

6 The file name for the distribution list has been entered automatically.

7 Type a subject.

8 Type a message.

9 Click the Send button.

Picking Up Mail

Most people log on to the Internet by connecting to their ISP several times during the course of the day or night. Then, they fire up their e-mail client program and have it pick up the messages that are waiting for them on their ISP's incoming mail server. Here's how to get them with Pegasus Mail.

Just click the Check Mail button. That's all the action you need to take; the rest is fully automatic. Pegasus Mail connects with your POP server and requests your username and password, unless you already requested that Pegasus remember your password. If you have no messages, that's the end of the process until next time. If you have messages waiting to be downloaded, Pegasus Mail gets them from the server, and it gives you a running play-by-play account in the status line while it's doing it. Once it's done downloading, the new messages are available for reading.

The new messages appears in bold, and stays that way until you select them for reading. If a message was sent with an urgent status, you'll be able to see it from this screen. Likewise, if an attachment is included with the message, you'll see it here as well. You can find out more about e-mail attachments in the next chapter.

TAKE NOTE

▶ **SORT ORDER**

As you can see by the figure on the lower right, new messages come in at the top of the list. You don't have to leave them that way, though; you can change their order in a variety of ways. Just select the Folder option from the menu and click your favorite sort method. Messages can be sorted by date, size, sender, or subject, just to name a few of the available methods. One of the most useful is the Sort unread before read option. This places the messages you haven't yet read at the top of the list, and you can just run down the line using the Next button to read them all in a row.

▶ **LEAVING MAIL ON THE SERVER**

Most of the time, you'll want the mail you pick up to be deleted from your ISP's incoming mail server. Otherwise, it'll still be there the next time you pick up mail, and you'll keep getting the same old messages over and over again along with your new mail. Your ISP won't appreciate it either when its hard drive begins to fill up with every message you've ever received. If you want to change that, however, you can. It's in the same dialog box as when you set your outgoing e-mail to go out right away (see the section titled "Eliminating the Queue"). The option is *Delete mail from host once successfully retrieved* — just deselect the checkbox and click the OK button.

CROSS-REFERENCE

See the section on configuring Pegasus Mail at the beginning of this chapter.

FIND IT ONLINE

SoftHome at **http://www.softhome.net/** has free e-mail service.

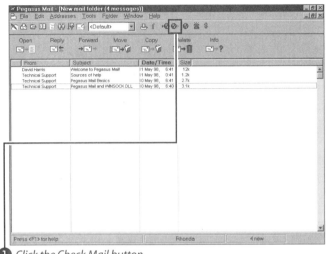

❶ Click the Check Mail button.

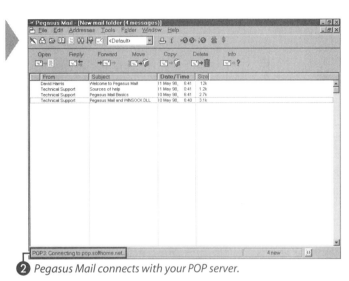

❷ Pegasus Mail connects with your POP server.

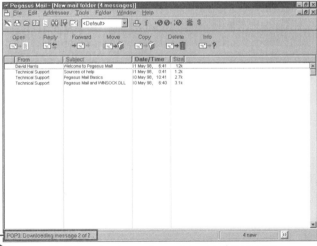

❸ Pegasus Mail downloads your incoming e-mail messages.

❹ The new messages are available for reading.

Reading Messages

Once you download your e-mail messages from the server, the next step is to open and read them. To get to a message, double-click it to open it for viewing (or you can highlight it and then press the Enter key on your keyboard if you prefer). To move on to the next message, click the Next button. Alternatively you can use your arrow keys to move up and down the listings in your new mail window. As you might guess, you click the Prev button to view the previous message. You might prefer, however, to close the message once you finish reading it, so you can return to the inbox view, and select another message from the list.

Messages that have been read already show a check mark next to them, as shown in the figure on the lower right. This enables you to tell at a glance the status of your e-mail messages.

TAKE NOTE

▶ **USING EMOTICONS**

Probably the biggest limitation of e-mail — or any written form of communication — is its inability to provide the emotional clues we normally get from body language. A simple comment can sometimes mean many different things depending on the intent of the writer, and it's not often easy to guess exactly what he or she had in mind. It's like in the old westerns where someone would say, "Smile when you say that, podner." Well, that's exactly what we do in e-mail. We use *emoticons* ("emotional icons") to add smiles, winks, and frowns to what we say. Emoticons are viewed sideways, and represent the human facial expression associated with various emotions. The most common emoticon is the smiley face, made with a colon, a dash, and a right parenthesis, like :-). Some people shorten it to just the colon and parenthesis, as in :). The opposite, to indicate sadness, is :-(. If you want to show that you're mad, try a "greater than" symbol added to the sadness emoticon, as in >:-(. To indicate that your comment is tongue-in-cheek, add a wink by changing the standard colon in a smiley face to a semicolon, as in ;-). Those four emoticons will get you through most situations, but there's a whole lot of variations on them. Check the link under Find It Online for many more.

CROSS-REFERENCE

See the section on closing messages at the end of this chapter.

FIND IT ONLINE

PC Doctor lists emoticons and abbreviations at **http://www.pcdoctor.co.uk/computing/emoticon.htm**.

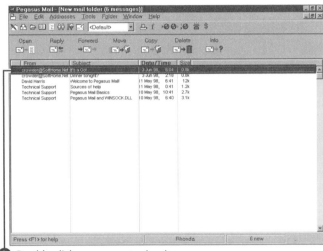

1 *Double-click a message to view it.*

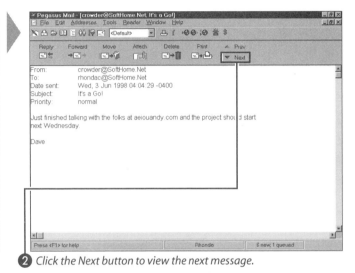

2 *Click the Next button to view the next message.*

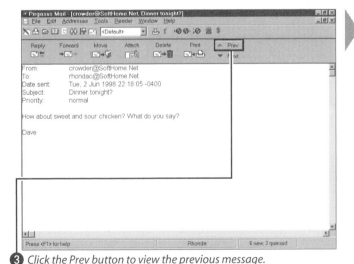

3 *Click the Prev button to view the previous message.*

4 *Messages you've read show a check mark next to them.*

117

Replying to Messages

While you probably don't want to do anything with some messages but delete them, e-mail is primarily about correspondence. Most of the messages you receive, other than junk mail, will need some sort of answer.

When you want to reply to a message, click the Reply button. You have four options in this dialog box. The first two involve other people than the addressee getting copies of your reply. The Copy original CC field into reply means that a carbon copy of your reply will be sent to anyone who received a carbon copy of the message to you. The Reply to all original addressees field means that a copy of your reply will go to everyone who was on a distribution list that you received the message from. The bottom two options are much more common. Make sure both checkboxes are checked. The first makes sure that the message to which you are replying is quoted so that the recipient will be reminded of exactly what they said to you. The second one is critical; it makes sure that the quoted material is marked with a ">" symbol at the beginning of each line, to set it apart from your own words in the reply.

You can delete the extraneous parts and reply to each section of the original message, which is a useful technique for lengthy messages.

CROSS-REFERENCE
See the section on using carbon copies earlier in this chapter.

FIND IT ONLINE
Check out E-mail Uses and Abuses at
http://www.tncrimlaw.com/pr_email.html.

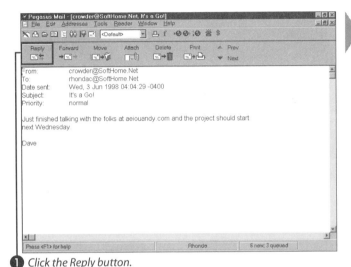

1 *Click the Reply button.*

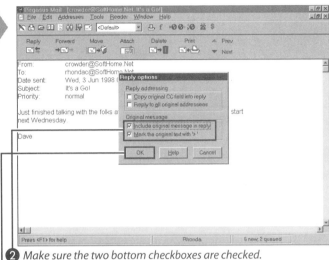

2 *Make sure the two bottom checkboxes are checked.*
3 *Click the OK button.*

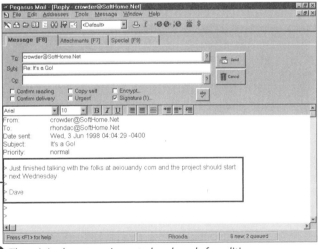

4 *The original message is quoted and ready for editing.*

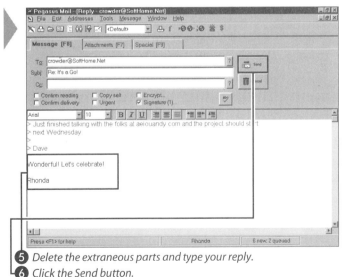

5 *Delete the extraneous parts and type your reply.*
6 *Click the Send button.*

Closing and Deleting Messages

Most messages just get read, acted on, and deleted. Everybody's e-mail box, though, seems to be as filled with undeleted messages as their closets are with coat hangers. Old messages can quickly add up to a lot of clutter. Granted, sometimes, you actually do need to hang on to some for a while for various reasons. Perhaps you need to copy something from it into a report you're working on, but you don't have time right now. You might want someone else in your family to read Aunt Mildred's description of the family picnic, or you may want to show your boss the message confirming you've won an award. Of course, you can always print out a hardcopy, but there's something special about reading it onscreen. Sooner or later, though, every message must go to data heaven.

You can delete each message as soon as you finish reading it by hitting the Delete button. To delete more than one message at a time, however, you'll need to close the message you're reading and get back into the New mail folder.

Close the message to return to the New mail folder view. You can select several messages here, and then click the delete button. If you're not sure that you want them all to be deleted immediately, you can

have Pegasus hold them in a queue until you're ready to get rid of them. Click the General tab on the Pegasus Mail Options dialog box (choose Tools ➪ Options) and check the box that says *Preserve deleted messages until end of session.*

TAKE NOTE

▶ GETTING THE RIGHT X

When you're closing the message window, make sure you click the X for it and not the one above that. The top X closes the whole program down. If you accidentally do this, just wait a moment and then start Pegasus Mail up again. Don't worry if you hit the wrong X before you're done writing a message, as Pegasus Mail will ask you to confirm the exit under those circumstances. Just tell it no and you'll be okay.

▶ FINDING MESSAGE SIZE

In addition to the basic information about sender, subject, and the message's date and time, Pegasus Mail tells you how much space the message is taking up on your hard drive in the Size column (see the figure on the bottom right). If you've got a lot of large messages and they're not really important, you can do yourself a favor by deleting them.

CROSS-REFERENCE

See Chapter 6 for instructions on how to recover deleted messages.

FIND IT ONLINE

You might need a bigger drive if you keep lots of messages. Check out **http://www.harddrives.com/**.

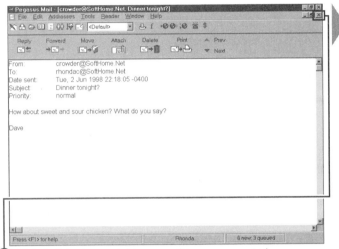

① *Click the X in the top-right corner of the message window.*

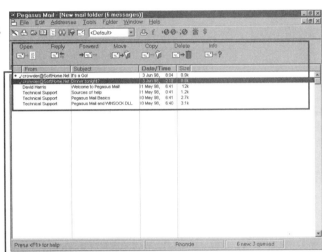

② *The message window is closed and the New mail folder is revealed.*

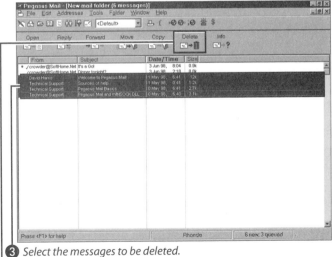

③ *Select the messages to be deleted.*
④ *Click the Delete button.*

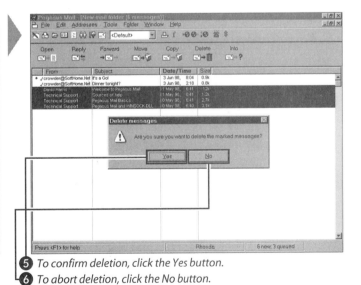

⑤ *To confirm deletion, click the Yes button.*
⑥ *To abort deletion, click the No button.*

Personal Workbook

Q&A

1 What is the @ symbol in an e-mail address?

_____

_____

_____

2 What is the difference between a *client* and a *server*?

_____

_____

_____

3 What is one way to send e-mail to more than one person?

_____

_____

_____

4 What does *bcc* stand for?

_____

_____

_____

5 When should you use your spelling checker?

_____

_____

_____

6 What is *netiquette*?

_____

_____

_____

_____

7 What is an *emoticon*?

_____

_____

8 What does *SMTP* mean?

_____

_____

ANSWERS: PAGE 379

EXTRA PRACTICE

1 Create a distribution list of your coworkers, classmates, family, or friends.

2 Make an e-mail message with deliberate misspellings and use the spelling checker.

3 Send a message to one person, carbon-copying two others.

4 Sort your messages by size.

5 Use emoticons and abbreviations in your e-mail.

6 Delete several messages at once (read them first!).

REAL-WORLD APPLICATIONS

✔ You're not at your home base and you're reading e-mails elsewhere, but still want to pick up all your other e-mail as usual when you get back home. You might change the settings on the e-mail program where you are so that the messages on the server aren't deleted, and pick them up later at home.

✔ You copy the e-mail address of a vendor from their business card and send them a message.

✔ You are teaching a class in a specialized subject. To save everyone trouble, you might add a long list of technical terms to the spell checker's dictionary and distribute the file to your students.

✔ Your new assignment at work is to coordinate the efforts of seven people who are located in different offices around the world. You could put them all in a distribution list and keep them up to date.

Visual Quiz

What does this checkmark next to a person's name tell you about the message?

_____

_____

_____

_____

_____

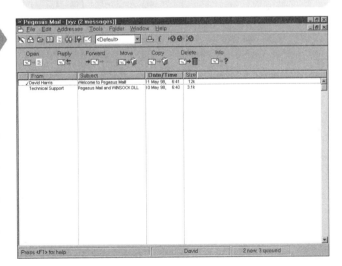

CHAPTER 6

MASTER THESE SKILLS

- ▶ Printing Messages
- ▶ Saving Messages to Disk
- ▶ Making Signature Files
- ▶ Using Signatures
- ▶ Using the Address Book
- ▶ Attaching Files to Messages
- ▶ Encrypting Your Messages
- ▶ Managing Folders
- ▶ Recovering Deleted Messages
- ▶ Filtering Out Junk Mail
- ▶ Finding Mailing Lists

Advanced E-mail

Now that you know how to send and receive e-mail messages, you're ready for the other skills that help make your e-mail experience more fulfilling. For starters, you doubtless want to keep copies of some of your messages. How many depends on what kind of messages you exchange or, at least, on what importance you attach to them. Some e-mail messages have no lasting value, and others need to be kept on hand for years. You could just leave them in your mailbox folders, but that would eventually mean that you had a bunch of useless clutter instead of organization. It's far better to either print them out or save them to disk.

You'll probably also want to personalize your messages with your own *signature* — usually a favorite quotation or two, but sometimes a business ad or a Web address — that's automatically added to the bottom of every message you send. And, if you're tired of typing in e-mail addresses, you can set up an address book that has addresses for all your family, friends, and business associates available at a mouse click.

Diving into deeper waters, you can send more than just text with e-mail — you can also send files attached to your messages, so you can send pictures, programs, or whatever can be digitized.

If you're sending sensitive material such as corporate financial data or personal secrets in an e-mail message, you might want to encrypt it so it can't be read by anyone but you and someone who knows the password.

If you don't want all your messages just landing in your new mail folder, then mastering message folders is the key to organizing your e-mail. You can set up several different mailbox folders and define rules for how incoming mail is sorted into them. Messages from different sources can be processed in different ways with mail filtering, and you can even set up your filtering rules to automatically delete junk mail so you don't even have to see it.

You can also copy and move messages between mail folders. Doing so not only lets you manually perform the same tasks as mail filtering does, but lets you retrieve accidentally deleted messages before they're lost forever.

Lastly, there's the fascinating world of mailing lists — topical discussion groups that work by interlinked e-mail and let you correspond with thousands of people around the world all at once.

Printing Messages

It's often a good idea to print at least your most important e-mail messages so you can refer back to specific information when you need it. Even if you have all your messages organized into special folders, you might have problems finding the messages, and a failure to back up your hard drive could permanently prevent you from finding your messages. You might find that having a hard copy of an important message helps out when you are away from work and don't have access to a computer.

Printing your messages involves setting up the printer and printing the messages. You could skip the first step, but if you just went straight ahead and printed without making a few choices, your hard copy probably wouldn't look exactly like you'd want it to. Once you've set your default printing preferences, things will be the way you want them. So it's best to take a few minutes to set up your printer first.

Setting Up the Printer

The dialog box that the Printer setup command invokes gives you several convenient options, as the figures on the right show. One detail that you might overlook is the checkbox labeled *Omit printed "footer" line*. When checked, it prevents Pegasus Mail from printing the page number, date, and time at the bottom of each page of your hard copy.

Another significant feature to examine more closely is the Font Selector, which enables you to

select the most legible font for your printed messages. Times New Roman is a good choice (it might be called Times or Roman or some other similar variation on your system, depending on what fonts you have installed). The default font size is also important. If you've got really good eyesight, you could go as low as 10, but 12 or even 15 is a good choice otherwise (the difference might seem small, but 12 is a full 20 percent larger than 10).

Continued

TAKE NOTE

▶ STORING HARD COPY

Some people keep their hardcopy printouts in file folders in an old-fashioned filing cabinet. Others keep shelves full of notebooks, organized by source and topic. If you're going to do the latter, you can do yourself a favor and use prepunched three-hole paper in your printer. It's available at any good office supply store and saves you the trouble of punching the notebook holes yourself.

▶ SETTING MARGINS

Because Pegasus Mail's margins are in millimeters, you need to set them to 25 or 26 to get about 1 inch for your margins (an inch is 25.4 mm, but you have to use whole numbers).

CROSS-REFERENCE

See the next section on using the Print buttons.

FIND IT ONLINE

There's a lot of information on printing on the Hewlett-Packard site at **http://www.hp.com/**.

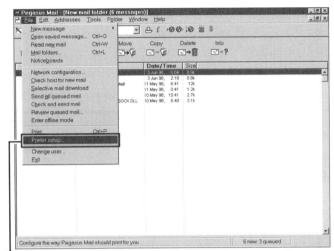

1 Select File ➪ Printer setup from the menu. This brings up the Print dialog box.

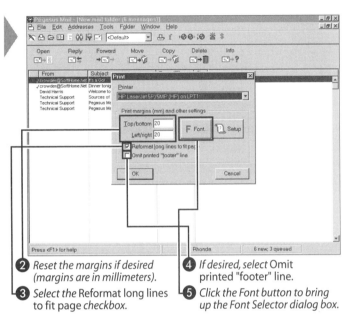

2 Reset the margins if desired (margins are in millimeters).

3 Select the Reformat long lines to fit page checkbox.

4 If desired, select Omit printed "footer" line.

5 Click the Font button to bring up the Font Selector dialog box.

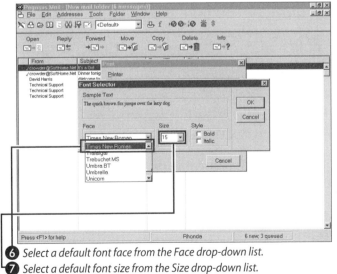

6 Select a default font face from the Face drop-down list.

7 Select a default font size from the Size drop-down list.

8 Click the OK button in the Font Selector dialog box.

9 Click the OK button in the Print dialog box to complete the task.

You can also access the paper's properties by clicking the Setup button. The dialog box gives you the options of changing the paper size and orientation, as well as the feeding source of the paper. You can even go to the printer's properties and modify the print quality or specific printer fonts. Your options will depend on the type of printer you have; some provide greater control over the functionality of the hardware than others.

Using the Print Buttons

If you have a lot of messages in your inbox, you have the option of printing the list of messages itself, without printing each message individually. This might be helpful when you are cataloguing all of your messages and need to get an overview of who has sent you what. In most cases, however, you'll be printing out individual messages. With Pegasus Mail, you have the option of including as much or as little as you want of the information about the sender or message by controlling the header printing.

The four choices for printing header information look confusing, but they're really quite simple. The significant headers are From, To, Date sent, Subject, and Priority. You can choose to print all of them by selecting Significant full (the default setting in Pegasus Mail) or, by selecting Significant first line,

you can print only their first lines if they are multi-line. If they're not multiline, then no difference exists between these two settings. If you choose to print All headers, then you're going to get a message that shows every detail of the message, including what e-mail client was used to create it, the path it took from the sender to you, and all sorts of technical details such as MIME-Version and Content-type that are of no interest to any but the most dedicated techno-nerd. The final choice, None, gives you only the text of the message itself, not even who it's from or the date.

TAKE NOTE

▶ **LIST PRINTING**

What if you have a message selected, but want to print the list? Choose Edit ⇨ Select all from the menu, and then click any message.

▶ **PRINTING OUT FORWARDED MESSAGES**

If you want to print out a message (such as a joke) that has been forwarded to you from a long list of recipients, you might want to delete the old headers that appear throughout the message, to create a more clean-looking message. Unfortunately, you can't edit the message directly, and then print it. You need to forward it to yourself, and edit it before you hit the send button. You can then open that message and print it.

CROSS-REFERENCE
See the preceding section on setting print preferences.

FIND IT ONLINE
Another major printer manufacturer is Epson at http://www.epson.com/.

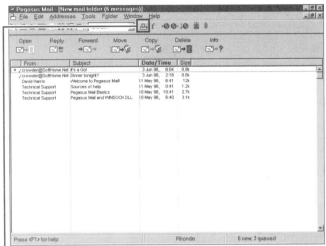

10 *If you click the Print button without selecting a message, Pegasus Mail assumes you want to print a list of the messages.*

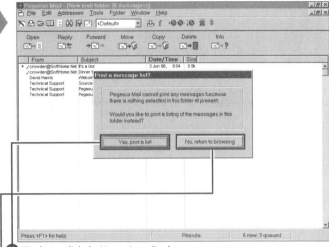

11 *To do so, click the Yes, print a list button.*

12 *If you don't want to, click the No, return to browsing button.*

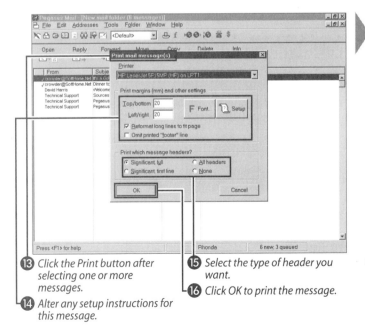

13 *Click the Print button after selecting one or more messages.*

14 *Alter any setup instructions for this message.*

15 *Select the type of header you want.*

16 *Click OK to print the message.*

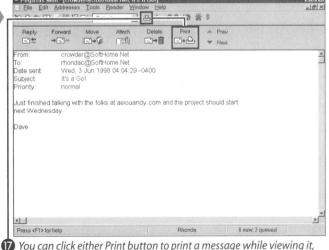

17 *You can click either Print button to print a message while viewing it, and then follow the procedure in Steps 13–16.*

Saving Messages to Disk

When it comes to backup, you're not stuck with the old-fashioned hard-copy approach; you can make a digital copy of messages as well.

While viewing a message, it's easy to save it to disk. Pegasus Mail keeps a list of "Recently-used directories" to which you can save your files, or you can add new directories for storing your messages. Of course, the first time you want to save a message to your hard drive, you'll have to add a directory anyway. It's best not to add too many directories, because it's easy to scatter your messages and lose track of important ones.

One reason to add directories is if you have multiple users that access Pegasus Mail on one computer. You certainly don't want to confuse your messages with those of your spouse or roommate. You might also want to create separate directories for your business and personal e-mail.

Regardless of how many directories you create, it's imperative that you name each message appropriately, reflecting important information, such as the subject of the e-mail, or the date it was sent. A combination of both, or a system you come up with might even suit you better. Without a clear system, each message could blend in with the rest, and you would have trouble locating the right one later.

CROSS-REFERENCE

See Chapter 4 for a discussion of disk space.

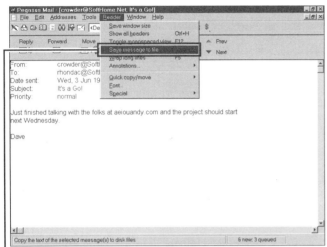

① Select Reader ➪ Save message to file from the menu. This brings up the Select a file dialog box.

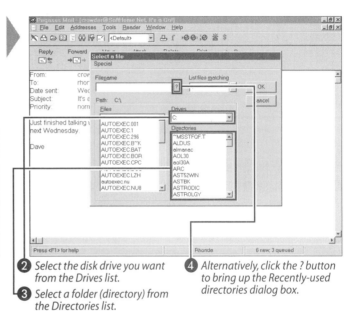

② Select the disk drive you want from the Drives list.

③ Select a folder (directory) from the Directories list.

④ Alternatively, click the ? button to bring up the Recently-used directories dialog box.

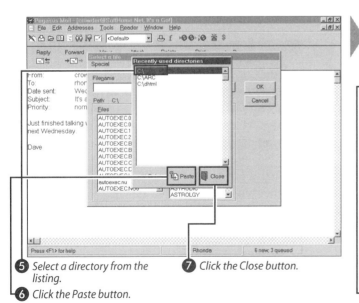

⑤ Select a directory from the listing.

⑥ Click the Paste button.

⑦ Click the Close button.

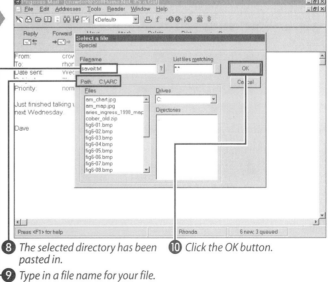

⑧ The selected directory has been pasted in.

⑨ Type in a file name for your file.

⑩ Click the OK button.

Making Signature Files

You might think from the name that *signature* (or "sig") files are a digitized version of your handwriting, but they actually have nothing to do with your signature. A sig is simply a few lines that are tacked on to the end of your messages when you send them out. A sig can be literally just your name, like a signature on a normal letter. Most often, though, your sig will be something short and meaningful to you, perhaps a quotation you like or your company's Web address. As you explore the world of e-mail, you'll see quite a few variations on the basic sig. Some people using corporate e-mail have a disclaimer in their sig stating that their opinions aren't necessarily those of their employers. Others include short poems they have written. Whatever your desires for your sig, Pegasus Mail lets you create up to nine different signature files and you can choose which one to use for each message before you send it.

A major reason that Pegasus Mail provides up to nine signature files is that you undoubtedly send messages to a variety of people, some of whom are more laid-back than others. Your business colleagues might not appreciate controversial quotes, but your friends might. By having several signature files, you won't have to keep changing what you've written to fit the audience; you just select the proper message for the proper occasion.

TAKE NOTE

▶ KEEPING IT SHORT

Some people's sigs take up a full screen of information. This is, to put it mildly, going overboard. There's no law against it, but most people think it's a bit ridiculous when the sig is longer than the message. Sigs traditionally are kept to about 4 to 7 lines. Anything longer is considered bad "netiquette."

▶ KEEPING IT CLEAN

Even though you might be sending most of your messages to friends or family, you should avoid profanity or crude sentiments. If a recipient prints out your message, or forwards it to someone else, it could fall into the hands of someone who doesn't appreciate your sense of humor, and you could find yourself with a bad reputation.

▶ GETTING CREATIVE

If you can't find a salient quote, but you want to add something creative to your e-mail messages, you could add some ASCII art. ASCII stands for American Standard Code for Information Interchange, and it's just a way of classifying the characters you can type with your keyboard. By using symbols (such as | or *), you can create simple, yet meaningful art. You can perform a Web search to see examples of good ASCII art. Remember not to attempt anything too elaborate, because it could take up a great deal of space in your e-mail message, and annoy your recipients.

CROSS-REFERENCE

See the following section for information on using the signature files in your messages.

FIND IT ONLINE

There's a great source of quotations for sigs at
http://www.columbia.edu/acis/bartleby/bartlett/.

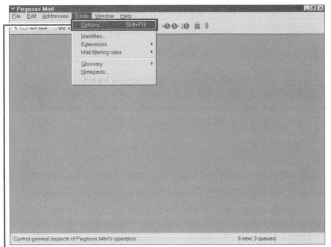

1 Select Tools ➪ Options from the menu.

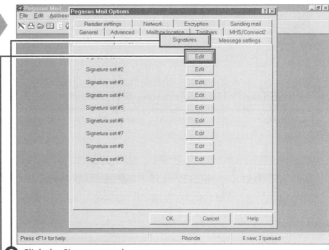

2 Click the Signatures tab.

3 Click the Edit button for the signature file you want to create or change.

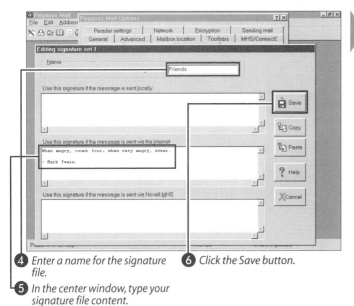

4 Enter a name for the signature file.

5 In the center window, type your signature file content.

6 Click the Save button.

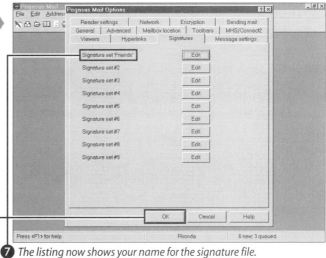

7 The listing now shows your name for the signature file.

8 Click the OK button to finish.

133

Using Signatures

Now that you have several signature files created, you probably want to use them immediately. You can select your message easily from the list you created. To select a sig for your message, any time between starting a new message (or replying) and before you click the Send button, click the Signature checkbox. It it's not checked, a single click does the trick. If it is already checked, you'll need to double-click it. This brings up the Select a message signature dialog box.

The drop-down list in this dialog box has all nine of the signature sets listed. Pick a signature from this list by clicking the name. It doesn't do any good to pick one of the ones you haven't defined because they're all still blank — just stick with the ones that have names you assigned and forget the ones that say "Signature set" followed by a number. Hopefully, you gave each signature file a meaningful name, rather than a number, so you can select the right one. If not, you should go back and rename them to make future selections easier.

You can choose to set the one you select as the default, or you can opt to send a message without a signature. Signatures are easy to forget when you are the sender, because you see them all the time, so it's important that you keep in mind which signature you have selected. If you are someone who tends to

forget about such things, you might want to select the *Add no signature to message* option, and add one only when you remember.

CROSS-REFERENCE

See the preceding section for how to create signature files.

FIND IT ONLINE

You can find even more sig quotations and humor at http://austin.brandonu.ca/~ennsnr/Tags/Welcome.html.

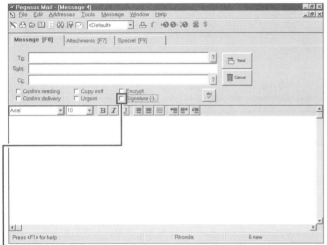

① *In an outgoing message, click the Signature checkbox. If it is already checked, double-click it.*

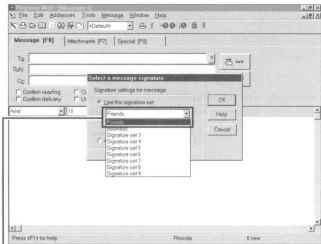

② *In the Select a message signature dialog box, pick a signature from the drop-down list.*

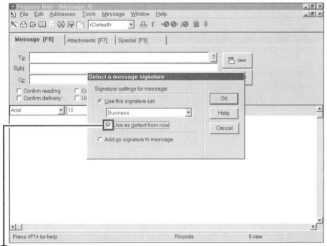

③ *If you want to make this your regular signature, click the checkbox labeled* Use as default from now.

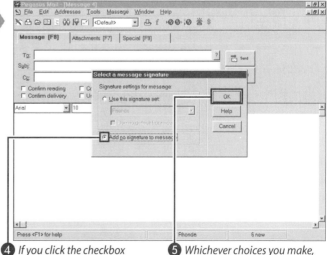

④ *If you click the checkbox labeled* Add no signature to message, *the options above it are deactivated.*

⑤ *Whichever choices you make, click the OK button to finish the signature selection options.*

Using the Address Book

Address books always make it easy to reference contact information for everyone you know. The most useful address books enable you to include information other than addresses and phone numbers, such as birthdays and anniversaries. Pegasus Mail address book entries provide similar features, with spaces for snail-mail addresses, phone numbers, and a box for notes. There's even a space to display a digital image of the person, if you have one.

Pegasus Mail also has the ability to create and use several different address books. You can have one for your friends and family, another for your coworkers, another for the people you need to contact for your high school reunion, and so on. Or, if you prefer, you can just keep a single one containing all your addresses.

The *Select an address book* dialog box provides you with a listing. At first, the listing is empty, because no address books have been created yet. Click the New button to create a new address book.

As you did with the signature files, make sure you enter a descriptive name for the address book. You can also enter a file name if you want to, but you don't really need to, because Pegasus Mail automatically creates it for you (that's why the Filename edit

box is labeled "optional"). The new address book is now listed with the descriptive name you gave it and now you just need to add entries to it.

Continued

TAKE NOTE

▶ CLICKING THOSE OTHER BUTTONS

Three of the buttons apply only to existing address books. The first of these is the Open button, which is covered in the procedure. The other two buttons are Rename and Delete. The Rename button lets you change the name of an existing address book (the one you assigned to it when you created it). Even if you specified a file name during that process, you cannot rename the file itself, only the long name for the address book. The reason for this is that Pegasus Mail knows this address book by that file name; the long name is just a convenience for you and other human users, and Pegasus Mail doesn't use it for anything. Delete, of course, deletes an entire address book, asking you for confirmation before doing so. The last button, Cancel, has no effect on any address books and just takes you out of the dialog box.

▶ MULTIPLE ADDRESS BOOKS

The example shows only one address book. If you have several and want to open one (or rename or delete it), then you must highlight that book before clicking any of the buttons.

CROSS-REFERENCE

Turn the page for information on address book entries.

FIND IT ONLINE

You can find lots of e-mail addresses at
http://www.four11.com/.

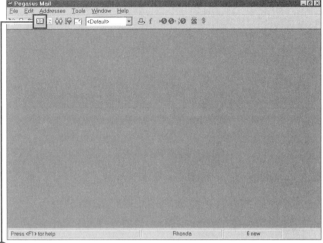

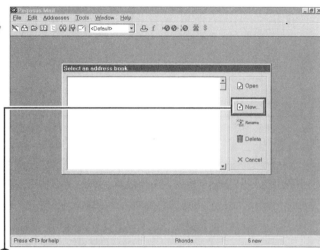

① Click the Address Books button.

② Click the New button to create a new address book.

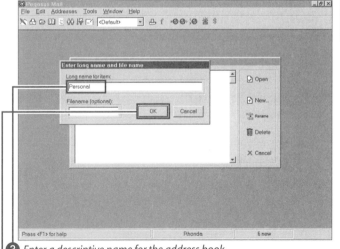

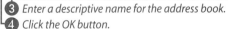

③ Enter a descriptive name for the address book.

④ Click the OK button.

⑤ The new address book is now listed. Click the Open button to make entries in it.

Using the Address Book
Continued

When you are ready to make an entry into the address book, click the Add button. The Edit address book entry dialog box appears. Type in the information for the person. You don't have to fill in everything, just the necessary parts. For example, if it's a personal friend, you don't need to list a company affiliation; if the person doesn't have a post office box, you don't have to fill in the Post address section. You can continue to enter as many people as you like.

If you'd like to include several people in an e-mail message using the Address book, you first have to start a new message. With the cursor in the To: field, open the address book, highlight as many people as you would like to include as recipients of the message, and click Paste. All the highlighted addresses will appear in the To: field of your message. You can also use this method to paste names into any field of your message, although it's most beneficial in the To: field.

In general, address books really help out when you're not sure whether a recipient's address requires a .com, a .net, or a .org. E-mail addresses can also be pretty lengthy, so it's beneficial to start learning how to use your address book as soon as possible.

TAKE NOTE

▶ **DELETING ADDRESS BOOK ENTRIES**

When you delete an entire address book, Pegasus Mail asks you to confirm that that's what you want to do. When you delete a single entry within an address book, however, you are not asked for confirmation. Once you hit that Delete button, the entry is just plain gone, right away and forever.

▶ **CHANGING THINGS IN ENTRIES**

If you need to update an entry, just highlight it and click the Edit button.

▶ **PICTURES**

If you have a digital photograph of the person in BMP format, you can add it to his or her entry by clicking the Set picture button. This opens a dialog box that is identical to the one you use for saving a message to disk, except that you use it to select a graphics file for loading.

▶ **PASTING ADDRESSES**

Any time you need to put someone's e-mail address in a message, you can open the address book, highlight the name, and click the Paste button. You can do this in any field, whether it's for the addressee, carbon copy recipients, or blind carbon copy recipients. Just make sure the cursor is in the appropriate box first.

CROSS-REFERENCE

See the preceding page for information on how to create address books.

FIND IT ONLINE

Another good site for finding e-mail addresses is
http://www.whowhere.com/.

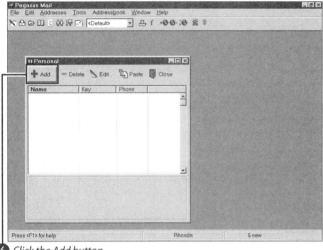

6 Click the Add button.

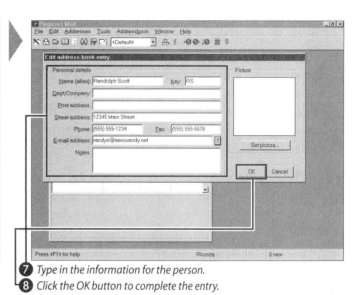

7 Type in the information for the person.

8 Click the OK button to complete the entry.

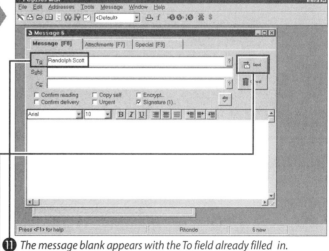

9 The entry is now listed as part of the address book. If you're finished, click the Close button.

10 If you want to send a message to the person before closing the dialog box, double-click the name to create a message addressed to that person.

11 The message blank appears with the To field already filled in.

12 When you've written your message, click the Send button to send it.

Attaching Files to Messages

Most e-mail messages have format limitations. ASCII text is all most e-mail applications will tolerate, so they include the capability of sending and receiving attachments. The attachments can essentially be anything—a picture, a sound bite, a complex word-processing document, or a mini application.

The attachment is typically not part of the message itself, but you have to indicate to Pegasus Mail that you'd like it that way. If you accept the default setting, Pegasus sends the attachment as part of the message as an enclosure rather than sending it as a "piggy-back" file, and other e-mail applications will not be able to acknowledge it.

Attachments are separate entities that are connected to messages, so it is possible for them to become fragmented and unreadable. In most cases, zipping up the files should prevent them from turning into garbage, but if your recipient still has problems, you can verify that the other person can accept attachments, and try breaking up the files into smaller chunks.

When you are finished typing a message, and you'd like to include an attachment, choose the directory and file on your hard drive. Click the Add button (or double-click the file name in the Files list) to add that file to the Current attachments. If you want to remove a file from the Current attachments, select it and click the Delete button. Ignore the File Type and Encoding settings. Finally, click the Message tab to return to your message.

TAKE NOTE

▶ ATTACHMENT SIZE

Limitations exist on how large a file you can send as an attachment to an e-mail message. Unfortunately, no hard and fast rules exist on just how big one can be. Each different server sets its own limits. Your ISP has one, and so does the ISP where you're sending your file. If the file is bigger than your ISP allows, then your message won't go out. If it's bigger than the recipient's ISP allows, then you'll get it back as rejected mail. Whichever server has the smaller file size allowed will determine how big your attachment can be. For instance, if your ISP lets you send a 1MB attachment, but the recipient's ISP won't let files larger than half a megabyte come through, you're stuck with the half meg file size.

▶ THE RIGHT STUFF

Just because you can send a file via e-mail doesn't mean that the recipient can use it. They'll have to have the appropriate software at their end. If you send them a graphics file, they'll need a graphics viewer to see it. If you send them a word processing file, they'll have to have a word processor that can read that format.

CROSS-REFERENCE

See Chapter 5 for information on how to send messages.

FIND IT ONLINE

Take a look at Common Internet File Formats at **http://www.matisse.net/files/formats.html**.

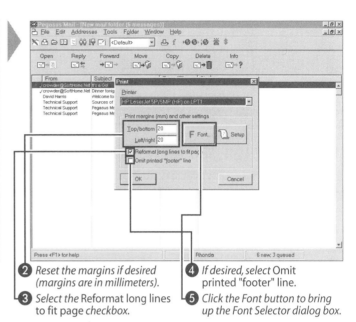

1 Select File ⇨ Printer setup from the menu. This brings up the Print dialog box.

2 Reset the margins if desired (margins are in millimeters).

3 Select the Reformat long lines to fit page checkbox.

4 If desired, select Omit printed "footer" line.

5 Click the Font button to bring up the Font Selector dialog box.

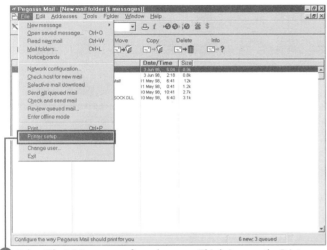

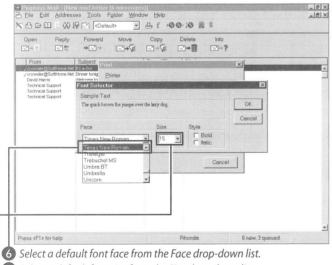

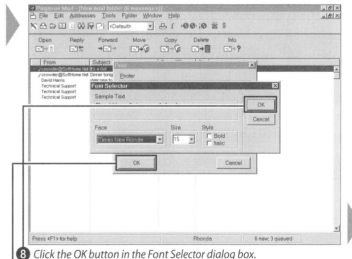

6 Select a default font face from the Face drop-down list.

7 Select a default font size from the Size drop-down list.

8 Click the OK button in the Font Selector dialog box.

9 Click the OK button in the Print dialog box to complete the task.

Encrypting Your Messages

When you send e-mail via the Internet, it doesn't just go straight to its destination. The message passes through other computers on the way, and they relay it along the line until it gets to the person it's addressed to. Although the practice is not widespread, it is possible to use *sniffer* programs to look for keywords in e-mail messages that are passing through a server. These programs can be set to copy any message with, for example, the words "VISA," "Master Card," or "American Express."

Fortunately, you can encrypt your messages — put them in a code that can't be read without a password. At any time before sending a message, click the Encrypt checkbox. You enter a password and send it. When the recipient gets it, he or she must enter the correct password, or the message will be gibberish. The headers, however, are not encrypted, so don't put any sensitive information in the subject line.

Most e-mail applications support PGP (Pretty Good Privacy), a free program you can use to encrypt your messages by entering a private "key." You can then distribute a public key for others to access your messages on their end. For more information, go to http://www.pgpi.com.

TAKE NOTE

▶ **OTHER APPROACHES**

If you don't want to bother with encryption, then you can do a few other things to make your e-mail more secure. If you're going to send credit card information via e-mail, don't put all the data in one message. Half a credit card number is useless to a thief; send the first part in one message and the second part in another. Send the expiration date in a third message. The odds that one person would be able to intercept all three messages are minimal.

▶ **PASSWORD SECURITY**

If you feel you need to encrypt a message, you face one catch-22 — the recipient has to have the password. Of course, you could send them the password in a separate message that is not encrypted, but that kind of defeats the purpose. The best way to deal with this is to decide on the password ahead of time and tell the recipient what it is in a telephone call or letter. A fax is an unsecure method unless the recipient is waiting by the fax machine as it comes in; otherwise, anyone who passes by can read it as it sits in the fax waiting for your recipient to come and get it.

CROSS-REFERENCE

See Chapter 4 for more information on Internet security.

FIND IT ONLINE

Check out the Cryptography FAQ (Frequently Asked Questions) at http://www.cis.ohiostate.edu/ hypertext/faq/usenet/ cryptography-faq/top.html.

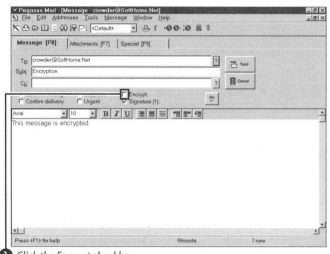

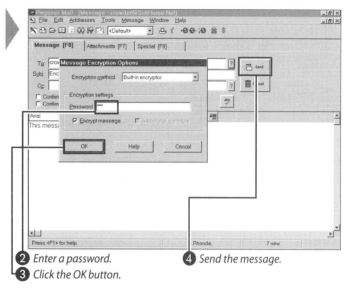

1 *Click the Encrypt checkbox.*

2 *Enter a password.*

3 *Click the OK button.*

4 *Send the message.*

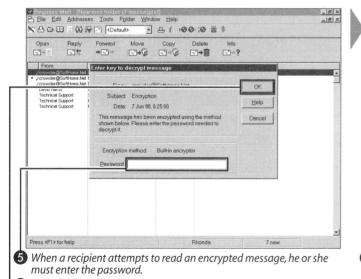

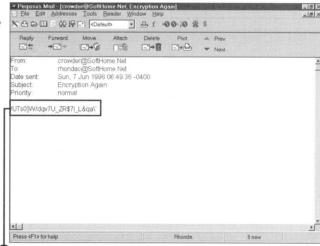

5 *When a recipient attempts to read an encrypted message, he or she must enter the password.*

6 *Click the OK button.*

7 *If the password is correct, the recipient will be able to read the message. If not, the message will be gibberish.*

Managing Folders

Think of a mail folder in Pegasus Mail as a mailbox. You can have as many different mailboxes as you want, and each one can hold different messages. This is highly recommended, especially if you find yourself in special situations, such as conducting business with your personal account. You don't want to have to wade through hundreds of messages just to locate an important announcement from your boss. Managing your folders ahead of time can save a lot of headaches later.

You can move or copy messages between folders, but you must first create at least one new folder to do this.

Creating a New Folder

When creating a new folder, you should provide a descriptive name that will mean something to you later. Make sure that the Message Folder radio button is selected and that the type of folder selected is *Pegasus Mail v2.x.*

If you want to create other folders, make sure that the My Mailbox folder is selected before you begin the process, or the new folders won't be created. You didn't need to do this the first time because the My Mailbox folder was the only one in existence and was therefore already selected.

Continued

TAKE NOTE

ONE EXCEPTION

You cannot move or copy a message into the My Mailbox folder from any other folder. However, you can move or copy messages from the My Mailbox folder into other folders that you create. This is because the My Mailbox folder is a *system folder* — a built-in part of Pegasus Mail — and cannot be deleted or treated as other folders can.

DIVIDING GROUPS OF MESSAGES

You might as well take advantage of folder creation. Once you get going on e-mail, you will fill up your inbox quickly. Organizing messages into new categories early and often really helps out. It's up to you how to divide them, but you could separate messages by dates, by sender names, or by topics. Adding a date somewhere in the folder name might help in any case, because it will give you an idea of which ones are old and need to be archived.

CREATING TRAYS

You can create both trays and folders in Pegasus Mail. The metaphor is that of a filing cabinet with separate drawers (trays) that contain folders that are not found in the other drawers. This introduces a level of complexity you don't have to deal with if you don't want to. You can just create all of your folders underneath the My Mailbox folder as shown in the example, treating it as the single tray.

CROSS-REFERENCE

See the section on recovering deleted messages later in this chapter.

FIND IT ONLINE

Mail System Converter adapts other e-mail folders to Pegasus format. Find it at **ftp://ftp.let.rug.nl/pegasus/ misc/mailconv.zip**.

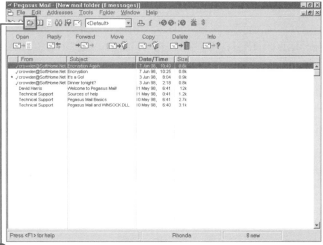

1 Click the Mail Folders button.

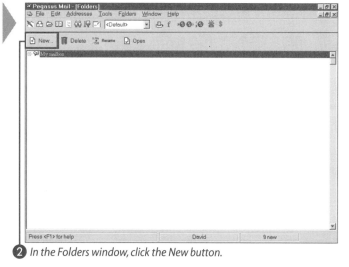

2 In the Folders window, click the New button.

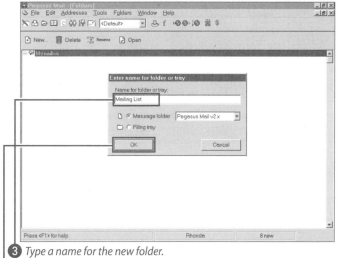

3 Type a name for the new folder.

4 Click the OK button.

5 The new folder now shows in the listing.

Managing Folders
Continued

Copying Messages to Another Folder

You might need to keep several copies of a message in a few places, depending on how you've organized your e-mail. If the body of the message includes information on several topics, it might be good to save the message in all folders where the message topic applies. Another helpful trick might be to place a copy of a message in a folder that contains messages you archive on a regular basis. Then, when you finish with the original, you can delete it without a problem, because the copy has been backed up.

Now that you've created a new folder, you can copy a message from the My Mailbox folder into it. The process is about as simple as it can get. To do the copying, select the message and then click the Copy button.

Pegasus Mail gives you no indication at all that a successful copy operation just took place, but don't worry; it did. A copy of the message now appears in the other folder. You can treat this copy just like the original; you can open it, delete it, or do whatever you want — even copy it to yet another folder. In most cases, your e-mail client wil give some indication, but it's always a good idea to manually confirm that the copy procedure took place.

TAKE NOTE

▶ **MOVING MESSAGES**

As mentioned in the first part of this section, you can move a message from one folder to another, too. The process is absolutely identical to the message copy process except that you click the Move button instead of the Copy button to start off. The only difference between the two methods is that, with Copy, you end up with the message in both the source and destination folders, but with Move, you end up with the message in the destination folder only.

▶ **USING OTHER SOURCE FOLDERS**

This example uses the My Mailbox folder for the source of the Copy operation, but any folder can be the source folder for a Copy or Move operation, just as any folder but the My Mailbox folder can be the destination folder (remember that only folders you have created can be destination folders). To select a message from any other folder, just click the Mail Folders button in the toolbar and then select the folder you want from the listing. You can either double-click its name or highlight it and click the Open button to view its contents. From there, just follow the same procedure as outlined for copying or moving a file from the My Mailbox folder.

CROSS-REFERENCE

See the preceding page for information on creating folders.

FIND IT ONLINE

There's a good page of Pegasus Mail add-ons at **http://www.aimnet.com/~jnavas/winpmail/ helpers.html**.

6 To copy a message from one folder to another, select the message and then click the Copy button.

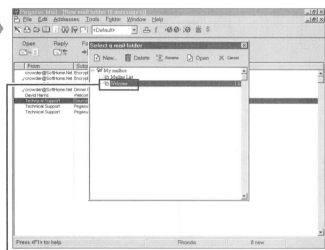

7 In the Select a mail folder dialog box, double-click the folder you want to copy the message to.

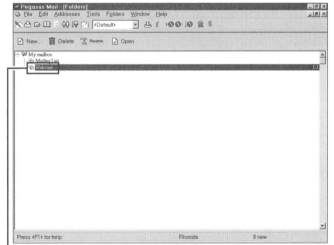

8 In the Folders window, double-click the folder to open it, or click the Open button.

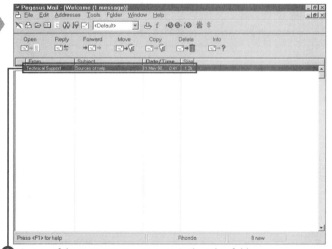

9 A copy of the message now appears in the other folder.

Recovering Deleted Messages

When you delete a message in Pegasus Mail, it's still kept around in a special folder (appropriately enough, it's called the Deleted Messages folder) — until you exit from the program. Up until that point, you can recover your deleted messages, but once you shut down the program, you're out of luck. When Pegasus Mail exits, your deleted messages are well and truly deleted. It's a really good idea to explore the process of deleted message recovery before you need to use it.

First, if you don't already have deleted messages to work with, pick a message to work with that you don't mind losing, select it, and then click the Delete button. Pegasus Mail is cautious about deleting messages and it protects you by asking, "Are you sure you want to delete the marked messages?"

After you've deleted at least one message, the Deleted Messages folder is automatically created and the deleted message is moved to it.

All you have to do if you want to rescue a message is move it out of the Deleted Messages folder to another folder. To do this, click the Move button, which brings up a listing of available folders, and then double-click the name of the folder you want to move it to. The process of moving messages between folders is illustrated in the earlier section on folder management. Just remember, you must do this before exiting from Pegasus Mail.

TAKE NOTE

▶ CREATE IT FIRST

You must have a folder other than the My Mailbox folder to move deleted messages into if you want to recover them. The My Mailbox folder is a special folder and cannot accept anything but incoming mail into itself. If you don't have a folder of your own already created, don't panic — just flip back to the section on folder management earlier in this chapter and make one, and then recover your deleted messages into it. Just as long as you don't shut down Pegasus Mail before you complete the recovery operation, you'll be fine.

▶ RECLAIMING SPACE

When you delete a message from a folder, Pegasus doesn't dump out the information in that space on your hard drive right away. Pegasus Mail is set to give back space after a certain number of messages have been deleted from a folder. This setting makes Pegasus Mail run more efficiently, but you probably won't notice a difference in your work on your PC. If you are concerned about space, however, you can select the *Recover deleted space* option to make sure the space is recovered immediately.

CROSS-REFERENCE
See the section on folder management earlier in this chapter.

FIND IT ONLINE
You can find the Pegasus Mail FAQ at **http://www .pegasus.usa.com/faq/winpmail.htm**.

① *To delete a message, select it and then click the Delete button.*

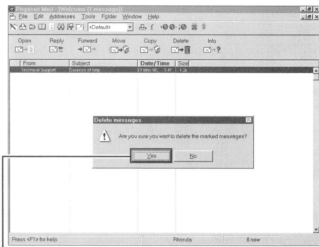

② *You must confirm the deletion. Click the Yes button if you mean it or the No button to back out.*

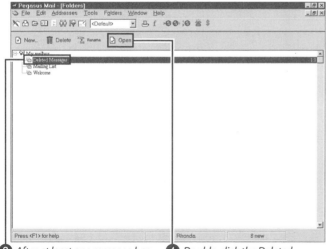

③ *After at least one message has been deleted, the Deleted Messages folder is automatically created and the deleted message is moved to it.*

④ *Double-click the Deleted Messages folder or highlight it and click the Open button.*

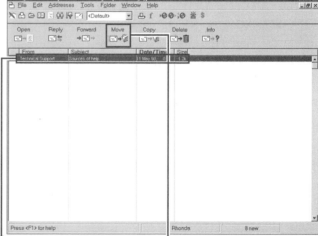

⑤ *The deleted message is accessible just like in any other folder.*

⑥ *Move the deleted message to another folder if you want to rescue it. You must do this before exiting Pegasus Mail.*

Filtering Out Junk Mail

Sooner or later, you're going to receive some e-mail that you don't want. Either it'll be spam (see Chapter 5) or you'll join a mailing list with a member you don't want to hear from. For whatever reason, you don't want to cut yourself off from the electronic world, but you need to get rid of some particular incoming messages, and you don't want to be bothered with manually deleting them every time they come in. That's where *mail filtering* comes in. Pegasus Mail lets you set up rules that govern its treatment of incoming e-mail messages. One very handy mail filtering rule you can set up is to automatically delete incoming messages with certain terms in their subject lines.

When you are typing the text you want Pegasus Mail to watch for, you might want to consider the terms "money," "opportunity," or various four-letter words. You have to select the header field where you want the application to check for the terms, and in most cases, this will be the Subject line. The action you choose for the "get rich quick" messages will likely be Delete, but you have options for what you want to do with filtered messages. Consult the Help menu to find out exactly what some of the actions do.

You can repeat the process to add as many rules as you want. See the Take Note area for other suggestions.

TAKE NOTE

▶ OTHER HEADER FIELDS

You're not limited to the Subject header when you filter mail. You can also select from five other headers (see the figure on the lower left). For instance, you may want to choose the From field to avoid all e-mail from a particular person. If your ISP has set things up for you to have e-mail relayed from other addresses to this one (called *aliasing*), you may have mail coming in to the same mailbox with more than one address in the To field, and you can treat them all differently.

▶ OTHER ACTIONS

You can also choose from a wide variety of responses to incoming e-mail. You could have Pegasus Mail play a song when a particular person's message comes in. You could automatically copy all messages that fit a particular pattern into a separate folder. You can have them automatically printed. The list is massive and you'll have fun trying out all the different things you can do.

▶ REPORTING THE SENDERS

One of the most annoying things about those who constantly spam others with messages is that the perpetrators usually get away with it. You would be doing yourself and others a great service by reporting these offenders to Internet organizations that specialize in reprimanding those who abuse the Internet's resources. Go to **http://www.abuse.net** to read more about what you can do.

CROSS-REFERENCE
See Chapter 5 for more information on spam.

FIND IT ONLINE
There's a Better Business Bureau article on junk e-mail at **http://www.bbb.org/alerts/spam.html**.

1 Click the Mail Filter button.

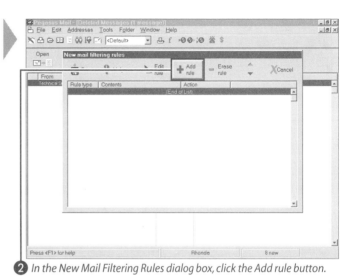

2 In the New Mail Filtering Rules dialog box, click the Add rule button.

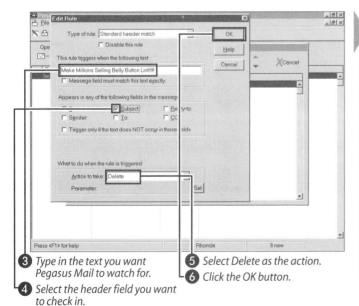

3 Type in the text you want Pegasus Mail to watch for.

4 Select the header field you want to check in.

5 Select Delete as the action.

6 Click the OK button.

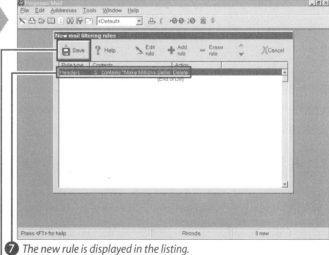

7 The new rule is displayed in the listing.

8 Click the Save button to complete the task.

Finding Mailing Lists

You're connected to the Net, you've got your e-mail software set up, you exchange occasional messages with a friend or two. Now what? Other than maybe saving a bit on the old phone bill, what's the big deal about e-mail for the average person? After all, unless you're pretty unusual, there aren't that many people you need to correspond with online. This is where mailing lists come in. Mailing lists are composed of groups of people from around the world who share common interests. The members of the list are called "subscribers" or just "list members." Instead of sending messages one at a time to each other, the subscribers send messages to a common address where the mailing list software (programs such as Majordomo and Listproc) automatically relays a copy of each message to every subscriber. When someone replies to the message, all the other subscribers also get the reply, and thousands of people living thousands of miles apart can share in the experience, combining their unique viewpoints and experiences (some mailing lists are set up so that replies go to the person who sent the original message, and those replies aren't seen by the other list members, but that's not too common).

One of the best ways to find mailing lists is the PAML Web site (PAML stands for Publicly Available Mailing Lists) at **http://www.neosoft.com/internet/ paml/**. PAML has two approaches to locating lists.

The first is an alphabetical listing you can browse, and the second is a search engine that can find topical lists for you.

TAKE NOTE

▶ FLAMES AND FLAME WARS

When a mailing list is at its best, it works for the enrichment of all the subscribers. Unfortunately, some people carry their anger, frustration, or ego problems online. When a subscriber sends an angry, obnoxious, or hate-filled message, it's called a *flame*, and flaming other subscribers can start a chain reaction of similar responses, reducing the formerly useful and pleasant mailing list environment to a *flame war*. If this happens, it's a good idea to institute some mail filtering rules at your end.

▶ REPORTING A MOVE

If you change ISPs, or your e-mail address changes for some other reason, make sure you follow the mailing list rules and unsubscribe your former name from the list. Sometimes rejected e-mails from an old address can hinder the workings of the mailing list.

▶ SENDING PERSONAL MESSAGES

Remember that hitting the Reply button means you send a message to the entire mailing list. If you have something to discuss "offline" with a specific member, it's a good idea to send a private e-mail to just that person.

CROSS-REFERENCE
See the section on mail filtering earlier in this chapter.

FIND IT ONLINE
You can also use the Liszt Web site at **http://www.liszt.com/** to find mailing lists.

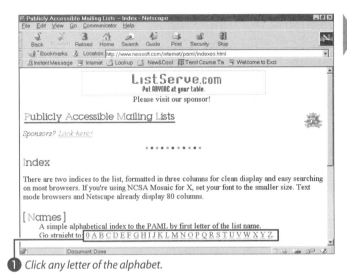

1 Click any letter of the alphabet.

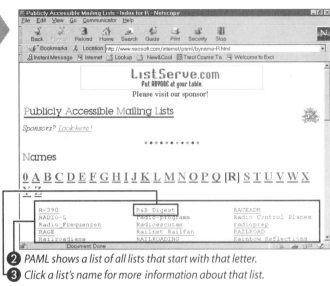

2 PAML shows a list of all lists that start with that letter.

3 Click a list's name for more information about that list.

4 In the PAML search form, type keywords that describe the topic you're interested in.

5 Click the Search button.

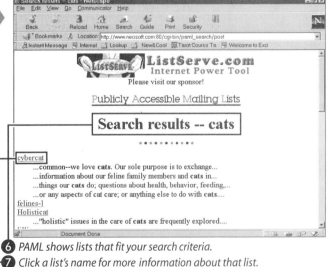

6 PAML shows lists that fit your search criteria.

7 Click a list's name for more information about that list.

Personal Workbook

Q&A

1 What kind of files can be attached to an e-mail message?

_____

_____

_____

2 What is *sig* short for?

_____

_____

_____

3 How long should a sig be?

_____

_____

_____

4 How do you put an e-mail address from an address book into a message?

_____

_____

5 Who needs to know the password for an encrypted message?

_____

_____

6 What are filtering rules?

_____

_____

7 Where do deleted messages go?

_____

_____

_____

8 What is a *mailing list*?

_____

_____

_____

_____

_____

ANSWERS: PAGE 379

EXTRA PRACTICE

1 Print a message and then save it to disk.

2 Set up a mail filter. Test it by sending a message to yourself that contains the trigger terms.

3 Create two new folders, and then copy a message into the first one. Move that message from the first folder to the second one.

4 Use Liszt or PAML to find three mailing lists that interest you.

5 Send an encrypted message to yourself and decrypt it.

6 Attach a copy of a file to a message and send it.

REAL-WORLD APPLICATIONS

✔ You begin receiving annoying messages about some get-rich-quick scheme. You might want to save yourself the trouble of deleting them by setting up mail filtering to take care of the problem automatically.

✔ You are negotiating a tricky deal, some of it via e-mail. You could consider it a wise move to make hard-copy printouts of the important messages.

✔ Your fax is on the fritz and you have to get some important diagrams to someone. If you have a scanner, you might turn them into graphics files and send them as e-mail attachments.

✔ You need to send some private information via e-mail. You may want to encrypt it to prevent anyone but the intended recipient from reading it.

Visual Quiz

What do these two buttons do? What is the difference between them?

155

CHAPTER 7

MASTER
THESE
SKILLS

▶ **Configuring Your News Client**

▶ **Subscribing to and Unsubscribing from Newsgroups**

▶ **Getting and Reading Messages**

▶ **Replying to and Posting New Messages**

Newsgroups

Newsgroups are similar to the mailing lists we talked about in Chapter 6. Like mailing lists, newsgroups enable people all over the world to communicate and everyone involved can see all the messages posted in them. They differ in important ways, however. Mailing lists deliver messages to your e-mail box automatically. With newsgroups, you have to go and get the messages. Also, mailing lists are available only by finding the source of the list and then subscribing. Newsgroups are open to everyone through the Usenet system, and most ISPs provide access to them as part of their basic package.

Tens of thousands of newsgroups exist, and they're carefully organized into categories and subcategories that help describe their content and purpose. That's why you'll find the computer science newsgroups named with "comp.sci" and the news announcements starting with "news.announce."

Newsgroups are created through a long and involved process. First, the new newsgroup has to be proposed, and then it's debated endlessly. Finally, if enough people agree that it might be a good idea, the whole thing is put to a vote. If it passes the first vote, the whole thing starts over again with amended names and such, until finally it passes another vote.

Many newsgroup creators, skip the official process, and just create them without committee approval. Although some ISPs won't accept any newsgroup that hasn't gone through the approval process, most don't really care and will add the newsgroup to their news server anyway.

Most newsgroups are unmoderated, meaning no one is in charge and anyone can say whatever he or she wants. As with mailing lists, the quality of any newsgroup depends on the people who participate in it.

We'll be using a news reader called Free Agent in this chapter. It's called that because, happily enough, it's free. There's a commercial version called Agent that has some more features to it, but Free Agent has everything you need to get into the world of newsgroups.

Configuring Your News Client

Before you can use Free Agent, or any news client, you have to tell it where to find your news server. A news server is a computer that relays newsgroup messages — pretty much the same thing as the e-mail servers you're familiar with from Chapter 5. As a matter of fact, you can even send e-mail messages from Free Agent (you can't receive them in it, though — you still need your e-mail client for that).

Most news clients show a Welcome screen right after installation and then ask you for your news server (NNTP) address, your outgoing mail server (SMTP) address, your own e-mail address, and your name. Generally, ISPs provide you with the information for the different servers when you sign up with their service. If you don't have it, you should contact your ISP. The names of the servers are usually very simple (such as smtp.yourisp.net for the NNTP server), and your ISP's support staff should be able to tell you over the phone. You don't have to enter your name if you don't want to. If you already have a news reader set up, and you would like to use Free Agent, you can click the Use Information From Another Program button and Free Agent will get the information for you from the other program.

Next, the News client typically asks you if you want to get the newsgroup listings from your ISP, as shown in the figure on the lower left. Click the Yes button, unless you don't have time right now (it takes a while because so many thousands of newsgroups are available). If you decide that you don't want to get the newsgroup listing at this time, you can select a listing update at any time, most likely from the File menu. Once the downloading is complete, the newsgroup names appear (see the figure on the lower right) and you are ready to start participating in newsgroup discussions.

TAKE NOTE

▶ GUESSING THE SERVER ADDRESSES

It's best if you contact your ISP to make sure you have the right server addresses. If it's late at night, or its line is busy, you still have a good chance of guessing the addresses. You can pretty well bet that, if your ISP is called *yourisp.net*, the address of the news server (NNTP server) is *news.yourisp.net* and the address of the outgoing mail server (SMTP server) is *smtp.yourisp.net*. If that doesn't work, you'll have to wait until you can contact your ISP.

▶ COPYING NEWSGROUPS

There's an option in the figure on the upper right that you should probably uncheck. If you leave the checkbox next to the words "Copy program's list of newsgroups" checked, you won't get the latest listings (they change constantly). Better to get the fresh listings yourself from your ISP in the following task.

CROSS-REFERENCE
See Chapter 5 for information on netiquette.

FIND IT ONLINE
You can get Free Agent at
http://www.forteinc.com/getfa/getfa.htm.

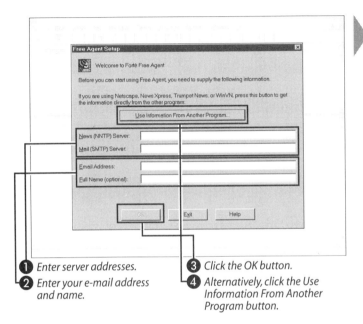

1 *Enter server addresses.*

2 *Enter your e-mail address and name.*

3 *Click the OK button.*

4 *Alternatively, click the Use Information From Another Program button.*

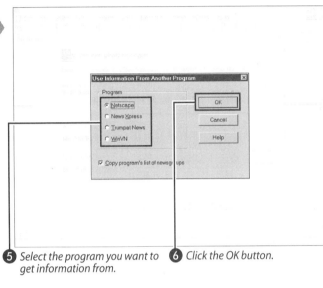

5 *Select the program you want to get information from.*

6 *Click the OK button.*

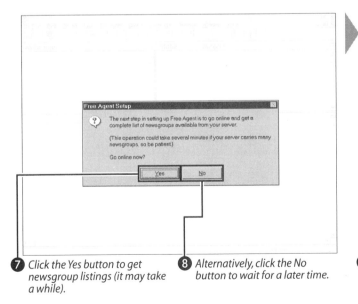

7 *Click the Yes button to get newsgroup listings (it may take a while).*

8 *Alternatively, click the No button to wait for a later time.*

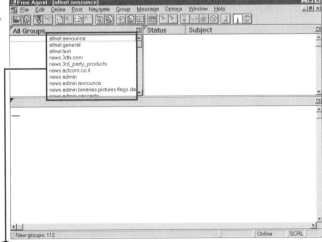

9 *Once the downloading is complete, the newsgroup names appear.*

Subscribing to and Unsubscribing from Newsgroups

You have to subscribe to newsgroups to get their messages. You can leave the windows as they are and scroll down the newsgroup listings only viewing about ten at a time, but you have an easier way. You can maximize the window so it fills your screen and shows a lot more newsgroups at a time.

Seeing more newsgroups at a time enables you to see more subcategories that exist within a large supercategory. For example, hundreds of newsgroups begin with "comp." — and the number is growing every day. Some of these newsgroups have long names, and a limited view might cause you to accidentally subscribe to "comp.os.microsoft.windows.32bit.applications" rather than "comp.os.microsoft.windows.16bit.applications." This misunderstanding could be troublesome when you try to download and run shareware from this group.

Now, you'll want to return things to a more useful setup. Because so many newsgroups exist, it's a practical impossibility to run down the whole list just to find the relative few you're subscribed to. Fortunately, Free Agent lets you limit the visible listings to those you're subscribed to, making life a lot easier.

Newsgroups for Newbies

It's been said that the Internet takes care of its own, and it's true that newcomers are welcomed with open arms. Among the tens of thousands of newsgroups that exist, some are dedicated to nothing but helping orient *newbies* (Net slang for newcomers). These are the places where you can ask anything you want, places where there truly is no such thing as a dumb question. They are: **alt.newbie**, **alt.newbies**, **news.announce. newusers**, and **news.newusers. questions**.

CROSS-REFERENCE

See Chapter 6 for information on mailing lists.

FIND IT ONLINE

See the Usenet Hypertext FAQ (Frequently Asked Questions) Archive at **http://www.faqs.org/faqs/**.

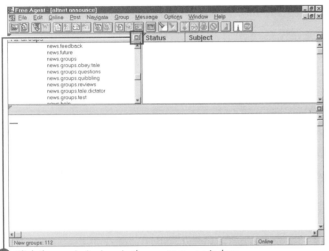

① Click the maximize icon in the newsgroup window.

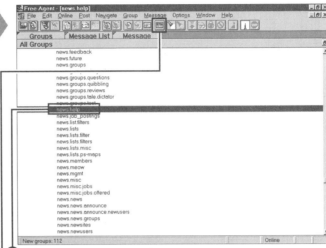

② Select a newsgroup you want.

③ Click the Subscribe button.

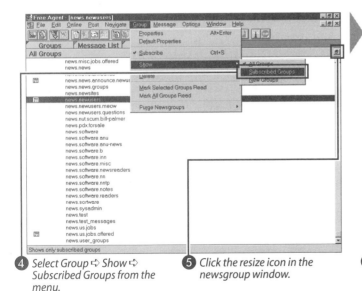

④ Select Group ⇨ Show ⇨ Subscribed Groups from the menu.

⑤ Click the resize icon in the newsgroup window.

⑥ The subscribed groups now show in their window.

Getting and Reading Messages

Before you can read newsgroup messages, you have to retrieve them from the news server — a two-step process. The reason for this is that so many messages fill the various newsgroups that it would overwhelm most computers if they tried to download them all, and you probably wouldn't be interested in all of them, anyway. The solution is to download only the *headers.* Headers provide you with basic information such as the title and size of a message. If, judging by the title, you're interested in the message, you can then download the specific one you want. Good titles save your system lots of wear and tear and save you lots of wasted time.

Once you're connected, most news clients give you two options. You can get headers for all the newsgroups to which you're subscribed, or just the headers for a particular newsgroup. You can typically select more than one newsgroup at a time, and its message headers will be downloaded in sequence the same way as when you get headers for all newsgroups.

Once you download the headers, the newsgroup window shows the number of messages in each newsgroup. The message list window shows the titles and sizes of messages, and the message window shows the title of the currently selected message.

Once you download a message, it's marked as read with a little page symbol next to it in the message list window. If you're not online, but you'd like to read a message the next time you log on, you can mark the message for later retrieval. The next time you are connected to the news server, you can click a button to transfer the designated files.

TAKE NOTE

▶ RETRIEVING IMAGES AND OTHER FILES

If the message indicates that it is an image file or a program, it will most likely prompt you that there is a binary attachment, and you can download it to your hard drive. In some cases, you might have to specifically tell your client that you want to access the binary file, and either view it immediately, or save it for later. You should consult your client's readme file for more information.

▶ AVOIDING THE GARBAGE

Newsgroups are often flooded with totally unrelated messages, advertising get-rich-quick schemes or pornographic sites. You can usually spot these messages by their headers, and easily ignore them, but be prepared to wade through several of these. If they annoy you enough, contact the newsgroup's administrator.

▶ EMOTICONS

Newsgroup messages use emoticons and abbreviations just like e-mail messages do — the same ones, for the same reasons.

CROSS-REFERENCE
See Chapter 5 for more information on emoticons.

FIND IT ONLINE
See the Usenet Info Center FAQ at **http://www.clark .net/pub/usenet-i/www/info-center-faq.html**.

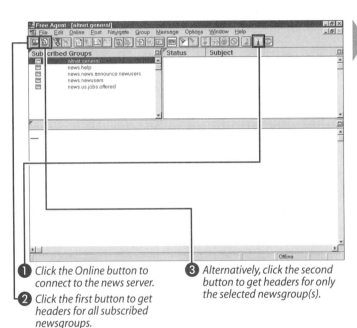

① Click the Online button to connect to the news server.

② Click the first button to get headers for all subscribed newsgroups.

③ Alternatively, click the second button to get headers for only the selected newsgroup(s).

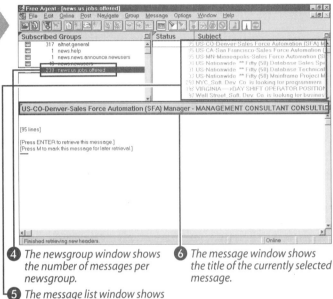

④ The newsgroup window shows the number of messages per newsgroup.

⑤ The message list window shows the titles and sizes of messages.

⑥ The message window shows the title of the currently selected message.

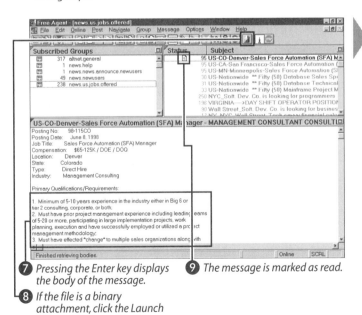

⑦ Pressing the Enter key displays the body of the message.

⑧ If the file is a binary attachment, click the Launch binary attachment button.

⑨ The message is marked as read.

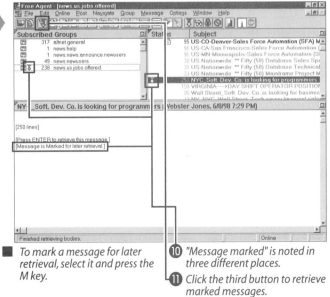

To mark a message for later retrieval, select it and press the M key.

⑩ "Message marked" is noted in three different places.

⑪ Click the third button to retrieve marked messages.

Replying to and Posting New Messages

I f you want to reply to a newsgroup message, just click the Reply button. As with an e-mail message reply, the original message is automatically quoted for you. The original is differentiated from the response you type because each line of the original is preceded by a greater-than symbol (>). Once you write your response, you can send your reply immediately, or save it in a queue to send out later.

If you're posting a new, original message instead of replying to one, the process is virtually identical. The only real differences are that you click the Post Message button, instead of the Reply button, and that, of course, there's no other message quoted. The name of the currently selected newsgroup is automatically inserted as the address you're sending to. You can enter the names of other newsgroups if you want the message to go out to more than one; just separate the names by commas. Enter a subject and then type your message. Your options for sending now or sending later are exactly the same.

Most newsgroups post a list of Frequently Asked Questions (FAQs) that outlines the newsgroup's policies. Also, as the name implies, such lists usually include answers to the most common questions people have on the newsgroup topic. It's a good idea to check the FAQ before asking questions on the newsgroup.

CROSS-REFERENCE
See Chapter 5 for advice on quoting and replies.

FIND IT ONLINE
See Rules for Posting to Usenet at **http://www.cis. ohio-state.edu/hypertext/ faq/usenet-faqs/ html/usenet/posting-rules/part1/faq.html.**

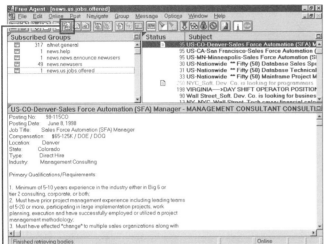

1 Click the Reply button to respond to a newsgroup message.

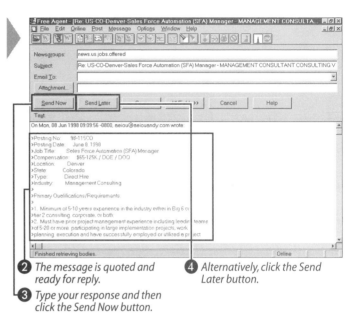

2 The message is quoted and ready for reply.

3 Type your response and then click the Send Now button.

4 Alternatively, click the Send Later button.

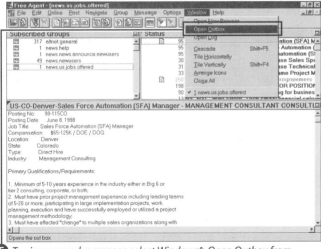

5 To view queued messages, select Window ➪ Open Outbox from the menu.

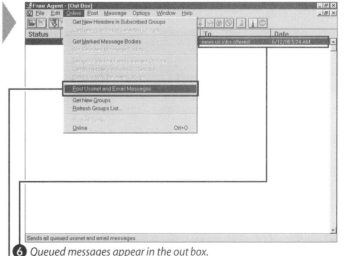

6 Queued messages appear in the out box.

7 To send queued messages, select Online ➪ Post Usenet and Email messages from the menu.

Personal Workbook

Q&A

1 How is the Usenet newsgroup system organized?

_____

_____

_____

_____

2 What is a *news server*?

_____

_____

_____

3 What is a news *reader*?

_____

_____

_____

4 What does *alt* mean?

_____

_____

_____

5 What is a *FAQ*?

_____

_____

_____

_____

6 Name one of the newsgroups for newbies.

_____

_____

_____

7 What is a *message header*?

_____

_____

_____

_____

8 How do you go online?

_____

_____

ANSWERS: PAGE 380

EXTRA PRACTICE

1 Post a message to one of the newbie newsgroups.

2 Find a newsgroup on a topic that interests you and subscribe to it.

3 Get the FAQ for a newsgroup and study its rules.

4 Reply to a message in a newsgroup of your choice.

5 Write a message while offline and send it when you go online.

6 Unsubscribe from a newsgroup and resubscribe to it.

REAL-WORLD APPLICATIONS

✔ You find an interesting job listing in one of the jobs newsgroups. You might want to note the phone number and immediately call the employer.

✔ You have a product you believe would be of interest to the readers of a particular newsgroup. You may want to check the FAQ for that newsgroup and see if it permits commercial offers before you post your message about.

✔ You really like a new TV show. If it's popular, odds are that a newsgroup exists for its fans. You might want to look under the alt.fan category to see.

✔ You have a question on a particular subject. Realizing that many FAQs have common questions already answered, you might look into it before posting your question.

Visual Quiz

What does this symbol mean (see box)?

_____

_____

_____

_____

_____

CHAPTER 8

MASTER
THESE
SKILLS

▶ **Configuring Microsoft Chat**

▶ **Logging On to a Chat Server**

▶ **Choosing a Chat Room**

▶ **Communicating with Other People**

▶ **Using Character Expressions**

▶ **Saving Chat Sessions to Disk**

▶ **Creating Your Own Chat Room**

▶ **Finding People**

Internet Relay Chat

Internet Relay Chat (IRC) is a way for different people to converse in real time. It's sort of like newsgroups or mailing lists, but you don't have to wait for minutes, hours, or even days to get responses. Everything takes place right away. The only real drawback to IRC, as compared to those other approaches, is that you don't have very much time to think about what you're going to say.

The way it works is that several people use chat programs to log on to a chat server, a computer that is dedicated to supporting these online conversations. Chat servers are divided into "rooms" and you pick which room you want to be in. You can wander from room to room to your heart's content, meeting and conversing with whomever happens to be there at the time. Everything you type is instantly relayed to all the other people in the room, and everything they type back is instantly relayed to you. Think of it as a huge mansion with a 24-hour party going on, and you have the run of the house.

Typically, each room is dedicated to a particular topic. You might find rooms where people are gathering to discuss football, baseball, haiku poetry, macramé, or pending legislation. In the unlikely event that you don't find a topic that interests you, you can create your own chat room. Many times, participants in mailing lists or newsgroups set up a time and place to meet and have live chats to supplement their e-mail discussions. Any group of people can do the same thing, whether they're a family, classmates, coworkers, or anything else. Sometimes, celebrities hold live chat sessions to answer questions from their fans.

Microsoft Chat is perhaps the easiest to use and most engaging IRC program available. While many other chat programs require you to memorize a set of commands and type them all on the command line to get anything done, Microsoft Chat works by means of buttons, icons, and menus. In addition to its ease of use, it offers a truly unique feature — chats can be illustrated like a comic strip instead of just being plain text.

Microsoft Chat comes with its own rather short list of chat servers already installed, but you can add others to the program and fully explore the IRC world through servers such as the Dalnet and Undernet systems.

Configuring Microsoft Chat

The comic strip design of Microsoft Chat makes it easier for members to express themselves clearly. The subtle nonverbal communication (such as facial expressions and body positions, as well as the ability to send thoughts and action statements) enhances the interactive nature of the chat environment. The comic characters might also make it easier to keep track of who is in each chat room, because a panel lists all the guests and the characters they have chosen to represent themselves.

This program is so easy to configure that you don't even have to do anything. Just fire it up and go. Your chat experience will be much more rewarding, though, if you take a few moments to set things up to your own satisfaction before you start chatting.

When you launch Microsoft Chat, the Chat Connection dialog box comes up. First, you need to provide some personal information. There's only one field that you really have to fill out: Nickname. Optionally, you can supply your Real name, your Email address, the URL of your WWW Home Page, and a Brief description of yourself.

The more information you provide, the easier it is for others to approach you and initiate a conversation. You might want to list your hobbies, the types of books you read, or a favorite quote. If you'd like to avoid giving others too much information about yourself, you can always leave these boxes blank, and

add things as you begin to feel more comfortable in your surroundings. The Characters that Microsoft Chat provides represent different men and women, along with a few purely cartoon types such as a cat in a lounging jacket. You can change the posture and expression by clicking the wheel of faces below the figure. You'll also find the face wheel on the main screen, so there's not much point to choosing an expression now — it can be changed at will during conversations.

You can also select a background on which the comic characters appear. Don't spend too much time agonizing over your choices. You can always change them in a few seconds later on, and you can change them as often as the fancy strikes you, but only while offline. You can either connect now or later, but your changes to your character will be saved either way.

TAKE NOTE

▶ EXTRA CHARACTERS AND BACKGROUNDS

If you don't like any of the characters or backgrounds, but you still like the idea of using them, you can get more — or even create your own. Just pop in to the Unofficial Microsoft Chat Add-On Page and download to your heart's content. They've got plenty of new characters you can add, along with a program for making your own. See "Find It Online" below for the URL.

CROSS-REFERENCE

See the section on using character expressions later in this chapter.

FIND IT ONLINE

Check out the Unofficial Microsoft Chat Add-On Page at **http://www.dido.com/chat/**.

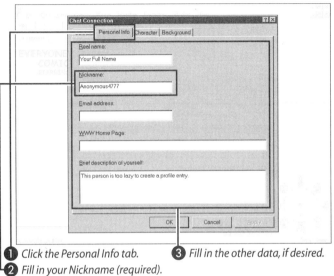

❶ Click the Personal Info tab.

❷ Fill in your Nickname (required).

❸ Fill in the other data, if desired.

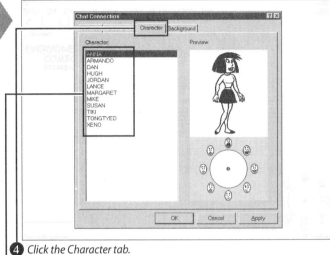

❹ Click the Character tab.

❺ Click the names to select a character.

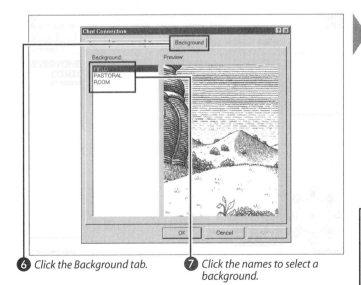

❻ Click the Background tab.

❼ Click the names to select a background.

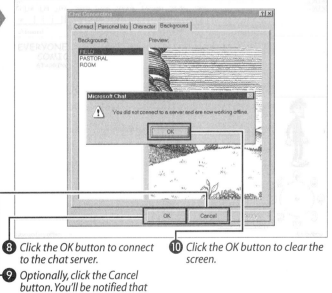

❽ Click the OK button to connect to the chat server.

❾ Optionally, click the Cancel button. You'll be notified that you're not online.

❿ Click the OK button to clear the screen.

Logging On to a Chat Server

Microsoft Chat enables you to connect to any chat server, whether it supports the comic format or not. Obviously, if you choose a non-Microsoft Chat server, you won't be able to use the comic characters, but you can still join conversations. The nickname you've chosen will still be used. Each server has several chat rooms, each usually covering a different topic area. See the next task on choosing a chat room.

If you're first firing up Microsoft Chat, you'll see the Chat Connection dialog box with the Connect tab selected, as shown in the figure on the upper left. If you're in offline mode, you need to click the Connect button to get to this dialog box. You'll see two radio buttons at the bottom. If you already know the name of a chat room you want to visit, leave the *Go to chat room* button selected and type the name of the chat room in the box. If you'd rather get a look at the room list on the chat server, select the *Show all available chat rooms* button.

The program comes with four different servers you can choose from. Just click the drop-down list and select one if you don't want to use the default one. You can also type in a new server and it will be permanently added to the list.

When you connect, you'll get the Message of the Day. This boils down to nothing more than a listing of statistics for the server and a disclaimer from Microsoft. If you really like statistics and legalese, this may be the high point of your day. If you're like most people and you don't want to see this every time you log on, deselect the checkbox that says *Show this whenever connecting*.

TAKE NOTE

▶ UNIQUE NICKNAMES

If you skipped the configuration step and just logged on right away, then you'll find that you need to do one thing before you can get on the chat server. You'll have to change your nickname, because the default nickname of "anonymous" is being used by someone else who did the same thing but got there before you, and no two people can have the same nickname. The shorter and more common a nickname is, the more likely it is that someone else has already chosen it. Stay away from names of popular movie or TV characters — "Mulder" and "Scully" are probably already taken, no matter what chat server you're trying to log on to. Be ready before you start with a few different nicknames you like, just in case. One simple trick is to just add some random number to the end of "Anonymous," as in "Anonymous4777."

▶ RECONNECTING TO A SERVER

You should make a note of the server and chat room that you have entered, in case you would like to return. Many chat rooms sound alike, so it's easy to get lost in future visits.

CROSS-REFERENCE

See the section on creating chat rooms later in this chapter.

FIND IT ONLINE

There's a good list of IRC servers at
http://www.megalith.co.uk/virc/servers.html.

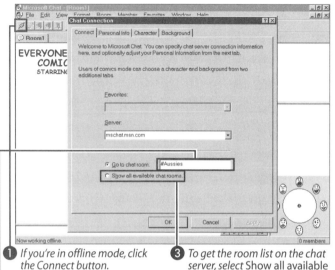

1 If you're in offline mode, click the Connect button.

2 If you know the name of the chat room you want, type the name.

3 To get the room list on the chat server, select Show all available chat rooms.

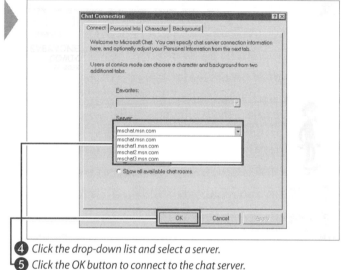

4 Click the drop-down list and select a server.

5 Click the OK button to connect to the chat server.

![Microsoft Chat window showing "EVERYONE'S A COMIC STARRING" and status line "Attempting to connect..."]

6 The progress of the connection appears in the status line.

![Message of the Day dialog box]

> There are 4134 users and 1019 invisible on 2 servers
> 3 operator(s) online
> 13 unknown connection(s)
> 1311 channels formed
> I have 2087 clients and 1 servers
>
> **Welcome to IRC.MSN.COM**
>
> The chats available in this area are not under the control of Microsoft.
> Microsoft does not control or endorse the content, message,

7 The Message of the Day appears. Click the OK button to view the room list.

Choosing a Chat Room

Chat Rooms run the gamut when it comes to topics of conversation. Some cover serious topics such as political issues, and some are geared toward young singles who want to meet potential mates. A lot of rooms have moderators that "listen in" to the conversations and kick out any members that use profanity. Often times, these moderators are nothing more than programs that are prompted by specific keywords. The serious chat rooms are more likely to have human moderators, whose main purpose is to keep all participants discussing the issue at hand, rather than going off on tangents.

It's important to realize that you can enter and leave chat rooms at will. Nothing says you have to stay in the first room you enter. You might find that new chat rooms splinter off the main room to start discussions within a subtopic. Generally, another member will create a room and invite members to join him or her in that room. If the creator designates the room to be private, however, it requires a password, and you might be out of luck.

When the room list first comes up, it includes the temporary rooms created by visiting users. If you want to see only the rooms that are registered with Microsoft, click the *Show only registered rooms* checkbox. Either way, you can just scroll down the list and read all the descriptions or you can search for particular keywords or phrases to narrow the list.

A significant search-narrowing option you can use is to specify a range for the number of people in the room. By default, it's set to anywhere from 0 to 9,999 people. Of course, this is so broad a range that it doesn't exclude anything at all. Unless you like talking to yourself, you should at the very least change the minimum members setting to 1 so you don't have to bother with empty rooms. If you use the scrolling arrows to raise or lower the minimum members setting, the listing is updated dynamically as you do so.

TAKE NOTE

▶ UPDATING LISTS

There's an Update List button at the bottom left of the room list. If you've chosen to show only the registered rooms, this doesn't do much, but if you're looking at the full display, then it has more impact. That's because the full list shows rooms that are created and closed by visitors on an ongoing basis. These rooms change every few minutes.

▶ CREATING ROOMS

You can create your own room from here by clicking the Create Room button. If you've narrowed your list to only registered rooms, this means that your created room won't show up on your room list. You have a few different ways to create your own room, and the process is explored in detail in a later section in this chapter.

CROSS-REFERENCE

See the section on creating your own chat room later in this chapter.

FIND IT ONLINE

Check out the IRC FAQ at **http://irc.msn.com/faq.htm**.

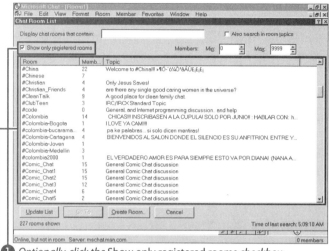

① *Optionally, click the* Show only registered rooms *checkbox.*

② *Scroll down the list to read all the descriptions.*

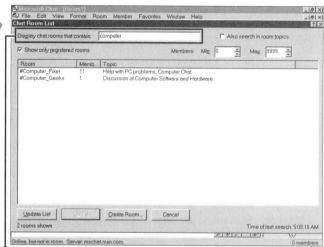

③ *To search for rooms, type your keywords into the box labeled* Display chat rooms that contain:.

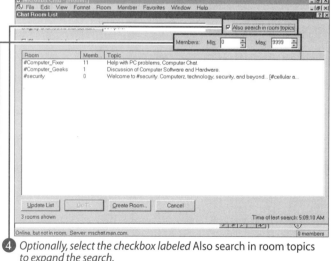

④ *Optionally, select the checkbox labeled* Also search in room topics *to expand the search.*

⑤ *Optionally, specify a range for the number of people in the room.*

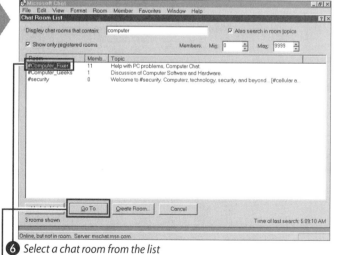

⑥ *Select a chat room from the list*

⑦ *Click the Go To button to enter the room.*

Communicating with Other People

Once you're in a chat room, the people in it are shown on the main screen and in a window on the upper right. To talk to the other people in the room, type a message in the box at the bottom of the screen, and then click the Say button.

The first thing to do is introduce yourself with a "Hello." Most members will greet you and make you feel at home with some basic "getting to know you" questions. If they don't, you shouldn't feel shunned—a heated discussion might be going on, or the network delays might inhibit normal communication. You should probably wait a few minutes for a response before trying again. If you still get no response after repeated attempts to introduce yourself, you might want to investigate another room.

As the people in the room talk back and forth, new cartoons are drawn, and their words appear in dialog bubbles. When you wish to show that your character is thinking something, but not saying it aloud, click the Think button instead of the Say button (see the figure on the lower left). Everyone in the room can still read it, but it's like they're reading the character's mind instead of hearing him (or her). This figure shows the screen from the man's computer. Notice that, in the character window, he does not have the woman selected, the way she has him selected on her computer. This is why, in the comic panels, she is shown talking to him, but he is shown

talking by himself. To show yourself talking to a particular person, select them in the character window before you send your message.

The action button is the third way of talking to the others in the room. It's used for nondialog communications, when you need third-party narratives.

TAKE NOTE

▶ **WHISPERING**

You can talk to just one person in the room so that no one else can "hear" your private conversation. Type your message, select the icon of the person you want to whisper to, and click the Whisper button (see the figure on the bottom left).

▶ **COUNT TO TEN**

When conversations take place in real time, tempers can flare more easily than with mailing lists or newsgroups, where the time lag enforces a certain cooling off period. If someone says something offensive, resist the impulse to jump right into an argument. If someone's really disruptive, you can use the whisper feature to quietly suggest to the host that they be kicked out for that session, or banned from the room permanently.

▶ **COMICS MODE**

If you go to other servers besides those few supplied by Microsoft, they can't see the comics, and you'll have to settle for communicating in plain text mode. To do that, click the Text button (identified in the figure on the lower right).

CROSS-REFERENCE

See the next section on using character expressions.

FIND IT ONLINE

The Microsoft Chat home page is at
http://www.microsoft.com/ie/chat/main.htm.

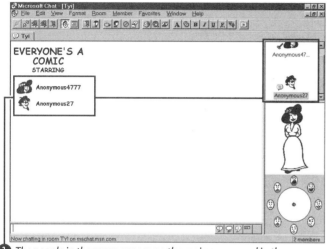

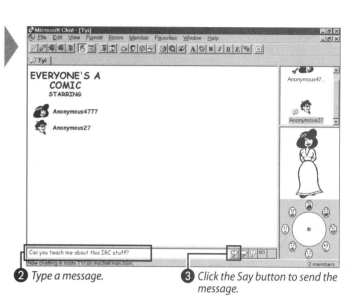

1 The people in the room appear on the main screen and in the character window.

2 Type a message.

3 Click the Say button to send the message.

4 To display a thought, type a message as usual, but click the Think button.

5 The message appears in a thought balloon.

6 To send a private message to a specific person, click the Whisper icon.

7 To create an action panel, type your message, and then click the Action button.

8 Your words appear in a box at the top of the comic panel, prefaced by your nickname.

9 To skip the comics version, click the Text button.

177

Using Character Expressions

The best advantage of Microsoft Chat is the characters, because they provide a lot of flexibility in conversations, thanks to their nonverbal expressions. The postures and facial contortions are somewhat analogous to the emoticons used in e-mail. Intentions or emotions such as sarcasm are often misconstrued in written media, because the subtleties of tone are missing. Emoticons attempt to add some of those subtleties back in. Here, tone can be added by things such as a coy grin or a shrug of the shoulders.

When you first log on, your character has its default expression, just like when you first chose it in the Chat Connection dialog box. Any time you want to return it to this look, just click the mark in the center of the face wheel, as shown in the figure on the upper left. The other eight settings are represented by the faces around the circle. You can click any one of them to change your character's expression. Starting at the top and moving clockwise, the options let you: shout or laugh, or look happy, coy, bored, scared, sad, or angry.

While you can't take back any words you've already sent, you can, oddly enough, change the posture and expression of your character after the fact. See the bottom-right figure. This only works for the most recent thing you sent; you can't go back to the earlier panels and change it.

TAKE NOTE

AUTOMATIC EXPRESSIONS

If you type certain words, your character automatically expresses the appropriate emotion to go along with them. Any time your sentence contains the word "I," your character points to itself. If you use "you," it points to the other person. Greetings ("Hello,""Hi,""Welcome,""Howdy") or farewells ("Bye") result in waves. If you use all caps, it's considered shouting, and your character demonstrates the appropriate angry expression. The abbreviations LOL ("laughing out loud") and ROTFL ("rolling on the floor laughing") make your character laugh, and the standard emoticons for happy, sad, and coy (wink) create the same reactions in your character. If you don't want this to happen, right-click the image of your character above the face wheel and select Frozen from the popup menu.

USING OTHER MEANS OF EXPRESSION

Microsoft Chat increases the fun of chatting by enabling you to play sounds. When you click the speaker icon (next to the action button in the lower left of the window), Chat requires that you select a sound from the media folder to play. Other members will hear the sound, provided they have the same file in their media folders. Sometimes there's a sound bite that fits an occasion perfectly, and now you can use it. See Chat's Help menu for more information.

CROSS-REFERENCE

See Chapter 5 for information on emoticons.

FIND IT ONLINE

You can download more characters from Microsoft at **http://www.microsoft.com/msdownload/ieplatform/chat/chat.htm.**

1 Click the mark in the center of the face wheel to show the default expression.

2 Click the faces to change your character's expression.

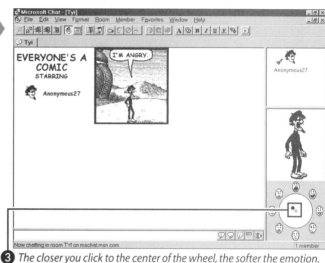

3 The closer you click to the center of the wheel, the softer the emotion.

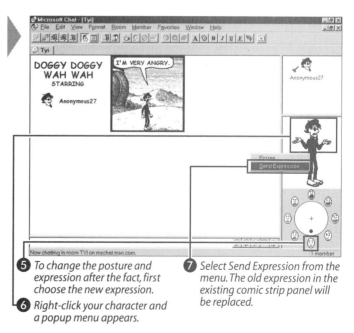

4 The closer you click to the face, the stronger the emotion.

5 To change the posture and expression after the fact, first choose the new expression.

6 Right-click your character and a popup menu appears.

7 Select Send Expression from the menu. The old expression in the existing comic strip panel will be replaced.

Saving Chat Sessions to Disk

Let's say you're in a private chat root discussing an important business topic — or in a public room where you wax particularly eloquently on a pet topic of yours. In either case, you might want to keep a record of your chat session's ideas or decisions. Whatever your reason, it's useful to be able to permanently save some of your chat sessions.

One problem with chatting is that conversations can go by very quickly, and it's hard to keep track of what things you said to which person. Microsoft Chat also lets you back up to earlier frames to check what you said earlier. But if you want to refer to the transcript later, you can save the entire chat session (at least the part in which you were involved) to your hard drive. The program itself makes it easy to save your chats.

The first time you save a chat session, you get the Save As dialog box. It's best to create a new folder for each chat room, and save each chat session from that chat room as a dated filename. This way, you will be able to distinguish between your sessions. When you want to recall them, you have to open them through the Microsoft Chat application. You'll be able to see the characters and their words.

CROSS-REFERENCE

See Chapter 6 for advice on disk storage.

FIND IT ONLINE

You can find out about mass storage at
http://www.iomega.com/.

1 *Select File ➪ Save from the menu.*

2 *The first time, you'll end up at the Desktop.*

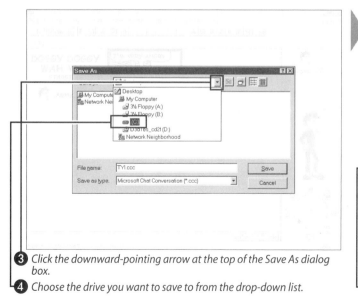

3 *Click the downward-pointing arrow at the top of the Save As dialog box.*

4 *Choose the drive you want to save to from the drop-down list.*

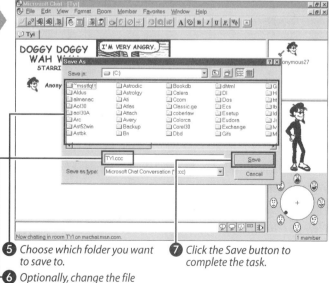

5 *Choose which folder you want to save to.*

6 *Optionally, change the file name.*

7 *Click the Save button to complete the task.*

Creating Your Own Chat Room

If you don't find a topic you like in the available chat rooms, or if you want to have a private meeting place, you can make your own instead of choosing one from the listings. You have at least four different ways to create a chat room. The most straightforward approach is to use the Create Room button (see the figure on the upper left). This brings up the Create Chat Room dialog box. The first thing you'll need to fill out, after *Chat room name*, is the name you want for the room. Next, fill in the topic, if desired; this is only necessary if you want to advertise the room in the room listings. You can also set some nonrequired options.

The Hidden option prevents the room from showing in the room listings. The Private option keeps the identities of the people in the room from being shown outside it. The Invite Only option means that nobody you don't ask in can come into the room. Set Maximum Users prevents the room from being overcrowded. Optional Password sets a password that must be entered by visitors before they can gain entry. The other two options, *Moderated* and *Set Topic Anyone*, are essentially useless. Click the OK button to complete the room creation.

You can also create a room by clicking the Enter Room button. This brings up the Enter Room dialog box. Where it asks you to enter the name of the room you want to enter, just enter one that doesn't exist. As with the Create Room approach, you can designate a password that will be required for anyone to enter the room. The room is automatically created for you using the name you typed.

You will probably find that new members will start popping into the room within a few minutes of the creation of a new room. If your room gets little response, you might want to go looking for guests. The next task covers finding people.

TAKE NOTE

▶ OTHER WAYS

You can also create a chat room when you first log on to the chat server. All you have to do is specify the name of a nonexistent chat room in the Connect dialog box when it asks you which one you want to enter; you'll go to a newly created room of that name. The room list also has a Create Room button.

▶ SENDING OUT INVITATIONS

You can contact other members and invite them to join your chat room by selecting Invite from the Members menu and entering the nicknames of those you would like to involve in your discussion group. If you don't know a particular nickname to look for, you can select User List from the Members menu and search for nicknames, identity, members of a group, or all users. You'll have to find out each user's nickname and then go back to the Invite dialog box to enter it for the invitation.

CROSS-REFERENCE

See the section on choosing chat rooms earlier in this chapter.

FIND IT ONLINE

Microsoft also has a 3D chat client. Take a look at http://www.microsoft.com/ie/chat/vchatmain.htm.

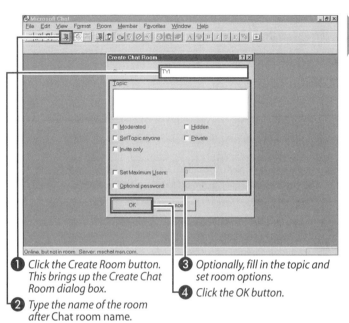

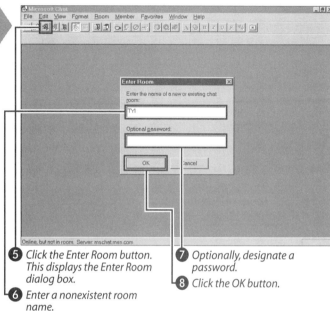

1 Click the Create Room button. This brings up the Create Chat Room dialog box.

2 Type the name of the room after Chat room name.

3 Optionally, fill in the topic and set room options.

4 Click the OK button.

5 Click the Enter Room button. This displays the Enter Room dialog box.

6 Enter a nonexistent room name.

7 Optionally, designate a password.

8 Click the OK button.

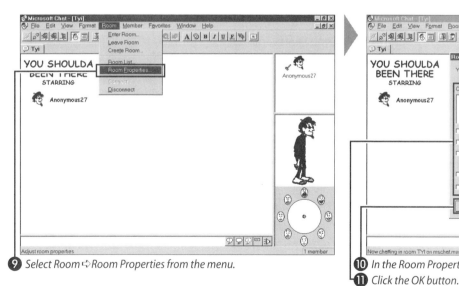

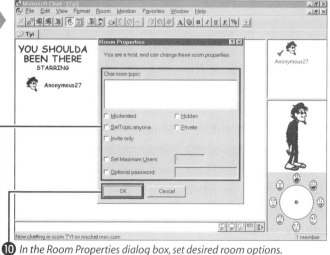

9 Select Room ⇨ Room Properties from the menu.

10 In the Room Properties dialog box, set desired room options.

11 Click the OK button.

Finding People

nternet Relay Chat is one of the most popular areas of the Internet, and thousands of users from all over the world are accessing hundreds of chat servers at any given time. Finding people in all of this talk soup is no easy task, but if you need to do it, Microsoft Chat offers the capability. All you need to do is access the User List.

The user list is a bit like the room list, and it works in much the same way. You can get a list of all users, or you can narrow your search down. The User List button brings up an empty user list. The Update List button, after several seconds during which the chat server checks to see who's currently using it, brings up a list of all users on all chat servers. The number of users in the list is shown on the lower left corner of the dialog box. You can scroll down to view the entire listing, or you can further limit your search.

The easiest way to find someone is to search by nickname. Nicknames are required for logging onto chat servers, and are thus more reliable than identities. Of course, the best way to find a friend is to ask him or her over the phone or e-mail what nickname he or she will be using. It eliminates the need to find a needle in a haystack. Another thing to keep in mind is that only the "#comic_chat" rooms let members see a cartoon image of one another. If you're looking for only those people who are using Microsoft Chat's comic feature, you can limit your search to just those rooms.

CROSS-REFERENCE
See the section on creating chat rooms for more information on hidden names.

FIND IT ONLINE
You can test your anonymity at the ARIN Whois page: http://www.arin.net/whois/arinwhois.html.

1 Click the User List button.

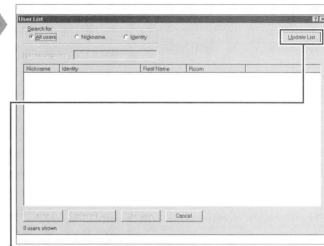

2 To get the full listing, click the Update List button.

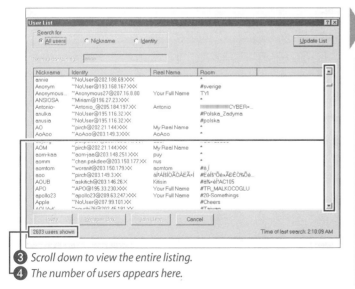

3 Scroll down to view the entire listing.
4 The number of users appears here.

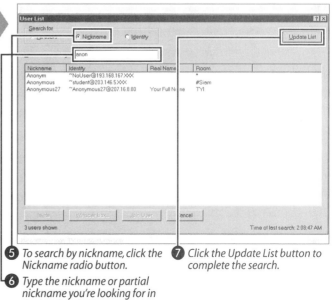

5 To search by nickname, click the Nickname radio button.

6 Type the nickname or partial nickname you're looking for in the box labeled Names containing.

7 Click the Update List button to complete the search.

Personal Workbook

Q&A

1 What does *IRC* stand for?

_____

_____

_____

2 What is a *chat server*?

_____

_____

_____

3 How do you add new chat servers?

_____

_____

_____

_____

4 What is a *host*?

_____

_____

_____

5 What is a *chat log*? How do you create one?

_____

_____

_____

_____

6 How many basic characters come with Microsoft Chat? How many backgrounds?

_____

_____

7 What is the difference between *kicking* and *banning*?

_____

_____

_____

8 How do you create a new chat room?

_____

_____

_____

ANSWERS: PAGE 381

EXTRA PRACTICE

1. Experiment with using comics versus text mode and see which you like best.

2. Go to the Microsoft Chat home page and download some new characters and/or backgrounds.

3. Try out a few other servers and see how you like their room selections.

4. Visit a chat room and use the whisper feature to speak privately to one person.

5. Make a log of a chat session on disk, and then print it out.

6. Join two rooms at once using two instances of Microsoft Chat.

REAL-WORLD APPLICATIONS

✔ You're traveling and want to get together with your friends back home. Instead of an expensive conference call, try using IRC to hold an online reunion party.

✔ You're a college professor conducting distance learning classes. You might want to consider setting up a private room on a chat server where you can hold lectures.

✔ You're hosting a chat room and it's visited by a disruptive character. You may consider banning that person from participation.

✔ If you're an artist, you might want to consider creating some of your own backgrounds or characters and submitting them to Microsoft.

Visual Quiz

What is this character's name? How do you find out?

_____

_____

_____

_____

_____

_____

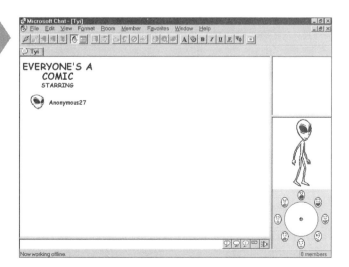

CHAPTER **9**

Online Communities

If the Internet is the new world, then online communities are its neighborhoods. What makes a particular set of Web pages into a community? Ultimately, as with so many other aspects on the Net, it's the people involved in them. If a site is designed to foster a feeling of belonging, rather than just visiting — a home on the vast network of networks — then it succeeds as a community.

Typically, online communities are Web-based places where many different people create Web pages that are clustered in groups by their themes, and the main page of the community directs visitors to the subjects they're looking for. Members of these communities gain all sorts of benefits when they join, and the good news is that the services are usually free. Free Web pages, free e-mail, free forums and chat rooms — you could spend years in one place such as GeoCities and never lack for novel experiences.

America Online is perhaps the most familiar example of an online community, with its famous forums and chat rooms. AOL features places such as Astronet that let people build close-knit relationships with others who may live thousands of miles away.

AOL, though, is a bit of a one-way street — it lets members of its community out onto the Internet, but it doesn't let the rest of the Internet in. True, AOL members' Web pages are accessible, and you can send e-mail to addresses that end in aol.com, but that's about it. AOL was originally designed as a standalone setup, and it remains so.

The Internet boasts its own online communities, accessible to anyone with an Internet connection. GeoCities, Tripod, Parent Soup, and the like are there for anyone to use, and Netscape is jumping into the game, expanding its Netcenter services to include free e-mail and a strong emphasis on the needs of people in small businesses. The free e-mail accounts alone are worth the effort of joining. If you wanted your ISP to provide you with extra e-mail boxes, it would cost you at least $5 or $10 a month for each one you added.

Something in the human spirit craves togetherness. Not surprisingly, millions upon millions of people are already members of online communities. It's a solid trend in the Internet world, and it's not likely to go away any time soon.

Joining the Community

GeoCities is one of the most popular and well known of the Internet communities. Its Join page offers you a choice of which GeoCities program you want to sign up for. Look them over and click whichever program interests you. The different packages offer various levels Web site storage space on the GeoCities servers, as well as different tools for maintaining your Web site. Unless you're thinking about starting a small business, you probably don't want GeoShops, which includes electronic transaction capabilities for selling goods. We're using the Homesteader program here — that's the one with a free Web page and free e-mail. If you pick the freebie and decide, partway through, that you'd rather go with one of the others, don't worry — you can always change your mind later in the sign-up process when you're filling out the final information.

The purpose of joining GeoCities is to link up with others who hold similar interests, so you need to select a neighborhood in which to place your home page. You have several choices, each divided into topical content, as shown in the figure on the lower left. They range from Area51 (for science fiction fans) to Yosemite (for outdoorsy types). We chose SiliconValley (that's not a typographical error, by the way; there are no spaces in any of the neighborhoods' names). The SiliconValley neighborhood is where computer buffs live at GeoCities. It's dedicated to the theme of hardware, software, and programming. If you have trouble deciding where you fit in, each neighborhood contains a more detailed description of its theme on its main page.

Once you've chosen a neighborhood and clicked its link, you go to a Web page where you pick an address in the neighborhood where you want your Web site to go.

TAKE NOTE

▶ ADVERTISING

The free online communities support themselves the same way free radio and television shows do — by advertising. In most cases, it's unobtrusive, just the usual small banner ads at the top of the Web pages. Increasingly, though, some of them use a popup JavaScript window that really intrudes, requiring the visitor to separately close it in order to view the Web page underneath. You can avoid this by disabling JavaScript in your Web browser when you visit such pages, but that's a bit of a drastic measure just to cope with one place on the Web, and it means you'll lose out if you go to any page that uses JavaScript for other purposes. To get rid of the ad window, just click the X in the ad's upper right-hand corner. Of course, if you're interested in the ad, by all means follow the link — those ads, after all, are what pay for your free home page and e-mail.

CROSS-REFERENCE
See Chapter 1 for more information on using Web browsers.

FIND IT ONLINE
The GeoCities home page is located at http://www.geocities.com/.

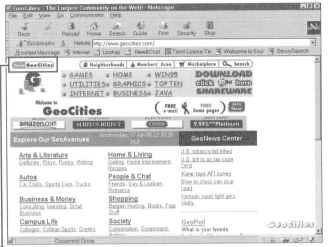

① Click the Join GeoCities button on the top left of the GeoCities home page.

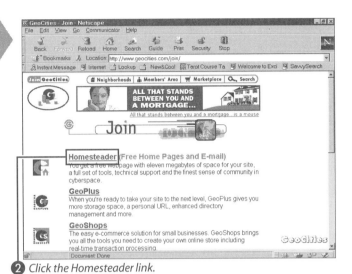

② Click the Homesteader link.

③ Click one of the neighborhood links.

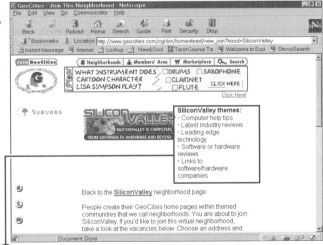

④ The neighborhood page has an expanded description of the associated themes.

Exploring GeoCities

Just like any normal neighborhood in the real world, the ones on GeoCities have different areas within them. Within the SiliconValley neighborhood, you might be in the heights, hills, lakes, and so forth. Scroll down until you reach the portion of the neighborhood Web page that shows which areas have vacancies. The number of vacancies in each area is shown next to its name. If no vacancies exist, click the link that says See More Vacancies to view other sections of the neighborhood.

If you decide at this point that you don't want to be in this neighborhood after all (or in the unlikely event that there are no vacancies), click the link to see the neighborhood descriptions and start over. Otherwise, click the link for one of the sections that has a vacancy. This will take you to a Web page where you can choose your "street address" in the neighborhood, as shown in the figure on the upper right. The occupied addresses will show a computer icon, while the vacant ones show a house icon. You can pick a plot of land to settle into (complete with street address), and fill out a New Member Application.

Once you settled in, you should take a look around through the other neighborhoods. The communities provide entertaining and informative pages that could be considered small libraries. Many neighborhoods include small businesses that have great store-fronts. They typically take orders online for your convenience. Chats and forums also exist here to promote social interaction with your friends and neighbors.

For topics that you might not find by cruising down the community avenues, a search utility exists at the GeoCities site. This search engine is powered by Lycos, but it is restricted to the parameters of GeoCities, so there's a manageable results pool to sift through. Search keywords follow the same structure set forth in Chapter 3, "Web Searching."

Continued

Continued

TAKE NOTE

YOUR HOME PAGE WEB ADDRESS

The URL of your home page is composed of the GeoCities main URL (**http://www.geocities.com/**) plus the neighborhood you choose, plus the area within the neighborhood, plus the "house number" you select within the area. Thus, if you chose to be at house number 4960 in the Sector area of the SiliconValley neighborhood, the URL of your GeoCities home page would be **http://www.geocities.com/SiliconValley/Sector/4960/**.

PERSONAL HOME PAGE

The free home pages in the Homesteader program are not for commercial use, but for your own personal use; you can't set up a free store at GeoCities. If you want to have a commercial site on GeoCities, you need to sign up with one of its paid programs. GeoCities has a section called GeoShops that offers all sorts of benefits to Web entrepreneurs (see Find It Online below).

CROSS-REFERENCE

See Chapter 1 for more information on URLs.

FIND IT ONLINE

Find out about GeoCities commercial pages at **http://www.geocities.com/join/geoshops/geoshops_faq.html**.

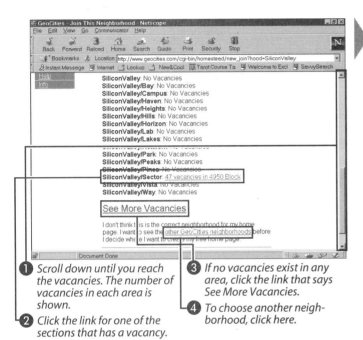

① Scroll down until you reach the vacancies. The number of vacancies in each area is shown.

② Click the link for one of the sections that has a vacancy.

③ If no vacancies exist in any area, click the link that says See More Vacancies.

④ To choose another neighborhood, click here.

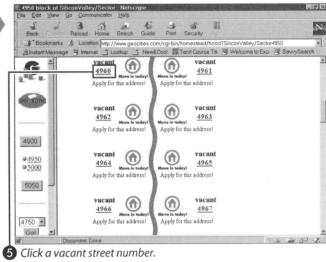

⑤ Click a vacant street number.

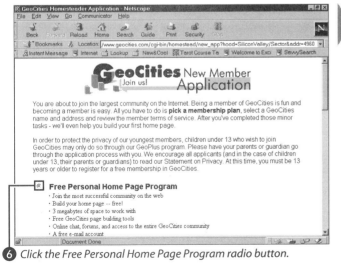

⑥ Click the Free Personal Home Page Program radio button.

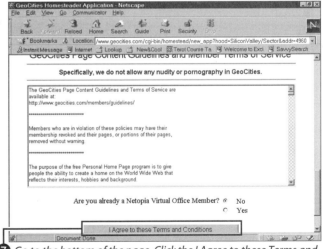

⑦ Go to the bottom of the page. Click the I Agree to these Terms and Conditions button.

Exploring GeoCities
Continued

Several areas have links to games, guidebooks to important or interesting sites, and contact information for community leaders, who can answer your questions about their home. Because all of these areas are based on real-life places or activities, interaction with the members can help you out when you need real items. Members of the Napa Valley area within the Home & Living neighborhood might be able to point you to the best gourmet food in your part of the country, for example.

When you become a little more familiar with the GeoCities neighborhoods, you might find that other people could benefit from your knowledge in one area or another. If this is the case, you should consider becoming a Community Leader yourself. Information pages describe what the position entails, and you'd have the support of your fellow leaders to guide you in the right direction.

Like America Online, GeoCities contains access to so many goods and services that it makes leaving this microcosm very difficult. The community places a major emphasis on sharing information between thousands of people, and GeoCities itself provides a lot of headline and sidebar news items. However, you still have links to major resources outside the GeoCities domain. For example, the Sports and

Recreation area has a link to ESPN's SportsZone, in case you don't get your fill of sports information on members' sites.

TAKE NOTE

▶ NOTE THAT PASSWORD!

When you receive the e-mail message with your password from GeoCities, make sure you print out the welcome message. You will need your password for just about everything you do as a GeoCities member. Without it, you won't even be able to modify your home page.

▶ IF YOU LOSE IT

GeoCities shows a rare degree of foresight among Web sites that require passwords. If you should ever find yourself suffering from the "I know I put it somewhere" syndrome, you can ask GeoCities to send you your password again. See the URL in Find It Online at the bottom of this page. This does not give anyone else access to your password. You can choose to have GeoCities e-mail you just your password or the entire welcome letter you initially received. The message is sent out automatically and immediately; it goes to the e-mail address they have on record for you in its member database.

CROSS-REFERENCE
See Chapters 5 and 6 for more information on e-mail.

FIND IT ONLINE
Find the GeoCities Password Look-Up page at **http://www.geocities.com/members/tools/ lost_password.html**.

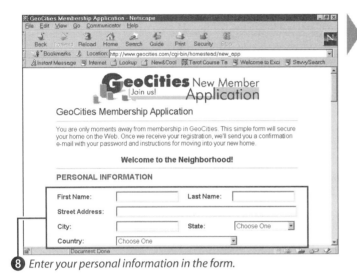

8 *Enter your personal information in the form.*

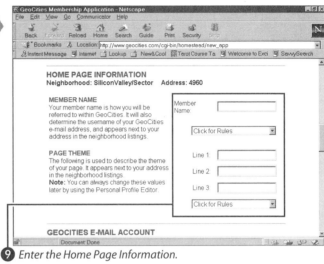

9 *Enter the Home Page Information.*

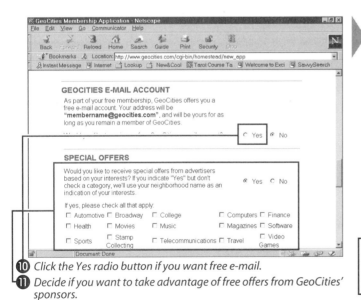

10 *Click the Yes radio button if you want free e-mail.*

11 *Decide if you want to take advantage of free offers from GeoCities' sponsors.*

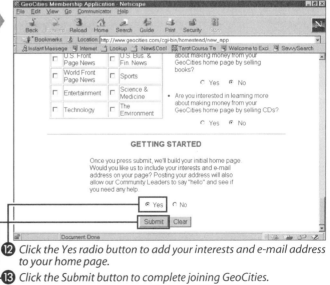

12 *Click the Yes radio button to add your interests and e-mail address to your home page.*

13 *Click the Submit button to complete joining GeoCities.*

Making a Personal Web Page

When you joined GeoCities, a basic home page was automatically created for you at the address you picked in the neighborhood of your choice. However, it's a generic Web page that GeoCities uses for any new member, and it's a bit bare at first, so you need to work on it to make it into what you want. Happily, GeoCities offers a lot of assistance to Web designers of all levels. Whether you've never even seen a Web page or you're an old hand at making them, you'll find what you need.

GeoCities has a File Manager page that assists you in creating and maintaining your Web site. You have to enter your username and password so File Manager can list your home directory and its contents. At the bottom of the page is a list of the total disk space you've used and the amount remaining to you.

Your home page is "index.html," which is a standard name for a site's root page. You can start editing this page, but you can't rename it, because it's a requirement that GeoCities imposes on all members. You might want to make a copy of your index page, in case you want to start from scratch later on, but a basic Web page is really easy to construct if you need to.

Continued

TAKE NOTE

▶ TIME LIMIT

There's no requirement to jump right in when you sign up, but you have to start work on your home page within two weeks of joining GeoCities, or they'll assume you're not going to stay, and it'll become vacant again. If this happens, then you'll need to start all over again, signing up as a new member.

▶ LIST FILES

Just above the spot where you type in your name and password, you'll see a set of radio buttons and checkboxes that tell File Manager which files in your directory to list. If you want to, you can make your file display choices here. However, you don't need to do anything with this at this point, because it's exactly duplicated in the File Manager itself. The default choices mean, in order, that all HTML pages will be in the listing, as well as all GIF and JPG images (the two most common graphics file formats on the Web). Because Other is also selected and, below that, Any is chosen, this means that every file in your home Web page directory will be listed. You could, if you wished, deselect Other so that only Web files and graphics files were listed. Or, you could deselect the graphics files and work only with HTML files. Instead of Any under the Other option, you could choose to have only files that started with a particular letter. Generally, it's best to just leave things as they are in the default settings, but you may have special needs and GeoCities has provided for that possibility.

CROSS-REFERENCE

See Part III for details on Web page creation.

FIND IT ONLINE

Tripod, at **http://www.tripod.com/**, is another online community.

1 On the GeoCities home page, click the Member's Area button.

2 Click the File Manager link under Quick Links.

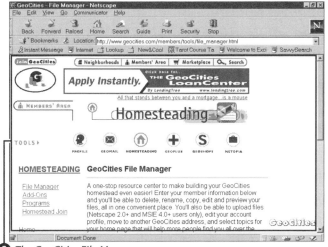

3 The GeoCities File Manager page appears.

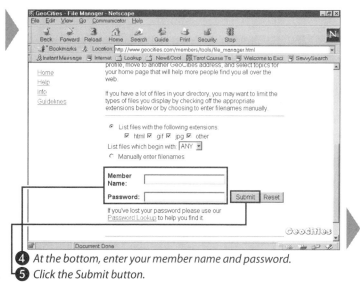

4 At the bottom, enter your member name and password.

5 Click the Submit button.

Making a Personal Web Page

Continued

When you're ready to build your site, you can either choose an editor from a list that the File Manager provides, or you can use your own. If you use your own, you can take advantage of the EZ File Upload option at the bottom of the page. The browse buttons are available to upload up to five files at a time. You can transfer files to your site with your own FTP (file transfer protocol) software as well, and avoid the hassle of sending only five files at a time. One distinct benefit of doing all your HTML editing through GeoCities is that the changes are instantaneous, and you can continually make improvements without having to constantly transfer files into your account. An advantage of using your own HTML editor, on the other hand, is that you can save copies of all your files on your hard drive. This way, you can be sure your hard work won't be lost forever in the event that something catastrophic happens to the server while you're making changes.

TAKE NOTE

▶ **TAKING THE MIDDLE ROAD**

Using an editor such as Microsoft's FrontPage or Netscape's Composer might be the best solution for most users. The close integration of these editors with their respective browsers enables you to see your changes immediately, but it's all done locally, so you can back up the files as many times as you need. Both of these editors are designed for users of all levels, and you don't need to know anything about HTML at all. To find out more about Composer, see Chapters 11 and 12. You can find more information on FrontPage at **www. microsoft.com/frontpage**.

▶ **HOW MUCH SPACE?**

If you browse around the GeoCities Web site, you'll find different amounts of Web space quoted for the free program (we noted 3MB, 8MB, and 11MB). As you can see from the figure on the upper right, the actual figure is 11MB, which is plenty of space for most Web site design purposes.

▶ **SHOWING YOUR PERSONALITY**

Regardless of which method you choose, you should try to let the Web site reflect your personality. Just make sure the style of the page doesn't obscure the content.

CROSS-REFERENCE

See the preceding page for instructions on using the List Files option.

FIND IT ONLINE

Netscape has an online community called Netcenter at **http://home.netscape.com**.

6 File Manager shows your home Web directory.

7 Either scroll down or click one of the links to get to the part you want.

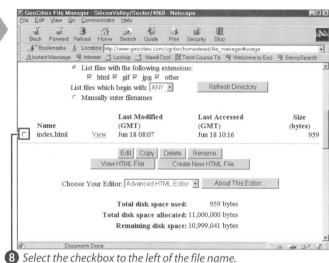

8 Select the checkbox to the left of the file name.

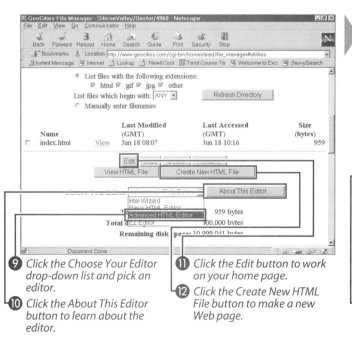

9 Click the Choose Your Editor drop-down list and pick an editor.

10 Click the About This Editor button to learn about the editor.

11 Click the Edit button to work on your home page.

12 Click the Create New HTML File button to make a new Web page.

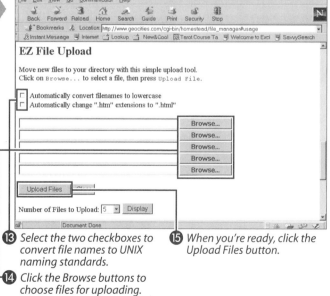

13 Select the two checkboxes to convert file names to UNIX naming standards.

14 Click the Browse buttons to choose files for uploading.

15 When you're ready, click the Upload Files button.

Managing Free E-mail

Why would anyone want another e-mail account? You've doubtless already got one, whether you got it from your ISP as part of your basic service or through your employer or school. Well, the simple fact is that people sometimes move or change ISPs, leave one employer for another, or graduate. Any time you do any of those things, your pending e-mail is going to be floating around looking for a place to land, and it's not going to find you.

Having an e-mail address at an online community offers you a higher degree of stability than the rest of life usually does. You can travel for business or pleasure, switch ISPs once a week, move every time your lease is up, change jobs so often you can't remember what company you work for, and still have one thing remain constant, because you'll always be at the same e-mail address no matter what else is going on in your life.

The e-mail accounts at GeoCities are the standard types already discussed in Chapter 5. You just set your e-mail client to the GeoCities POP and SMTP servers. Both are named mail.geocities.com — don't preface them with pop or smtp. You can also opt to cancel the e-mail account or to have your GeoCities e-mail messages automatically forwarded to another e-mail address. The GeoMail Tools page is the resource you'll use to make changes to your e-mail account. There's not much more that the page lets you do besides forwarding or canceling your account, but many services don't even provide you this much control.

TAKE NOTE

▶ ALTERING SUBSCRIPTIONS

When you change or cancel your e-mail address, you should contact any mailing lists that you belong to and change your status with them. Having messages bounce back to their automated e-mail systems could cause a lot of trouble. Make sure you also let your friends and family know of your e-mail changes so they can update their address books.

▶ JUGGLING YOUR IDENTITIES

Free e-mail can be a great thing, but it's easy to sign up for several different services and forget which ones you belong to. Unless you really have uses for several e-mail accounts, you should probably have no more than two (one for work-related correspondence and one for personal correspondence).

▶ OTHER FREE E-MAIL

Many other places on the Internet besides online communities offer free e-mail accounts to anyone who wants them. Most of these only give Web-based e-mail, but some, such as SoftHome.Net, offer standard POP and SMTP servers for nothing. You can get Web-based e-mail accounts from Excite and Yahoo! (see Chapter 3).

CROSS-REFERENCE

See Chapters 5 and 6 for more information on e-mail.

FIND IT ONLINE

Parent Soup is an online community for those with children. Find it at **http://www.parentsoup.com/**.

1 In the Quick Links Area, click the GeoMail Manager link.

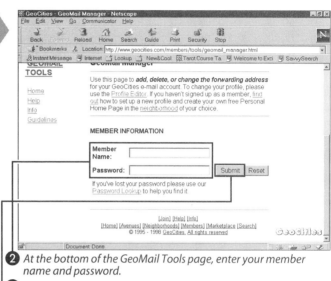

2 At the bottom of the GeoMail Tools page, enter your member name and password.

3 Click the Submit button.

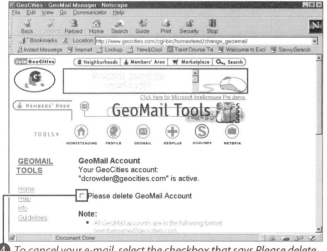

4 To cancel your e-mail, select the checkbox that says Please delete GeoMail Account.

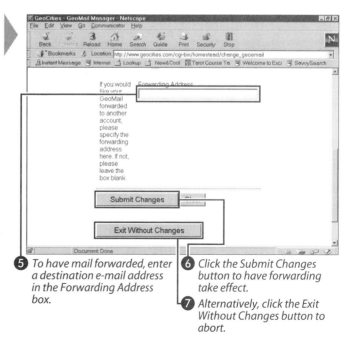

5 To have mail forwarded, enter a destination e-mail address in the Forwarding Address box.

6 Click the Submit Changes button to have forwarding take effect.

7 Alternatively, click the Exit Without Changes button to abort.

Using Chat Rooms and Forums

The chat rooms on GeoCities are much the same as those you're already familiar with from the preceding chapter. They don't use the same software as IRC chat rooms (the ones on GeoCities are Web-based), so you can't use Microsoft Chat or other IRC clients with them. GeoCities provides its own chat software, and it works like all chat clients — you type your messages in at the bottom and read the chat in the main window.

Forums are pretty much the same thing as newsgroups (see Chapter 7). You read messages that other people have left and leave your own messages for other people to read. Unlike the Usenet system, though, the GeoCities forums take place in real time. Whatever message you send is instantly posted right there on the GeoCities system and available to other members, instead of having to go through the complex worldwide routing system that Usenet newsgroups suffer from.

To access either chat rooms or forums, go to the GeoCities home page and scroll down to the bottom. The chat area has several chat rooms you can join, and you can pick your own chat name, which is different from your GeoCities user name. You need to use special chat software, and you can choose between Java or plain HTML chat programs.

The forums page lists all the available forums. Just click the one you want and you're off and running.

The name you use here is your GeoCities user name. The forums require no special software — just your browser.

CROSS-REFERENCE

See Chapter 8 for more information on chat rooms.

FIND IT ONLINE

The folks who brought you Parent Soup provide a women's community at **http://ivillage.com/ TWN/FrontDoor/net/**.

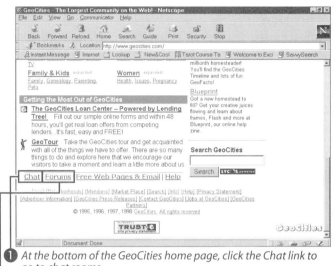

① At the bottom of the GeoCities home page, click the Chat link to go to chat rooms.

② To go to the forums, click the Forums link.

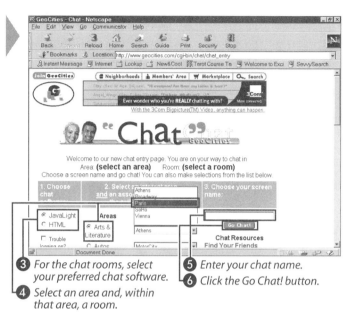

③ For the chat rooms, select your preferred chat software.

④ Select an area and, within that area, a room.

⑤ Enter your chat name.

⑥ Click the Go Chat! button.

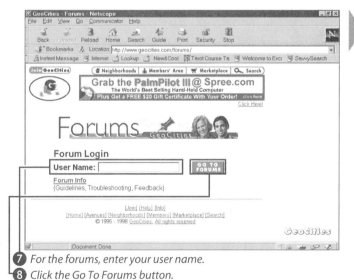

⑦ For the forums, enter your user name.

⑧ Click the Go To Forums button.

⑨ Click the desired forum.

Personal Workbook

Q&A

1 What is the difference between an ordinary Internet site and an online community?

_____

_____

_____

2 What is one advantage of free e-mail, other than the cost?

_____

_____

_____

_____

3 Name two online communities.

_____

_____

4 What is an _online neighborhood_?

_____

_____

5 How do online communities support themselves financially?

_____

_____

6 What is the structure of a GeoCities Web page address?

_____

_____

_____

_____

_____

7 What type of e-mail servers does GeoCities use?

_____

_____

_____

8 Can you use Microsoft Chat in GeoCities chat rooms?

_____

_____

ANSWERS: PAGE 381

EXTRA PRACTICE

1 Visit and explore at least three of the online communities listed in this chapter.

2 If your computer supports Java, try both of the chat programs.

3 Work with the different HTML editors and see which one you like best.

4 Add another Web page to your site and link to it from your home page.

5 Set up your e-mail client to use your free account.

6 Forward e-mail from your GeoCities account to your other one.

REAL-WORLD APPLICATIONS

✔ You have multiple interests that won't all fit into one of GeoCities' categories. Consider joining more than one neighborhood and setting up several different home pages.

✔ You find that you like working with the GeoCities setup, but you want a commercial operation. You might want to take a look at GeoStores to see if you like the idea.

✔ You have one particular interest, such as parenting or business. You might be better off joining a more specialized community such as Parent Soup or Netscape's Netcenter than one of the generalized communities.

Visual Quiz

What do these choices mean (see box)? What other Web page are they duplicated on?

_____

_____

_____

_____

_____

_____

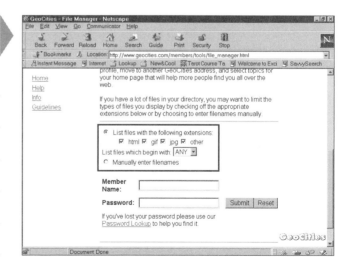

CHAPTER **10**

Internet Telephony

Forget those dime-a-minute long distance rates! Now your Internet connection is your long distance connection, too. Because you're already connected to the Internet, your long distance calls don't need to cost you a thing.

Internet telephony has a couple of drawbacks. For one thing, you can only call people who are on the Internet and using compatible software (some companies will relay Internet calls to regular telephones, but such a service costs about as much as placing the call yourself the regular way).

The other major consideration is sound quality. You won't get the kind of perfectly clear signal you're used to on a regular telephone, but you'll have no problem understanding the person you're talking to.

Unlike the other programs in this book, you'll need some special equipment to use this—a SoundBlaster 16–compatible sound card and speakers. If you've got a recent model computer, the odds are pretty good that you've already got these as part of your basic setup for multimedia purposes. You can skip the speakers and just use a regular Walkman-type headset in place of them; in fact, you might prefer headphones to speakers for Internet telephony. And one more thing—you have to have a microphone to talk into. You can use just about any mike, including one from that old tape recorder you have in the closet. Just plug the headphones and the mike into your sound card and you're ready to go. You can also pick up a special headset with a mike on a boom in front of your mouth at any good office supply or computer store for around $15 to $40. Make sure it's designed to plug into a sound card instead of a telephone.

We're using a program called FreeTel in this chapter. Unlike similar programs, it's fully functional right out of the box and doesn't cost you a dime, no matter how many minutes you talk on it. Most Internet telephony programs are pretty much like FreeTel, but cost money. Don't forget that anyone else you want to call on the Internet has to be using FreeTel also, but at the cost, there should be no problem there. FreeTel maintains a live, online Internet phone directory you can tap into the instant you install it.

Configuring FreeTel

A nice feature of FreeTel is that it provides an online directory of other FreeTel users. While using the application, you can find out information about anyone with whom you wish to speak, including alternate means of communication (such as an e-mail address), in case you have trouble with the audio channels. For this reason, it's best for you to fill in as much information about yourself as possible.

When you start FreeTel for the first time, it asks you to supply some basic information such as your first and last name. You can also include an optional comment. This comment appears in the FreeTel online phone directory after your name. If you include your e-mail address, the address appears after the comment in the directory. The bottom portion of the form asks for demographic data for FreeTel's own benefit; this data, although required, will not appear in the directory.

FreeTel goes online and connects with the FreeTel phone directory server. At first, it displays the word [Empty] in the directory window, but in a few seconds it fills with listings. It may not look like it at first, because some people have filled in their names as a blank space and included no comments — or used exclamation points as comments. In the ASCII code — the code of letters and numbers that computers use — blank spaces come before any letters or numbers and exclamation points come next, which is why these listings appear before those that start with normal letters.

When completing the configuration, you should probably also select the Automatically Reject File Transfer Requests checkbox unless you are only going to connect with people you know and trust. (Never accept a file transfer from a stranger, because they could conceivably send you a program infected with a virus.)

TAKE NOTE

▶ HOBBIES, SPORTS, AND ACTIVITIES

The final field under User Info asks you to list at least three hobbies, sports, or activities that you enjoy. This field can cause difficulties sometimes, refusing to accept a simple hit on the Enter key. If this happens, a way around the problem is to hold down your Ctrl key and then press the Enter key to go to the next line.

▶ LISTING YOUR E-MAIL ADDRESS

Including your e-mail address when you first sign on to FreeTel's services might seem like it sacrifices some of your privacy, but you should consider the benefits: If you are trying to have a conversation with a new person and you are having technical difficulties, you might need to find another way to "talk" to each other and figure out the problem. Listing your e-mail address in the directory is an easy way for the other person to locate you immediately.

CROSS-REFERENCE

See the section on understanding the directory later in this chapter.

FIND IT ONLINE

The FreeTel home page is located at **http://www.freetel.com/**.

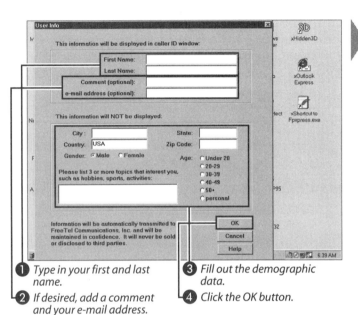

① *Type in your first and last name.*

② *If desired, add a comment and your e-mail address.*

③ *Fill out the demographic data.*

④ *Click the OK button.*

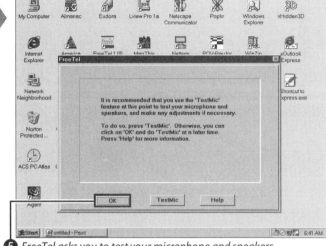

⑤ *FreeTel asks you to test your microphone and speakers. Click the OK button to skip this step for now.*

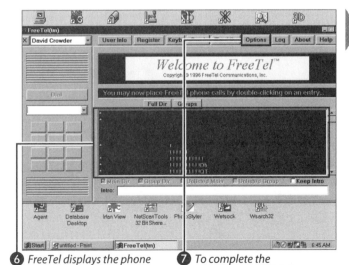

⑥ *FreeTel displays the phone listings in the directory window.*

⑦ *To complete the configuration, click the Options button. This brings up the Options dialog box.*

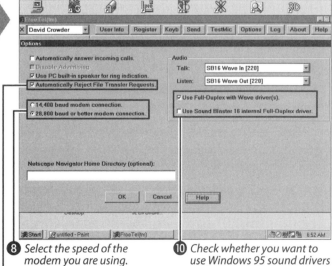

⑧ *Select the speed of the modem you are using.*

⑨ *Select the Automatically Reject File Transfer Requests checkbox.*

⑩ *Check whether you want to use Windows 95 sound drivers or the SoundBlaster 16 drivers.*

Testing Your Microphone and Speakers

Before attempting to use the application in a real conversation, you should test your equipment to make sure it's working properly. You can perform a test on your mike and speakers (or integrated headset) at any time while using FreeTel.

You can, if you want to, just click the Test Mic button and talk into your microphone and wait a couple of seconds to hear the results from your speakers. To gain the full benefit of testing, however, you need to pay attention to the left side of your screen. There, hiding under the visual representation of a normal telephone as you would see it if you lifted the handset, are some special controls. At the top left and bottom left are a series of horizontal lines. If you click either group of lines, the underlying controls are revealed (see the figure on the bottom left). The top set of controls is for your speakers and the bottom set is for your microphone. You'll be testing the microphone first. Speak into it and observe the readings on the gauges in the bottom controls. Most likely, they'll be fine, and the only settings you'll need to adjust will be for your speakers. However, you may want to adjust the mike volume. Lower microphone volume is to the left; higher is to the right. The VOX setting (the top slider) controls the amount of background noise the microphone picks up. If you're getting too much, move the slider to the left.

After a couple of seconds, the words you spoke will emanate from your speakers, and the gauges in the upper controls will reflect the results (see the figure on the upper right). You'll probably need to turn the volume down.

TAKE NOTE

▶ ADJUSTING BASS AND TREBLE

FreeTel is one of the only Internet Telephony products at any price that lets you adjust the bass and treble settings on your speakers or headphones.

▶ FULL DUPLEX AND HALF DUPLEX

Full duplex operation enables both parties to talk at the same time, like on a normal telephone. Half duplex operation means that only one can talk at a time, like on a CB radio.

▶ OVERLOOKING THE OBVIOUS

Many times the obvious solutions are overlooked when problems in software performance occur. This includes simple things such as sound that require many parts to be working well. To start off on the right foot, make sure your sound card is installed and working, and your speakers and microphone are plugged in. Then check your sound settings to make sure the volume is at the right level and the mute button is unchecked.

CROSS-REFERENCE

See the introduction to this chapter for information on speakers and microphones.

FIND IT ONLINE

See **http://www.deltathree.com/doorway.html** for a company providing PC-to-phone services.

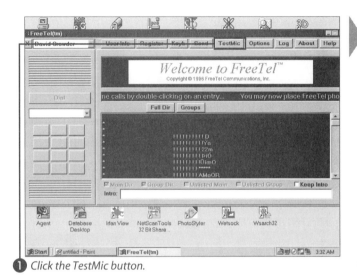

1 *Click the TestMic button.*

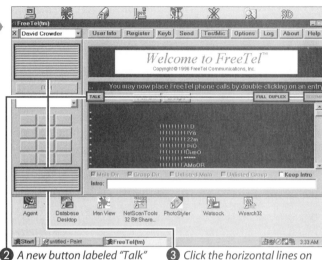

2 *A new button labeled "Talk" appears, along with the words Full Duplex (or Half Duplex) and the word TestMic.*

3 *Click the horizontal lines on the left side of your screen.*

4 *Speak into your microphone. Adjust the mike volume and the VOX setting as needed.*

5 *Adjust the speaker volume, treble, and bass controls as desired.*

Making Calls

Once you find someone to call, whether you have reached that listing by scrolling or searching (or if you just knew someone's FreeTel name by other means), you have a few options on how to place the Internet phone call.

The first method is selecting a name from the directory. If you don't have the patience to wait to move step by step down the listings, waiting at each move, or if you're looking for someone in particular, you can use FreeTel's Find feature to locate Internet telephone listings in the directory. All you have to do is type in the text string you're searching for in the edit box above the keypad. If you already know the name of the person you are calling, you can type it in above the keypad and click the Dial button. If the person is someone you have called or who has called you, his or her name is kept in your personal phone directory, so you can click the drop-down list and select the name and then click the Dial button.

When you have initiated dialing, the top window shows that you are dialing, and to whom you are dialing. Your computer beeps repeatedly while the dialing of the call is in progress. If that number is being used at the moment, then — just like with a regular telephone — you will get a busy signal. Unlike with a normal phone, you won't hear it — the busy signal shows in the upper window. Otherwise, you connect to the number and the upper window shows the identity of the person you have connected to.

TAKE NOTE

▶ UNLISTED NUMBERS

People who have upgraded to one of the commercial versions of FreeTel (either $29.95 or $39.95, depending on the features you want) can have unlisted numbers. The names of those with unlisted numbers will not show in the FreeTel online directory, but anyone who knows the name that the person is using with FreeTel can still call them by typing that name into the edit box on the left side of the screen and clicking the dial button.

▶ REJECTED CALLS

If the person you're calling isn't using the line, but doesn't click their Accept button, then your call still won't go through. In this case, the upper window will say "Cannot Connect." This may mean the recipient refused your call, or that he or she just wasn't near the computer.

▶ BUSY SIGNALS

You can save yourself a lot of busy signals by noting the left side of the directory listings. If the listing is preceded by an asterisk, then that number is in use at the present time and you will get a busy signal if you attempt to call it (see the figure on the upper left).

CROSS-REFERENCE
See the section on using the keyboard chat feature later in this chapter.

FIND IT ONLINE
Find links to different Internet telephony products at **http://davecentral.com/phone.html**.

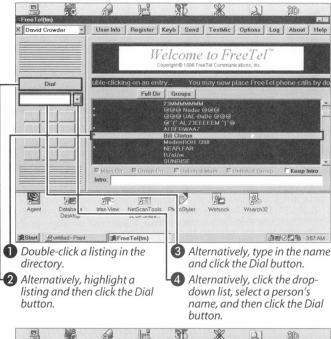

❶ Double-click a listing in the directory.

❷ Alternatively, highlight a listing and then click the Dial button.

❸ Alternatively, type in the name and click the Dial button.

❹ Alternatively, click the drop-down list, select a person's name, and then click the Dial button.

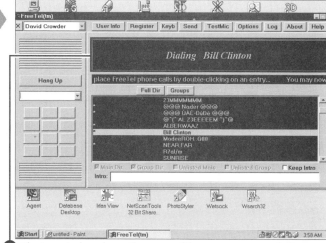

❺ The top window shows the name of the person you are dialing.

❻ If the number is busy, a busy signal appears in the upper window.

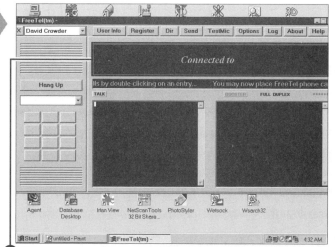

❼ Otherwise, you will connect to the number and the upper window shows the identity of the person you have connected to.

Receiving Calls

During the course of a day, you might get phone calls from several people, interrupting various work or home activities. The same interruptions might happen as you are working with a computer application. You have the option of picking up the call or ignoring it. FreeTel makes this easy to do, and it even includes a caller ID function to help you decide whether or not you'd like to take a call.

When a call comes in to you from someone who either knew the name you were using or who picked your name out of the FreeTel directory, your computer beeps repeatedly until you either accept or reject the call (click the Accept or Reject buttons, respectively, on the left side of your screen). If the caller terminates the call before you decide what you want to do, your computer stops beeping and the top window in FreeTel displays the words "Hung up." During the time when the call is coming in, the top window shows the identity of the caller (this is the FreeTel "caller ID" feature) and the words "is calling."

If you click the Accept button, the chat windows automatically open and, if the person calling doesn't want to (or can't) use the voice features, he or she will then type a message to you. Normally, the caller will speak into his or her microphone and you will hear him or her on your speakers or in your headphones.

CROSS-REFERENCE

See the section on using the keyboard chat feature later in this chapter.

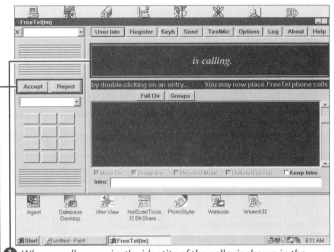

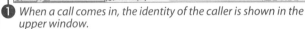

① When a call comes in, the identity of the caller is shown in the upper window.

② Click the Accept or Reject button.

③ If you click the Accept button, the chat windows open.

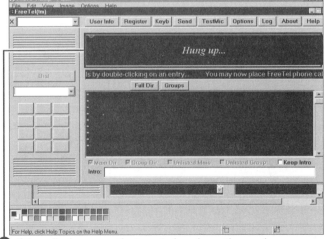

④ If the caller hangs up, the top window shows the words "Hung up."

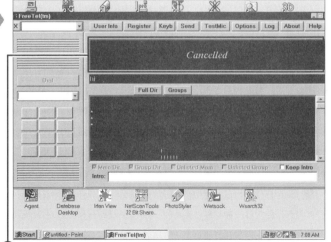

⑤ If you hang up, the top window shows the word "Cancelled."

Using the Keyboard Chat Feature

One of the best features of FreeTel is the capability of chatting online with someone in a text-based environment. This feature is helpful because: 1) it increases the number of potential people you can talk to, because the other person doesn't need additional hardware (such as a microphone) to communicate, and 2) it lets you talk to only one person in a real-time Internet chat environment, without all the extra "noise" created by other occupants of a chat room.

The Keyboard Chat feature comes in handy for those users who experience a lot of static interference in the voice environment. It's also a benefit for those users who are hearing impaired.

At any time when you are connected to other FreeTel customers, whether they have called you or you have called them, the chat screens will be activated, as shown in the figure on the upper left. This gives you the option of typing a message to them and receiving messages from them in a like manner if you'd rather not talk, or if one of you doesn't have the required equipment for normal Internet telephony conversations (some of the listings in the online FreeTel phone directory will say something like "no mike" to let you know in advance that you'll need to use the chat feature).

TAKE NOTE

▶ THE BOOSTER BUTTON

When you're online with another FreeTel customer, a button labeled Booster appears above the right-hand chat window. This button activates a special feature of FreeTel. When you're attempting to carry on a conversation with someone during peak Internet usage hours, the quality of the connection can deteriorate due to the amount of traffic competing with the digital voice signal you're generating. Clicking the Booster button increases the quality of the sound, but it comes at a slight price. The conversation will suffer some delay in transmission as a result.

▶ THE TALK BUTTON

As mentioned in the previous section, if you want to switch from chat to voice, click the Talk button that appears above the left-hand chat window.

▶ OLDER COMPUTERS

If your computer lacks the sound card typically found in the newer multimedia capable models, you can still use FreeTel. You just have to use the chat feature instead of communicating by voice. It still beats the high cost of regular long-distance calls, and it's a lot simpler to use and understand than IRC (Internet Relay Chat) programs. To have a private conversation with IRC, you'd have to both log on to the same IRC server, one of you would create a private chat room set to exclude anyone else, and then you could both meet there. With FreeTel, all you have to do is for one person to call the other person.

CROSS-REFERENCE

See Chapter 8 for information on Internet Relay Chat.

FIND IT ONLINE

Visit VocalTec at **http://vocaltec.com/homep.htm** for Internet voice mail information.

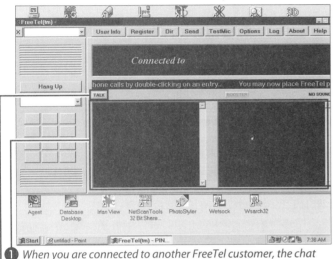

1 When you are connected to another FreeTel customer, the chat screens are activated.

2 Click the Talk button if you would rather use voice.

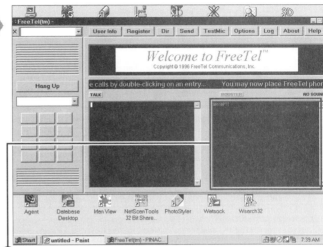

3 The other person's input appears in the right-hand chat window.

4 Your input shows up in the left-hand chat window.

5 Click the Dir button to restore the phone directory.

6 Click the Keyb button to restore chat mode.

217

Sending Files

One problem with speaking to someone on the phone is that you can only describe objects; you can't very easily show someone a picture or have him or her experience a multimedia presentation. This problem is especially frustrating for those who have to collaborate on work-related projects over a long distance. FreeTel solves this problem by enabling its users to send files back and forth to each other. Once you scan an image, record a sound, or compress an application, you can send it on its way with the simple click of a button. The recipient must have a means of opening these files, of course, and must also have the "Automatically Reject File Transfer Requests" checkbox unchecked (see sidebar).

You should avoid sending very large files to someone, as they take longer to transmit, and they might cause delays in your conversation. You should also take advantage of this chat environment to discuss the files after the recipient has had a chance to open them.

Many people using Internet telephony want to send each other pictures of themselves. If the file you receive is a GIF or JPEG file (these end in .gif and .jpg or .jpeg, respectively), then they are not computer programs, but image files in one of the two most popular formats that you can safely display using most normal graphics programs.

TAKE NOTE

▶ BASIC SECURITY PRECAUTIONS

It's not really a good idea to accept file transfers from someone you don't know very well. Malicious strangers could easily send you a file infected with a virus that could infect your entire system. If you do receive a file from someone you don't know, don't panic — a normal virus must be contained in a program file and it cannot affect your system unless you run the program that is in the file you received. Some newer viruses can be put into normal program files if the programs that use those files have the capability to run *macros*. Macros are mini-programs that run within programs such as Microsoft Word and Excel. You still have to load that file into the program before the virus can work. If you're in doubt about the validity of any file, use a virus-detection program to check the file to verify whether it is safe or not. Better yet, just delete the file.

▶ RECEIVING FILES AND FREETEL OPTIONS

If you follow our recommendations about configuring FreeTel at the beginning of this chapter, your system is set up to automatically reject all attempts to send you files. To change this so you can receive files, click the Options button and then deselect the checkbox labeled "Automatically Reject File Transfer Requests." You'll need to click the OK button at the bottom of the Options dialog box to complete the change.

CROSS-REFERENCE

See the beginning of this chapter for information on how to set FreeTel to reject incoming file transfers.

FIND IT ONLINE

A premier Web site for antivirus software is at **http://www.nai.com/default_mcafee.asp**.

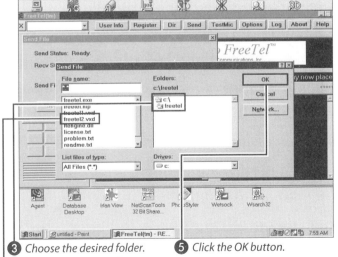

① Click the Send button to bring up the Send File dialog box.

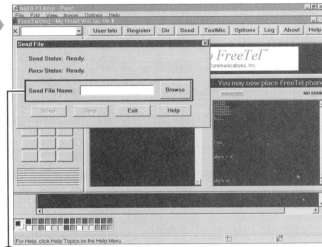

② Type in the file name or click the Browse button.

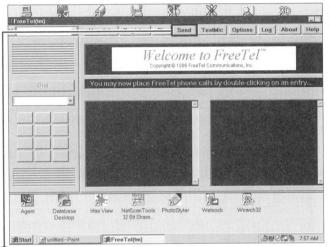

③ Choose the desired folder.
④ Choose the desired file.
⑤ Click the OK button.

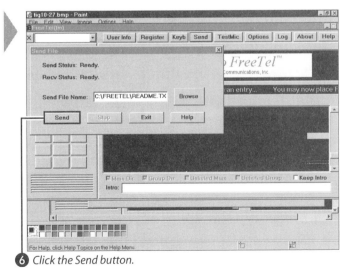

⑥ Click the Send button.

Personal Workbook

Q&A

1 What are the three items of special equipment you need for Internet telephony?

_____

_____

_____

2 In what way can two of the three Internet telephony items be combined?

_____

_____

_____

3 What is the minimum modem speed required by FreeTel?

_____

_____

_____

4 What are the two ways to find names in the directory?

_____

_____

_____

5 What does the Intro do?

_____

_____

6 How do you set the Intro to remain for multiple calls?

_____

_____

7 How do you adjust the microphone and speaker settings?

_____

_____

_____

_____

8 How do you call an unlisted FreeTel user?

_____

_____

_____

ANSWERS: PAGE 382

EXTRA PRACTICE

1. Find an interesting listing in the directory and place a call to it.

2. Leave FreeTel running until you get a call. Decide whether to accept or reject it.

3. Get an ASCII chart and experiment with variations on your name to move it higher and lower in the directory listings.

4. Search for a name in the directory using the Find button.

5. Send a file to a friend with FreeTel.

6. Adjust the bass and treble settings on your speakers or headset.

REAL-WORLD APPLICATIONS

✔ You have a friend who lives in a distant city or country. You both may want to get FreeTel to reduce your telephone bill.

✔ Someone you're talking to is using a poor-quality microphone. You might want to adjust the speaker settings to get a clearer signal.

✔ You don't like getting Internet phone calls from strangers. Consider upgrading to the commercial version of FreeTel so you can have an unlisted number.

✔ You're talking during a busy time on the Internet. Try using the Booster button to increase the signal strength.

Visual Quiz

What is different about this screen compared to the normal one? What button did you push to get here?

_____

_____

_____

_____

_____

_____

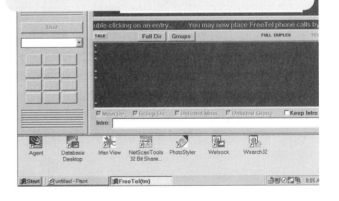

HTML and Web Content

This part shows you how to graduate from looking at other people's Web pages to designing your own. We'll cover the basics of using Web-page creation tools that don't require any knowledge of HTML at all, and show a bit of what's "under the hood" as well. All along the way, we share tips and tricks to help you create Web pages that truly shine.

You'll see how to create Web pages from scratch or from templates, how to save and upload your pages, how to poke into the HTML source code, and work with it directly if you want to. We look into manipulating text on your pages, from changing text size and style to using color for dramatic effect.

Next, we delve into adding images to make your pages graphically appealing. You'll find places to get free, high-quality artwork you can use, find out about the different types of graphic files that are available, and understand which ones to use for fastest Web-page display or best appearance. We show you how to mix images and text, as well as how to set background images for your pages.

You'll get to know the ins and outs of hyperlinks, how to use them to tie your own pages together into a full-blown Web site, and how to connect with the rest of the Web.

Finally, we tell you how you can use tables and lists to organize your Web pages.

CHAPTER 11

Basic Composer

The Hypertext Markup Language, called *HTML* for short, is what makes the World Wide Web work. The reason it's called a *markup language* is that it's composed of *tags* that mark the contents and tell Web browsers what formatting or functionality the Web designer intended. The tags, in turn, contain *attributes* that further define the designer's intent. The tags may hold *content*, as well, such as text. Together, tags, attributes, and content compose the *elements* of HTML.

You can sit down at your keyboard and use a plain old text editor to type in all the different HTML tags, their attributes, and even their contents if you wish. You have an easier way, though. Special HTML editors exist that are designed to make your Web page creation tasks much easier than they were way back in the prehistoric days of Web design (say, about five or six years ago).

Both of the major Web browsers come with their own HTML editors. Microsoft's Internet Explorer comes with FrontPage Express, a stripped-down version of the commercial program, FrontPage. Netscape Communicator, which includes the Web browser Navigator, also includes Netscape Composer, another HTML editor.

Both programs let you create Web pages with point-and-click simplicity. You don't have to know or ever learn anything about HTML to use either program. Just point at buttons on the toolbar with your mouse, click them, and fill out a couple of really simple forms to get things going.

FrontPage Express has better form handling than Netscape Composer — Composer, in fact, ignores forms entirely. This is not so much a problem with Composer as it is with HTML's poor implementation of forms. Forms generally require a separate program using the Common Gateway Interface (CGI) to process their information.

FrontPage Express, like the commercial FrontPage, has a couple of problems of its own, though. We've chosen Netscape Composer for the chapters in this part because it generates HTML code that is usable by any Web browser, while FrontPage Express, in many cases, generates code that can only be used by Microsoft Internet Explorer.

Setting Your Web Page and Image Editors

You might find, at times, that it's easier or more accessible to tweak HTML code in a source code editor such as Notepad. An example would be if you are not at your own computer, but your need to fix something on one of your Web pages. Rather than searching for an editor such as Composer, you could instead download the page's source code, make the minor changes, and upload it to the Internet again. If it's a significant change you're making, however, you might opt to use Composer to start again from scratch.

You can use Composer without an HTML editor if you want to. If all you're ever going to do is use the toolbar buttons to work on your Web page, if you're never going to want to view or print the HTML source, you can skip choosing an HTML editor. Even so, it's probably best to play it safe and pick one.

The one thing you need for sure in any HTML editor is the ability to save in plain-text ASCII format. It's best to use a text editor that does this by default, because saving an HTML file in a word processing format (such as Word or WordPerfect) results in a file that no Web browser can read. Beyond this, different editors have various features such as color coding to make your HTML programming easier. Check out the link under Find It Online below to see what's out there. Otherwise, Notepad is a suitable option that comes with Windows.

Continued

TAKE NOTE

▶ THE SHORT COURSE

If you definitely want to use Notepad and not another editor, and you have the standard Windows setup on drive C, it's very simple. Just type **C:\WINDOWS\Notepad.exe** in the edit box in the figure on the lower right, and then click the OK button. The entire procedure is outlined here for the benefit of those who might want to use some other editor, instead.

▶ THE ADVANTAGES AND THE DETRIMENT

Notepad is available right away without bothering to download it, as it's a basic part of Windows. It saves pure ASCII files, which is perfect for HTML coding, although you'll have to specify the ".htm" or ".html" file extension, because it defaults to a .txt file extension. Its one downside is that it won't load or save any file larger than 32K, but few HTML files in the world even begin to approach that size.

▶ LEARNING HTML

Regardless of what system you use to create and post Web pages, it is a good idea to familiarize yourself with HTML. Besides enabling you to fix things when an editor such as Composer is unavailable, it helps you understand what other Web designers have done with their sites. You might discover, after viewing other people's sites on the Web, that you have new ideas for your own site. You can view online (or print) someone's source code, and see which techniques he or she used.

CROSS-REFERENCE

See Chapter 4 for information on setting Navigator preferences.

FIND IT ONLINE

You'll find lots of HTML editors at **http://www.winfiles.com/apps/98/html.html**.

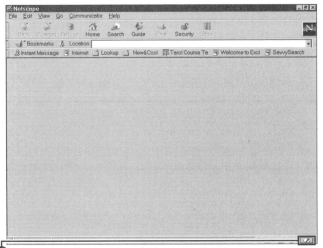

1 *Click the Composer icon in the bottom right-hand corner of Navigator.*

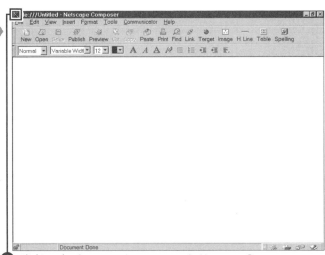

2 *Clicking the Composer icon puts you in Netscape Composer.*

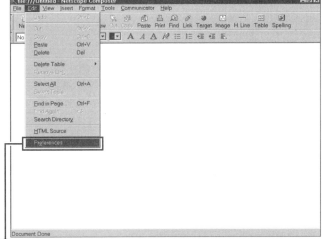

3 *Select Edit ⇨ Preferences from the menu.*

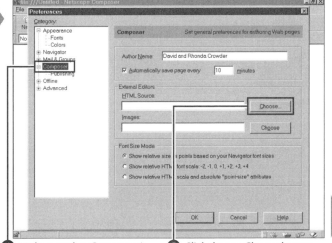

4 *Make sure that Composer is selected in the Preferences dialog box under Category.*

5 *Click the top Choose button to begin the HTML editor selection process.*

227

Setting Your Web Page and Image Editors *Continued*

Image editors are very important because they give you the power to liven up your Web pages. You can add all types of pictures to your sites as background art, decorative fringes, or image maps that guide users to other areas of your site.

The more elaborate the image editor, the better the final images will appear on your site, because of the additional levels of refinement that you can impose on them. The quality comes at a cost, however. The image editor will likely take up more space on your hard drive, and the time you spend in manipulating the artwork will no doubt increase. The best image editor out there is probably Adobe Photoshop, because it lets you open almost any image, apply hundred of filters and other tools to it, and save images in several different formats. The downside is that Photoshop is expensive, and typically intended for advanced users who are willing to put in a great deal of time to learn the software. Some image editors out there do perform some similar functions as Photoshop, however, and they are worth investigating further.

The process for setting your image editor is absolutely identical, except that you use the lower of the two Choose buttons and the path to the image editor program appears in the Images edit box. As with a text editor, you don't have to have an image editor specified if you're never going to make changes to any images within Composer, but it can't hurt to be prepared just in case.

TAKE NOTE

▶ EXECUTING FILES

You'll notice that "Executable (*.exe)" is already chosen for you at the bottom of the Choose HTML Editor Application dialog box where it says Files of type. That's because you're looking for a program, and programs are referred to as *executable files*. Don't change this setting while you're looking for your text or graphics editor.

▶ IMAGE EDITORS

Also called *graphics editors* or *paint programs*, image editor applications vary in sophistication. Some are simple programs that convert images from one format to another. Others let you create or modify your own artwork, and these are the ones you'll be most interested in for your Composer image editor. The bottom-line requirement is that they be able to handle GIF and JPEG (often shortened to JPG) files, as these are the two most common graphics file formats on the Web, although PNG (Portable Network Graphic) files are likely to become much more common in the future. If your image editor supports PNG in addition to GIF and JPG, it's a nice plus.

▶ STEALING IMAGES

Many images that you'll find online will be tempting to save to your hard drive and use later for your own pages, but beware: Often those images are copyrighted, and the owner of the original artwork will probably be unhappy that you have copied images without prior written consent.

CROSS-REFERENCE

See Chapter 14 for more information on images.

FIND IT ONLINE

A good listing of image editors appears at **http://www.winfiles.com/apps/98/graph-editors.html**.

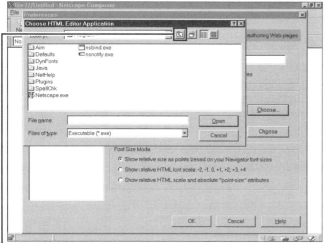

6 *Click the Up One Level button until you reach the folder you want.*

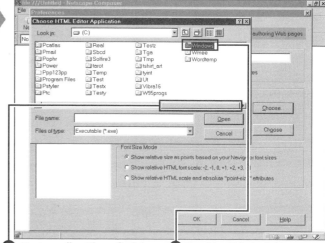

7 *Next, scroll until you find the folder that contains the text editor you want to use.*

8 *Double-click the folder name to open it (or select it and click the Open button).*

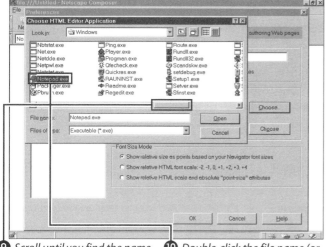

9 *Scroll until you find the name of the file.*

10 *Double-click the file name (or select it and click the Open button).*

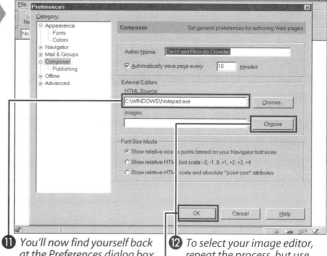

11 *You'll now find yourself back at the Preferences dialog box, and the path to the text editor you've chosen is filled in under HTML Source.*

12 *To select your image editor, repeat the process, but use the lower of the two Choose buttons.*

13 *Click the OK button to finish.*

Using the New Page Command

To access the New Page command, click the New button. This brings up the New Page dialog box (see the figure on the upper right), which has three basic choices. The first is to create a blank page, which looks just like the first figure.

The next option for creating new pages is to use templates. Templates are predesigned Web pages. All the fundamental elements are in place, and all you need to do is replace the template's text, images, and so forth with ones of your choice. In this segment, we explore how to use local templates of your own creation. Netscape also provides online templates for various purposes, and we explore these in the next segment.

It's a pretty simple matter to create a template. Just break down your tasks in Web page creation to their common factors and label them. Thus, if you constantly create a page that features the name, title, and duties of executives of a corporation, make a template that includes the name of the company, plus a few bits of text that say such things as "Executive's Name," "Executive's Title," and "Executive's Duties." Save it as a normal HTML file, perhaps in a special folder set aside for templates, and you've got the basis for your future pages ready to go.

Continued

TAKE NOTE

▶ **MULTIPLE INSTANCES**

Every time you click the New button, whether it's to create a blank page or use templates or the Page Wizard, you launch a new instance of Netscape Composer. The only exception is if you click the Cancel button in the Create New Page dialog box (see the figure on the upper right). If you don't want to have two copies of the program running at the same time, select the first one in the taskbar and shut it down. The new instance will be unaffected.

▶ **CHANGING PROPERTIES**

Other than typing over the existing text in templates, most of what you'll be doing is simply changing the properties of the various elements. For how to do that with links, see Chapter 15. For images, see Chapter 14.

▶ **PREVIEWING WEB PAGES IN NAVIGATOR**

You can test your ongoing or finished work by viewing it with Netscape Navigator. First, make sure the file has been saved. Next, just click the Preview button. If you have forgotten to save your file, you'll be reminded to do so. Your Web page will be displayed in Navigator. If the Web browser is not active at the time you click the button, it automatically launches with your Web page loaded. How is it possible to have Navigator shut down while Composer is open? That's because they're both part of the suite of programs called Netscape Communicator. If any part of Communicator is running, all its parts are immediately accessible.

CROSS-REFERENCE

See the section on using online templates later in this chapter.

FIND IT ONLINE

Find the Composer home page at **http://home.netscape .com/communicator/composer/v4.0/index.html**.

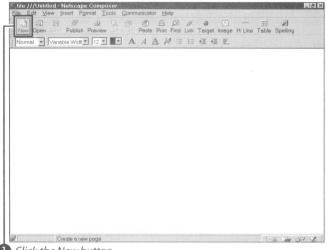

❶ *Click the New button.*

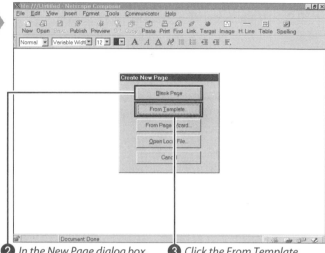

❷ *In the New Page dialog box, click the Blank Page button to create a blank page.*

❸ *Click the From Template button to use templates.*

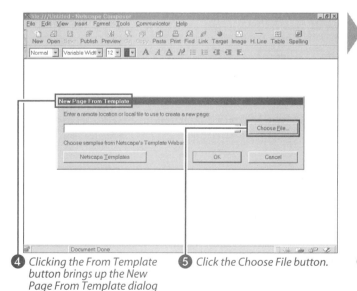

❹ *Clicking the From Template button brings up the New Page From Template dialog box.*

❺ *Click the Choose File button.*

❻ *Clicking the Choose File button displays the Choose New Web Page Template File dialog box.*

❼ *Navigate to the folder that holds the template file you want to use.*

The template is now displayed in Composer. All that remains is for you to replace the template's text with your own, and then save the resulting Web page under a new file name. You're free to change the template any way you want, including adding new elements and modifying or even totally removing the old ones, because you're working on a copy of the template, and not affecting the original.

Unlike when you open an existing HTML file with the normal method, this new file created from the template has no name showing in the title bar. That's a simple, practical precaution because templates are not supposed to be saved back under their own file names; the idea is to save them under a different file name after you use it as a basis for a new Web page. Of course, nothing prevents you from saving a modified version of a template under the same file name by using File ➪ Save As, but if that's your intention, it's simpler to just open it in the usual way and save it in the usual way, too.

TAKE NOTE

▶ REALLY, IT'S A URL

The path to the template file is not really a proper file path. If you take a close look, you'll notice that it starts with "file:///C|/" instead of the usual "C:\" and that all the slashes lean the wrong way. That's because you're opening a Web page in Composer, regardless of the fact that it's on your local system, and this is actually a Web address — in this case, a *file* URL — and the path to the file must follow the usual Web standards just as if it had started with "http://" as with a normal address out there on the World Wide Web. Web addresses, as you've no doubt noticed, use backslashes instead of DOS-based forward slashes to separate directory levels. The technical specification for file URLs (and other kinds as well) can be found at the link given in Find It Online below.

▶ VIEWING INVISIBLE ELEMENTS

You might notice a little target icon at the top of a Web page created in Composer. This particular item does not show up if you view this page in Navigator because the element it represents (a *target*, which is used with links and is explained in Chapter 15) is not visible on the Web page when displayed in a Web browser. Composer, however, because it is a development environment, must have some way of letting you know where every element is, and that's why it shows icons for the invisible ones.

CROSS-REFERENCE
See the section on saving HTML files later in this chapter.

FIND IT ONLINE
Read about file URL technicalities at **http://info .internet.isi.edu:80/in-notes/files/rfc1738.txt**.

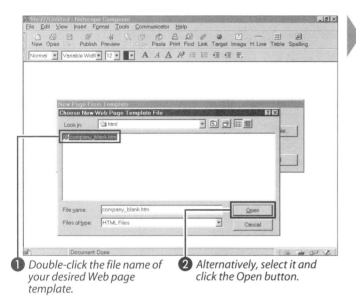

1 Double-click the file name of your desired Web page template.

2 Alternatively, select it and click the Open button.

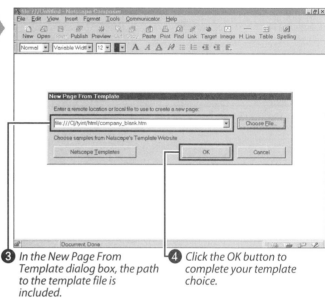

3 In the New Page From Template dialog box, the path to the template file is included.

4 Click the OK button to complete your template choice.

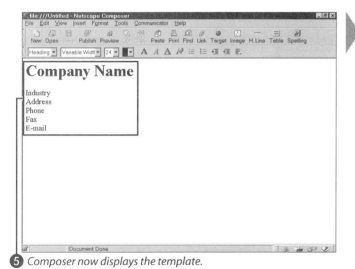

5 Composer now displays the template.

6 Replace the template's text with your own.

Using Online Templates

In addition to being able to create your own templates on which you can base a variety of similar Web pages with slightly different elements, you can use online templates created by Netscape. The online templates that Netscape maintains for your use on its Web servers have exactly the same function as any local templates you might create on your own. The only real difference is that Netscape has saved you the trouble of developing them.

The procedure for obtaining an online template is similar to using one for a local template. The difference is that online templates require the activation of the Netscape Navigator Web browser, which connects to a designated Netscape server that stores the templates. The Netscape Web Page Templates home page will guide you to a variety of templates.

Netscape arranges these templates into five different categories: Personal/Family Templates, Company/Small Business Templates, Department Templates, Product/Service Templates, and Special Interest Group Templates. This listing may change from time to time as Netscape adds or removes templates. Clicking one of the template links (we use "My Home Page," the first choice under Personal/Family Templates, for the example) brings up the template on your browser screen.

Continued

Continued

TAKE NOTE

ONLINE TEMPLATES AND DEFAULT BROWSERS

Netscape Navigator responds to the Netscape Templates button even if it's not the default Web browser on your system, because it's being called from another Netscape Communicator program.

OLD VERSION OF NAVIGATOR

The instructions under How To Use A Template on the Web page shown in the figure on the lower right are for an older version of Navigator called Netscape Navigator Gold; the Netscape Web page has not been updated for the new version of Navigator (4.0 and above) that's a part of the Netscape Communicator suite of programs. Things still work pretty much the same, though, but in the new version, you select File ⇨ Edit Page from the menu instead of Edit ⇨ Document (see the next page for details).

TEMPLATES FOR TEMPLATES

You can create your own templates based on the ones that Netscape has on its Web pages. Just go ahead as though you were going to use them as per normal procedure, but save them without making any changes to them. Then, reload the templates from your own system as local files (see the preceding section), alter them to suit yourself, and then resave them as your own custom templates under new names.

CROSS-REFERENCE

See the preceding section for information on using local templates.

FIND IT ONLINE

Find the Netscape templates at **http://home .netscape.com/browsers/templates/index.html**.

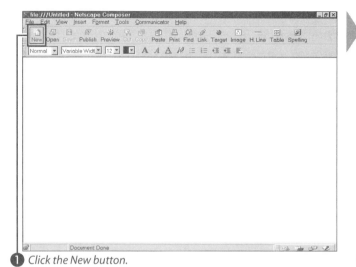

1 Click the New button.

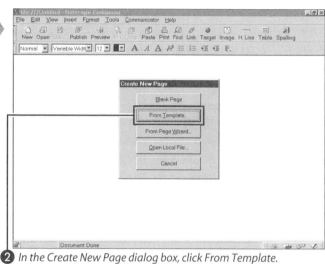

2 In the Create New Page dialog box, click From Template.

3 The New Page From Template dialog box appears.

4 Click the Netscape Templates button.

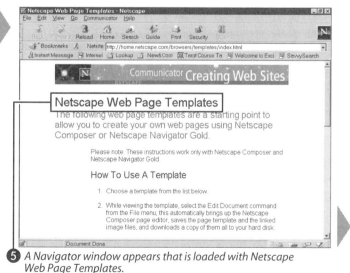

5 A Navigator window appears that is loaded with Netscape Web Page Templates.

Using Online Templates
Continued

You have to get the template out of Navigator, where it's doing you no good, and into Composer where you can work on it. Once you are back in Composer, all you have to do is put your own words and images in place of the ones that come with the template, save the page on your local system, and hit the Preview button to see your completed home page in Navigator.

It's probably a good idea to give credit to Netscape on the page in which you used the template. Some Netscape employees had to design all of these, and they would surely appreciate recognition, at least so they know that the templates are helpful to beginners. In addition, in the source code, you might want to put a comment to yourself (or someone who is viewing your source code) about which template you used and where you got it. This might be useful when you want to create additional pages with a similar look and feel.

Although Netscape has a long history of keeping earlier files online for its users, a possibility does exist that the company might decide to get rid of or modify a template that you'd like to use. To cover yourself against that eventuality, it might be worthwhile to go online and get every last one of them right away. Then you can save them to your local hard drive, floppy disk, zip disk, or whatever storage medium you prefer so you have a backup just in case.

TAKE NOTE

▶ **THE CREATING WEB SITES PAGE**

At the bottom of the listings of templates on Netscape's Web Page Templates page, you'll find a link to its Creating Web Sites page, which contains links to valuable Web site design products.

▶ **GETTING RID OF THE INSTRUCTIONS**

Don't forget to delete the leading paragraph and its horizontal lines in the home page template shown in the figure on the upper right, as well as any of its elements that you don't use.

▶ **DOUBLE INSTANCES**

The online template process creates two instances, not only of Composer, but of Navigator as well (you can see this in your taskbar as you proceed). When you're done with all of it, make sure to close down at least the second instance of each program. If you're totally done and want to shut down your online activity, you'll need to close both instances of both programs.

CROSS-REFERENCE

See Chapter 6 for more information on storage media.

FIND IT ONLINE

Netscape has lots of graphics available at **http://home .netscape.com/navigator/vgold3.0/using/index.html**.

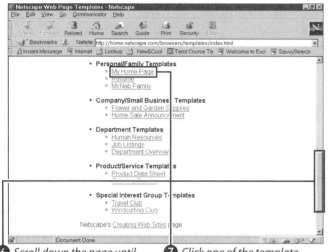

⑥ Scroll down the page until you reach the listing of available online templates.

⑦ Click one of the template links.

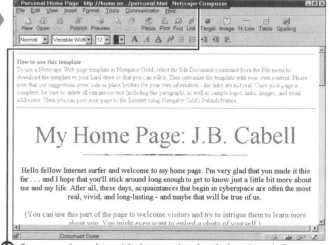

⑧ This brings up the template on your browser screen.

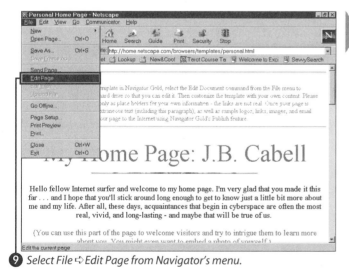

⑨ Select File ⇨ Edit Page from Navigator's menu.

⑩ Composer launches with the template loaded and ready for editing.

237

Using the Online Page Wizard

Perhaps the idea of creating Web pages intimidates you. Templates make it easy. They give you a framework, and assume that you need to design your Web page in a certain way. What if you have no idea what you want, and need a "blank canvas" to work from instead?

Templates, of either the local or online variety, provide you with a basic format that you can type over or otherwise modify. In contrast, the online Page Wizard is a program that actually walks you step by step through the creation of a simple Web page. You can choose to use as many or as few of the features in the Page Wizard as you desire. Use one or use them all; you'll still end up with a basic Web page at the end of it.

Just like with the online templates, choosing the Outline Page Wizard sends Navigator to a Netscape page (if Navigator isn't already active, it launches automatically, even if you have another Web browser such as Microsoft Internet Explorer set as your default browser). The Page Wizard Web page, though, is a bit different from the online templates page. It's divided into three frames. At first, the only frame with anything in it is the one on the right, which describes the Page Wizard and gives simple instructions for using it, but the other two will come into play shortly, as you can see on the next page.

The next step is to scroll down the page until you reach the bottom. There, you will find the Start button

shown in the figure on the lower right (feel free to read through the instructions on the way down). You need to click the Start button to launch the Page Wizard into action.

TAKE NOTE

▶ THE OTHER PAGE WIZARD

One of the links on the Netscape Creating Web Sites Tool Chest page (see Find It Online on the preceding page) simply leads to another online location for the very same Page Wizard. If, for any reason, you can't get to the main one, you might try going to the other one. See Find It Online below for the main address and Find It Online on the next page for the other one.

▶ NAVIGATOR GOLD

If you're using the older version of Navigator called Navigator Gold, it's true that you have some decent Web editing capabilities, but you'd be well advised to upgrade to Communicator, which includes not only the newer version of Navigator, but Composer as well, with much-improved HTML editing capacity.

▶ USING OTHER WIZARDS

Most other HTML editors that you might run across have Page Creation Wizards, much like that of Composer. It's a good idea to try these out before you start creating a page from scratch. You may have forgotten elements that the Wizard will point out for you as it runs its course.

CROSS-REFERENCE
See Chapter 2 for more information on frames.

FIND IT ONLINE
Page Wizard is located at **http://home.netscape.com /home/gold4.0_wizard.html**.

① Click the New button.

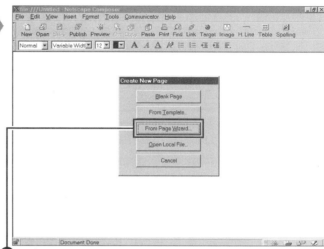

② In the Create New Page dialog box, click the From Page Wizard button.

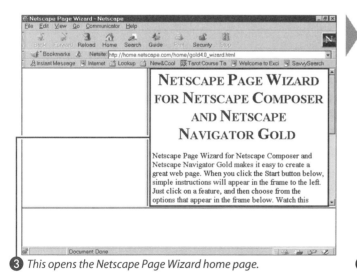

③ This opens the Netscape Page Wizard home page.

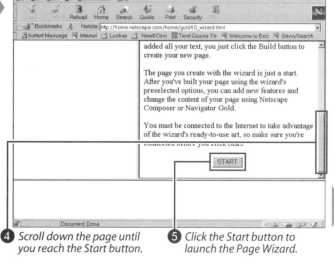

④ Scroll down the page until you reach the Start button.

⑤ Click the Start button to launch the Page Wizard.

Launching the Online Page Wizard

The Online Page Wizard involves three frames that guide you through the process. One frame contains detailed instructions, one contains a preview of your Web page, and one contains options from which you select the page components. As you go through the Wizard, your page begins to fill out and look more like a real Web page. When you finally finish, you will have to transfer the page from Netscape's server to your hard drive.

The first thing you need to fill out is the title. You might think that you can set the title later (changing it from the default "Type your title here" to something of your choosing), but you need a unique title to distinguish it from others on the Netscape server and so you can download the proper page.

The Online Page Wizard enables you to add elements that come from either the Content group or Looks group. As is the case when using any method to create a Web page, you should think in terms of these two categories: Content and Looks. Content deals with the text and links forming a cohesive map to follow throughout your site. The logistics of the site is the most important thing, because you are providing information, and a user must be able to access that information easily. The aesthetic qualities of the site are almost as important, because a good-looking site attracts more visitors. A page's design also takes into account things such as eye fatigue. People don't often think about both of these factors when creating their pages. Many sites have animated pictures, or really complex image maps, which tend to be distracting. Some sites go the other direction, and are too text-heavy. The Online Page Wizard tries to make sure you keep the design intriguing, without overwhelming the content inside.

You can start over at any time by clicking the Start Over button. If you are satisfied with what you have created, click the Build button, and the Page Wizard loads your page into Navigator.

Continued

Continued

TAKE NOTE

▶ BUILDING BEYOND THE BASICS

Although the Web page created by the Page Wizard is fully functional, you'll probably want to add to it. You can continue to build on the foundation it presents by using Composer to improve on the simple design.

▶ LOSING YOUR PAGE

If you happen to close Navigator before you click the Build button, you'll lose everything you've been working on, and you'll have to start over. The page isn't finished until you click the Build button, and it's not saved until you bring the finished page into Composer and save it.

CROSS-REFERENCE

See Chapters 13 through 15 for more information on modifying Web pages.

FIND IT ONLINE

You can find Page Wizard at **http://home.netscape.com/ assist/net_sites/starter/wizard/index.html**.

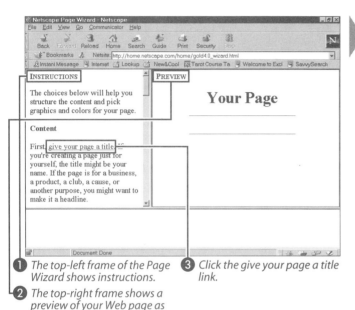

① The top-left frame of the Page Wizard shows instructions.

② The top-right frame shows a preview of your Web page as you design it.

③ Click the give your page a title link.

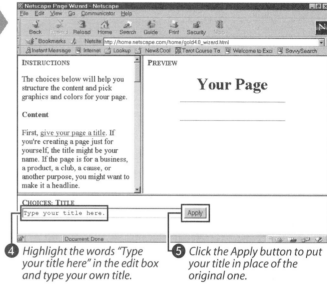

④ Highlight the words "Type your title here" in the edit box and type your own title.

⑤ Click the Apply button to put your title in place of the original one.

⑥ Scroll down the top-left frame and continue to click the links.

⑦ To make your Web page, click the Build button.

⑧ To begin again, click the Start Over button.

⑨ To go to the beginning of Page Wizard, click the Back to Introduction button.

⑩ If you click the Build button, your completed Web page appears.

Launching the Online Page Wizard *Continued*

Now that you're finished using the Page Wizard and you've got everything just the way you want it on your basic page, you're not really finished with it just yet. You still have something to do, especially if you want to add more elements or embellishments to it. Once again, you find yourself faced with a situation where you have a Web page you want to edit, but it's in Navigator, not in Composer where you need it if you're going to work on it. To solve this problem, select File⇨Edit Page from Navigator's menu, as shown in the figure on the upper left. This brings the page into Composer, where you can work with it (see the figure on the upper right). However, the page is still not on your local system; as you can see from the title bar, it's still on Netscape's server. We'll cover how to save it on your local system in the next segment.

If you make the mistake of saving the file you built with the online Page Wizard in Navigator instead of in Composer, you'll end up with an incomplete page. This is because Composer grabs all the files you need, including the image files, but Navigator saves only the main HTML file. If you want to save all the image files, too, in Navigator, you'll have to select them one by one and save them individually, which is a lot more unnecessary work.

TAKE NOTE

▶ THOSE LITTLE QUESTION-MARK ICONS

The icons with a folded corner and a question mark in the center, as shown in the figure on the lower right, represent missing image files. That is, they are image files that are references in the HTML source code of the Web page, but aren't found at the specified location. You might be surprised, if you know a bit of HTML, to find that the horizontal lines are image files, but this is not really unusual. The basic horizontal lines (or horizontal rules, to give them their proper name) that HTML supports are not enough for most people. Many Web designers prefer to use graphical images as page dividers instead, and you can find lots of them to choose from. Some of them are simply variations on simple lines (like the dotted line images in the figure on the upper left), while others are artistic items such as flowering vines or clever twists on the theme like a chainsaw ripping through the page. Check out the link in Find It Online below for a source of graphical line replacements.

▶ USING LOCAL IMAGES

Sometimes you'll find Web pages that have images from other sites, and those images appear on the page because of a link to that site. This is not a good idea, because the disappearance of the second site would cause a broken image icon on the page. If you see an image that you'd like to have on your page, make sure you have a copy of it in the same directory in which your page resides.

CROSS-REFERENCE

See Chapter 2 for more information on saving Web pages from Navigator.

FIND IT ONLINE

You can find some horizontal rule graphics at **http://www.littletechshoppe.com/linehrindex.html**.

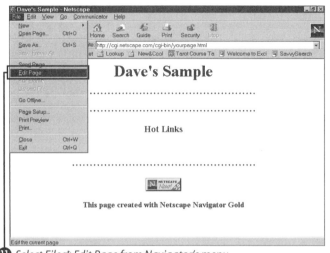

⓫ *Select File ⇨ Edit Page from Navigator's menu.*

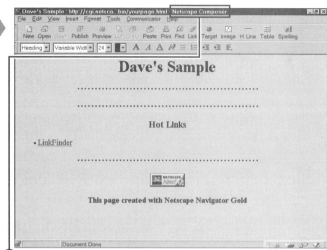

⓬ *This brings the completed page into Composer.*

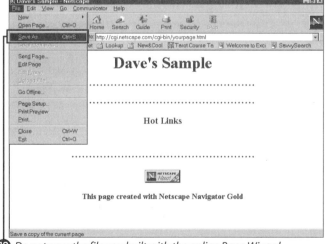

⓭ *Do not save the file you built with the online Page Wizard in Navigator.*

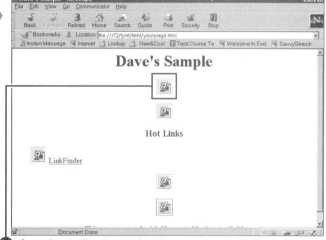

⓮ *If you do, you'll end up with an incomplete page, indicated by missing graphics.*

Saving HTML Files

You can't just click the Save button when you've got a file in Composer, except in certain circumstances. While you may say, and we may agree, that this is not the best way of doing things, it's one of those regrettable facts of life we all have to deal with.

In all likelihood, the reason Composer forces you to use Save As is so you will be able to distinguish between different pages right away, and not accidentally replace old pages with new ones. Be sure to name the page something significant, rather than "index1.html." You're not really limited by the length of a name, so you should assign it a name that is related to the page's content.

It's only when you make a change to a file (in the figure on the lower right, we've changed "Dave's" to "David's") that the Save button becomes active. It doesn't matter what the source of the file is; it can be a previously saved file, a newly created file, or an online file you're editing (any online files can be edited, even if they're not on your own Web site, but you can only save them to your local disk). Once the Save button is active, you can just click it to save the file under either a new name (in the case of a new file or an online file) or the same name as it's been saved under before (in the case of a previously saved file).

TAKE NOTE

THE TITLE BAR

Once you've typed in a name for the file and saved it, the title bar reflects that fact. In the example on the facing page, we're saving the file that was created with the online Page Wizard in the preceding task. Note that the title bar in the figure on the upper left shows a normal Web URL (the location of the file on Netscape's Web server). The title bar in the figure on the lower right, after the save operation, shows a local file URL.

FRAMES

If you attempt to edit on online file that is frame-based, you'll need to edit each frame separately, and save them separately, too. This is because each frame on the screen of your Web browser holds a totally separate Web page, even though it appears to be a single one with different parts. To edit the frames, click anywhere within the one you want to edit (anywhere, that is, but on a link), and then select File ⇨ Edit Frame from the menu in Navigator. To edit the frameset (the overall controlling page, which is not visible on the Web browser), you need to select File ⇨ Edit Page instead.

CROSS-REFERENCE

See Chapter 2 for more information on frames.

FIND IT ONLINE

Another good source of horizontal rule graphics is **http://www.barndog.net/tazem/free.htm**.

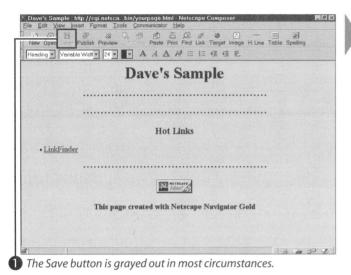

❶ The Save button is grayed out in most circumstances.

❷ Select File ➪ Save As from Composer's menu.

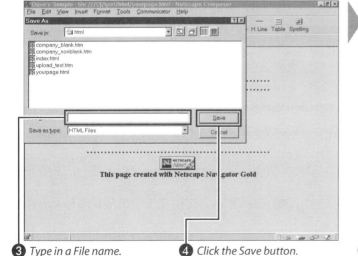

❸ Type in a File name.　　❹ Click the Save button.

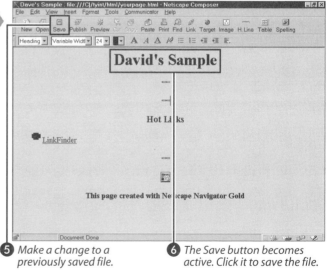

❺ Make a change to a previously saved file.

❻ The Save button becomes active. Click it to save the file.

Publishing Your Web Page

The point of creating all these pages is so you can provide information and entertainment to the public, right? Well, it's not doing any good to have the files stored on your hard drive. You have to upload these files to a server that anyone on the Internet can access. The act of uploading your HTML file and all its attendant files from Composer to a Web site is called *publishing*.

Before you start publishing, you must take care of a few things. First, make sure you have access to a server that will store your pages. In most cases, this will be an ISP where you have a membership. You must know your username and password, and which directory to upload to. It's also a good idea to see that you're not exceeding the space limit that ISPs enforce on their servers. In most cases, you won't be in any danger, but if you want to include a lot of images or a QuickTime movie, you might need more room.

Next, make sure that all of your files for the site are together and properly referenced within each page. Links between your pages should have relative URLs, as opposed to absolute URLs, because you might not always have the account with one particular ISP. You'll need the flexibility to change locations without going back through your documents and fixing all the references. Composer automatically includes all files associated with the Web page you're

uploading, but it's a good idea to verify that everything is complete before you start uploading.

Continued

TAKE NOTE

▶ FTP AND HTTP

Both the File Transfer Protocol (FTP) and the Hypertext Transfer Protocol (HTTP) can upload files to your Web site. Use of HTTP for file uploads is a fairly recent development, however, and some Web space providers don't support it. Composer supports both methods, so you're covered regardless.

▶ WHY IT ASKS FOR BOTH

In the Preferences dialog box, Composer still wants to know your HTTP address (Web URL) even if you're going to be using FTP to upload with. The reason for this is that, after you upload your files, Composer will ask you if you want to view the Web site. If you do, it needs to know where to find it. This address should be for the home page of your Web site. When you add new pages, make sure to add links to them from your home page; you can then follow the links to your newly uploaded pages.

▶ WHAT IF THERE'S NO HOME PAGE?

If there's no home page for the Web address you uploaded to (in other words, no file named "index.html" or "index.htm"), then Navigator lists all the files in the Web location in the form of hypertext links. To view the one you just uploaded, click the link to it and it will be displayed in Navigator.

CROSS-REFERENCE

See the following section on uploading via an FTP program.

FIND IT ONLINE

There's a FAQ for Composer at **http://www.swbell.net/download/composer_faq.html**.

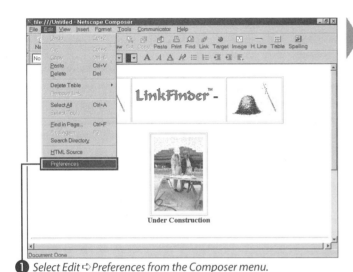

1 Select Edit ➪ Preferences from the Composer menu.

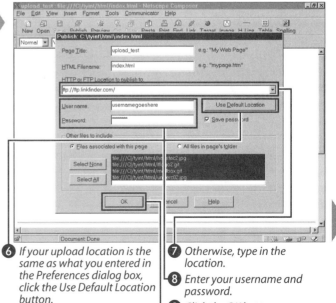

2 In the Preferences dialog box, make sure that Composer ➪ Publishing is selected.

3 Under Default publishing location, enter the FTP site or the Web address where you will store your HTML files.

4 Click the OK button.

5 Click the Publish button.

6 If your upload location is the same as what you entered in the Preferences dialog box, click the Use Default Location button.

7 Otherwise, type in the location.

8 Enter your username and password.

9 Click the OK button.

Publishing Your Web Page

Continued

You also have the option in Composer to transfer individual files (without the supporting documents) to a server, in case you made some adjustments that only affect one page. This way, you won't have to resend everything.

If bad links occur in your documents, Composer tells you so when you try to publish them. If you get this error message, go back in and make sure all the links are correct. You can ignore the error message if it doesn't apply to you.

Once you complete the publishing phase, Composer gives you the opportunity to go right to the URL where you placed your page. It's a good idea to check it out so you can check for errors one more time.

Once you publish your site, you should inform the Internet search engines (such as Yahoo! and Excite) that you have a new site that needs to be "advertised." Typically, you have to describe what category your site falls into, such as "sports" if it's a page about your favorite football team, for example. Often, pages don't really have a central theme other than "who I am, and here are my interests." If this is where yours falls, don't worry — the search engines have a category just for personal pages.

CROSS-REFERENCE

See the following section for information on uploading via FTP.

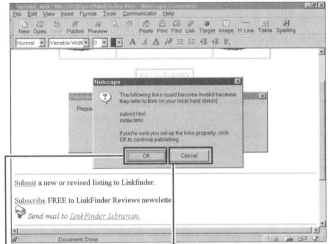

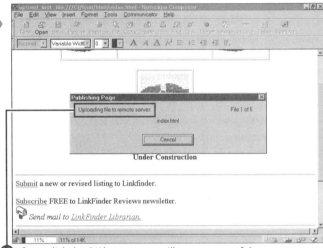

10 *If you get a warning message about invalid files, click the OK button to proceed anyway.*

11 *Alternatively, click the Cancel button to abort.*

12 *If you click the OK button, you will see a report of the upload progress.*

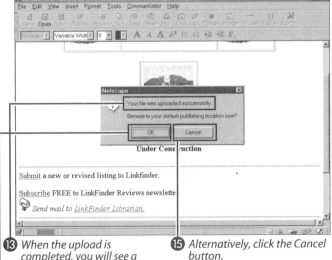

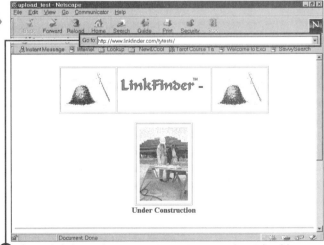

13 *When the upload is completed, you will see a dialog box showing success.*

14 *Click the OK button if you want to see the Web location you uploaded to.*

15 *Alternatively, click the Cancel button.*

16 *If you click the OK button, Navigator jumps to the Web address you uploaded to.*

Uploading Files with FTP

Either because you prefer to use it or you have no other uploading method, you can always fall back on the old standard method of uploading Web pages and use an FTP client to do it. FTP, the *file transfer protocol*, is an older method than modern HTTP publishing for both uploading and downloading files, but it is still much in use today.

Most FTP clients have two boxes within a window. One box shows the contents of your hard drive, and the other displays the contents of a remote computer (in this case, it's the server of your ISP). To see the contents of the remote computer, you have to log on to the server and tell the FTP client which directory you'd like to start in. When transferring files for your Web site, you will probably log on as you normally do, and automatically be taken to your own directory. You can then begin transferring files one at a time or in blocks.

If you're transferring HTML files, then you don't need to do anything because ASCII is selected by default; if you're transferring image files, then you'll need to click the Binary radio button. If the file you're uploading is an HTML file — an ASCII file — then the receiving system needs to know this. Both Windows and UNIX treat graphics files the same, so GIF and JPG files are sent as binary files instead (if you're transferring an executable file, it should be sent as binary, also).

TAKE NOTE

UPLOAD THOSE IMAGES, TOO

When you upload your HTML files via FTP, don't forget that you also need to upload any graphics files they reference. If you do forget, your Web pages won't have all the parts they need to look the way you intended.

GRANTING PERMISSION

For many Web servers (especially UNIX-based ones), you will need to specify who has permission to read, write, and execute your Web pages. The levels of permissions are typically broken into owner, group, and public. Obviously, the public needs to be able to see your pages, but not write to them. Check with your ISP to see how to set the permission levels. Some ISPs do it for you automatically.

USING EXTENSIONS

FrontPage is an editor that has special extensions you can implement that increase the functionality of your site. If you decide to use FrontPage, check with your ISP to see if it supports the application's extensions.

DELETING REMOTE FILES

It's easy to delete files from a remote directory, but it's not something you want to do unless you have backups of the original files on your hard drive. If you have updates that will replace old files, you can go ahead and transfer them, having them write over the old files.

CROSS-REFERENCE

See Chapter 14 for more information on images.

FIND IT ONLINE

You can get WS_FTP at **http://www.ipswitch.com/ downloads/ws_ftp_LE.html**.

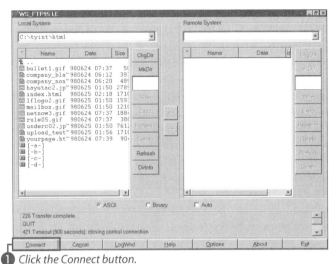

1 Click the Connect button.

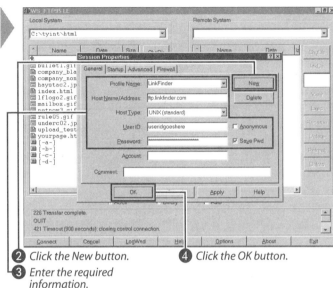

2 Click the New button.

3 Enter the required information.

4 Click the OK button.

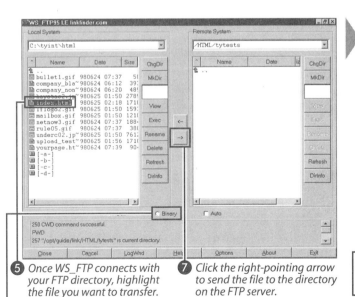

5 Once WS_FTP connects with your FTP directory, highlight the file you want to transfer.

6 If you want to transfer an image file, click the Binary radio button.

7 Click the right-pointing arrow to send the file to the directory on the FTP server.

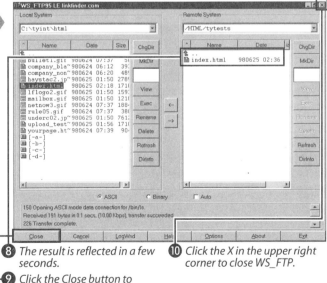

8 The result is reflected in a few seconds.

9 Click the Close button to finish.

10 Click the X in the upper right corner to close WS_FTP.

Personal Workbook

Q&A

1 What are your three basic options when creating a new page?

_____

_____

_____

2 What is a *template*?

_____

_____

_____

3 Why shouldn't you save a page created with the Page Wizard from Navigator?

_____

_____

4 What does *FTP* stand for?

_____

_____

_____

5 What is the advantage of using Notepad as your HTML editor?

_____

_____

_____

6 What does *publishing* mean in Composer?

_____

_____

_____

7 What icon does a Web page use for a missing image file?

_____

_____

_____

8 Do you have to use an image editor with Composer?

_____

_____

_____

ANSWERS: PAGE 383

EXTRA PRACTICE

1 Try another program such as HomeSite for your HTML editor.

2 Try creating different pages with the online Page Wizard.

3 Experiment with a few different image editors.

4 Make your own templates.

5 Upload some Web pages via both the Publish button and FTP. See which you prefer.

6 Upload an HTML file with FTP and set it for binary file transfer instead of ASCII. Take a look at the source code on the Web server.

REAL-WORLD APPLICATIONS

✔ You have to make a Web page that uses simple elements. You may want to try the online Page Wizard to create the basic page.

✔ You have to create a number of different pages on a similar theme. You might consider creating your own template to save time.

✔ You're not satisfied with Notepad as an HTML editor. Maybe you should try out some of the more specialized ones.

✔ You're planning on creating an entire Web site with several different pages. You might want to think about uploading the index.html file last so you can get a simple listing of all the files when you publish them.

Visual Quiz

How do you get to this dialog box? What are your two main options from here?

_____

_____

_____

_____

_____

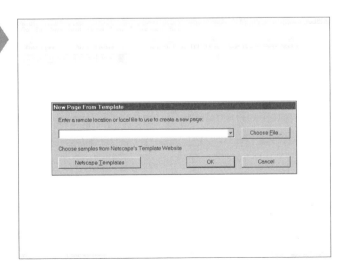

CHAPTER **12**

MASTER
THESE
SKILLS

▶ **Viewing, Editing, and Printing HTML Source**

▶ **Adding Metadata**

▶ **Adding Composer Plug-Ins**

▶ **Using the Document Info Plug-In**

▶ **Using the Frame Editor Plug-In**

Advanced Composer

Composer has many features that go way beyond the simple make-and-save-the-page functionality described in the preceding chapter. You can get by with Composer just using the toolbar buttons. If you want to get into the heart of your Web page instead of just pointing and clicking, though, you're going to need to view, print, and edit your HTML source code. This chapter shows you how to use the HTML editor you installed in the previous chapter.

Metadata is information contained in the HTML source code that does not display onscreen when someone looks at your Web page in their browser. Composer automatically adds your name to the HTML source code as *author* metadata. Some search engines use metadata called *keywords* and *categories* that describe your pages' content to index your Web site; others ignore them and go only with the actual displayed text on your pages. Although several proposed uses for metadata are floating about, no real consensus exists on how it should be used.

As with the Navigator Web browser, Composer has its own set of plug-ins that can enhance its capabilities. Out of the box, you might find that Composer doesn't have some of the resources to help you design the kind of pages you'd like. The plug-ins that Composer uses are essentially upgrades to the basic software package that you really shouldn't be without. In this chapter, we tell you which ones are available, show you where to find them, how to add them, and how to use two of them. We'll be exploring some of the other plug-ins in subsequent chapters.

The first plug-in we cover is Document Info, which gives you more useful information than the document information available from the regular Composer menu. It presents such data as the number of words and images in your document. The second plug-in we look at in this chapter is a powerful improvement over normal Composer functionality called the Frame Editor. It lets you create and edit framed pages in addition to the regular, nonframed kind.

Viewing, Editing, and Printing HTML Source

Viewing the source code of your Web page is the best way to fix any problems that occur. This is particularly necessary when you start implementing scripts and other advanced components. Although parts of your site that involve things such as Java or JavaScript are self-contained units that fall out of HTML's scope, you need to make sure that you have invoked these applications or scripts properly.

You actually have two different ways to view the HTML source code of a document in Composer, but only one of them lets you edit it. To edit the HTML code in Notepad, simply type in the code you want or delete the code you don't want. Notepad has all the basic needs of an HTML text editor. You can cut, copy, paste, and delete in addition to just plain typing (you can set font styles, too, but that's strictly cosmetic and temporary — that information doesn't get saved with the file). When you're done with your modification, select File ⇨ Save from the Notepad menu. Notepad saves plain ASCII files, which is what you need from an HTML editor.

Composer can display a listing of the source code, but it can only be viewed. This is only useful for a quick peek at the source code, which cannot be edited or printed.

CROSS-REFERENCE
See Chapter 11 for information on setting your HTML editor.

FIND IT ONLINE
There's a great HTML language page at
http://www.stars.com/Authoring/HTML/.

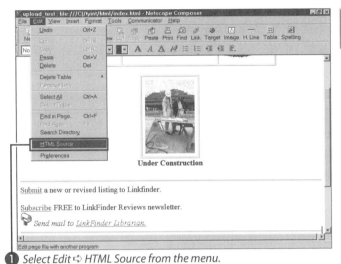

1 Select Edit ➪ HTML Source from the menu.

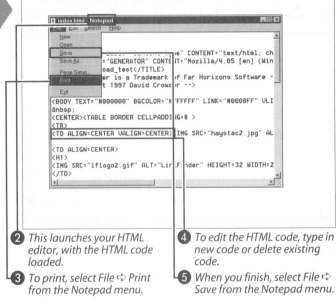

2 This launches your HTML editor, with the HTML code loaded.

3 To print, select File ➪ Print from the Notepad menu.

4 To edit the HTML code, type in new code or delete existing code.

5 When you finish, select File ➪ Save from the Notepad menu.

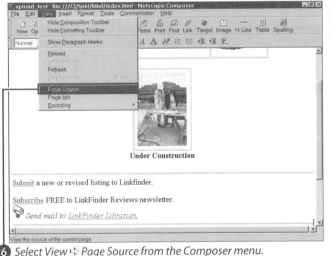

6 Select View ➪ Page Source from the Composer menu.

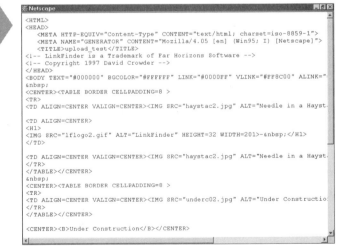

■ The Page Source command displays the Netscape page source window.

Adding Metadata

Metadata is information that does not appear on the visible Web page. Some of the most useful metadata involves refreshing pages, pointing a browser to a new URL, and listing keywords so that search engines have help in finding sites. Composer makes it easy to enter such keywords for your site. Some search engines also accept categories in addition to keywords, and you can also enter these in the META dialog box that Composer uses.

If you want to enter other metadata, you'll have to do it with META tags. The HTML code for author metadata looks like this:

<META NAME="Author" CONTENT="David and Rhonda Crowder">

Composer already enters author metadata for you, but all META tags follow the same format, stating first a name for the metadata, and then its content. Technically, these types of relationships are called *name/value pairs*, and Composer uses this terminology in this dialog box. Instead of having to concern yourself with the exact syntax, just enter the name of the metadata where it says Name, and then enter the content part where it says Value. As we stated in the opening of this chapter, metadata has no hard and fast rules, and you can feel free to make up anything you want.

TAKE NOTE

▶ **DELETING META TAGS**

To delete a META tag in Composer, just select it and click the Delete button.

▶ **PLANNING FOR SEARCH ENGINES**

Some search engines pay attention to keywords, but the biggies index Web pages by their actual content. Although it's not a bad idea to include keywords, it's best to put most of your energy into designing content-rich Web pages.

▶ **TWEAKING THE META TAG NAMES**

You can provide other useful bits of information by substituting alternates in place of the "keywords" designation in a META tag's Name attribute. These are "description", which will provide a description of the page to search engines, and "robot," which you can use to tell search engines not to list your page, or to list only portions of it. Go to the URL listed in the "Find It Online" section below for more information on the Name attribute of the META tag.

▶ **COMMANDING YOUR BROWSER**

Besides the Name attribute of the META tag, there is HTTP-EQUIV, which goes in the header section of your page. HTTP-EQUIV issues directives to your browser to do something. Most often, Web designers use this to refresh a page (as when updated sports scores are posted to a page) or to redirect visitors to a new URL (if an old address is no longer in use).

CROSS-REFERENCE

See Chapter 13 for information on page colors.

FIND IT ONLINE

Check out **http://www.submiturl.com/metatags.htm** for information on META tags.

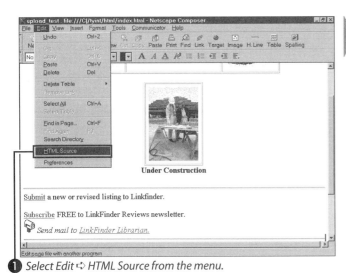

① Select Edit ➪ HTML Source from the menu.

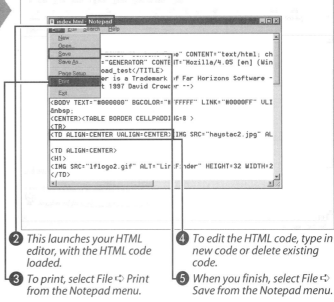

② This launches your HTML editor, with the HTML code loaded.

③ To print, select File ➪ Print from the Notepad menu.

④ To edit the HTML code, type in new code or delete existing code.

⑤ When you finish, select File ➪ Save from the Notepad menu.

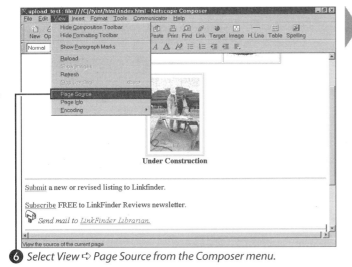

⑥ Select View ➪ Page Source from the Composer menu.

■ The Page Source command displays the Netscape page source window.

Adding Composer Plug-Ins

If you take a look at your available tools by selecting Tools from the Composer menu, you'll see that the only one that comes as a part of Netscape Composer is the spelling checker. Fortunately, Composer, like Navigator, can take plug-ins to expand its capabilities. The most useful plug-ins include things such as an Image Map editor, a Frame Editor, and a Document Info tool. To add to your toolbox, you need to go to the Composer Plug-in Samples Page (see Find It Online below for the URL) and download some plug-ins specially designed for use with Composer. Grab everything; plug-ins don't take up much space, and you never know when you'll need one of them.

Download the plug-ins into the same folder as your Navigator plug-ins. If you're using the latest version of Navigator that's part of the Netscape Communicator suite of Internet programs, and you did a normal installation on a typical system, that folder will be C:\Program Files\Netscape\Communicator\Program\Plugins. Do not unzip the plug-ins — they are supposed to be zip files and should stay that way.

The tools aren't available right away. First, you have to shut down the program (and Navigator, if it's running), and then launch Navigator again. That's because the plug-ins are loaded every time you start Communicator, and they need to be loaded before you can use them. Once you do so, you can check the Tools menu in Composer again and you'll see that you have a lot more than you started with (see the figure on the lower right). Even more plug-ins are available than it first appears, because each of the menu options opens a submenu with even more choices.

TAKE NOTE

DON'T DISABLE JAVA

The plug-ins you download are Java applets, so if you've disabled Java, they won't work. You'll notice that, after you install them, Composer takes a few more seconds to start up the first time you use it, and Navigator displays the message "Starting Java" in the status bar during this time (unless your home page uses Java, in which case the "Starting Java" message is a part of your normal Navigator startup process and you won't see it again when you switch over from Navigator to Composer).

MORE ON THE WAY

Netscape has developed an application programming interface (API) for software developers to use in creating more Composer plug-ins, so expect a whole lot of new ones in the near future. Among the anticipated plug-ins are a thesaurus, grammar checker, and image editor.

CROSS-REFERENCE
See Chapter 2 for more information on plug-ins.

FIND IT ONLINE
Get Composer plug-ins at **http://developer.netscape.com/docs/examples/plugins/composer/**.

1 Select Tools from the Composer menu; you'll see that you have only one tool: the spelling checker.

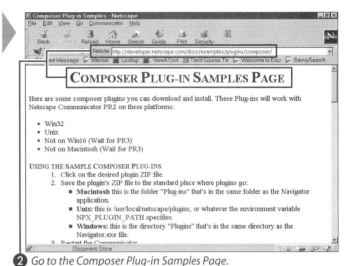

2 Go to the Composer Plug-in Samples Page.

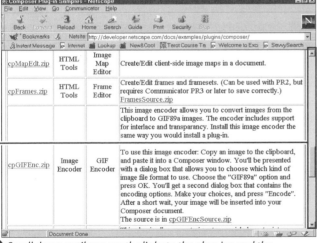

3 Scroll down until you see the links to the plug-ins and the descriptions of them. Download them.

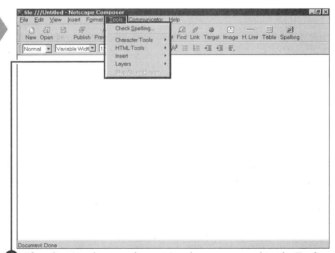

4 After shutting down and restarting the program, select the Tools menu in Composer again to see your new list of plug-ins.

Using the Document Info Plug-In

As an HTML author, you need to design your pages in a manner that is most efficient for the viewer. To do that, you need to have the relevant information about your site at your fingertips, so you can make any necessary adjustments. Some of the most useful information is the size of the page and how long it will take to download to a viewer's screen. The way to access your page's properties is by examining the document info.

Composer already has a built-in document info feature — the same one that's in Navigator, and it's just as useless to you as that one is. It mainly consists of the words "no" and "unknown," providing little information of any value. That's why the Document Info plug-in is a real treasure for Web designers.

Once the Document Info plug-in is ready, select Document Info from the Composer menu. The resulting Document Statistics window is chock full of useful information for HTML authors, showing the number of characters and words in the HTML file, the number of images and their total size in bytes, and the number of bytes taken up by the entire HTML file. It also gives projected time to display on a visitor's screen ("minimum time to download") and the file location in both the Windows standard folder notation and file URL notation.

When you are finished calculating your page's statistics make sure that you click the X in the upper right-hand corner of the Document Statistics window before you close down Composer. Just clicking the X in the upper-right corner of Composer would shut down the program but leave the Document Info Java Applet running by itself.

TAKE NOTE

▶ NAVIGATOR MENU DIFFERENCE

The built-in document info feature has the identical menu option as used in Navigator for the same purpose except that the shortcut key is different: In Navigator, press Alt+V for the View menu, and then "I" for Page Info; in Composer, press Alt+V for the View menu, and then "N" for Page Info.

▶ MODEM DOWNLOAD SPEEDS

The Document Statistics window shows the minimum time to download the Web page using a 14.4 Kbps modem. To get the download time for a 28.8 Kbps modem, just cut the time in half. For a 33.6 Kbps modem, multiply by 0.43. For a 56 Kbps modem, it would be one fourth of the time. Bear in mind that this is the minimum download time, assuming a perfect connection, with no data dropouts and barring any other problems. You might want to arbitrarily add, say, 10 percent more to the time to account for practical considerations in the real world.

CROSS-REFERENCE

See Chapter 11 for more information on file URLs.

FIND IT ONLINE

Find information on high-speed modems at
http://www.usr.com/home/online/main_page.htm.

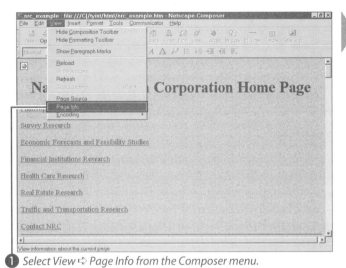

1 *Select View ⇨ Page Info from the Composer menu.*

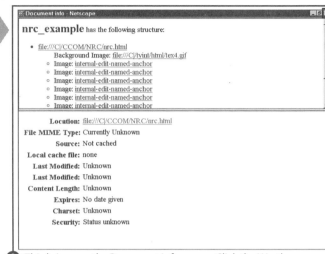

2 *This brings up the Document Info screen. Click the X in the upper-right corner to close the window.*

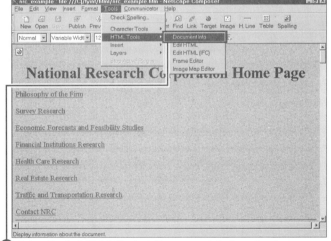

3 *Select Tools ⇨ HTML Tools ⇨ Document Info from the Composer menu.*

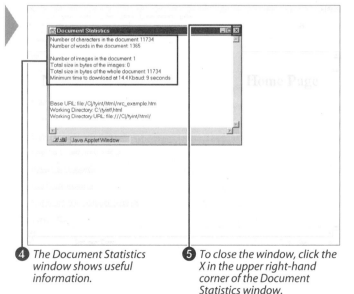

4 *The Document Statistics window shows useful information.*

5 *To close the window, click the X in the upper right-hand corner of the Document Statistics window.*

Using the Frame Editor Plug-In

Frames add a great deal of functionality to a Web site. The best use of one of the panes in a frameset is as a navigational menu, or table of contents. In this system, users can navigate to different areas of a site easily, by just a click of a hyperlink. Then, when they get to another area, the navigation pane stays where it is, so they can continue to jump to another section of the site again, without having to click the Back button and select another path. You might find other good reasons to implement frames in your pages.

One of the major shortcomings of Netscape Composer is that it only works with regular, non-framed Web pages. The Frame Editor plug-in, however, solves this problem handily.

When you first launch the Frame Editor, nothing appears in the Frame Editor window, because no frames have yet been created. To get started, you need to split your page into parts, which will become separate entities. The first split option (Edit ⇨ Split|) creates two frames side by side (a vertical split, symbolized by the "|" character), while the second option (Edit ⇨ Split–) creates two frames, one on top of the other (a horizontal split, symbolized by the "–" character). It's up to you to decide which layout you prefer.

Whichever orientation you choose, Frame 2 is always the frame that is selected after a split. At this stage, although two frames exist, no real information exists about them.

Continued

TAKE NOTE

▶ **FIXING HTML SOURCE CODE**

The HTML source code generated by the Frame Editor plug-in gives purists a fit. For one thing, framesets replace the BODY element in HTML. However, because this frameset is added to a Composer page, and Composer already has a BODY element in place from the start on any page, you end up with both. Netscape Navigator is perfectly capable of ignoring the extra element, so everything works out fine in practice, but if it makes you feel better, you can delete the start (<BODY>) and end (</BODY>) tags for the unneeded BODY element from the source code. If you're really finicky, you might want to move a few of the other elements around, too, so that the NOFRAMES element is outside the FRAMESET element, and you'll probably want to delete the nonbreaking space ( ). Nevertheless, it's still functional as is.

▶ **USING NOFRAMES**

The NOFRAMES element appears for the benefit of those people who don't use one of the two major Web browsers (both Navigator and Internet Explorer can handle frames). Between the <NOFRAMES> start tag and the </NOFRAMES> end tag, it encapsulates all the information you want people to see even when they don't have frames-capable browsers. Usually, this is advice to get one of the better browsers, because frames are a big part of the Web today.

CROSS-REFERENCE

See Chapter 1 for more information on frames.

FIND IT ONLINE

There's an excellent frames tutorial at
http://ttlc.net/webtutor/frames/index.htm.

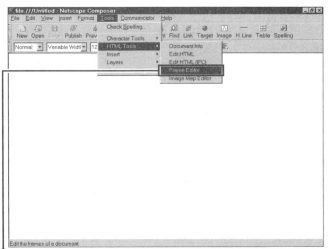

① *Select Tools ➪ HTML Tools ➪ Frame Editor from the Composer menu.*

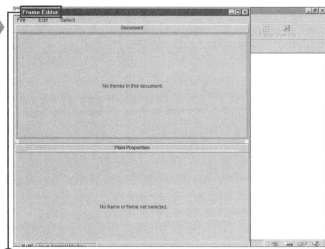

② *The Frame Editor window launches.*

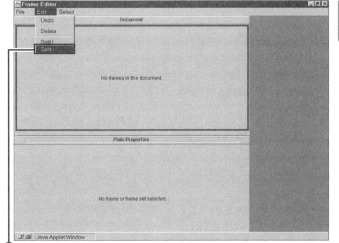

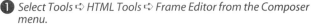

③ *Select Edit ➪ Split– from the Frame Editor menu.*

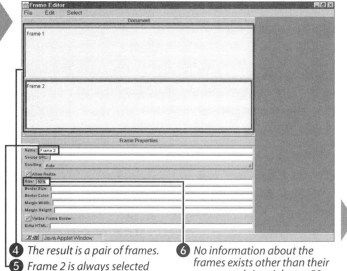

④ *The result is a pair of frames.*

⑤ *Frame 2 is always selected after a split.*

⑥ *No information about the frames exists other than their names and sizes (always 50 percent at this point).*

Using the Frame Editor Plug-In
Continued

Although you can choose to do a bit more with frames, such as setting the border color and size or the margin width and height, the major thing is to say where the information in them comes from. Remember that a frame is only a regular Web page, and those Web pages need to be created separately from the frames and frameset that contain them. You need to explicitly state the location of the Web page that will appear in each frame. Do not enter the full file URL to these Web pages; the source file URLs are relative to the frameset. This means, basically, that you should keep all the Web pages relating to this framed page in the same folder and simply refer to them by name.

When you return to Composer, you will see what seems to be a blank page because Composer doesn't show framed pages.

Now, you'll need to save the frameset, so you have to click the Save button and save the file. Make sure you choose a file name for the frameset that reminds you of its purpose. Click the Preview button to view the framed page you've created in Navigator. Despite the blank appearance of the framed pages in Composer, they display properly in Navigator.

CROSS-REFERENCE

See Chapter 15 for an explanation of relative URLs.

FIND IT ONLINE

Read Netscape's introduction to frames at http://www.netscape.com/assist/net_sites/frames.html.

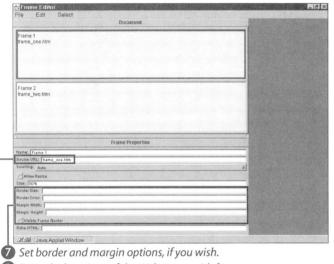

⑦ Set border and margin options, if you wish.

⑧ Enter the locations of the Web pages with frame content.

⑨ Select File ➪ OK from the Frame Editor menu.

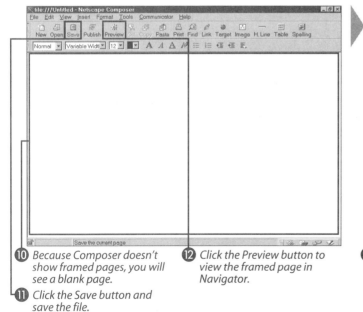

⑩ Because Composer doesn't show framed pages, you will see a blank page.

⑪ Click the Save button and save the file.

⑫ Click the Preview button to view the framed page in Navigator.

⑬ The framed pages display properly in Navigator.

Personal Workbook

Q&A

1 How do you print HTML source code?

_____

_____

_____

2 What is *metadata*?

_____

_____

_____

3 What's the best way to get document information in Composer?

_____

_____

_____

4 How do you access plug-ins in Composer?

_____

_____

_____

5 What Composer bug causes a Web search?

_____

_____

_____

6 What are *keywords* used for?

_____

_____

_____

7 Why would you use "reboot" in a Meta tag's Name attribute?

_____

_____

_____

8 What is the source for a frame composed of?

_____

_____

_____

ANSWERS: PAGE 383

EXTRA PRACTICE

1. Add words to the personal dictionary.

2. Put keywords and categories into your Web pages.

3. Use the Frame Editor to make a page with three frames, and then view the bad HTML source code. Compare it to the HTML code when you only create two frames.

4. Resize a frame by pointing to its border and dragging it.

5. Check out how long it takes to download your Web page with a 33.6Kbps modem.

6. Print the HTML source code to your Web page.

REAL-WORLD APPLICATIONS

✔ You might not be satisfied with Composer's capabilities. Consider adding some plug-ins to increase its functionality.

✔ You have to create Web pages for a particular industry. You might want to add terms peculiar to that industry to your personal dictionary.

✔ You may want to submit your Web site to some search engines. You should probably add keywords before you do so.

✔ You'd like to create a page with a table of contents and a main page. Consider using framed pages to solve the problem.

Visual Quiz

What is this window? Why is it useful?

_____

_____

_____

_____

_____

_____

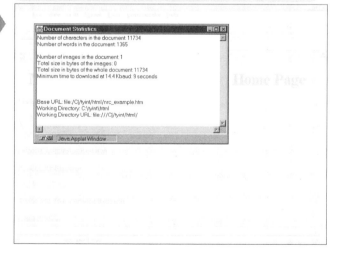

CHAPTER **13**

Handling Web Text

When all is said and done, when all the buzz about multimedia, Java and JavaScript, and the browser wars is stripped away, one fundamental truth remains about Web pages — they're almost all text. No matter what pretty wrappings we put around them, the words remain as our fundamental method of communication with one another.

The ways you choose to use Web text affects the look of your site more than any other single factor. The variety of different approaches is surprising, and many of them can be a hindrance, rather than a help, to your design scheme.

At its most basic, Web text was simply black lettering on a medium gray background, and the only real variance was the size of the lettering. Major headings were very large, lesser headings weren't quite as large as that, and regular paragraphs were smaller.

As the Web grew more sophisticated, and an audience used to the glitzier look of CD-ROMs demanded more of the same from HTML, the basic look began to change. Today, you have your choice of font faces, styles, and sizes, not to mention all the colors of the rainbow for both text and background.

A font face is the actual look of the basic lettering. For instance, in this book, the headings are in a different face from the text. Font faces can be simple and clear, ornate and stylish, or — in some cases — downright ugly. The *style* of a font is whether it is normal, bold, italic, and so forth. Font sizes range from microscopic to poster-sized. In this chapter, we show you how to apply all of these factors to your Web pages and cover a few of the pitfalls you might face as well.

You'll also use a couple more of the Composer plug-ins you installed earlier. This time, we look at the special character plug-in for those times when you need to use nonstandard characters in your Web text, and we have a bit of fun with the small caps special-effect plug-in, too.

In addition, we discuss the use of color to enhance the appearance of your Web site, and put up a few warning signs about abusing color, too. You'll also find coverage of headings and horizontal rules to set off different areas of your Web page from the rest so that it's more readable.

Using the Special Character Plug-In

At times the characters available on your keyboard just won't do what you need. Where, for instance, is the copyright symbol? Sure, you've got a dollar sign, but what about the symbols for the British pound or the Japanese yen? You won't find them on your typical American keyboard. It's true that you can learn and type in arcane codes for them if you want to actually edit the HTML source code, but there's a much easier way to solve the problem, thanks to Composer's plug-in modules.

The figure on the upper left is a Web page describing an island paradise in the Caribbean Sea called Curaçao. That little mark under the "c" is called a *cedilla* and means that you pronounce the "c" like an "s." The "ç" is one of those characters that doesn't appear on your keyboard unless you're in France (oddly enough, the island of Curaçao was discovered by a Spaniard and belongs to the Netherlands). To insert the "ç" character, you need to access the Insert Special Character dialog box. Click the character you want. It is automatically inserted where the cursor is on the Web page, and then the dialog box closes by itself, and you can continue typing.

For all special characters, you'll have to access the Insert Special Character dialog box, which might seem to be a time-waster. The alternative, however is memorizing esoteric character codes, which is undoubtedly a bigger time-waster.

TAKE NOTE

▶ THE CHARACTERS

The Insert Special Character dialog box has just about any character you'll need for international communication, at least in Europe. It has the Spanish "ñ," the German "ü," and the ubiquitous diphthong "æ." What's a diphthong? That's a pair of vowels that's pronounced as a single sound, like the "ou" in sound.

▶ CHARACTER CODES

If you want to, you can always edit the HTML source code and type in the character codes for the special characters. The one for "ç" is *ç* — you have to start all of them with an ampersand (&) and end them all with a semicolon (;). The code for the capitalized version "Ç" is *Ç*. This is a vast improvement over the earlier approach, where each character was assigned a number — "Ç" was *&199;* and "ç" was *&231;*. Actually, they still are, and you can use the numbers if you want to go back to the roots of the system. The more word-like approach is called *character entity referencing*. Fortunately, it just keeps getting easier for Web authors with each new stage, and the point-and-click approach is the best so far. For a complete listing of character codes and references, check the link under Find It Online below.

CROSS-REFERENCE
See Chapter 12 for information on getting the Composer plug-ins.

FIND IT ONLINE
Find the complete character entity references at **http://www.w3.org/TR/REC-html40/sgml/entities.html**.

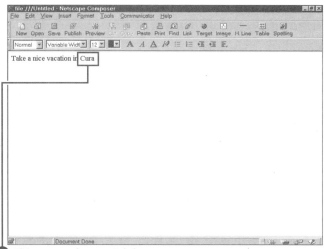

1 *This text needs a special character.*

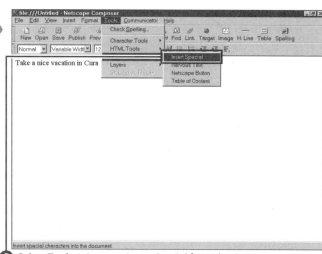

2 *Select Tools ⇨ Insert ⇨ Insert Special from the Composer menu.*

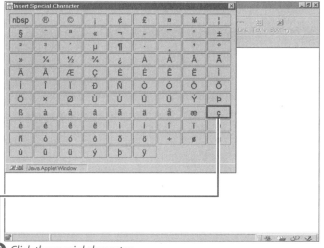

3 *Click the special character.*

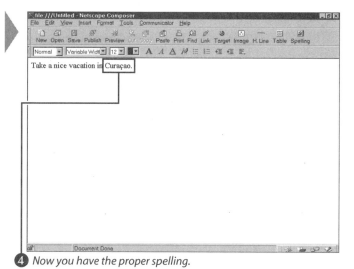

4 *Now you have the proper spelling.*

Aligning and Indenting Text

Aligning and indenting text are helpful ways to make any document legible for a reader, and this is especially true with Web pages. When using a bare-bones text editor for HTML coding, it's easy to forget that text runs together, unless you insert the proper tags for clarity. You should remember that the placement of text is part of a site's design, and it should be as easy to follow as possible.

All text on a Web page is by default left-aligned. This means that the beginnings of any paragraphs are on the left margin of the Web page. The other two possible alignments are centered and right-aligned. Centered paragraphs extend the same distance to the left and right of the center point of the Web page. Right-aligned paragraphs place the ends of each line on the right margin.

To change alignments, click anywhere in a paragraph, and then click the alignment button. A drop-down button menu appears. The top, middle, and bottom buttons in the menu are for left alignment, center alignment, and right alignment, respectively.

In addition to setting the alignment of paragraphs, you can also set their indentation. The figure on the upper left shows some text that, despite the contents, is not actually indented yet. To make it tell the truth, you need to click the second paragraph, and then click the Increase Indent button. Next, click the third paragraph, and then click the Increase Indent button twice.

Continued

Continued

TAKE NOTE

▶ WATCHING THE LENGTH

Text alignment, although it takes place on a paragraph level, is best used with short bits of text such as headings. When used with full paragraphs of text consisting of several sentences, center and right alignment can render them difficult to read, because the beginnings of the lines end up at different locations depending on the sentence length.

▶ WHAT'S THE LEFT-ALIGN BUTTON FOR?

Text on a Web page is automatically left-aligned, so there doesn't seem to be much use for a left-align button. The reason for it is to let you change any paragraphs that are centered or right-aligned back to the default.

▶ HOW ABOUT OTHER LANGUAGES?

With some languages, the natural order of sentences is from right to left rather than from left to right. Simply changing the paragraph alignment won't do the trick. You need to go into the HTML code and set the *dir* attribute to *rtl*. The code to set an entire Web page to right to left text would be in the HTML element: <HTML dir="rtl">.

The value of the dir attribute can also be set to *ltr* so the text runs left to right, but there's no point in that as that's the default direction anyway.

However, this whole thing is a relatively new development in HTML and neither Internet Explorer nor Netscape Navigator support it at the current time.

CROSS-REFERENCE

See Chapter 14 for information on aligning text with images.

FIND IT ONLINE

Language issues in HTML are covered at **http://www.w3.org/TR/REC-html40/ struct/dirlang.html**.

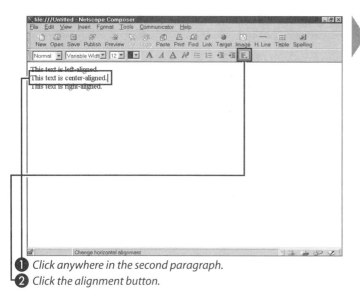

1 Click anywhere in the second paragraph.

2 Click the alignment button.

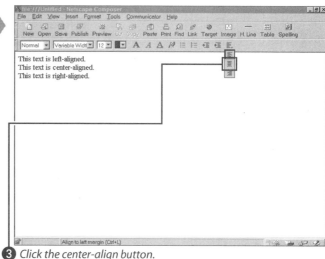

3 Click the center-align button.

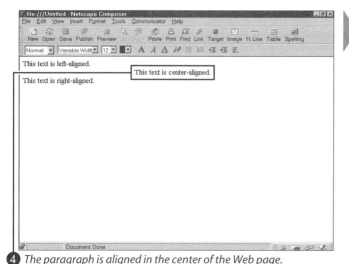

4 The paragraph is aligned in the center of the Web page.

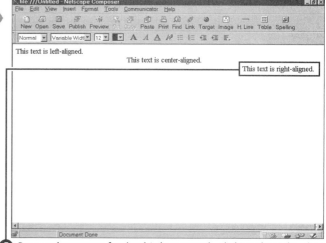

5 Repeat the process for the third paragraph, clicking the right-align button. The paragraph is right-aligned.

Aligning and Indenting Text
Continued

The HTML source code is most informative. The BLOCKQUOTE element is invoked once for the single indentation and twice for the double indentation. Further clicks on the Increase Indent button will result in further increases in the number of BLOCK-QUOTE elements involved.

The indentation is done by putting the selected text inside <BLOCKQUOTE> and </BLOCK-QUOTE> tags (as with most HTML elements, BLOCKQUOTE requires both start and end tags, and the end tag is identical with the start tag except for the beginning slash in its name). The BLOCK-QUOTE element is designated in the official HTML specification for use in quoting large segments of text from other sources, but because it has the effect of indenting the quotation, it is most often used by Web designers for its indentation properties instead of its quotation purposes. The World Wide Web Consortium is not happy about this abuse of their intended usage, but it is commonplace and they are powerless to do anything about it because they are merely a standards-setting body and not a ruling body (standards are merely official suggestions, not requirements, and may be ignored at will). Indenting more than one time is done by nesting multiple BLOCKQUOTE elements within one another.

CROSS-REFERENCE

See Chapter 16 for more information on structuring Web pages.

FIND IT ONLINE

Read about the BLOCKQUOTE element at **http://www.w3.org/TR/REC-html40/struct/text.html**.

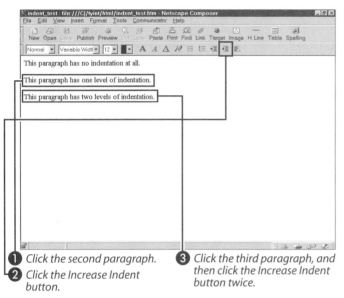

① Click the second paragraph.

② Click the Increase Indent button.

③ Click the third paragraph, and then click the Increase Indent button twice.

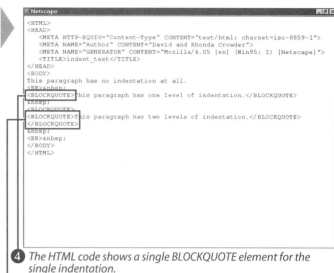

④ The HTML code shows a single BLOCKQUOTE element for the single indentation.

⑤ The HTML code shows two BLOCKQUOTE elements for the double indentation.

⑥ Click the third paragraph.

⑦ Click the Decrease Indent button.

⑧ The HTML code shows that one BLOCKQUOTE has been removed from the code.

Setting Paragraph Style

Where font styles affect only the particular characters they're applied to, and can be limited to as little as a single letter or number, paragraph styles change every single character in the paragraph.

Headings, which are used for starting off different sections of Web pages, come in a variety of sizes ranging from the H1 element (the largest) to the H6 element (the smallest). The ADDRESS element's official specification says that it's supposed to contain "information on author." However, it's not usually the author of the Web page that's at issue. It's usually used to provide the physical address, e-mail address, phone number, fax number, and so forth where further information can be obtained. In addition to simply making the text italic, it also sets it off from surrounding text by adding a space between it and the preceding lines.

The Formatted style invokes the PRE element (short for "preformatted"). Preformatted text is displayed in a monospaced font such as Courier, and white space, which is usually ignored by Web browsers, is treated like any other character. Thus, if you begin a sentence in a normal paragraph on a Web page with three spaces, it shows up in a Web browser just as though it had no leading spaces at all. An identical sentence within a PRE element, though, will start off three spaces to the right of the other sentence. Likewise, carriage returns and all other types of formatting that are normally ignored in HTML are significant in a PRE element.

TAKE NOTE

OTHER PARAGRAPH STYLES

You'll no doubt have noticed that we've skipped three paragraph styles here. The List Item, Description Title, and Description Text styles are specific to lists and are covered in a later chapter.

CHANGING STYLES LATER

You might find it easier to type out all of your text and then go back and apply the styles. You don't even have to highlight each line; you can click anywhere in the line and select a new style. The entire line will reflect your modification.

UNDERSTANDING SOURCE CODE

This is an excellent opportunity to familiarize yourself with the container relationships that form the bulk of HTML. The figure on the bottom right shows the source code for the preceding Web page. Note that the Heading 1 paragraph shows a start tag of <H1> and an end tag of </H1>. Each of the other paragraphs is similarly contained within start and end tags.

CROSS-REFERENCE

See the section on text styles later in this chapter.

FIND IT ONLINE

Learn more about heading elements at
http://www.w3.org/TR/REC-html40/struct/global.html.

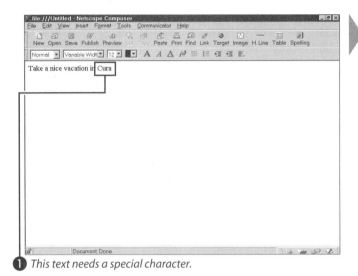

① *This text needs a special character.*

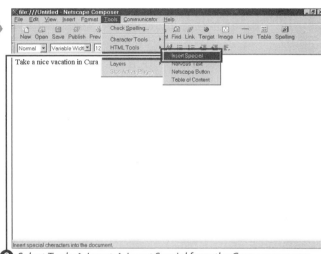

② *Select Tools ⇨ Insert ⇨ Insert Special from the Composer menu.*

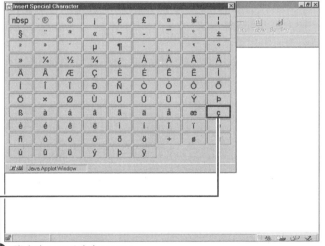

③ *Click the special character.*

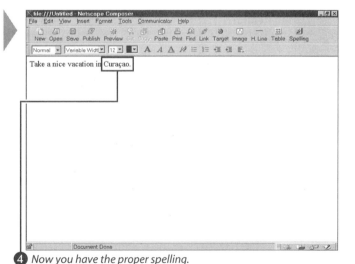

④ *Now you have the proper spelling.*

Changing Text Style

One way to spice up your page's text is to change its style. Composer provides buttons in its toolbar to help with this. You can add emphasis to your statements quite easily by making certain words stand out. The key, however, is not overdoing it. Too much bold can be like writing in all caps, as if you're yelling at the reader. Special formatting can also start to lose its effect, if the whole page is in bold text. If done well, text styling can be the minor adjustment that makes a significant improvement to your site.

You may click multiple buttons if needed. For example, you click both the bold and italic buttons to create bold italic text; if you then click the underline button, you'll have text that's bold, italic, and underlined.

To remove text style formatting, just select the text you want to change and click the same button you used to format it to begin with. For italic text, click the italic button to change it back to normal; for bold text, click bold, and for underlined text, click the underline button.

If you select text that's had one of these styles applied to it, the corresponding button in the toolbar looks like it's pressed in. For instance, if you select some bold, underlined text, these two buttons will look pressed, but the italic button won't be. If you have different kinds of formatting applied to different parts of a sentence and you select the entire sentence, then all the buttons that are affected by any of the characters in that sentence will look pressed. For example, if you have one word that's in italics and another one elsewhere in the sentence that's bold, then selecting that sentence causes both the italic and bold buttons to look pressed. When you select text that's been formatted and then click a button to remove formatting, the button comes back up.

Continued

TAKE NOTE

▶ FORGET UNDERLINING

It's not a good idea to underline text on a Web page. The World Wide Web Consortium, the closest thing to a ruling body that the WWW will tolerate, is officially against it for a sound reason — links on a page are normally indicated by underlining, and anything else on a Web page that's underlined is bound to be confusing. If you underline words on your Web pages, visitors will click those words and wonder why they're not going anywhere. If you want to emphasize words, it's best to use bold or italic styles.

▶ BLINKING TEXT

If there's one thing more people on the Web agree on than any other, it's that the <BLINK> tag was a step in the wrong direction. Blinking text does initially attract a viewer's attention, but it quickly becomes irritating, and your visitors' irritation can easily be transferred from the annoying blinking text to you, your product or service, or whatever it is you're trying to get across. If you feel you must use it, use it sparingly.

CROSS-REFERENCE

For more information on styles, see the section on paragraph styles earlier in this chapter.

FIND IT ONLINE

Find font style technicalities at **http://www.w3.org/ TR/REC-html40/present/graphics.html**.

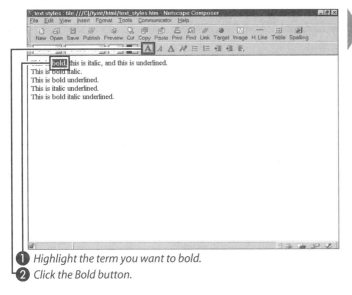

1. Highlight the term you want to bold.
2. Click the Bold button.

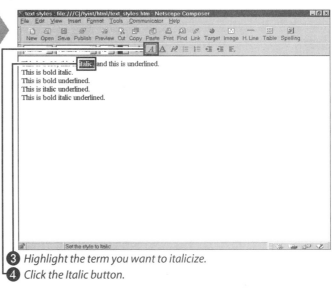

3. Highlight the term you want to italicize.
4. Click the Italic button.

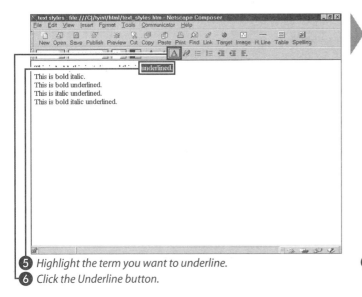

5. Highlight the term you want to underline.
6. Click the Underline button.

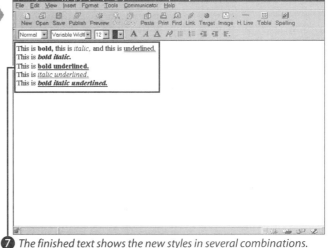

7. The finished text shows the new styles in several combinations.

Changing Text Style

Continued

Although you'll probably only use the bold and italic text styles under normal circumstances, more text styles are available than appear in the toolbar. To get to the other ones, you need to select the text you want to change, and then right-click within that selection. This brings up a popup menu, where you can click Character Properties. Under Style, in addition to the three styles you already have in your toolbar (Bold, Italic, and Underline), you have Strikethrough, Superscript, Subscript, Blinking, and Nonbreaking. The latter two are exceptions to Composer's pure HTML code, and are Netscape-specific, but have limited utility in any case. See the notes below. Of the remaining three, strikethrough has very few uses on the Web, but you may well need superscripts or subscripts.

TAKE NOTE

▶ THE NOBR ELEMENT

Nonbreaking text, as you can see in the source code if you use it, puts the selected words between <NOBR> and </NOBR> tags. This prevents the text within from being word wrapped when seen in a browser. If the nonbreaking text is wider than the browser's screen, this forces the viewer to scroll horizontally to see the remainder. You will almost never have a reason to do this, but if you have some unusual situation and don't mind limiting the effect to Netscape users, it's available.

▶ THOSE OTHER PARTS

In addition to the font styles, you can also see that the Character Properties dialog box duplicates the Font Face, Color, and Font Size options from the toolbar. The font face choices are as limited as the ones in the toolbar. The Don't change color option becomes active when you select text that already has a color assigned. The Remove Style Settings button clears all the style checkboxes at once, and the Remove All Settings button resets everything in the dialog box at once.

▶ GATHERING OPINIONS

The best way to find out if a text style works is to ask members of the target audience. After all, they're the are's you've trying to please.

CROSS-REFERENCE

For more information on color, see the section on text color later in this chapter.

FIND IT ONLINE

Netscape discusses the NOBR element at **http://home. netscape.com/assist/net_sites/html_extensions.html**.

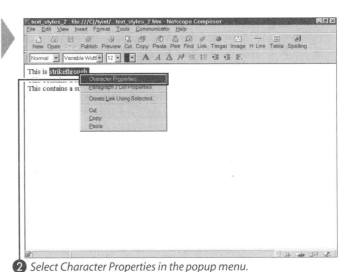

① Select the text you want to change, and then right-click within that selection.

② Select Character Properties in the popup menu.

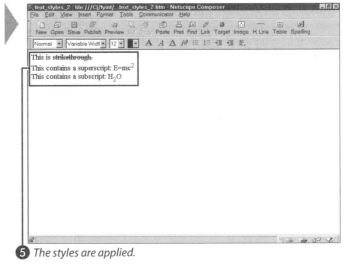

③ Click the checkbox for the text style you want.

④ Click the OK button.

⑤ The styles are applied.

Changing Text Size

Changing the size of a given word or character isn't usually meaningful. Generally, the only time you want some words larger than the norm is in a heading, and the best way to take care of that is to use the Heading elements. In some cases, though, changing the size of a particular character can improve the appearance of Web text. You may notice that many books (like this one) begin a chapter with the first letter of the first word enlarged. Some even use elaborate fonts for this purpose, as was done in medieval illuminated manuscripts. That enlarged first capital letter is known as a *drop cap*, by the way.

If you do want to change the size of some of your text, the procedure is similar to setting text styles. First, highlight the characters you want to change. Next, click the drop-down size menu, and then pick the size you want from the listing.

One other way to change the size and appearance of text is to use the Small Caps plug-in, which changes all the letters in the selected text to capitals, with the first letter of each word being a larger size than the rest. Using small caps might work well with a different typeface. See the task later in this chapter that discusses using different fonts.

TAKE NOTE

▶ FONTS AND POINT SIZE

The numbers in the drop-down menu are a bit misleading. They specify the size of the fonts in *points* (72 points equal an inch, so 12 points is a sixth of an inch, 36 points is half an inch, and so on). HTML does not actually permit you to specify an exact point size for fonts. HTML has 7 sizes for fonts, ranging from very small (1) to very large (7). The default setting is 3. The exact size of the default font and, therefore, of the other sizes in relation to it, is determined by the user's preference settings in his or her browser. If you want control over exact font size in points, you'll have to use Cascading Style Sheets (CSS), which are beyond the scope of this book. For a good starting point to learning CSS, see Find It Online below.

▶ SLOPING WORDS

You can emphasize a short word by making it slope up toward the center, and then down toward the end. To do this, start increasing the font size with the second letter and increase it one more time until you reach the center letter; from there to the end, decrease the font size letter by letter.

CROSS-REFERENCE

See Chapter 4 for more information on setting Web page font sizes.

FIND IT ONLINE

Find the W3C CSS page at **http://www.w3.org/Style/CSS**.

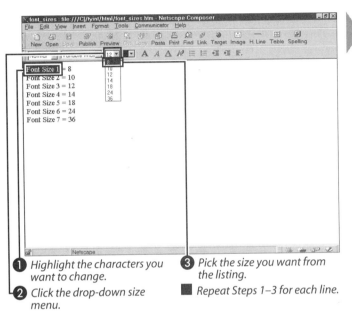

1 Highlight the characters you want to change.

2 Click the drop-down size menu.

3 Pick the size you want from the listing.

■ Repeat Steps 1–3 for each line.

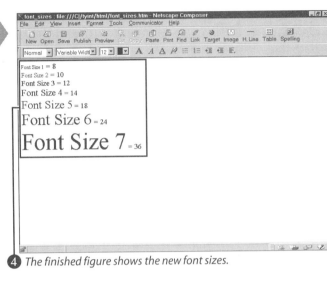

4 The finished figure shows the new font sizes.

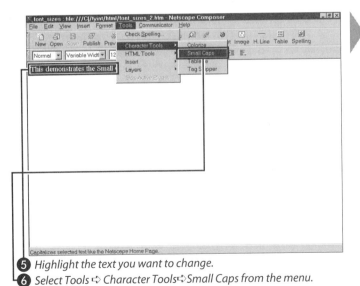

5 Highlight the text you want to change.

6 Select Tools ➪ Character Tools ➪ Small Caps from the menu.

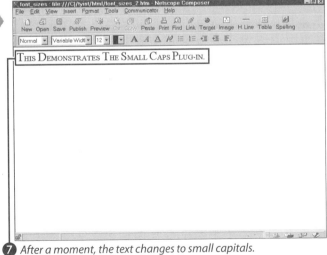

7 After a moment, the text changes to small capitals.

Changing Text Color

Although many people would argue that the main purpose of a Web page is to convey information, there's no denying that color plays a distinct role in how appealing your design is to your visitors. As with text styles, you can use color to emphasize certain words, or you can use it simply to make a dull stretch of text prettier. It can also be misused to make a site totally unreadable, especially in combination with background color (see the next section).

As with the text styles, you can change anything from a single character up to the entire page. If you're going to use the sloping text technique from the previous section, adding color changes to it can really liven things up.

One clever Composer add-on is the Colorize plug-in. Like the color menu, it changes the color of text, but instead of setting the selected text to a single color, it produces a rainbow effect from a range of colors. It does this by changing the color of each character just a little bit from the preceding one. The result is called a *gradient*, because the color changes gradually. The larger the amount of text selected, the more pronounced the effect of the color gradient.

Coloring text with plug-ins such as Colorize should be kept to a minimum. Reading text affected by color gradients can make reading difficult, and your visitors might get annoyed if it's overused.

TAKE NOTE

▶ SETTING ONE MORE OVERRIDE

Like font size, color is one of those things that you may set, but your visitors may override. Notice in the color menu, in the figure on the upper left, that the default color says it's the one "from browser preferences." If you've left the default color as black, but your visitor has set his or hers to blue, then you'll see black and they'll see blue.

▶ THE "OTHER" BUTTON

The Other button at the bottom of the color picker lets you create and assign custom colors. The procedure for doing so is identical to the one we detailed in Chapter 4 for creating custom colors in your Web browser preferences. It's generally best to avoid using custom colors and stick with the basic ones unless you're aiming strictly for an audience of people with high-quality video cards.

▶ USING COMMON SENSE

Text color is sometimes used to spice up boring statements, but it can be almost as difficult to read or annoying as the blink tag. If you need a lot of color, consider changing the background or adding some interesting pictures. Too much colored text can be hard to read.

CROSS-REFERENCE

See Chapter 4 for more information on setting custom colors for Web pages.

FIND IT ONLINE

Read about basic and custom colors at **http://www. connect.hawaii.com/hc/webmasters/Netscape. colors.html.**

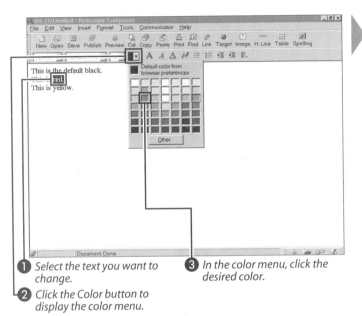

1 Select the text you want to change.

2 Click the Color button to display the color menu.

3 In the color menu, click the desired color.

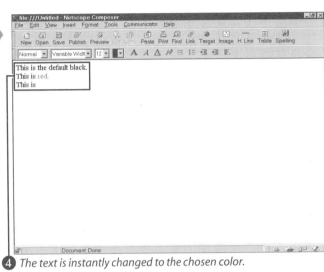

4 The text is instantly changed to the chosen color.

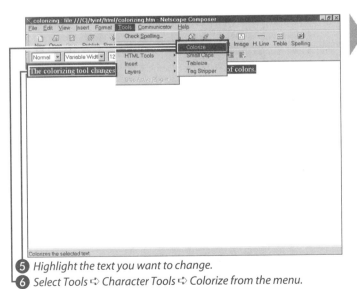

5 Highlight the text you want to change.

6 Select Tools ➪ Character Tools ➪ Colorize from the menu.

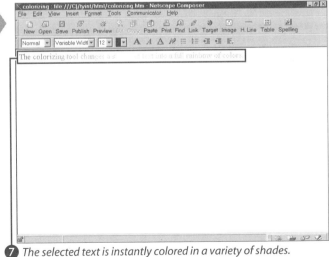

7 The selected text is instantly colored in a variety of shades.

Setting the Background Color

The default background color for Web browsers used to be a medium gray. Today, that's changed to white. You don't have to stick with the default, though. The best color scheme for readability is a pale variation of yellow or beige for the background color, with black text. A black background with yellow text isn't bad either. A bad combination would be two different shades of the same color.

If you compare how well the text and links showed up when the background color was white with the situation when the background color is darker, you'll see that the combination is not good. If you're dead set on going with the darker background color, you'll have to make changes to the text and link colors to accommodate the background (but see the note below first).

You can experiment with different colors endlessly before committing to a particular one. Until you click the OK button, your choices aren't cast in stone. All you have to do to return to the defaults is to click the Cancel button.

Chapter 14 goes into more detail on the interplay of the background color, background images, and coloring text work with different schemes.

TAKE NOTE

▶ USING BACKGROUND IMAGES

Background images can clash with text color as well, so keep this in mind when you are working on your color scheme. You might need to lighten the images before you set them up in the background.

▶ DIFFERENTIATING BETWEEN LINK AND TEXT COLORS

Just as you could with your browser preferences, you can change the color settings for text and for hypertext links in the Page Properties dialog box. Although you might want to change the text color at times, it's best not to mess with the link colors for the same reason that you shouldn't use underlining — people are used to the default values and, if they don't see what they're used to, they're likely to consider your Web site confusing. If you do decide to change these colors, click the color button next to the one you want to change and follow the same procedure as for changing the background color.

▶ SETTING DEFAULT COLORS

To make your color choices the defaults for any future Web page you create in Composer, click the checkbox labeled *Save these settings for new pages*.

CROSS-REFERENCE

See Chapter 14 for information on using background images.

FIND IT ONLINE

Find another good site about colors (from a Mac point of view) at **http://130.212.8.138/msp/Instructors/ rey/FINPAL.HTM.**

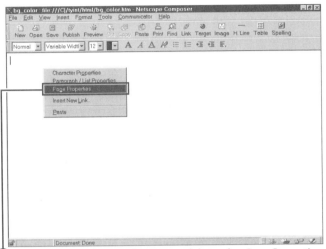

1 Right-click anywhere on the page and then select Page Properties from the popup menu.

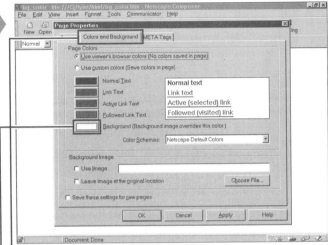

2 Click the Colors and Background tab.

3 Click the Background button to display the color picker.

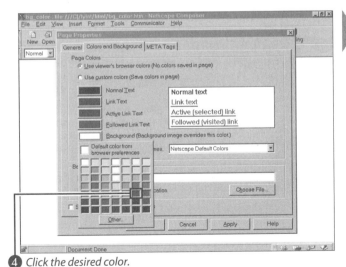

4 Click the desired color.

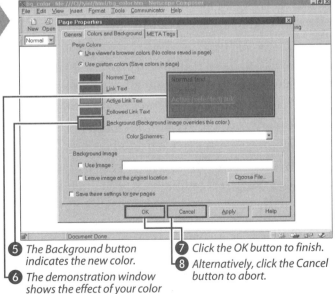

5 The Background button indicates the new color.

6 The demonstration window shows the effect of your color choice.

7 Click the OK button to finish.

8 Alternatively, click the Cancel button to abort.

Changing Font Faces

Although you can specify that your Web page contain any font at all, there's not really much use for this capability. The reason is that nobody can view your Web page with the fonts you specify unless they have those fonts on their own system. Three basic font faces can be found on practically anyone's computer, whether they're using a PC, a Mac, or a UNIX box. Other than that, it's pretty much a grab bag. Every popular computer has some variety of Helvetica (called Arial on PCs), Times (called Times Roman or Times New Roman on PCs), and Courier (or Courier New on PCs). The figure on the upper left shows the three common font faces.

If you specify one of the common font faces, you'll have no trouble. On the other hand, if you have a large collection of fonts and you decide to use some such as Merlin or Zurich Calligraphic, you're not going to get the results you want, because those are quite a bit less likely to be found on other people's computers. Remember that HTML is a markup language, and it simply specifies to the Web browser how to construct the Web page on the visitor's screen. If the Web browser can't find the fonts you specify, it can't construct the page the way you intended, and it'll substitute some other font for the one you wanted, probably Times, the default font for Web page text.

If you want to set some text to Arial, highlight it and click the Font Face button. The drop-down menu allegedly shows the fonts available on your system, but it's flawed and doesn't show the complete list. If Arial is shown on yours, simply click it. If not, scroll down to the bottom of the listing and click Other. This brings up a standard Font dialog box, as shown in the figure on the lower right. Unlike the one in Composer's toolbox, this one shows all the fonts. Click the font you want, and then click the OK button (the other settings for Font style and Size have no effect whatsoever on your Web page).

TAKE NOTE

COVERING ALL THE BASES

If you do specify a particular font, take a look at the HTML source code. If you've specified Arial, for instance, you'll see that Composer also listed Helvetica in the code. If people using Mac or UNIX systems look at your page, they don't have the Arial font, but they do have Helvetica, which is virtually identical, so their browser will take the second choice and they will still see the text as you intended.

CROSS-REFERENCE

See Chapter 4 for more information on Web fonts.

FIND IT ONLINE

There's a good font site at **http://coolsound/simplenet.com/Free/fonts.htm**.

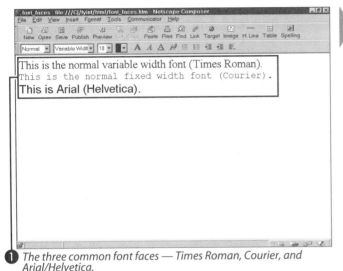

❶ The three common font faces — Times Roman, Courier, and Arial/Helvetica.

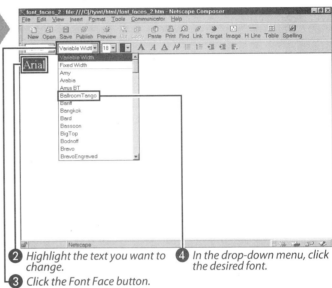

❷ Highlight the text you want to change.

❸ Click the Font Face button.

❹ In the drop-down menu, click the desired font.

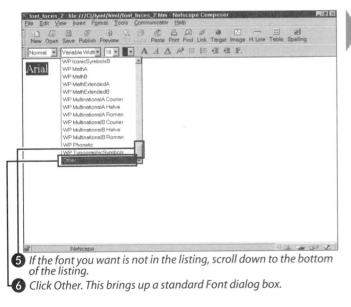

❺ If the font you want is not in the listing, scroll down to the bottom of the listing.

❻ Click Other. This brings up a standard Font dialog box.

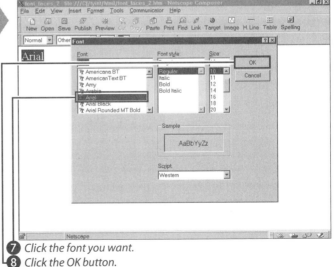

❼ Click the font you want.

❽ Click the OK button.

Using Horizontal Rules

Although, strictly speaking, horizontal rules are not textual, they are mainly used to separate one section of text from another to emphasize short segments or break large stretches of text into more readable sections. Composer refers to them as *horizontal lines*, but the proper terminology in HTML is *horizontal rule*, and the element's name is abbreviated HR (after you create one, you can check the source code to see this name).

To insert a horizontal line, place the cursor where you want to put the line, and then click the H.Line button. You can't put a horizontal rule on the same line as any other element, because the HR element is a *block level element* (elements that can coexist on the same line are called *inline elements*).

The default horizontal rule in Composer is 2 pixels in height, takes up the entire width of the Web page, and has the 3D shading set (meaning that it is hollow rather than filled-in, although this is impossible to see with such a thin line). To change any of these settings, place your mouse pointer on the line and right-click. You'll probably have to jockey the pointer around a bit to get it on the line, because it's so thin (the tip of the pointer may actually be above the line before it works). From the resulting popup menu select Horizontal Line Properties.

Continued

TAKE NOTE

► ALIGNMENT AND LINE WIDTH

The default Composer horizontal rule is set to 100 percent of the Web page's width, yet is also center-aligned. This has no particular meaning, because a line that stretches from one side of the page to the other cannot actually be said to be aligned in any way whatsoever. If you want any type of alignment — left, right, or center — to show up, the line itself has to be less than the width of the Web page.

► WHAT'S A GOOD HEIGHT?

The right height value depends on your Web page design. A 1-pixel-high line is virtually invisible, while a 20-pixel-high line is overpowering. It also depends on whether you're going to take advantage of 3D shading. Shaded (hollow) horizontal rules require more room to properly show up than does a solid line. A good range in most cases is from 2 to 4 pixels for a solid line and from 4 to 6 pixels for shaded lines.

► USING AN IMAGE INSTEAD

You can create an elaborate horizontally-oriented graphic to take the place of a horizontal rule. This way, you can break up sections of your page through more creative means.

CROSS-REFERENCE

For more information on alignment, see the section on aligning text earlier in this chapter.

FIND IT ONLINE

Read the specs about horizontal rules at http://www.w3.org/TR/REC-html40/present/graphics.html.

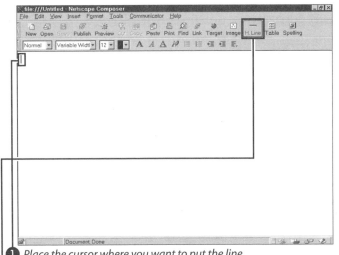

① *Place the cursor where you want to put the line.*

② *Click the H.Line button.*

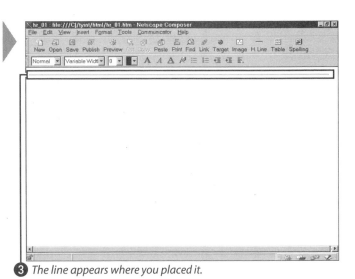

③ *The line appears where you placed it.*

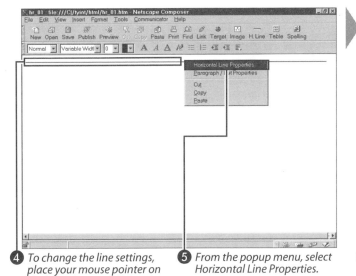

④ *To change the line settings, place your mouse pointer on the line (aim carefully) and right-click.*

⑤ *From the popup menu, select Horizontal Line Properties.*

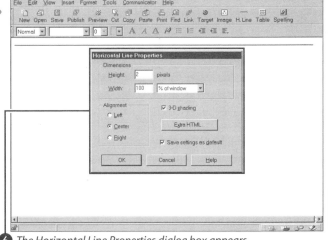

⑥ *The Horizontal Line Properties dialog box appears.*

Using Horizontal Rules

Continued

The Width setting for horizontal lines has two different approaches. The first approach in Composer (the default) is to set a percentage of the Web page's width. However, you can also specify that the horizontal rule has a specific width in pixels. With the percentage approach, the horizontal rule is the same proportional size on any computer screen regardless of the resolution; 50 percent is half the screen whether your visitor is using a screen resolution of 640 × 480 or 1,280 × 1,024. With the absolute size approach, however, the proportional size of the horizontal rule will vary from one computer screen to another, but the actual width will never vary. A fixed-size 320-pixel-wide horizontal rule, for instance, is 50 percent of the width of a 640 × 480 screen, but only 25 percent of the width of a 1,280 × 1,024 screen. The figure on the upper right shows a 100-pixel horizontal rule.

One odd bit about Composer is that it doesn't properly display shading for horizontal rules. In the figure on the lower left, the horizontal rule has 3D shading, so it should show as hollow, and it's large enough (6 pixels in height) that the effect should be visible. However, Composer shows it as a solid line. Clicking the Preview button to show the Web page in Navigator, as shown in the figure on the lower right, shows that the horizontal line is indeed hollow as it's supposed to be. There's no HTML code for 3D shading, only for its absence — the noshade attribute.

TAKE NOTE

▶ ONE TECHNICAL DETAIL

With all the variations in the way different monitors display anything, not even the exact size of pixels, those tiny colored dots that form the screen image, is constant. The smaller the monitor's *dot pitch* (the size of the pixels), the smaller an absolute horizontal line will be.

▶ SAVE SETTINGS AS DEFAULT

If you click the *Save settings as default* checkbox, then all the settings you have chosen will be applied to any new horizontal rule you create afterward. This checkbox is selected by default, so if you don't want to apply your changed settings to every horizontal rule from this point on, make sure to deselect it before you click the OK button.

▶ SIZE AND HEIGHT

If you take a look at the source code for a horizontal rule on your Web page, you'll notice that there's no height attribute in the HR element. The actual HTML attribute for the height (or thickness) of the line is called *size*. The attribute for width is more sensible — it's simply called *width*.

CROSS-REFERENCE
See Chapter 11 for information on horizontal rules and images.

FIND IT ONLINE
Find more graphical replacements for horizontal lines at **http://www.fsap.com/ehi/bars/lines/**.

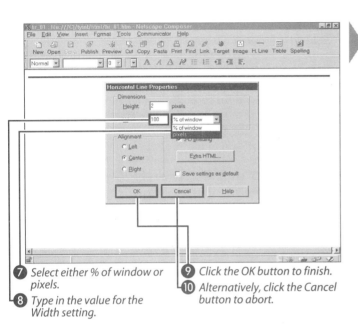

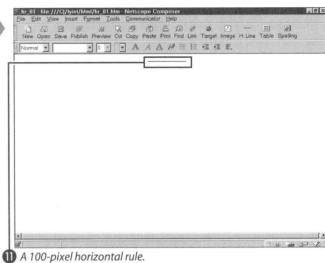

7 Select either % of window or pixels.

8 Type in the value for the Width setting.

9 Click the OK button to finish.

10 Alternatively, click the Cancel button to abort.

11 A 100-pixel horizontal rule.

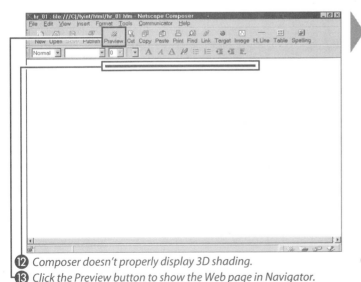

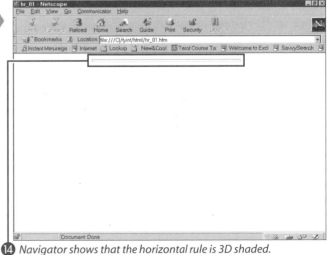

12 Composer doesn't properly display 3D shading.

13 Click the Preview button to show the Web page in Navigator.

14 Navigator shows that the horizontal rule is 3D shaded.

Personal Workbook

Q&A

1 Why is there a left-align button?

_____

2 What three font faces are common to most computers?

_____

_____

_____

3 How do you make a default setting for Web page colors and background images?

_____

_____

_____

_____

4 What is the difference between a _horizontal line_ and a _horizontal rule_?

_____

_____

_____

5 What is a _character code_?

_____

_____

_____

6 What is a _character entity reference_?

_____

_____

_____

7 What HTML element is used for indenting?

_____

_____

_____

8 Why is underlining text frowned upon?

_____

_____

_____

ANSWERS: PAGE 384

EXTRA PRACTICE

1. Make a Web page with different heading levels.

2. Pick up a foreign-language text and type a sentence from it into a Web page using the special character plug-in.

3. Experiment with the PRE element by applying the Formatted style to a paragraph full of white space and carriage returns. Compare it to an identical paragraph formatted as Normal.

4. Change the color of text on your Web page.

5. Try out several different background colors.

6. See what effect changing the font size has on a heading element.

REAL-WORLD APPLICATIONS

✔ You may want your headings to really stand out. Try centering them, coloring them, and putting a horizontal rule underneath them.

✔ You have some computer code you want to add to your Web page. You might try using the Courier font face for it so that the spacing is clearly defined.

✔ You have to quote some text from a book for your Web page. You might want to use the indentation buttons to set it off from the rest of the text.

✔ You have a background color against which the text barely shows. Bearing in mind that different monitors and color cards show colors in slightly different shades, you may want to scrap the color combination and go for one with more contrast.

Visual Quiz

What is this menu? What would this particular menu choice do to the selected text?

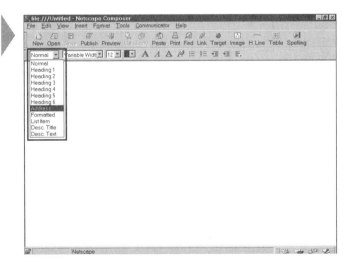

_____

_____

_____

_____

_____

_____

CHAPTER **14**

Adding Images

If you're an accomplished artist who is comfortable with electronic media, you'll have no problem populating your Web pages with fabulous graphics. For the rest of us, there's *clip art*. The term comes from back in the days when every type of printed material was put together with scissors and paste, and then shipped to a professional printer for compositing. Organizations with low budgets would save money by buying books of preprinted artwork on various themes instead of hiring an artist. An appropriate image was clipped out of the book with scissors and pasted into place. Once photocopiers became commonplace, the artwork was usually photocopied instead of being clipped, but the name stuck, and it's carried over into the world of digital images.

Lots of talented artists maintain Web sites where you can get tons of really wonderful material. The caliber of much of this material is way better than what most people are capable of creating. Other sites called *image archives* have large collections of clip art from various sources available for download. Where an artist's Web site usually has very high-quality graphics for you to use, the image archives tend to go more for quantity than quality, and you have to pick through a lot of primitive or simplistic material to get to the good stuff. On the plus side, many of them offer their own search engines that let you find images by topic or title instead of having to browse through several Web pages filled with images. The vast majority of the artists' sites don't have search engines or topical databases, but they are generally well organized. Whatever the source, once you download the art, all you have to do is add it to your Web page.

Much of the clip art on the Web is in the *public domain* — that is, nobody holds the copyright to it, so anyone can use it. Even most of the copyrighted artwork is available at no cost; the artists would simply like you to put in a link to their home page in exchange for using it. That way, commercial organizations who like their work and want to hire them can find them more easily. It works out well for both you and the artists, because you get high-quality graphics for nothing and they get free advertising and increased exposure.

Downloading Clip Art

The first step in downloading clip art is to find a good site. We've included several to get you started in the Find It Online portions of this chapter. Most artist's sites have a series of links leading off from their home page to various categories of artwork. Click the links to get to the images. The categories usually have several different images in them, and you'll need to scroll down the page to see all of them.

It's easy to search for clip art using popular search engines such as Yahoo!, Lycos, Excite, and WebCrawler. A quick way to locate the right image is to search for sites related to a particular topic. For example, if you were searching for images of dolphins, use the following phrase to narrow your search: "Clip art AND dolphins."

Some of the Web sites that have amassed large collections of public domain clip art charge fees for downloading — or even browsing — the images. In most cases, the proprietors of these sites have not actually created any of these images, but simply downloaded them just like you do, and are charging you more for the work of others than for any labor of their own. In almost every case, the same images are available for nothing at some other Web site, so think twice before you pay for something you can get for free elsewhere.

Regardless of where you go for your images, make sure you understand the artist's wishes about whether you can redistribute his or her images. In most cases you will need permission from the images' owner.

TAKE NOTE

▶ IF IT'S ZIPPED

The majority of Web sites that offer downloadable clip art display the images for you to see and download one at a time. Some, however, have compressed the files for downloading and you'll need to follow the normal procedures for nonimage file downloads. This is not that common, however, because the average image file is pretty small to begin with.

▶ WEB RINGS

Practically every category of human endeavor online has some kind of *Web ring* going, and artists are no exception. A Web ring is a series of sites on a similar topic, each of which has a link pointing to the next one in line. By following the links in the ring, you can visit hundreds of Web sites on any given subject. The ring links usually give you the option of visiting the next or previous ring member, or of taking a random leap somewhere into the ring. When you're on a graphics site, check out the home page for any mention of a Web ring. If you find one, it's worth your time to follow the links. Web rings are usually mentioned near the bottom of the home page, but sometimes at the top.

CROSS-REFERENCE
See Chapter 2 for more information on downloading files.

FIND IT ONLINE
You can find Jasmine's Gallery at
http://www.twostar.com/gallery/.

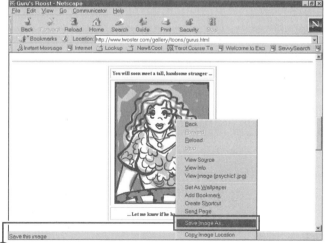

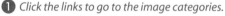

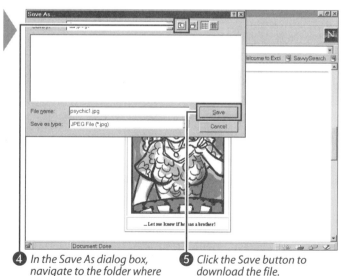

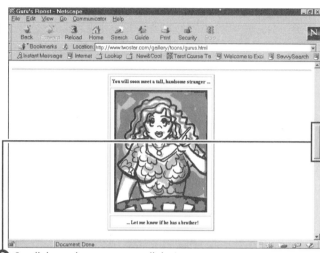

① Click the links to go to the image categories.

② Scroll down the page to see all the images.

③ To download an image, right-click it and then select Save Image As from the popup menu.

④ In the Save As dialog box, navigate to the folder where you want to put the file.

⑤ Click the Save button to download the file.

Inserting Images

Once you decide on the type of image you want to include in your Web page, the next step is actually inserting the image.

Images come in different formats. Most of the clip art you'll find, however, is available in one of the two most common formats for Web graphics — Graphic Interchange Format (GIF) or Joint Photographic Experts Group (JPEG). Composer is designed to plug both of these file formats right into your Web page.

So how do you determine which format of graphic will suit your Web page best? Here are a few guidelines for choosing between GIFs and JPEGs. A GIF file can be a better choice if your images are small, such as image thumbnails, or if your images are solid colors. A JPEG is perhaps a better choice for large photographs or graphics with many different colors. The choice is yours.

Inserting an image in your Web page with Composer is relatively simple. It's a matter of letting Composer know what you want to insert (an image) and where it can be found — either from a URL or from your hard drive, floppy disk, or CD-ROM.

You have many choices of how you can use images in your Web sites. For example, you can choose one image to be the background of your page, or you can insert graphics as smaller links.

Continued

TAKE NOTE

▶ IMAGE LINKS AND SERVER LOADS

If you're going to use graphics that you find on another Web site, make sure you download them and put the actual file on your own Web site. It's just as easy for you to use HTML to link to the original image anywhere on the Web as it is to link to a copy of it on your own Web server, but it's not nice to ask someone else's server to bear the load every time someone looks at one of your pages. A thousand copies of an image on a thousand different servers is a tribute to the artist. A thousand hits on their server from people who have thoughtlessly linked to the original image is a major irritation. When you look at the Image Properties dialog box, you'll see a checkbox labeled *Leave image at the original location*. Use this only if the original location is a server you control. Using this option to achieve a link to someone else's server is a serious violation of netiquette. Also, because graphic artists are aware of this problem, they're likely to change the file names and/or directories on occasion, which can leave you in the lurch if you violate this caution. If that happens, you won't have the image on your Web page anymore, which is another reason to have your own copy.

CROSS-REFERENCE

See the section on background images later in this chapter.

FIND IT ONLINE

Check out the Clip Art Connection at **http://www.clipartconnection.com/home/php3**.

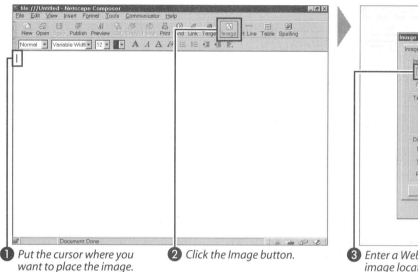

① Put the cursor where you want to place the image.

② Click the Image button.

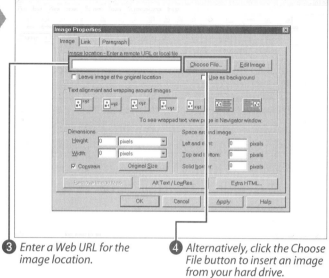

③ Enter a Web URL for the image location.

④ Alternatively, click the Choose File button to insert an image from your hard drive.

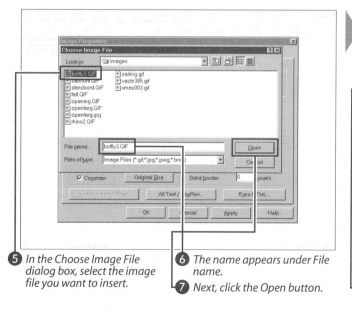

⑤ In the Choose Image File dialog box, select the image file you want to insert.

⑥ The name appears under File name.

⑦ Next, click the Open button.

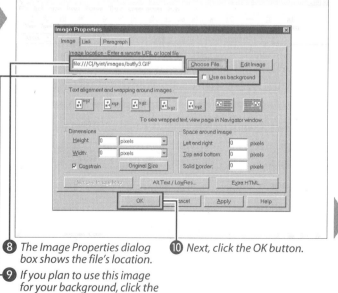

⑧ The Image Properties dialog box shows the file's location.

⑨ If you plan to use this image for your background, click the Use as background checkbox.

⑩ Next, click the OK button.

303

Inserting Images
Continued

The image is inserted into the Web page, as shown in the figure on the upper left of the facing page. To finalize things, you have to save the altered Web page. Once the changes have been saved, you can see the way Composer handles the new images you inserted.

Check the properties of your image to see the height, width, and name of your image, among other things. The height and width of images is important because that notation lets your browser set aside space for them on the Web page before it's finished loading.

Images, as we mentioned, can serve many different uses in a Web page. Large graphics can be used as backgrounds; smaller graphics can be tiled and also used as backgrounds. You can incorporate graphics such as product or company logos to add some visual element to your page.

You'll sometimes find small clip art items called *icons*. Other than the size, the main distinction between regular art and icons is that icons are used to symbolize things or actions. For instance, you might find a small pair of binoculars or a magnifying glass as icons for searching. A great number of icons symbolize home, and these are ideal for using on pages throughout your Web site for links back to your home page.

Thumbnail images are another type of smaller image. Basically, thumbnail images are previews to larger versions of themselves. These images can save a site visitor from downloading each large image individually or from waiting for all the images to download when he or she enters the site. Consider using thumbnails if your site contains many graphics.

TAKE NOTE

▶ ALPHABET SOUP

GIF stands for *Graphics Interchange Format*, a file format popularized by CompuServe, an online entity that was a forerunner of America Online. JPEG is named after the *Joint Photographic Experts Group* (JPEG is often abbreviated to JPG because of the old DOS and Windows 3.*x* limit of three characters for file extensions), and BMP (strictly a Windows file format) is short for *bitmap*. Many people think a newer file format called PNG is likely to become the common graphics format on the Web. PNG stands for *Portable Network Graphic*. The PNG format was developed as a result of a legal debacle. It's designed to replace the GIF file format, because the Unisys Corporation, owner of the GIF approach, after years of letting graphics professionals and amateurs use the format without restriction, suddenly announced that it would be charging for using it. Even after they clarified that they would only be charging people who developed image editing programs, graphics personnel banded together to create a better approach that would be free of restrictions.

CROSS-REFERENCE

See the next section for more information on graphic file formats.

FIND IT ONLINE

Surf to the PNG specification at **http://www.boutell.com/boutell/png/**.

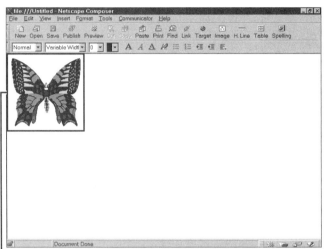

⓫ The image is inserted into the Web page.

⓬ Click the Save button to save the altered Web page.

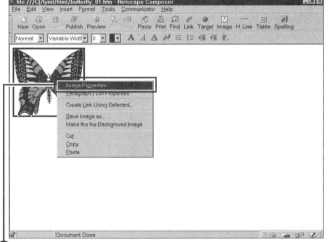

⓭ Right-click the image. From the popup menu, select Image Properties.

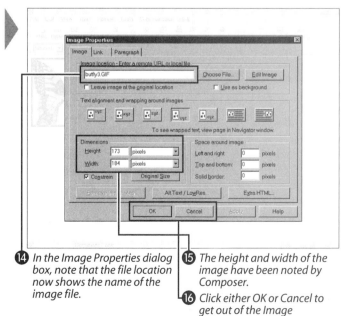

⓮ In the Image Properties dialog box, note that the file location now shows the name of the image file.

⓯ The height and width of the image have been noted by Composer.

⓰ Click either OK or Cancel to get out of the Image Properties dialog box.

305

Choosing GIF or JPEG

You have a choice of either GIF, JPEG, or BMP files when inserting images into a Web page in Composer. A BMP file is a Windows Bitmap file. These files are not used that frequently because of their very large size.

You can choose which kind of files to insert. The kind you choose depends partially on the shape of the image. Although all images are actually rectangular, GIF images can appear to be otherwise, due to a property called *transparency* that lets the background of a Web page show through. Any color in the GIF can be transparent, but it's usually the background color of the image, not a color that appears in the main image.

The figure on the upper left shows a Web page that has a background color. A GIF image with transparency appears in the figure on the lower left. The figure on the lower right shows a JPG image without transparency. The rectangular nature of the image is clearly demonstrated in the JPG image, while the transparency factor of the GIF image shows its versatility in Web design.

If the background color of the JPG image is the same as the Web page's background color, then the transparency issue doesn't come into play, and the fact that JPG files are usually smaller than the equivalent GIF file could be a factor in deciding which to use. Bear in mind, though, that users can set their own background colors for Web pages through their browser preferences regardless of what you put in your HTML code. If they do that, the rectangular nature of the JPG image will become readily apparent.

TAKE NOTE

▶ GIFS AND GIFS

Two different kinds of GIFs exist. The older version, that follows the GIF87 standard, cannot show transparency. The newer version follows the GIF89 standard. Most GIF images will be the later version, but one factor about the Internet is that it has given us practically limitless storage. It's kind of like the biggest closet or garage in the world, and all sorts of old odds and ends lie around in it, some of them very old. If you have a GIF image that doesn't use transparency, just load it into a graphics program and add the transparency. Also, many graphics programs let people save images in both the GIF87 and GIF89 versions, and some people, not understanding the difference, save new images in the old format. If you've got a GIF image that won't hold the transparency you set in the program, make sure you're saving it in GIF89 format.

▶ USING QUALITY IMAGES

A lot of times, JPG quality can be less than that of GIFs, but at the screen resolution of 72 dpi, the image quality doesn't have to be that high.

CROSS-REFERENCE

See the following section for information on handling BMP files.

FIND IT ONLINE

Laurie McCanna has a good art site at http://www.mccannas.com/.

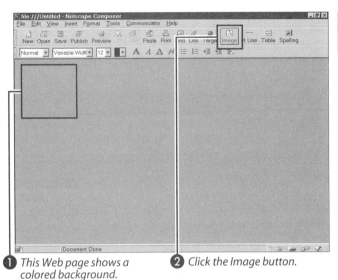

1 *This Web page shows a colored background.*

2 *Click the Image button.*

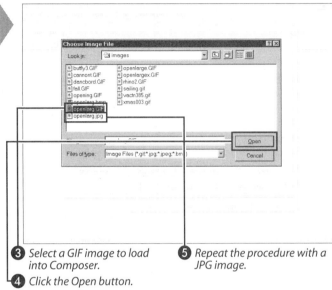

3 *Select a GIF image to load into Composer.*

4 *Click the Open button.*

5 *Repeat the procedure with a JPG image.*

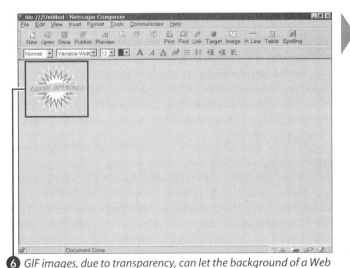

6 *GIF images, due to transparency, can let the background of a Web page show through.*

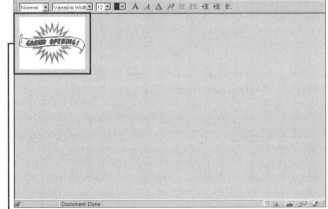

7 *JPG images, lacking transparency, invariably show their rectangular shape.*

Using the JPEG Encoder

JPEG stands for Joint Photographic Experts Group, the consortium that invented the format. They intended JPEG to be a royalty-free, high-quality image format that could support millions of colors while compressing well. JPEG is great for photographs, complex art, and images with subtle shading and colors. But for small line drawings, icons, low-resolution graphics, and charts, use GIF instead.

Generally, it's best to prepare an image in a graphics program, save it as a GIF or JPG file, and then insert it via the Image button. But if you have an image in the Windows clipboard and want to put it into a Web page in Composer, you can insert it as a JPEG image. Paste it in, as shown in the figure on the upper left. The Image Conversion dialog box appears, as shown in the figure on the upper right. The JPEG encoder is selected by default. Just click the OK button to get things going.

The statement in the JPEG Image Quality dialog box that the image size will be larger at higher qualities is misleading. It's actually the file size, not the image size, that increases; the image size stays the same regardless of quality. The file size in this example was 41K for high quality, 12K for medium quality, and 7K for low quality. All the quality levels produced an acceptable image, and smaller files download faster, so it's best to go for the smallest file size that gives you an image with quality you can live with.

CROSS-REFERENCE

See Chapter 12 for more information on Composer plug-ins.

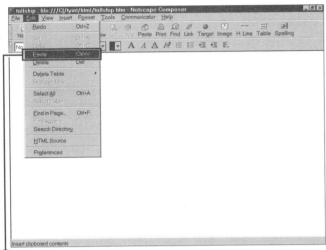

① Select Edit ➪ Paste from the menu.

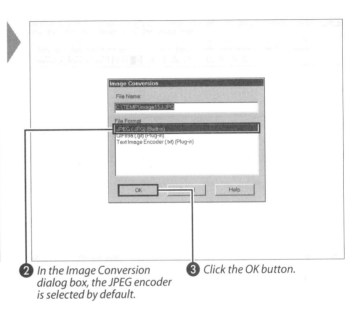

② In the Image Conversion
dialog box, the JPEG encoder
is selected by default.

③ Click the OK button.

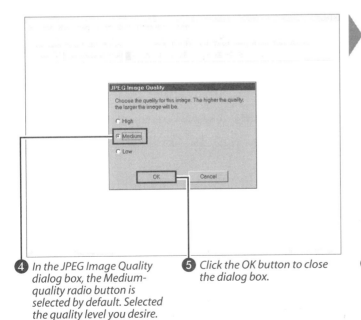

④ In the JPEG Image Quality
dialog box, the Medium-
quality radio button is
selected by default. Selected
the quality level you desire.

⑤ Click the OK button to close
the dialog box.

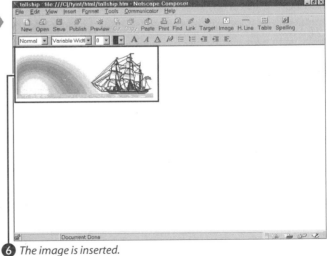

⑥ The image is inserted.

Resizing Images

Once you insert your images and save them as part of your Web page, you may decide you want to make some adjustments to the images themselves. For example, your design scheme may determine that you want your image to be either increased or decreased in size. That is the aim of this task.

You can change the size of an image on the Web page without having to change it in a graphics program. Once an image has been inserted, you can adjust its size using the Image Properties menu, which takes you through all your options.

When you resize an image, the proportions of that image stay intact. In other words, when you change one dimension, the other is automatically calculated for you so the shape and look doesn't distort. You have an option of turning this feature off, so you can change height and width independently of one another, but you'll end up with a funny-looking image that way. Click the OK button to complete the change.

One important distinction to keep in mind is image size and file size. Reducing the size of the image as it appears on your Web pages will not necessarily affect the size of the file itself in any way. Image file size is an important factor of the type of art you choose to include in your site; the larger the file, the longer it will take to download. Image size, on the other hand, simply has to do with the appearance of the graphic on your page itself.

Continued

TAKE NOTE

▶ IMAGE SIZE AND FILE SIZE

Changing the size of the image on the Web page does not affect the file size at all; it merely changes the way the image is displayed. If you want to reduce the file size itself, and thus speed download time, you'll have to do it in an image editor or by using a color reduction tool such as the GIF Wizard (see Find It Online below).

▶ PIXELS AND PERCENTAGES

In addition to setting the exact pixel dimensions of the image, you can choose to set the height and width as a percentage of the window size. This definitely results in a distorted image, especially considering that different visitors to your site will be using different screen resolutions, so it's best to stick with the normal method unless you're experimenting with bizarre effects. If you do want to play with these settings, you can get some really weird-looking distortions by setting the height to pixels and the width to a percentage of the window, or vice versa.

▶ RESIZING BY DRAGGING

You can also change the size and shape of the image by dragging the edges or corners of the image with your mouse (drag by the corners to maintain the image's proportions in their original ratio). This approach lacks the precise control of the dialog-box method, but it's available.

CROSS-REFERENCE
See Chapter 13 to compare using window percentage for horizontal rules.

FIND IT ONLINE
You can find the GIF Wizard at **http://gifwizard.com/**.

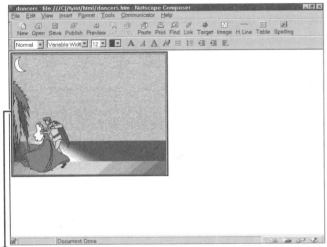

1 First, insert an image.

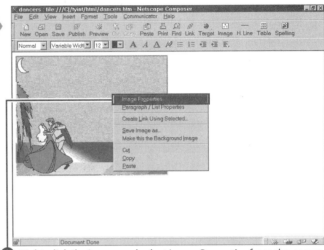

2 Right-click the image and select Image Properties from the popup menu.

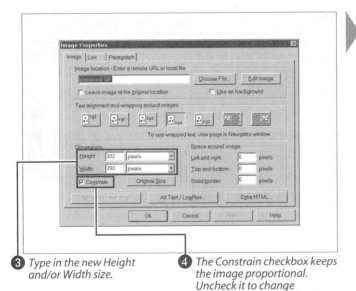

3 Type in the new Height and/or Width size.

4 The Constrain checkbox keeps the image proportional. Uncheck it to change dimensions independently.

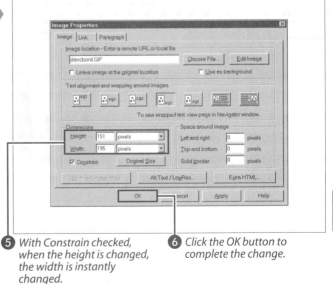

5 With Constrain checked, when the height is changed, the width is instantly changed.

6 Click the OK button to complete the change.

Resizing Images

Continued

So what happens if you resize your image and you aren't happy with the results? Say, for example, you resize an image and then you figure out that most of your site's visitors are viewing your images at a much higher resolution than you. This affects how your images appear to other people — they would seem much smaller than you intended.

Like so many actions, resizing images is completely reversible. If you want to return your image to its previous state, you have a few ways to do so. You can adjust the image properties to suit the specifications you desire, or you can use the Undo command.

You have another way to reverse the size change, but it has a limitation. You can select Edit ⇨ Undo from the menu (or use the Ctrl+Z key combination). The problem with this technique is that you have to do it right away if you want it to work. The Undo command can only undo the single most recent thing you did. If you do anything else at all after changing the image size, then that's the thing the Undo command will reverse. Fortunately, changing the size back in the Image Properties dialog box can be done at any time, no matter how many other things you do in between.

Another option for returning an image to it previous size is to use the Original Size button. When you change the size of the image in the Image Properties dialog box, you're simply adding a command in the HTML source code that tells a Web browser to display it in that size. However, as mentioned previously, the original image file is totally unaffected by this operation, thus Composer can find the original size to reset it to from that file.

TAKE NOTE

▶ **SHRINKING AND ENLARGING**

Very few images look better enlarged. The images used in Web pages (both GIF and JPG) are bitmaps, which are collections of colored dots. When bitmaps are enlarged, they're grainy and unclear because the dots are spread out and the Web browser has to fill in the areas between the known dots. If you're going to change image size, it's better to go smaller rather than larger. If you must enlarge an image, make the enlargement minimal. If you absolutely must enlarge an image to a high degree, you're a lot better off using a high-end graphics program that can do a better job than a Web browser of interpolating the new pixels needed to fill in the gaps created when you enlarge it. Even then, the results often aren't worth the trouble. You might be better off looking for another image to replace the small one with.

▶ **IMAGES AS BUTTONS**

You can shrink down images to small hyperlinked squares to create buttons.

CROSS-REFERENCE

See Chapter 11 for information on image editors.

FIND IT ONLINE

Try the GIF animations at **http://members.aol.com/ Lor1466/animations.html**.

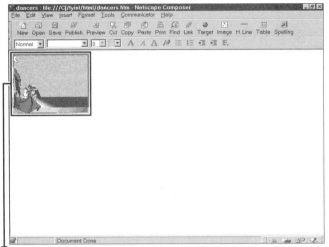

7 The image is now the size you specified in the dimensions panel.

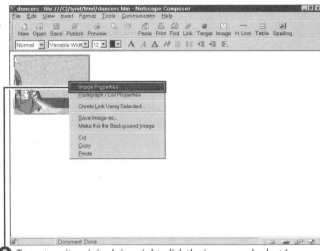

8 To restore its original size, right-click the image and select Image Properties from the popup menu.

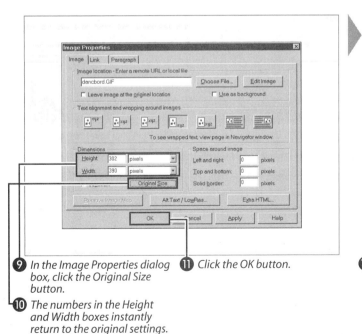

9 In the Image Properties dialog box, click the Original Size button.

10 The numbers in the Height and Width boxes instantly return to the original settings.

11 Click the OK button.

12 The image on the Web page is restored to its original size.

Setting Text Alignment

While images make great contributions to your site on their own, you may choose to accompany your images with text. For example, if you are publishing an online account about your trip to Europe, you may want to include captions that go along with photos, explaining to visitors of your site what they are seeing, where the photo was taken, and what the significance is.

Aside from captions, you may want to add labels to your images. Say you have a gardening site that includes a page of images, each of a different type of flower. You can include text with these images to provide the name of each particular one.

Aligning text with your images is a fairly simple process that really involves only inserting your image, typing your text, and choosing the way you wish to align the text. You are given basically three options of how to align your text: top, middle, and bottom.

The majority of the images on the Web appear independently, but they can have text associated with them. Normally, the text would be either above or below the image, but text alignment lets you place text in a variety of positions next to an image. Flexibility in placement enables a designer to prevent confusion by placing a lot of images with captions consecutively on a page.

TAKE NOTE

▶ THE FIVE SETTINGS

Although essentially three settings exist for text alignment — top, middle, and bottom — two other ones add a little extra. The middle and bottom alignments have variations that rely on a normal part of letters that you probably never think about. While most letters fit neatly along the typed line, some letters have parts that drop below the line. Take a look, for example, at "g" or "j" and you'll see that they're a bit different from letters like "a" and "r." The first group has *descenders*, those fiddly bits that won't fit in the normal space allotted for letters, but that drop below the line. The text alignment buttons illustrate how these descenders are handled in the middle and bottom alignments by showing a red line that's drawn under the letters. They don't matter with top alignment, because the line in that case is above the letters. The second button shows that, in the pure middle alignment, the line goes right through the middle of the letters. The third button shows the letters still centered, but here the descenders drop below the line. The fourth button shows a similar arrangement with the bottom alignment, and the fifth button shows the letters at the bottom of the image, but with the descenders on the line instead of under it. These subtle differences don't show up with small size fonts, but can matter a lot if you use large font sizes.

CROSS-REFERENCE

See the following section on setting word wrap.

FIND IT ONLINE

Check out the Clip Art Searcher at
http://www.webplaces.com/search/.

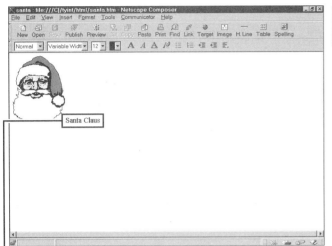

1 *Insert an image and type the associated text immediately following it.*

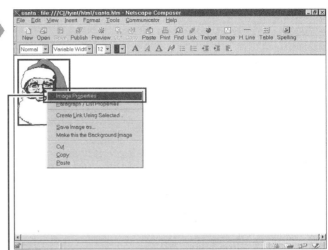

2 *Right-click the image and select Image Properties from the popup menu.*

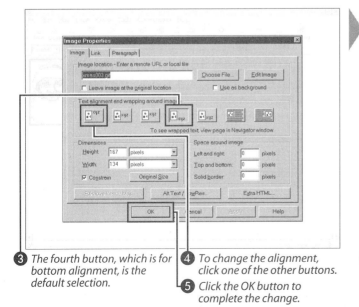

3 *The fourth button, which is for bottom alignment, is the default selection.*

4 *To change the alignment, click one of the other buttons.*

5 *Click the OK button to complete the change.*

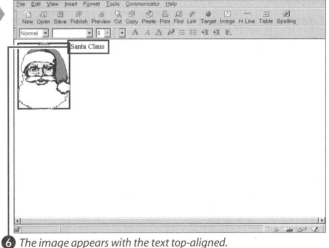

6 *The image appears with the text top-aligned.*

Setting Word Wrap

Text alignment is only useful with a word or short phrase such as an image caption. Word wrap, however, functions with whole paragraphs at a time, and it can help improve a Web site's appearance.

You would want to use word wrap, for example, if you were producing an online newsletter. As with a newspaper or magazine article in the print world, you can incorporate photos and images into your Web pages and flow the text around the graphics.

If you use text alignment with more than a phrase or a very short sentence, the paragraph breaks at the right side of the Web page and wraps around to the bottom of the image instead of continuing along the side of it the way it does with word wrap. This results in an ugly gap in the paragraph that makes it difficult to follow the flow of the words. Word wrap lets you create a nice flow while still mixing images and text together.

As with word alignment, you insert an image and type the text immediately following the image, as shown in the figure on the upper left. You'll recall from the section on text alignment that seven buttons appear in the Text alignment and wrapping panel. The first five are for text alignment, and the last two buttons control word wrap.

Back in Composer, the image looks no different. To see the changes in word wrap, you have to view the Web page in Navigator. To do this, save the Web page and then click the Preview button in the toolbar, as shown in the figure on the lower right.

Continued

TAKE NOTE

▶ THE ALIGNMENT BUTTONS

You might notice, if you poke into the HTML source code while using word wrap, that you're actually setting the alignment of the image. Why not just use the alignment buttons in the toolbar instead of going to the trouble of working with the Image Properties dialog box? The reason is that the toolbar's alignment buttons are for text, and don't affect the alignment of images. You might also wonder why there are only two choices for image alignment in word wrap. That's because of a limitation in HTML — the IMG element has left and right alignment attributes, but no center alignment attribute.

▶ USE TABLES TO ALIGN TEXT

HTML tables can be excellent layout tools. If you have to place text in an exact position relative to a photo or other graphic, keep in mind that you can use borderless tables to lay out your text. A borderless table is a table with its table borders turned off. In HTML, you do this with the BORDER=0 attribute in the <TABLE> tag. In general, all tables in Web pages should be borderless (the borders are often distracting). But particularly remember to turn them off if you are using a table to format text around a graphic.

CROSS-REFERENCE

See the preceding section on setting text alignment.

FIND IT ONLINE

Moyra's Web Jewels is a great art site at
http://www.mysticpc.com/jewels/.

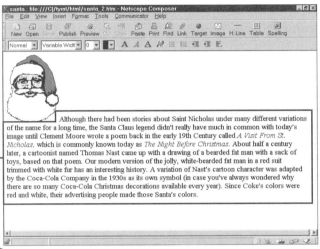

❶ Insert an image and type text immediately following the image.

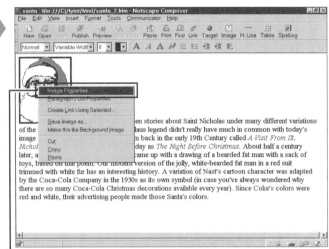

❷ Right-click the image and select Image Properties from the popup menu.

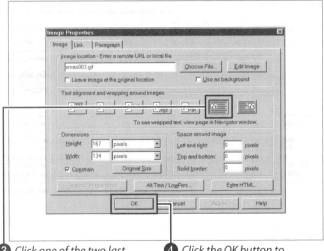

❸ Click one of the two last buttons in the Text alignment and wrapping panel.

❹ Click the OK button to complete the choice.

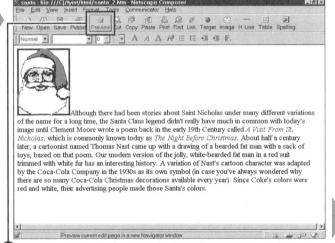

❺ Back in Composer, the image looks no different. To see the changes in word wrap, click the Preview button in the toolbar.

Setting Word Wrap

Continued

You should always preview your page, especially after making insertions, adjustments, or edits, before releasing it to cyberspace. You can check your page with the Preview button. First, though, always save your work before attempting to preview; actually, there's no way around it. Navigator will not be able to load the Web page unless you have saved it to disk first.

The figures on the facing page show previews of different layouts: image on the left and text on the right, image on the right and text on the left, and image in the middle of the paragraph and text all around it. You won't always know which looks best until you see the preview.

So far, we've only dealt with the two options where the top of the image is on the same line as the first sentence of the paragraph. If you want the image to appear in the midst of the text, you can also drag the image to somewhere other than the beginning of the paragraph and the words will wrap around it, as shown in the figure on the lower right. You'll still have to settle for the image being on either the left or the right side because, as noted previously, no center alignment option exists for images.

After you drag and drop the image, you sometimes need to reset the word wrap alignment. If it isn't showing up the way you want it, go back into Composer, right-click the image, select Image Properties from the popup menu, and make sure that the image alignment hasn't been changed by Composer behind your back. This is only a problem if you move the image after setting the word wrap.

TAKE NOTE

▶ RESIZING THE IMAGE

While your image may be a fine size as a stand-alone page element, you may need to resize it to get it to fit better as a part of a paragraph. As mentioned earlier in this chapter, enlarging an image usually results in poor quality, so it's good that images usually need to be downsized to fit in with a paragraph.

▶ PUTTING IT IN THE MIDDLE

You can actually have an image that is neither left-nor right-aligned, but sits anywhere you want on any line in the paragraph. Just place the image where you want it and don't set the text alignment or word wrap (the default is no alignment at all). However, the resulting paragraph will look pretty bad, because the line it sits on will be the height of the image, not the height of the lettering.

▶ HOW DOES IT FLOW?

Images are great tools to break up monotonous text, but they can be distracting if they interrupt the flow of text. If it's hard for your eyes to follow the text, consider redesigning the layout.

CROSS-REFERENCE

See Chapter 11 for information on saving Web pages in Composer.

FIND IT ONLINE

Fantasy Graphics has fabulously beautiful art at **http://members.aol.com/litesrealm/enter.html**.

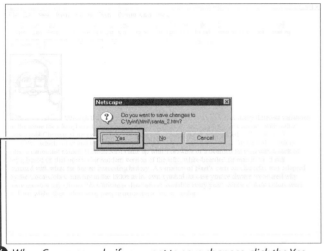

6 When Composer asks if you want to save changes, click the Yes button.

7 The image appears in Navigator. This shows the image on the left and the words wrapping to the right.

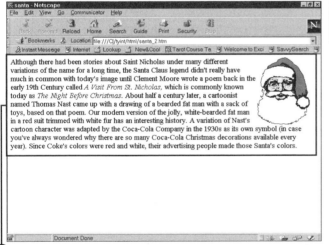

8 This shows the image on the right and the words wrapping to the left.

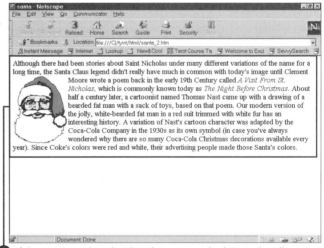

9 If the image is placed within the paragraph, the words will wrap above and below it.

Using Spacing and Borders

Images have two further features you might find interesting and useful in your Web design repertoire. The first is the ability to specify a certain amount of space between the image and anything surrounding it. The second is to place a border of specified thickness around the image.

The spacing is a matter of choice and a matter of layout. It is up to you how you want your images to appear in relation to the page or in relation to each other. Borders are often used with hyperlink graphics; many browsers will put borders around these graphics. You can also use borders to create navigation bars on your site.

You can set spacing for either above and below the image or to the left and right of it. Of course, you can feel free to set both horizontal and vertical spacing at the same time. The spacing is measured in what are called *pixels*. (If you're not familiar with this term, a pixel is a unit of measurement used in layout.)

You can also control how much space your image takes up on your Web page as a whole. If you specify the dimensions of your image, your browser will know exactly how much room to leave for the image when downloading your page. This prevents your site's visitors from having to stare blankly at a white screen while your browser determines how much space your image requires.

The figure on the upper left has text to the immediate right of and just below the image; it has no

border. You can set the image's spacing and/or border properties (these are known in HTML as *attributes* of the IMG element) by right-clicking the image and moving through the options in the Properties menu.

You have setting options for Left and right, Top and bottom, and Solid border. These deal with, respectively, the horizontal spacing, vertical spacing, and the border width. You can enter the numbers you want (the spacing is in pixels) and implement the settings.

Continued

TAKE NOTE

LINING UP IMAGES

If the amount of space on the Web page and the size of the images allows, you can put one image after another after another, all on the same line. To do this, all you have to do is to insert one image, and then just keep right on inserting more until you run out of space. If you want to put in one image, and then put another image under it, just insert the first image and then hit the Enter key to put in a carriage return before inserting the next image. In either case, you might want to take advantage of the spacing feature to place the images some distance apart from one another.

CROSS-REFERENCE
See Chapter 13 for information on text alignment.

FIND IT ONLINE
Heikki's Free Stuff has lots of free art at
http://njet.net/heikki/FREESTUFF_link.shtml.

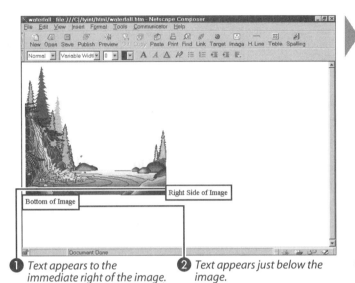

1 *Text appears to the immediate right of the image.*

2 *Text appears just below the image.*

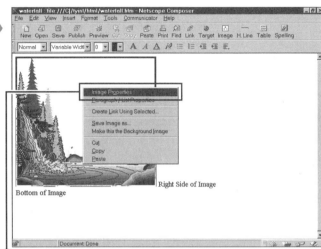

3 *Right-click the image and then select Image Properties from the popup menu.*

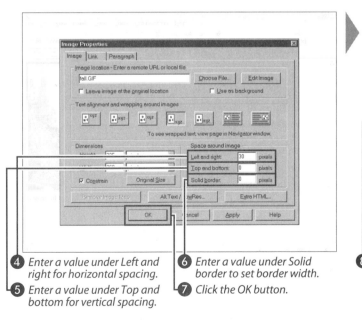

4 *Enter a value under Left and right for horizontal spacing.*

5 *Enter a value under Top and bottom for vertical spacing.*

6 *Enter a value under Solid border to set border width.*

7 *Click the OK button.*

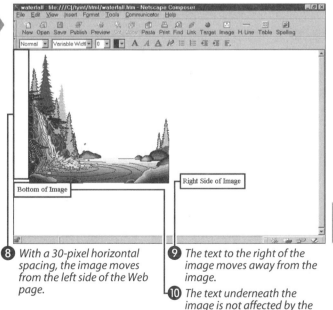

8 *With a 30-pixel horizontal spacing, the image moves from the left side of the Web page.*

9 *The text to the right of the image moves away from the image.*

10 *The text underneath the image is not affected by the horizontal spacing.*

Using Spacing and Borders

Continued

If we go back into the Image Properties dialog box and set the vertical spacing (Top and bottom) to 30 pixels as well, then you'll see both expected and surprising effects (see the figure on the upper left). As you'd expect, the image moves down on the Web page and the text underneath is pushed down from the image as well. Surprisingly, the text to the right of the image also drops down. The reason for this is that anything following the image is affected by the vertical spacing, even other elements on the same line as the image.

You can use the Image Properties dialog box to set the border. You just decide on the border width you want and enter it. The figure on the upper right shows a border width of 1 pixel. We've eliminated the text from the Web page so we can focus on the border changes. The image on the lower left shows the same image with a border width of 5 pixels, and the image on the lower right has a border width of 10 pixels. How wide you set your border is a personal choice that depends entirely on the image being used and how it fits into your Web site's design scheme.

You can use the vertical spacing setting that causes anything to the right of an image to drop down if you want to have an interesting effect with a line of images. Setting each image so that it has some degree of vertical spacing around it can create a staircase effect, with each succeeding image dropping a little bit more. The higher the number, the greater the drop and the steeper the staircase. Unfortunately, you can't use negative numbers to reverse the staircase effect. The values have to range from 0 to 1000 for spacing or borders.

TAKE NOTE

▶ TRANSPARENCY

The decision to use a border depends in part on the shape of the image itself. While every image is rectangular, remember that GIFs have a property called *transparency* that lets the background show through. This results in an image that doesn't look rectangular. Such images can, under some circumstances, benefit from the addition of a border.

▶ BORDER COLOR

The color of the border around an image is the same as the text color on your Web page. If your text is the default black, the border is black, too; if it's green, the border's green, and so on. If you change the text color in the Page Properties dialog box, the border color changes at the same time.

▶ MORE WAYS TO ADD SPACE

Both Microsoft Internet Explorer and Netscape Communicator will shove text and other elements right up against your image on the user's screen, and it's kind of awkward that adding vertical and horizontal space adds space on both sides of the image. Sometimes it's easier and more accurate to use an image editor such as Paint Shop Pro to add "space" to just one side of an image. Make the space pixels transparent and forget about adding space in Composer altogether.

CROSS-REFERENCE
See the section on choosing GIF or JPEG images earlier in this chapter.

FIND IT ONLINE
Drop in to the Free Graphics Store at **http://ausmall.com.au/freegraf/index.htm**.

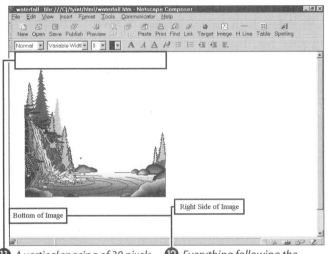

Bottom of Image

Right Side of Image

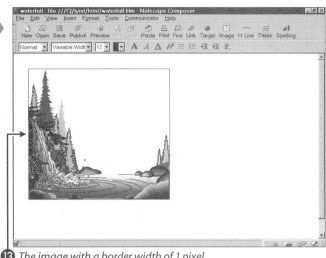

11 *A vertical spacing of 30 pixels moves the image down on the Web page.*

12 *Everything following the image is also affected by the vertical spacing.*

13 *The image with a border width of 1 pixel.*

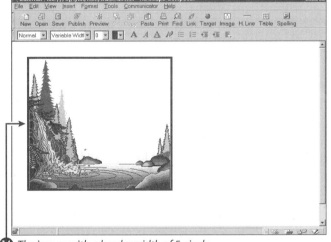

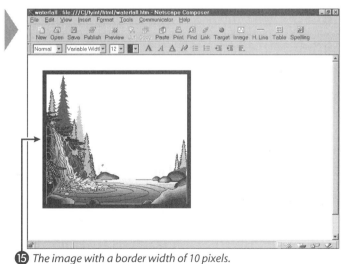

14 *The image with a border width of 5 pixels.*

15 *The image with a border width of 10 pixels.*

Using Alternate Text and Low-Resolution Images

Probably the first thing you ever noticed when you visited your first Web site was that images load more slowly than text. Even with a really fast modem, arriving at a graphics-intensive site can be an occasion to get up, stretch, and maybe even catch up on reading *War and Peace* or have a quick snack. To make the experience easier on your site's visitors, you can use one of two techniques.

The first way to make image-use more user-friendly is with *alternate text* (often called *alt* because that's the actual HTML attribute used in the source code). Its purpose is to provide a brief description of the graphics on your site. The alt text shows up in place of your image while the image is loading. This lets visitors decide if they care to wait for the image or to just go ahead and do other things such as clicking links or scrolling down the page. This much-appreciated tool helps protect your viewers from unknowingly clicking an image that will take way more time than they were willing to spend to download.

The other approach is to provide two versions of the image and let your viewer choose which they want to download. One would be the normal image, while the other is a lower-resolution version of it. The low-res image lacks the fine detail of the regular image and has fewer colors, but it loads faster. If visitors to your site are really interested in the intricate details of your image, they might decide it's worth the wait. Otherwise, it's nice to have the option to view the slightly lesser quality version that downloads more quickly.

Setting both of these options is easy to do. It's a matter of working your way through the options in the Image Properties popup menu, shown on the figure on the upper left of the facing page. You simply indicate the option you want.

TAKE NOTE

▶ ALT TEXT AND DISABLED ACCESS

The World Wide Web is primarily a visual experience, so it doesn't cross the minds of most people — even most Web designers — that sightless people also use the Web. The speech output screen readers they use depend heavily on alt text for nontextual Web page elements such as images. Without it, the visually impaired have no way to know what the image represents.

▶ INTERLACED GIFS

GIF images offer an alternative to the low-res approach. GIFs can be *interlaced* — that is, every third or fourth line of the image is displayed as it loads. The result is similar to the low-res method, in that a low-quality version of the image appears very rapidly, but with interlaced GIFs, only a single image is involved, and that image gradually reaches its full quality when all the lines that make up the image fill in.

CROSS-REFERENCE

See the section on GIFs earlier in this chapter.

FIND IT ONLINE

There's a lot of information on blind Web access at
http://www.visi.com/~dtanner/.

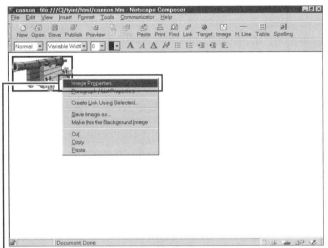

1 Right-click the image and select Image Properties from the popup menu.

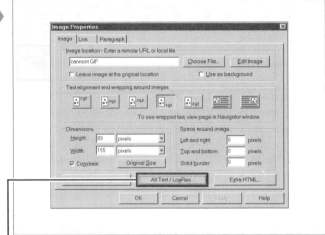

2 In the Image Properties dialog box, click the Alt Text/LowRes button.

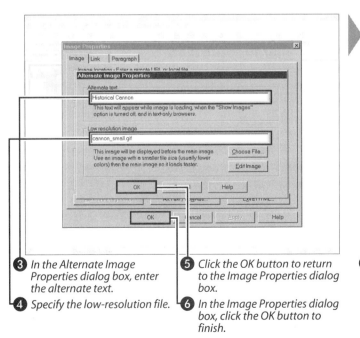

3 In the Alternate Image Properties dialog box, enter the alternate text.

4 Specify the low-resolution file.

5 Click the OK button to return to the Image Properties dialog box.

6 In the Image Properties dialog box, click the OK button to finish.

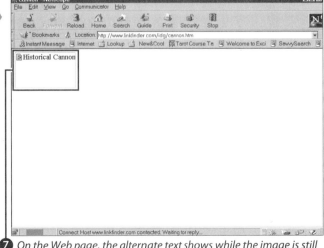

7 On the Web page, the alternate text shows while the image is still loading.

Adding Background Images

Background images can, like most Web design choices, either add to or detract from the appearance and utility of a Web site. On one hand, using a background can save your visitors from the monotony of the plain white background, adding more character and finesse to your page. On the other hand, it is very possible to go overboard. If you've ever visited a Web site with a background so bright, busy, and distracting that it made the text virtually impossible to read, you know the problem.

You have three different ways to add a background image. You can, as mentioned earlier in this chapter, specify while inserting an image that it will be the background image. The other methods will be covered in this section.

Because you don't know what screen resolution your Web visitors will be using, you need to give some advance consideration to the width of your background images. Many people use a screen resolution of 640 × 480 or 800 × 600; others use 1,024 × 768, and some use 1,280 × 1,024. Because you want your background images to come out evenly and you have to account for all the likely resolutions, you have to use some common denominator of the popular screen widths. The possible widths of good background images in pixels for all the resolutions except 800 × 600 would be: 2, 4, 8, 16, 32, 64, or — at the absolute largest — 128. In a practical sense, 2, 4, 8,

and probably 16 are too small to hold any meaningful picture information, and 128 allows only five repeats of the background image on a 640-pixel-wide screen. The best range to stick with would be 32 or 64 pixels for the width. If you factor in the 800 × 600 users, then you have to go with 32, as that's the highest common denominator for all four resolutions. The actual image size has to be 32 pixels wide, by the way — you can't alter the size the way you can with normal images.

Continued

Continued

TAKE NOTE

▶ SAVE THESE SETTINGS

If you do click the *Save these settings for new pages* checkbox option, all the settings in the Page Properties Colors and Background dialog box, not just the background image, will be the defaults for your new Web pages.

▶ IMAGE LOCATION

The location of the file you choose for your background image is first shown as a file URL. After you save the Web page, if you check the Page Properties, it simply lists the file name. Because it's saved in the same folder as your Web page, that's all that's needed to find it; it's called a *relative URL*, because its location is relative to your Web page.

CROSS-REFERENCE

See the section on inserting images earlier in this chapter.

FIND IT ONLINE

Find some great background graphics at **http://www. apocalypse.org/pub/u/batalion/backgrounds.shtml**.

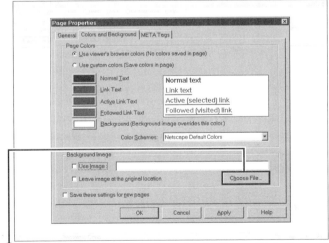

① *To make an existing image into the background image, right-click it, and then select Make this the Background Image from the popup menu.*

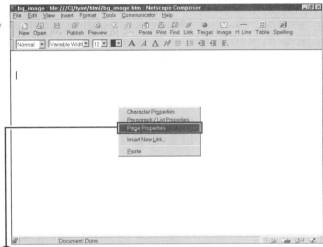

② *To select a background image, right-click anywhere on the page, and then select Page Properties from the popup menu.*

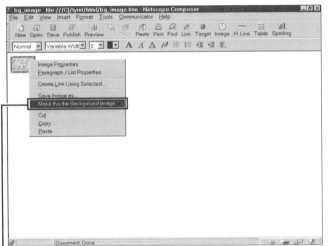

③ *In the Page Properties dialog box, click the Choose File button on the Colors and Background tab.*

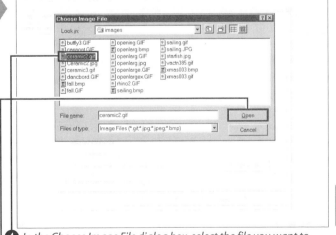

④ *In the Choose Image File dialog box, select the file you want to use.*

⑤ *Click the Open button.*

Adding Background Images
Continued

Back in the Page Properties dialog box, the file you have selected is now listed, as shown in the figure on the upper left. The Use Image checkbox has been auto-matically selected. If you want to use this image as the background on all your future pages, select the *Save these settings for new pages* checkbox. Click the OK button to set the background image. The figure on the upper right shows the background image in place.

Bear in mind that the background image is a small picture that is *tiled* (repeated) all across your Web page. While tiling is a cool capability, and also makes most backgrounds possible, the background image you want to tile should be chosen carefully. Not just any old image will work as a good Web page background. Sometimes you have to experiment a bit.

Another commonly used background is a vertical bar, usually seen running along the left side of the page. You can choose the color and border width, and even fancy it up a bit by adding a blended edge instead of the sharp vertical one. This simple background makes your site more visually interesting while not interrupting the text.

The figure on the lower left shows the effect of tiling an image that has high contrast between its own elements. It creates a tiled background against which it is not easy to read the overlying text, even when the color of that text has been carefully chosen (and the problem gets worse when the text is small). A low-contrast image, on the other hand, such as the one in the figure on the lower right, tiles nicely and

smoothly, creating a background that does not compete with the overlying elements.

TAKE NOTE

BACKGROUND COLOR AND BACKGROUND IMAGES

If you're going to use a background image that overrides the background color, should you bother with choosing a background color? The answer, surprisingly, is yes, especially if you're also using a light color for your text. The reason for this is that a Web page loads into a browser in stages — the text loads first, then the background color, and then the background image. If you have light text that shows up well against your background image, but doesn't show up well against a white background color (the default in most people's browsers), then your Web page will be unreadable for the first several seconds while it's displaying. Because of the loading sequence, if you had specified a dark background color, then your text would be readable during the interim before the background image is loaded.

RIGHT-CLICKING

Right-clicking is a common way to access popup menus to perform certain tasks. Be careful when you right-click that you're not clicking any page elements, such as images, but the page itself.

CHECK DIFFERENT BROWSERS

Always test the appearance of your background choice in different browsers, to make sure your text is still legible.

CROSS-REFERENCE
See Chapter 13 for details on how to set the background color.

FIND IT ONLINE
Try Texture Land for more backgrounds at
http://www.meat.com/textures/.

328

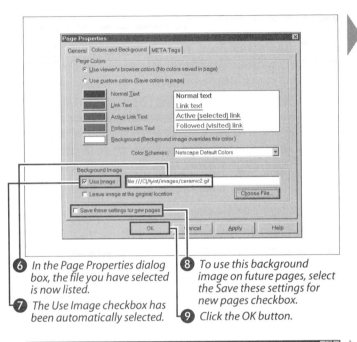

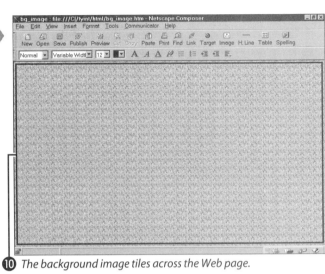

6 In the Page Properties dialog box, the file you have selected is now listed.

7 The Use Image checkbox has been automatically selected.

8 To use this background image on future pages, select the Save these settings for new pages checkbox.

9 Click the OK button.

10 The background image tiles across the Web page.

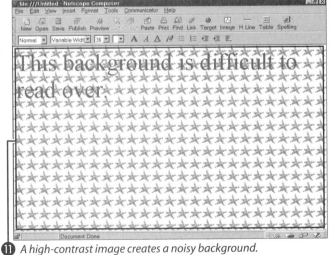

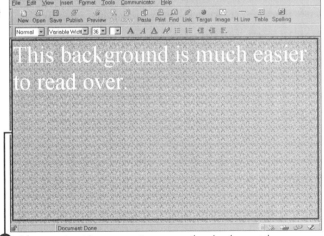

11 A high-contrast image creates a noisy background.

12 A low-contrast image creates a smoother background.

Personal Workbook

Q&A

1 What was the original meaning of *clip art*?

_____

_____

_____

2 What does *JPEG* stand for? Why is it sometimes called *JPG*?

_____

_____

_____

3 Does a JPEG file have the property of transparency?

_____

_____

4 What is a *Web ring*?

_____

_____

_____

5 What is a major difference between the GIF87 and GIF89 formats?

_____

_____

_____

6 What happens to the file size of an image when you resize the image in Composer?

_____

_____

_____

7 What is *alternate text*?

_____

_____

_____

8 What determines the color of a border in HTML?

_____

_____

_____

ANSWERS: PAGE 384

EXTRA PRACTICE

1. Visit several graphics Web sites. Browse through their offerings and download images you like.

2. Insert different types of images. Use some GIFs, some JPEGs, and paste from the Windows clipboard.

3. Resize an image so it's larger. See how large you can get it and still maintain its recognizability.

4. Use all three methods of inserting background images.

5. Try several different background images. Experiment with using different text colors on top of them.

6. Apply a border to several different images. See which ones look best with thin or thick borders.

REAL-WORLD APPLICATIONS

✔ You have an image you'd like to use, but it's in some unusual format. You could convert it to GIF or JPEG in a graphics program, or copy it to the Windows clipboard and paste it into Composer.

✔ You want to find just the right image for your Web page. Consider using one of the graphics search engines on the Web.

✔ You have an image that's not the right size. You could resize it in Composer or a graphics program.

✔ You're trying to speed download time of your Web pages as much as possible. You might try converting all your GIF images into JPEGs to see if they'll be smaller. If you need the transparency property of the GIFs, try the GIF Wizard or a good graphics program to reduce the number of its colors.

Visual Quiz

What is this button for? How is it different from the one to its right? How do you get to this dialog box?

_____

_____

_____

_____

_____

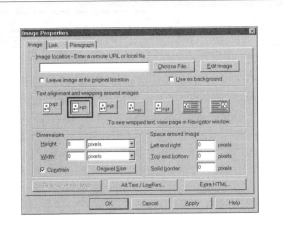

CHAPTER 15

Creating Links

You're already familiar with using Uniform Resource Locators, called *URLs* for short, to get from one Web page to another. They're the addresses of Web pages on the Internet. Hyperlinks, usually just called *links*, form the strands that hold the World Wide Web together. A link is nothing more than the address of a file on the Web that is put into a format that tells Web browsers to go to that address when a user clicks the link.

If you want to dig into the HTML code for it, links use the *A* (anchor) element, and that element has an attribute called *href* (hypertext reference). The href attribute contains the Web address of the page to which you're linking. In Composer, though, you don't need to worry about the details. Just click a button, fill in the address, and you're off and running.

Most links are text-based, but they can also originate in an image. Image links are distinguishable from normal images because they have a thin border around them that's the same color as the text links. As with normal links, users click an image link and their Web browser takes them to the linked page.

This chapter shows you different techniques for using both kinds of links, covers the differences between them, and shows you a few tricks that'll make your life as a Web designer a little bit easier. We also show how you can test your links in both Composer and Navigator, and how you can modify or remove links as necessary while you develop and change your Web page.

Next, we dive into using targets. While a link to a normal URL only takes you to the beginning of a Web page, targets are a special kind of URL called a *fragment URL*. You can use targets to jump straight from one Web page right into the middle of another one instead of coming in at the top all the time, or you can create a set of links at the top of your page called a hyperlink menu that lets visitors jump to just the part of your page they want to see.

Finally, we take a look at the Table of Contents plug-in, a handy tool that automatically builds a hyperlink menu for you based on the headings in your Web document.

Creating Text Links

Text links can be shortcuts to another place in your Web site or to another site on the Web. In either case, clicking on a link moves you to a specific location in another Web page. Links to other places on your site can save users from scrolling through pages and pages to find the information they want.

For example, to order a new product, you go to the home page of the company that makes it. But many times there's a lot of material on a home page. People visit the site for different reasons: to learn about the company itself, to place orders, to search for jobs, and so on. Links on the page leading to different areas, such as About Our Company, Online Catalog, or Join Our Staff, direct visitors where they want to go in one simple click.

Or, say you want to research Greek mythology. You visit one site, but want to find more. Often, sites on a specific topic include links to other sites on the same subject. So, rather than search for several sites individually, you can use one site's links to lead you to further information on the same topic.

Products such as Netscape Composer offer straightforward ways to place text links — the software actually gives you five separate methods from which to choose. Toolbars and popup menus and dialog boxes take you through all the steps; with one method, you just point your cursor where you want the link to go, and then click a button.

Continued

TAKE NOTE

▶ SPACES BEFORE AND AFTER

Composer puts a space before and after any link you create. This can be disruptive to your site design if everything else starts flush with the left margin. Fortunately, all you have to do is delete the offending spaces.

▶ RELATIVE AND ABSOLUTE URLS

If your link is going to some place on your own site, that's called a relative URL. Just enter the name of the file (instead of an entire URL) or use the Choose File button to locate and insert the file name. Web browsers automatically check the same directory on the server for the file called for in your relative URL. For example, if you have a home page at **http://www.myownsite.com/index.html**, and that page has a link to just the filename resume.html, the Web browser just chops off the name of the current file from the end of the URL it's starting from (**http://www.myownsite.com/**) and then adds resume.html to it to get the full address, **http://www.myownsite.com/resume.html**. If you're linking to a page on another site, though, you need to enter the full URL, called an absolute URL. No Web browser in the world, no matter how smart it is, can guess which Web site contains that file unless you tell the browser the location with the absolute URL. For instance, **http://whatever-site.com/whicheverpage.html** would be an absolute URL.

CROSS-REFERENCE

See Chapter 1 for more information on URLs.

FIND IT ONLINE

Find technical specifications on links at **http://www.w3.org/TR/REC-html40/struct/links.html**.

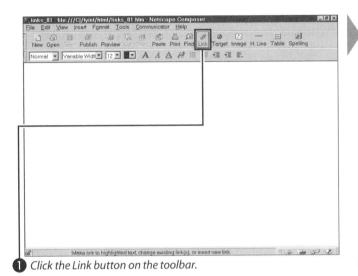

➊ Click the Link button on the toolbar.

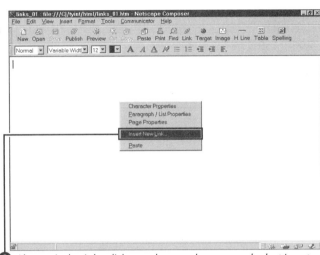

➋ Alternatively, right-click anywhere on the page and select Insert New Link from the popup menu.

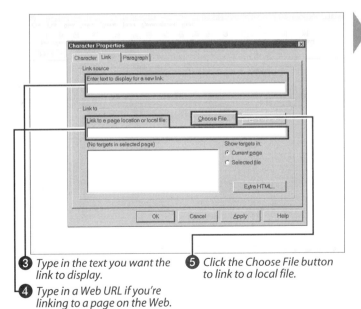

➌ Type in the text you want the link to display.

➍ Type in a Web URL if you're linking to a page on the Web.

➎ Click the Choose File button to link to a local file.

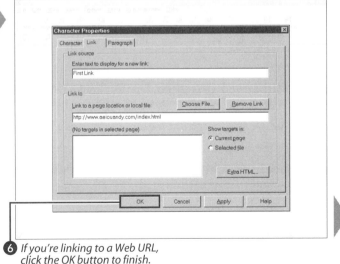

➏ If you're linking to a Web URL, click the OK button to finish.

Creating Text Links

Continued

It may not seem as though there's any point to linking to a local file instead of a Web URL. However, most people develop their Web sites on their local computer before publishing them to a remote Web server, and this approach lets them use relative URLs, making the site more portable. By *portable*, we mean that the entire Web site can be moved from one Web server to another by just copying the files to the new server. If you have your own domain name (like idg-books.com), then this isn't as important, because you'll move the domain name along with the files, but most of the pages on the Web are in someone's personal directory on an ISP's Web server, and the URL of your personal directory will change if you change ISPs. If that happens, and all your links are absolutely tied in to the old URL, you'll have to go in and manually change each and every one of them before your site will work at your new address on the new Web server. Composer lacks a search and replace function, so that's a lot of work. If you find yourself in this position, just load the file into Windows WordPad (or other text editor of your choice) and select Edit ⇨ Replace from its menu. Enter the base URL of the old server under Find what and the URL of the new one under Replace with. Next, click the Replace All button. When it's done converting the URLs, save the file as a text document.

TAKE NOTE

▶ IF YOUR REMOTE LINK STOPS WORKING

If your absolute URL suddenly doesn't work any-more — that is, if what was a Web page yesterday is an Error 404 message today — it doesn't necessarily mean that the whole Web site is gone. It may mean that the page's filename changed or the file was moved to a different directory. Delete everything after the last slash in the URL and try loading that. Usually, at least something will come up in your browser that can give you a clue where the page (or graphic) went, whether it's a different default HTML file for that directory or a plain list of files in a directory that has no default HTML file.

▶ BACKUP COPIES

There's also another tremendous advantage to this approach — if you make and test your Web site on your computer, and then upload the files to the Web, you have a backup copy of your site in case anything should go wrong with your Web server. Of course, whoever maintains the Web server where your pages reside should be making a backup of their own at least once a day, but you could still lose a full day's work in the event of a disaster if you rely on someone else to make your only backup.

CROSS-REFERENCE

See Chapter 11 for information on publishing your Web pages.

FIND IT ONLINE

Read about relative URLs at **http://www.w3.org/Addressing/URL/4_3_Partial.html**.

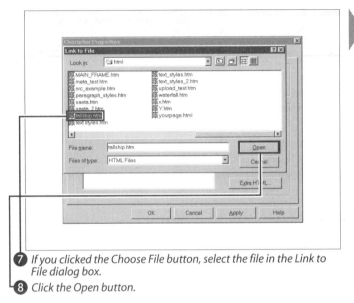

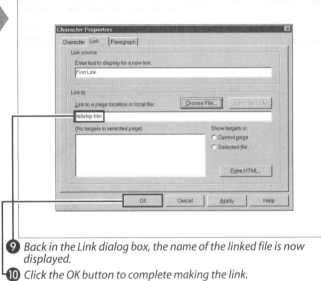

⑦ *If you clicked the Choose File button, select the file in the Link to File dialog box.*

⑧ *Click the Open button.*

⑨ *Back in the Link dialog box, the name of the linked file is now displayed.*

⑩ *Click the OK button to complete making the link.*

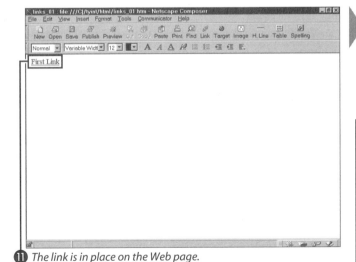

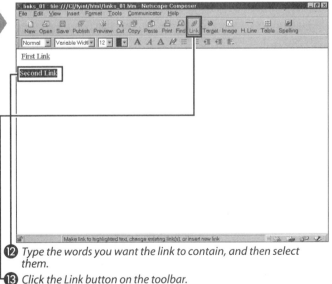

⑪ *The link is in place on the Web page.*

⑫ *Type the words you want the link to contain, and then select them.*

⑬ *Click the Link button on the toolbar.*

Alternative Methods

The third method for creating a text link is to first type the words you want the link to contain, as shown in the figure on the lower right, and then to select them and click the Link button in the toolbar.

The fourth method is very similar. You select the words, but instead of using the toolbar button, you right-click the highlighted text and select Create Link Using Selected from the popup menu.

Both of these approaches result in a Link dialog box. Because the text was entered and selected in these two methods, the Link source in the dialog box is already cast in stone. Other than that, the rest of the linking procedure — entering a URL or choosing a file — is the same as the first method.

The fifth way to put a text link into your Web page in Composer is to drag and drop a link from some other source. For example, say you have Composer open and you're viewing a Web page in Navigator. If you decide you want to grab a link from it to add to your own Web page, click the link and, instead of releasing the mouse button as usual, continue to hold it down. Drag the link down to the Composer button on the taskbar. Hold it there for a moment until Composer comes up, and then move the pointer to the place on your page where you want to drop the link before releasing the mouse button. The link drops right into your own Web page.

TAKE NOTE

▶ NO DRAG AND DROP FOR IMAGE LINKS

The drag-and-drop approach only works for text links. If you try to drag and drop an image link into Composer, the image comes along all right, but its link doesn't come with it. If you do want to add an image link, you can still drag and drop the image, but make a note of the URL of the file it links to and then follow the procedure for creating an image link that's detailed later in this chapter.

▶ RELATIVE URLS AND DRAG AND DROP

Dropping a link to an absolute URL into your Web page from someone else's site is certainly no problem, but what if the link is to a relative URL? The page the link goes to doesn't exist on your site, so a relative URL won't do any good. But there's good news: Relative URLs are automatically converted into absolute URLs during the drag-and-drop process.

▶ DON'T OVERDO IT

A Web site cluttered with too many text links can be more distracting than useful. Be conservative in the number of links you place on a given page. Create categories to reduce the number of links. For example, if you post a paper and want to cite your sources, include one link called Bibliography and put the sources there instead of providing a separate link for each source.

CROSS-REFERENCE

See the following section on modifying link text.

FIND IT ONLINE

The official standard for relative URLs is at
http://www.w3.org/Addressing/rfc1808.txt.

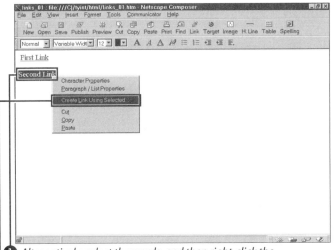

① *Alternatively, select the words, and then right-click the highlighted text.*

② *Select Create Link Using Selected from the popup menu.*

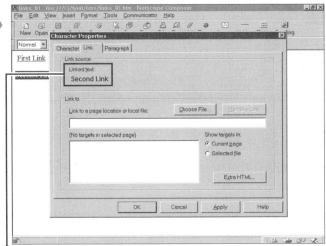

③ *The Link dialog box already has the Link source filled in.*

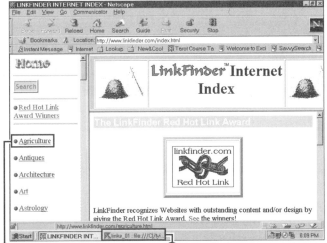

④ *To drag and drop a link from a Web page in Navigator, click the link and hold the mouse button down.*

⑤ *Drag the link down to the Composer button on the taskbar. Hold it there for a moment until Composer comes up.*

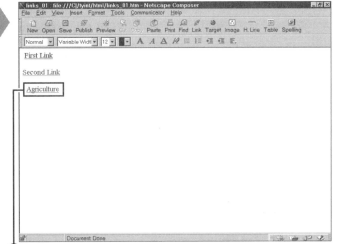

⑥ *Move the pointer to the place on your page where you want to drop the link, and then release the mouse button.*

Modifying Text Links

Although you can easily change the file that a text link points to, Composer doesn't have any facility for modifying the text itself. You can see the problem in action if you check the link.

You could copy the URL in the *Link to* panel, delete the link, and remake it, pasting the URL back in. Fortunately, you can get around the limitation more easily, but you have to be a little bit careful to pull it off. Just select the text, as shown in the figure on the lower left. Note that the first character in the text is not selected. This is very important, because you cannot replace the entire link text at once — if you select the whole thing, and then start typing, the link gets deleted automatically along with the text you're replacing. Go ahead and type in your replacement text, and just delete the first character and your link text will be changed to the way you want it without affecting the link itself.

Of course, you can use the same technique to change part of the link text instead of replacing all of it. If you want to replace some text in the middle, for instance, just select the part you want to change and type over it. If you want to insert some text in the link, just do it normally. The only place you can't add text is at the very beginning; text typed at the beginning of a text link is just plain text, and won't be a part of the link itself.

CROSS-REFERENCE

See the section on removing links later in this chapter.

FIND IT ONLINE

Find a tip on selecting text at **http://www.chami.com/ tips/internet/112096i.html**.

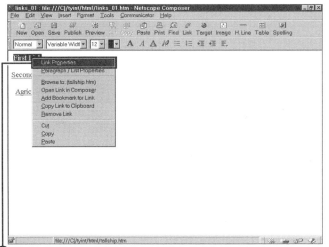

1 Right-click a text link, and then select Link Properties from the popup menu.

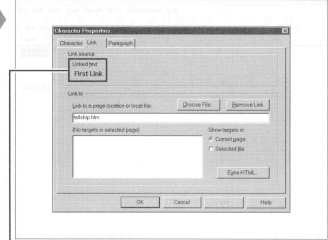

2 The Link source is already filled in and cannot be modified.

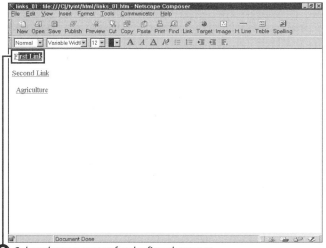

3 Select the text except for the first character.

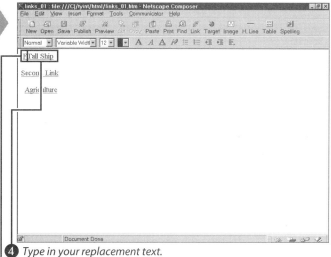

4 Type in your replacement text.
5 Delete the first character.

341

Creating Image Links

A picture is worth a thousand words, and this is also true on the Internet. Even the most informative and detailed Web page can seem uninviting and even uninteresting without graphics. One simple and functional way to incorporate graphics into your Web page is to create image links.

Image links work just like text links on a Web page, but they're graphical instead of textual. For example, say you have a Web site that's all about pets. Your site contains several pages, each covering a different animal. You could show a list of text links: Dog, Cat, Snake; or you can show a picture of each to serve as the link instead. Or, say you want to include a link to your company or organization. A logo can be a far more eye-catching link than simple text.

You can get images to use as graphic links from many different sources: you can take them from clip-art galleries on the Web, you can scan an image, or you can draw your own with any drawing program.

While you have five different ways to make text links, you can create image links in only two ways. Both processes are essentially identical to adding a text link, except that you don't need to add any text. Just choose an image you want to use and then follow the steps to set up the link.

The name of the selected image is already filled in just as selected text would be (see the figure on the lower left). The remainder of the process for choosing which file to link to is identical with that for text links.

CROSS-REFERENCE

See Chapter 11 for information on using the Preview button.

FIND IT ONLINE

Read about anchors and image links at **http:// ise.ee.uts.edu.au/ise/hyptech/Essay97s/sun.htm**.

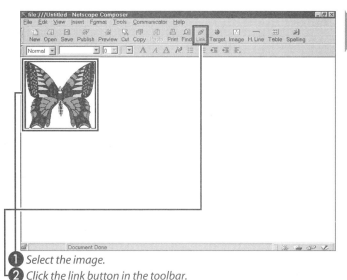

1 *Select the image.*
2 *Click the link button in the toolbar.*

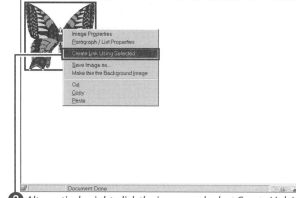

3 *Alternatively, right-click the image and select Create Link Using Selected from the popup menu.*

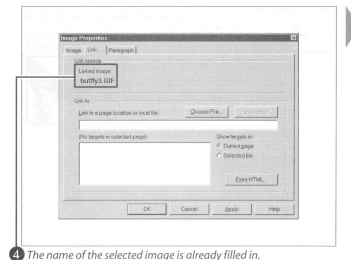

4 *The name of the selected image is already filled in.*

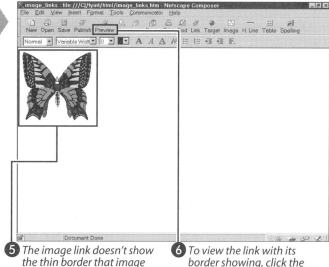

5 *The image link doesn't show the thin border that image links show on the Web.*

6 *To view the link with its border showing, click the Preview button in the toolbar and view it in Navigator.*

Testing and Removing Links

I t's a good idea to test your links before you post your page to make sure they are functioning. But you also need to keep testing them once your site is live. Some links stop working after a while, and in those cases you will want to remove them.

You have two options for testing links. The first option is Browse to, which opens the linked file in Navigator (if Navigator isn't already active, it'll be launched automatically). The second option, Open Link in Composer, is self-explanatory. This option isn't terribly useful for testing links, though, because it opens the linked page for editing instead of just confirming that it's there.

When you delete the link, you do not delete the text; it is left intact, but any associated link is removed.

Interestingly, if you right-click an image link, you don't have the same options in the popup menu. However, a workaround solution to this problem does exist. Simply add some text next to the image (or just use some that's already there), and then select the image link and the adjoining text. Next, right-click the selection. The popup menu now shows both link testing options and has a *Remove all links in selection* option. This option differs from the Remove Link option only in that it's intended to show up if more than one link is selected. Apparently, Composer assumes that if you've selected both an image and text with a link somewhere in them, then there's more than one link involved. Be that as it may, the technique still works, so feel free to use it.

CROSS-REFERENCE

See the section on modifying text links earlier in this chapter.

FIND IT ONLINE

Find a great page on links at **http://www.en.polyu. edu.hk/~enhoyung/yung/Links.html**.

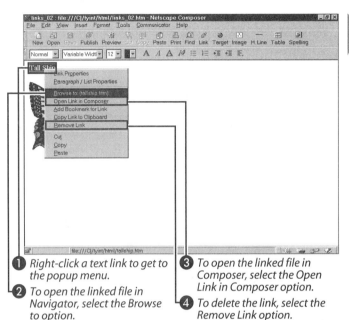

① *Right-click a text link to get to the popup menu.*

② *To open the linked file in Navigator, select the Browse to option.*

③ *To open the linked file in Composer, select the Open Link in Composer option.*

④ *To delete the link, select the Remove Link option.*

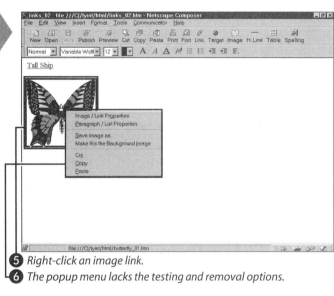

⑤ *Right-click an image link.*

⑥ *The popup menu lacks the testing and removal options.*

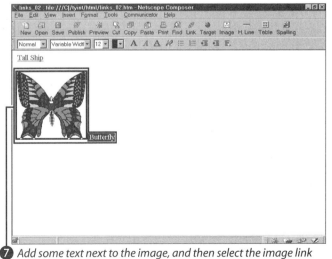

⑦ *Add some text next to the image, and then select the image link and the adjoining text.*

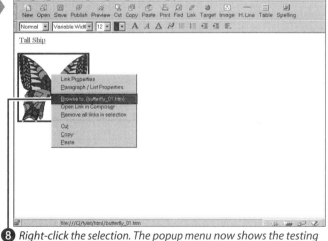

⑧ *Right-click the selection. The popup menu now shows the testing and removal options.*

Creating Targets

What Composer calls *targets* are generally referred to as *named anchors* in HTML. The reason for this, if you want to take a look at the HTML source code, is that targets use the A (anchor) element, just like links do, but targets don't need to have a link associated with them. They're simply an A element with a *name* attribute attached; hence the term *named anchors*. However, *target* is as good a term as any to describe the function of these elements.

Targets are destinations for links within Web pages. Say you have four main headings in a long Web page. You can set a target at each heading and provide four links at the top of the page, each link leading to one of the targets at the main headings. This way, readers can move quickly from the top of the page to whichever sections most interest them, without having to scroll through the whole thing to find what they want. Targets speed up the browsing of Web pages and make it easier to get around. They make Web pages friendlier and more usable.

Composer enables you to set targets easily via the Target button on the toolbar. The anchor, which isn't visible on a Web page but has a presence anyway, is shown in Composer by a target icon, as you can see in the figure on the lower left. Remember: The anchor is the A element you use in HTML to set targets.

TAKE NOTE

► CHANGING THE NAME OF TARGETS

If you want to change the name of the target, Composer enables you to right-click the target icon and select Target Properties from the popup menu, as shown in the figure on the lower right. For efficiency's sake and to keep the HTML clean, target names should be as short as possible while still remaining functional.

► ANCHOR ELEMENTS AND TARGETS

If you put a target before a link, and then look at the HTML source code, you'll see that you've got two A elements right next to each other. In HTML, you can put a target inside a link — all you have to do is add a *name* attribute to the A element in addition to the *href* attribute — but if you try to put a target inside a link in Composer, you'll run into a little problem. Because Composer treats the target as a separate element, you'll have one A element inside another — and nested A elements are intolerable in HTML. Both of the A elements have an <A> start tag that tells Web browsers where they start and both have a </A> end tag on them that tells Web browsers where they end. Because the target's end tag is in the middle of the link's A element, it confuses a Web browser into thinking the link ends there.

CROSS-REFERENCE

See the following section on linking to targets.

FIND IT ONLINE

Read about anchor elements and targets at **http://www.wdvl.com/Authoring/HTML/Body/anchor.html**.

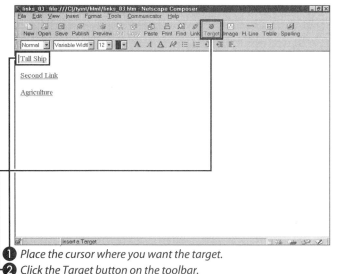

1 *Place the cursor where you want the target.*
2 *Click the Target button on the toolbar.*

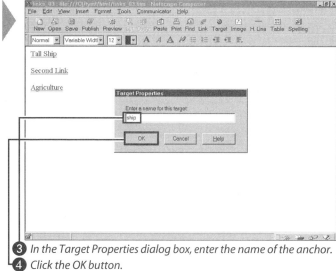

3 *In the Target Properties dialog box, enter the name of the anchor.*
4 *Click the OK button.*

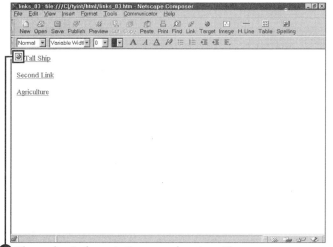

5 *The anchor is shown in Composer by a target icon.*

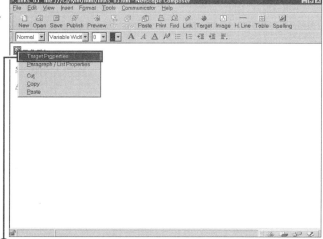

6 *To change the target's name, right-click the target icon and select Target Properties from the popup menu.*

Linking to Targets

Targets are of little use without their corresponding links. When viewing a Web page, you never notice targets themselves because they are simply names for sections hidden in the HTML. Targets exist only as landing pads for links. Composer makes it easy to link to the targets you create. Linking to a target involves following the normal procedure for creating a link, except that you pay a little bit of extra attention to the Link Properties dialog box. The figure on the upper left shows a Web page in Composer that contains several targets, which makes it easy to simply select the one you want the link to point to.

You can also select targets from another file. If you select some other file, then the Selected file radio button is automatically selected, and the targets that are listed are the ones found in that file instead of the one you're starting from. If you select one of the targets in that listing, the target name is appended to the URL of the selected file, again preceded by a hash mark.

You can identify a target because it always begins with a hash mark (#), also known as the pound sign. The part from the hash mark on is known as a *fragment URL*, and it tells a Web browser to find that referenced Web page and then look for the target with the name following the hash mark. When the target's on a local page, the same thing happens except that the page doesn't have to be found first.

CROSS-REFERENCE

See the preceding section on creating targets.

FIND IT ONLINE

Read the semi-official fragment URL description at **http:// www.w3.org/Addressing/URL/4_2_Fragments.html**.

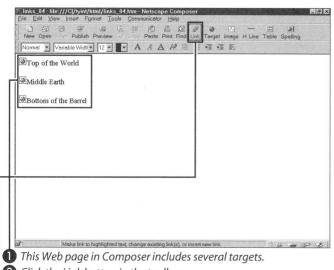

1. *This Web page in Composer includes several targets.*
2. *Click the Link button in the toolbar.*

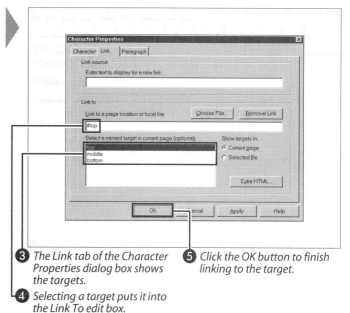

3. *The Link tab of the Character Properties dialog box shows the targets.*
4. *Selecting a target puts it into the Link To edit box.*
5. *Click the OK button to finish linking to the target.*

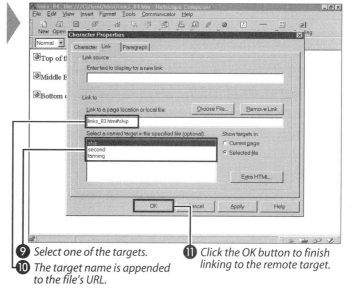

6. *Alternatively, choose another file.*
7. *The Selected file radio button is selected automatically.*
8. *The targets listed are the ones found in that file instead of the one you're starting from.*
9. *Select one of the targets.*
10. *The target name is appended to the file's URL.*
11. *Click the OK button to finish linking to the remote target.*

Using the Table of Contents Plug-In

Hyperlink menus are a common feature of many Web pages. While most links are buried somewhere in the main text of a page, menus provide a collection of links in one place. Usually, menus appear at the top of a page and provide a jumping-off place to the page's different parts, although they can also be links to other pages entirely. Although menus of links are very useful, they can be extremely tedious to construct. Putting in the first link, then the second, then the third, and so on, is dull, repetitive work.

The Table of Contents plug-in is a clever solution that can help you create your own hyperlink menu without going to all the trouble of handling each link individually. It only builds such a menu for the one Web page you're using it on, though — it can't add anything from other Web pages. The reason for this is the way it works. It searches through your Web page looking for Heading elements (H1, H2, H3, and so forth), as shown in the figure on the upper left. If you want to add any other kind of element to the hyperlink menu, you have to do so manually.

Be sure to leave some space in your design for the Table of Contents near the top of your page. Also, note that because the Table of Contents plug-in searches only for heading elements, that means you must use heading elements in your Web page. If, for example, you have been using images of text in fancy typefaces for heading, such as the *New York Times*

Web site does, the Table of Contents plug-in won't find those headings.

Wherever the plug-in finds a heading, it puts in a target, and then builds a set of links to all targets, putting the links wherever the cursor is at the time you generate the table of contents. The table of contents it builds takes nice advantage of the heading hierarchy and indents each lower heading level so that the Web page structure appears correctly in the contents (see the figure on the lower right).

CROSS-REFERENCE

See Chapter 12 for more information on Composer plug-ins.

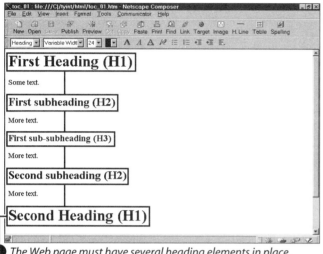

❶ The Web page must have several heading elements in place.

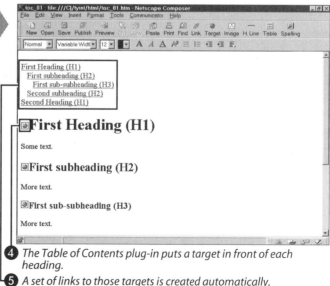

❷ Make a space above the headings you're going to index. Leave the cursor there.

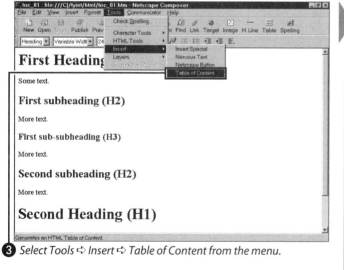

❸ Select Tools ➪ Insert ➪ Table of Content from the menu.

❹ The Table of Contents plug-in puts a target in front of each heading.

❺ A set of links to those targets is created automatically.

Personal Workbook

Q&A

1 What is the difference between a *relative URL* and an *absolute URL*?

_____

_____

_____

_____

2 What does the *href* attribute do?

_____

_____

_____

3 What kind of links does drag and drop work for?

_____

4 What methods does Composer provide for modifying the words in text links?

_____

_____

_____

5 What are the three methods for removing links?

_____

_____

_____

_____

_____

_____

6 What is a *fragment URL*?

_____

_____

_____

7 What HTML element do links and targets both use?

_____

8 How does the Table of Contents plug-in set up a link menu?

_____

_____

_____

ANSWERS: PAGE 385

EXTRA PRACTICE

1. Use the Table of Contents plug-in to make a hyperlink menu for your Web page.

2. Create a hyperlink menu to both local targets and Web URLs.

3. Use two images to create links to different Web pages.

4. Alter the text in a text link.

5. Test a link in both Navigator and Composer.

6. Create a target in one of your Web pages.

REAL-WORLD APPLICATIONS

✔ You want to link to several different Web pages. You might think about whether text links or image links would better represent the remote links.

✔ You're surfing the Web when you find a page with several links you'd like to add to your own Web page. Maybe drag and drop would be the best method for adding them.

✔ You've put in several image links. You might want to preview your page in Navigator to see whether they work as expected.

✔ You've designed a page with several different levels of headings. The Table of Contents plug-in may be your solution for a hyperlink menu.

Visual Quiz

What is this dialog box? How do you get to it? Why is the link text already filled in? What is special about the Remove Link button?

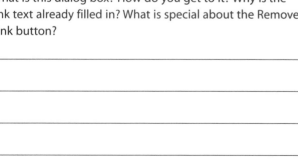

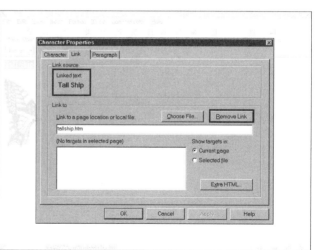

CHAPTER **16**

MASTER
THESE
SKILLS

▶ **Using the Insert Table Button**

▶ **Inserting and Deleting Rows, Columns, and Cells**

▶ **Setting Cell Width**

▶ **Setting Cell Span**

▶ **Using Text in Tables**

▶ **Adding Background Color and Images**

▶ **Creating Lists**

Organizing with Tables and Lists

Tables, at their simplest, can present data on your Web pages in neat rows and columns. Savvy Web designers, though, have realized that tables can also structure the entire look of a Web page.

Tables are HTML elements that contain *rows*, and rows contain *cells*. The cells are what contain the viewable data on your Web page. Each cell in a table is essentially a miniature Web page within your Web page. Like the overall page, cells can hold text, images, links, lists, horizontal rules — even other tables.

This chapter shows you how to put tables into your Web pages, how to modify, add, and remove the various elements that make up tables, and how to use the tools Composer provides for tables.

Tables can have their own background colors and background images, just like Web pages. In fact, every row and cell within the table can have its own separate background color or image. Because the size of tables and cells can be changed at will, and you can alter the position of cells within the table or the alignment of anything within them, the possibilities for using tables in Web-page design are virtually endless.

We show you how to use the different features of tables and cells, and suggest different ways you can take advantage of both their features and their quirks to help you create great Web pages.

Text within table cells can be modified to your heart's content, not only on the character level in ways such as changing the color, size, or style, but on the paragraph level as well, thus letting you use tables in concert with heading styles. The Tableize plug-in tool makes this task about as easy as it gets.

In the last part of this chapter, we show you how lists, like basic tables, are used most often for presenting simple information in a coherent format. During the history of HTML, various list formats have come and gone, but we cover three useful ones here: bulleted lists, numbered lists, and description lists.

Lists can also contain many things other than text, including images and hypertext links. So, just as with tables, the use of lists in Web page design is not limited to the simple presentation of text. As with so many things about the Web, the only real limit is tradition — or imagination. Feel free to be creative.

Using the Insert Table Button

Before you can do anything with a table, you've got to put it in the Web page first. If other page elements are already in place, you need to put the cursor where you want the table to end up before you start. If you don't have anything else on the page yet, just click the Table button on the toolbar, as shown in the figure on the upper left. Composer displays a dialog box that already has some default values filled in for a new table, such as alignment, border line width, and table width and height. You can simply click the OK button if you want to accept these values and modify the basic table later on. In this task, we change a few of the more important settings. We deal with the others settings in later tasks.

You can set the number of rows and columns you want to have in the table, as shown in the figure on the lower left. Remember: You can always add more rows and columns to your table later on if you need to. Or you can delete some later if you add too many at this stage. If you want a caption, click the Include caption checkbox. Change the Table width setting if desired; the default setting is 100 percent of the window width. Click the OK button to finish.

The figure on the lower right shows the finished table with a blank caption above it. You can fill in the caption whenever you want.

TAKE NOTE

TWO DIALOG BOXES

The New Table Properties dialog box is nearly identical to the Table Properties dialog box used for modifying tables after they're inserted. The only difference between them, as far as the table segment is concerned, is the ability to set the number of rows and columns. The Table Properties dialog box also lets you control the features of individual rows and cells.

CAPTIONS

The caption can be placed above or below the table by clicking the appropriate radio button next to the Include caption checkbox (see the figure on the lower left). The text in captions is automatically centered with reference to the table, and this alignment can't be changed.

HOW IT WORKS

If you dig into the HTML source code, you'll find the table between the <TABLE> and </TABLE> tags. The caption is contained between <CAPTION> and </CAPTION> tags. Each row is defined by <TR> and </TR> tags, and the cells are between the <TD> and </TD> tags. The TR element stands for Table Row and the TD element is short for Table Data.

PLAN IT OUT

Before you start with a table, it's a good idea to review what you want to put in it and figure out how many rows and columns you'll need.

CROSS-REFERENCE

See the following section on inserting rows, columns, and cells.

FIND IT ONLINE

Read official table specifications at **http://www.w3.org/TR/REC-html40/struct/tables.html.**

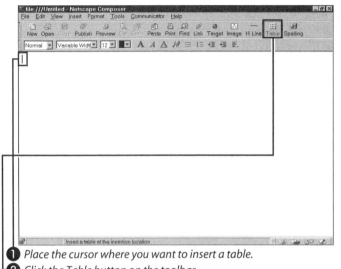

1 Place the cursor where you want to insert a table.

2 Click the Table button on the toolbar.

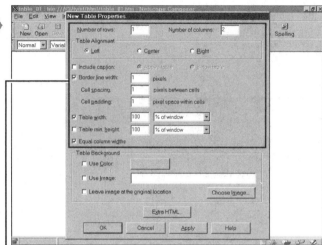

3 The New Table Properties dialog box shows the default table settings.

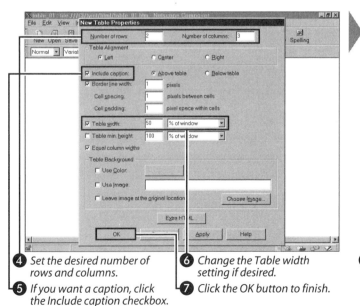

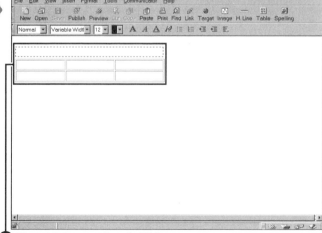

4 Set the desired number of rows and columns.

5 If you want a caption, click the Include caption checkbox.

6 Change the Table width setting if desired.

7 Click the OK button to finish.

8 The table is created on the Web page.

357

Inserting and Deleting Rows, Columns, and Cells

Composer makes it easy to modify the structure of your tables. In fact, the ease with which HTML editing programs like Composer enable you to work with tables is one of their greatest values in Web-page creation. In Composer, you can add or delete whole rows and columns or individual cells. To add a row, you place the cursor in the row before the one you want to add and then right-click it and select Insert ⇨ Row from the popup menu. You add new columns in exactly the same manner, except that you place the cursor in the column to the left of where you want to add one and then select Insert ⇨ Column instead.

Although new rows and columns maintain the symmetry of the table, new cells don't. Adding a single cell makes the table a bit uneven, so be sure you have a reason for adding only one cell. To add a cell, place the cursor in the cell to the left of where you want the new cell to go. Follow the same procedure that you do for inserting new rows or columns, except select Insert ⇨ Cell from the popup menu. The new cell is automatically added to the row, making the row longer than the other rows. We now have a table with two rows of four cells each and a third row with five cells.

Deletions of rows, columns, and cells are handled similarly. The cursor must be placed in the row, column, or cell to be deleted. You select Delete instead of Insert from the popup menu; the submenu is identical to the one used for insertions. Deleting cells can affect the symmetry of the row they're in in the same way adding them does.

TAKE NOTE

▶ TABLES, TOO

You can insert an entire table into a cell, though you'd rarely have a reason to do this. You can, of course, also delete entire tables just as you can delete the elements the table contains. By the way, be very careful when deleting rows, columns, or cells. If you accidentally click the Table option in the Delete submenu, you can wipe out your work. There's no warning, no dialog box asking if you're sure you want to delete the entire table — it's just plain gone right away. If you do delete a table by accident, you need to immediately select Edit ⇨ Undo from the main menu (or use the Ctrl+Z key combination). It's very important to take this action right away before doing anything else, because you can only undo the most recent action. Never develop an entire table without saving the page it's on at least once at some point early on. This way, if you do lose the table, you can reload the page and salvage at least some of your work.

CROSS-REFERENCE
See the preceding section on inserting tables.

FIND IT ONLINE
Check out the Table Tutor at **http://junior.apk.net/~jbarta/tutor/tables/index.html**.

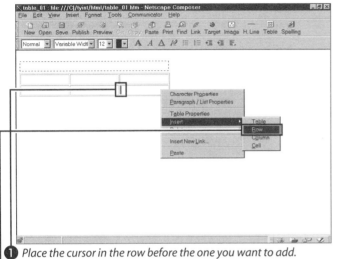

1 Place the cursor in the row before the one you want to add.

2 Right-click the cell where the cursor is and select Insert ➪ Row from the popup menu.

3 The new row is added to the table.

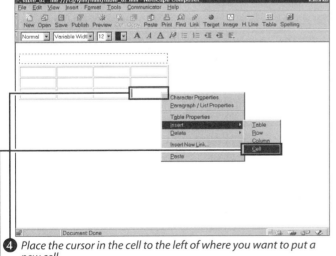

4 Place the cursor in the cell to the left of where you want to put a new cell.

5 Right-click the cell where the cursor is and select Insert ➪ Cell from the popup menu.

6 The new cell is added to the row.

Setting Cell Width

By default, if you select Equal column widths in the Table tab (see the figure on the upper right), all cells in a table are the same width. For example, in a row with two cells, each cell is 50 percent of the table width. If a row has four cells, they're each 25 percent of the table width, and so on. But beware: This default makes things difficult when you want to change the width of individual cells, so we advise you to change the default in this task. Whatever you do, don't try to change the width of individual cells with Equal column widths selected. If you leave the column widths set to equal and then try to adjust individual cells, you'll get some strange results — the cell widths will change, but not to the settings you choose.

When you want to change the width of individual cells, make sure the Cell width checkbox is checked in the Cell tab, as shown in the figure on the lower left. Enter the percentage of the table width you want the cell to be (say 10 percent). The figure on the lower right shows the resized cell. The other two cells also resize automatically to take up the slack created by making the first cell smaller. All three cells were 33.3 percent of the table width to start with (because of the default setting that we asked you to change), but the width of the first one is now 10 percent, and the widths of the second and third are 45 percent each.

TAKE NOTE

► PERCENTAGES AND PIXELS

Like the horizontal rule, widths in tables can be either percentages or precise pixel widths, and they have the same liabilities and restrictions. Setting width in pixels gives you precise control over the exact size of the table or cell, but can cause problems when the table is viewed by visitors using different video resolutions. If you design a table that's 800 pixels wide, people with resolutions of 800 × 600 or higher have no problem, but those with a resolution of 640 × 480 have to scroll the page horizontally to see the rest of the table. In general, tables are easier to deal with in percentages than in pixels.

► ONE HUNDRED PERCENT

If you manually set the width of all the cells in a row using percentages, and the total of those widths doesn't equal 100 percent, then the automatic resizing feature won't work. In fact, none of your cells will be the right size. For instance, if you set the first cell to 10 percent of the table width, the second to 10 percent, and the third to 80 percent, there's no problem, because the total equals 100 percent. If, on the other hand, you set them to 10 percent, 5 percent, and 28 percent, you'd have a row with erratically sized cells, none of them looking the way you wanted them.

CROSS-REFERENCE

See Chapter 13 for more information on horizontal rules.

FIND IT ONLINE

Check out the Crashcourse in Tables at http://www.webhelp.org/tables/.

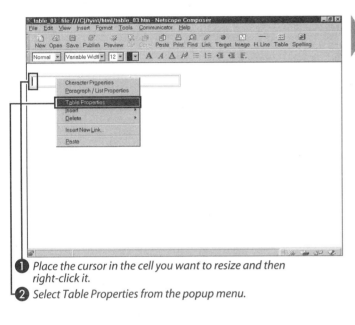

1 *Place the cursor in the cell you want to resize and then right-click it.*

2 *Select Table Properties from the popup menu.*

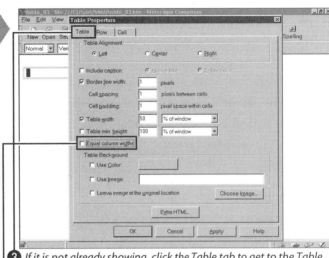

3 *If it is not already showing, click the Table tab to get to the Table dialog box.*

4 *Click the Equal column widths checkbox to deselect it.*

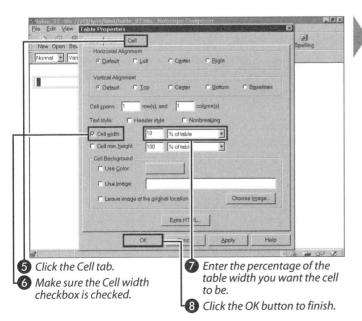

5 *Click the Cell tab.*

6 *Make sure the Cell width checkbox is checked.*

7 *Enter the percentage of the table width you want the cell to be.*

8 *Click the OK button to finish.*

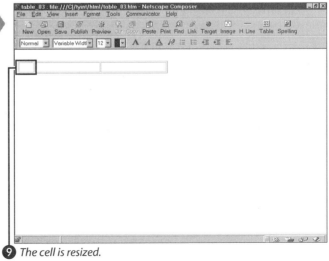

9 *The cell is resized.*

Setting Cell Span

Standard cell dimensions have a couple of other variations besides width and height. As part of the default symmetry of tables, each cell normally occupies one column across and one row high. A single cell, though, can span more than one column or more than one row. To make a cell span across rows or columns, you have to make sure the cursor is in the cell you want to span, and then change the standard settings in the Table Properties dialog box (see the figure on the upper right).

The figure on the bottom left shows a table three rows by three columns, where the first cell has been set to span two columns. The third cell, although there is no room left for it, doesn't disappear, but is shoved off to the side and vastly reduced in size, and the table expands just a bit to accommodate it.

The figure on the bottom right shows the same table with the first cell expanded to span two rows as well as two columns. All three cells on the second row have been shoved aside to make room for it.

A good use for the span feature is table headings. Another popular use for a cell that spans rows or columns is to hold an image. The image can be part of a table yet still be as wide or tall as the table itself if you make the image span all the rows or columns.

TAKE NOTE

▶ INVISIBLE CELLS

Cells that have no content do not display in a Web browser, so you don't really have to worry about the cells that are shoved off to the side. Just don't put anything in them and they'll stay invisible except in Composer. You can deliberately leave out content in some cells as a part of your design. Viewers of your Web page will never know the cells are there at all.

▶ MIXING CELL WIDTH AND CELL SPAN

It's generally a good idea to use either cell width or cell span, because you can get some strange effects if you set both values. For instance, if you have a cell width set to 10 percent and then set a two-column cell span for it, it won't enlarge to be the size of the two cells underneath it. Instead, they will each shrink to 5 percent so they'll both fit under the top one. Something similar happens when you insert new rows. Normally, when you insert a new row, it has the exact same settings as the first row. If the new row is inserted under one with cell span, though, it also changes to accommodate the fixed-width cell with cell span. The results can be chaotic, so it doesn't make sense from a Web-design standpoint to mix these options.

CROSS-REFERENCE
See the preceding section on setting cell width.

FIND IT ONLINE
To see a clever use of tables, see **http://www.shef. ac. uk/uni/academic/A-C/chem/web-elements/ web-elements-home.html.**

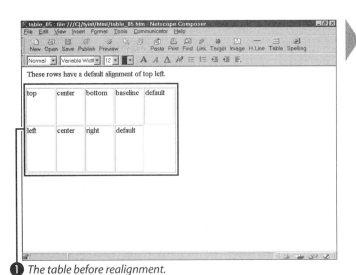

❶ The table before realignment.

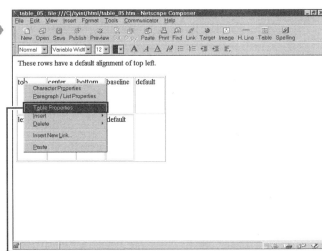

❷ Right-click within the first cell and select Table Properties from the popup menu.

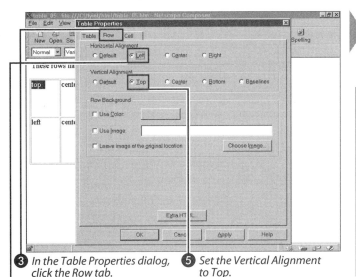

❸ In the Table Properties dialog, click the Row tab.

❹ Set the Horizontal Alignment to Left.

❺ Set the Vertical Alignment to Top.

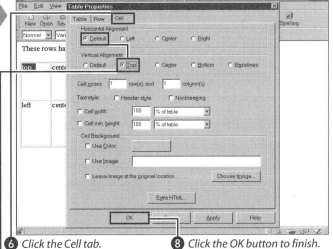

❻ Click the Cell tab.

❼ Set the Horizontal Alignment to Default and the Vertical Alignment to Top.

❽ Click the OK button to finish. Reset the Vertical Alignment in each cell, and then reset the Horizontal Alignment in the cells in the second row.

363

Using Text in Tables

You can format text in tables the same way you do text on a plain Web page: change its color, italicize it — whatever you want to do. Tables, though, have some special text-handling options of their own. One of these options is the capacity to align text not just horizontally, but vertically as well. The figure on the upper left shows a table before any alignment is assigned to the text in its cells. Each cell has a term in it that corresponds to the settings in the Table Properties dialog box. In this task, we're going to change the alignment in each of these cells to illustrate the effect of those settings.

You can set the Horizontal Alignment of text in cells to be Left, Center, Right, or Default. Vertical Alignment can be set for Top, Center, Bottom, Baseline, or Default. You can set Horizontal Alignment for a cell or for a complete row. To align a row, click the Row tab (see the figure on the lower left) and set the Horizontal Alignment to Left and the Vertical Alignment to Top. This sets the default alignment for the row, and all the cells in that row will inherit this alignment unless you specify differently in each individual cell's settings.

On the Cell tab you can also set the Horizontal Alignment to Default and the Vertical Alignment to Top. In this task, you can repeat the procedure for each cell in the first row, setting the Vertical Alignment to match the term (the test in the cell) —

that is, you would choose Center for the cell with "center" in it, and so forth.

Text alignment plays a big part in the attractiveness of your page's design. You can achieve interesting looks by playing with the alignment of the text in the cells of your table. All Left and Top alignment can become boring quickly.

Continued

TAKE NOTE

▶ RIGHT ON THE WORDS

When you select a cell that is only partially filled with text, it's necessary to click the text, not in the white space, or the cell won't be selected.

▶ NO DEFAULT FOR TABLES

Despite the fact that the Row dialog box shows a Default setting for alignment, this is not based on the table's alignment the way the cell's default alignment is based on the row's alignment.

▶ TABLE HEIGHT

To make room to show the effects of vertical alignment in this task, we changed the minimum height of the table (Table min. height) to 50 percent of the window size in the Table tab of the Table Properties dialog box. You can also adjust the minimum height of a cell (in relation to the containing table, not the window) with the Cell min. height option on the Cell tab. You have no way to set the maximum height, however.

CROSS-REFERENCE

See Chapter 13 for more information on text alignment.

FIND IT ONLINE

There's another good table tutor at
http://www.quadzilla.com/tables/tabletutor.htm.

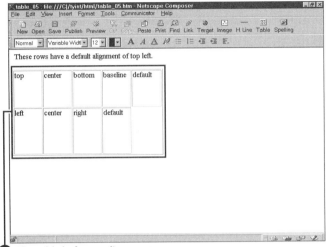

① The table before realignment.

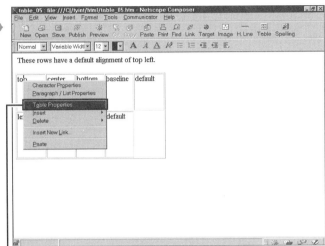

② Right-click within the first cell and select Table Properties from the popup menu.

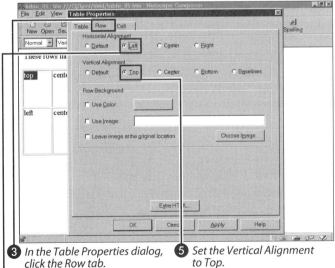

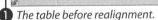

③ In the Table Properties dialog, click the Row tab.

④ Set the Horizontal Alignment to Left.

⑤ Set the Vertical Alignment to Top.

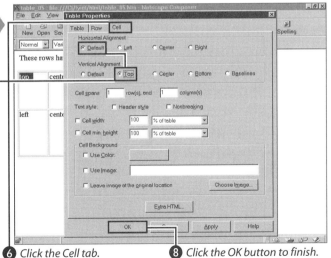

⑥ Click the Cell tab.

⑦ Set the Horizontal Alignment to Default and the Vertical Alignment to Top.

⑧ Click the OK button to finish. Reset the Vertical Alignment in each cell, and then reset the Horizontal Alignment in the cells in the second row.

Using Text in Tables

Continued

When you're done, your table will look like the one shown in the figure on the upper left, giving you a clear illustration of the meaning of the various alignment options. Notice that in each row, the Default setting simply inherits the row's own alignment values, but the other settings override the row's default values.

So far, we've only dealt with text that's been carefully chosen to fit within the cells. But what about situations in which cell contents aren't so cooperative? The figure on the upper right shows how cells expand vertically to handle content that is larger than the original cell size. If you don't want the text to break and make the cell grow vertically, you can use another feature of cell text: the nonbreaking text style. When you select the Nonbreaking checkbox in the Cell tab, the cell grows horizontally to accommodate overflowing text.

The other checkbox after Text style is Header style. To see what it looks like, select the third cell in this task and then repeat the procedure you used for nonbreaking text, except select the Header style checkbox instead.

The results appear in the figure on the bottom right. The two end cells have changed size due to the stretching of the center cell, and the text in the third cell is bold and horizontally centered. Be aware that the longer your text is in the nonbreaking style, the bigger the cell will grow.

TAKE NOTE

▶ BASELINE

The baseline vertical alignment setting is not consistent, but changes with the size and structure of the table. If you want definite consistency, avoid baseline vertical alignment and use the other settings.

▶ LONG WORDS AND IMAGES

Although normal text with average-sized words and spaces between them wraps around, as shown in the figure on the upper right, this wraparound doesn't happen if a single word is longer than the cell is wide. In such cases, because no space occurs in the middle of the word, the cell stretches to accommodate it, just as if you had used the nonbreaking text option. Try typing a long string of letters into a cell without hitting the spacebar to see this effect in action. This is also true with images. If you insert an image into a cell, and the image is larger than the cell, the cell stretches so that the image will fit within it. And the rest of the cells in the table resize themselves accordingly.

▶ FONT SIZE AND CELL HEIGHT

Cells increase their height to accommodate large font sizes. And when one cell in a row increases in height, every cell in the row increases to the same height. You can't override this behavior; if you increase the font size, you increase the cell height, and you increase the row height.

CROSS-REFERENCE
See Chapter 14 for information on inserting images.

FIND IT ONLINE
For a good example of using images in cells, look at
http://www.ssas.com/webstars/01_05_98.html.

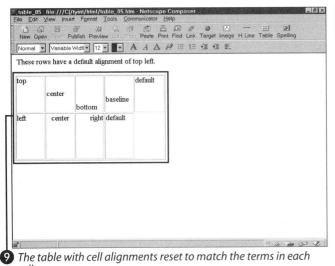

9 The table with cell alignments reset to match the terms in each cell.

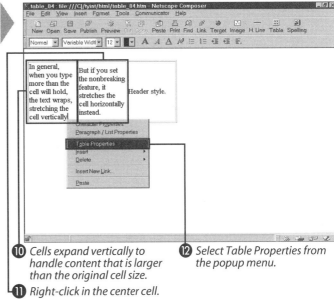

10 Cells expand vertically to handle content that is larger than the original cell size.

11 Right-click in the center cell.

12 Select Table Properties from the popup menu.

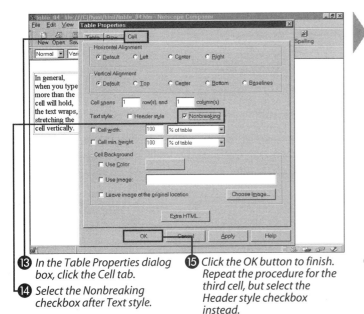

13 In the Table Properties dialog box, click the Cell tab.

14 Select the Nonbreaking checkbox after Text style.

15 Click the OK button to finish. Repeat the procedure for the third cell, but select the Header style checkbox instead.

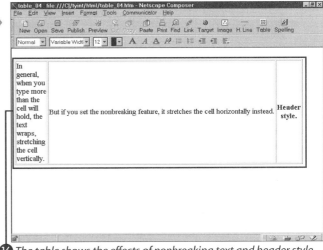

16 The table shows the effects of nonbreaking text and header style text.

Adding Background Color and Images

Tables, like other Web pages, can have background colors and background images. Except for the start, the procedures for adding background colors and images to a table are identical to setting the background options for the page as a whole (see the figure on the upper right).

Adding color and images is an excellent way to spice up a plain-looking table. If you're using a table to create the whole Web page, placing different-colored backgrounds and images in cells is pleasing to the eye and provides an unequalled opportunity to really add visual interest to the page. If you're mixing images and backgrounds, it's a good idea design-wise to select one or two colors from the image and use those (or colors close to them) as the colors for the backgrounds in the other cells.

To set colors and images for your table, use the Table Properties dialog box. You set the backgrounds and images in the Table tab. In either case, you follow the exact same process as for Web pages, clicking a color box or selecting a graphics file. The figure on the lower left shows a table with one of the same background images that we used for a Web page in Chapter 13.

You can also set the same features for individual rows or even just single cells. Just click the appropriate tab in the Table Properties dialog box (the Row tab for rows and the Cell tab for cells) and perform the same operations for the row or cell as you did for the table as a whole.

TAKE NOTE

▶ BACKGROUND COLOR USES

The figure on the lower right shows one use of background color. In it, every other row has been assigned either a green or a white background to simulate a computer printout. Borders and the space between cells have been set to zero, for a seamless simulation of a printout. This shows that you can format text in tables just like in a Web page — in the top row, the text is bold, italic, and underlined (an exception to the no-underlining rule — the text here is obviously for table headings).

▶ A MATTER OF PRECEDENCE

Background images override background colors. Cell backgrounds override row backgrounds, row backgrounds override table backgrounds, and table backgrounds override Web-page backgrounds.

▶ THE TABLEIZE PLUG-IN

One of the Composer plug-ins uses a table background color to emphasize text. If you really want a heading to stand out, highlight it and then select Tools ⇨ Character Tools ⇨ Tableize. The text is placed in a single-cell table, surrounded by its own background color, which is initially dark green. You can change the color in the Table Properties dialog box. Don't bother to do anything special with the text first, because Tableize resets it to normal, unformatted text when it creates the table. After that, you can manipulate the text to suit yourself.

CROSS-REFERENCE

See Chapters 13 and 14 for more information on background colors and images.

FIND IT ONLINE

You can find excellent background textures at http://www.steveconley.com/kaleid1.htm.

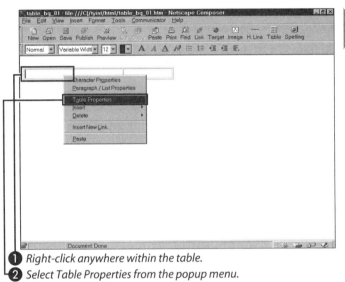

① *Right-click anywhere within the table.*
② *Select Table Properties from the popup menu.*

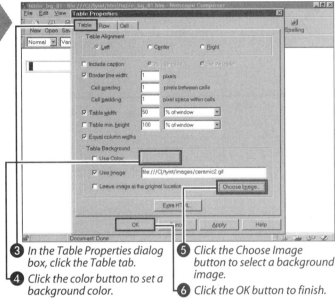

③ *In the Table Properties dialog box, click the Table tab.*
④ *Click the color button to set a background color.*

⑤ *Click the Choose Image button to select a background image.*
⑥ *Click the OK button to finish.*

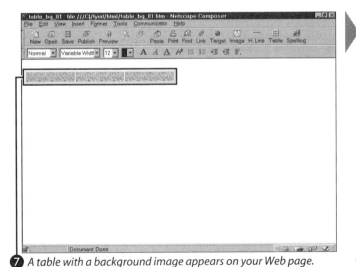

⑦ *A table with a background image appears on your Web page.*

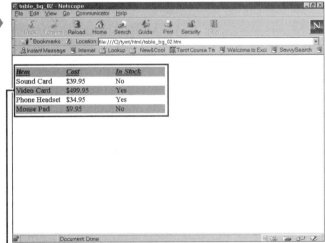

⑧ *A table with background colors in each row.*

Creating Lists

You can use lists, like tables, to present information in a clearly structured and easy-to-understand manner. Bulleted lists set off each item in the list with a symbol. Numbered lists do the same thing with numbers or letters, except that conceptually numbered lists are ordered (meaning the steps happen in a particular sequence). For a word (or phrase) followed by its definition, you can use description lists for a definition-style approach.

You create a bulleted list by putting the cursor where you want the list to go and then clicking on the Bullet List button on the toolbar. The bulleted list is inserted. Because the list doesn't have content yet, it looks like the one in the figure on the upper right, just a lonely dot sitting on the Web page. Entering the items in the list by hitting the Enter key after each item completes the bulleted list entries. Each new line begins with a bullet, as shown in the figure on the lower left.

When you finish the list, you run into a little problem. The only way to create more useable space under the list for putting in other page elements is to hit the Enter key, but hitting the Enter key only creates another line for a bulleted list item. Consequently, you're locked into the list format. To solve this problem, first select the paragraph after the last list item. All you need to do to change it back to normal is to again click the Bullet List button on the toolbar.

Continued

Continued

TAKE NOTE

▶ RESETTING A LIST ITEM

The same technique that you use to end a list is also useful if you want to break up an existing list. Simply place the cursor in any list item you want to change back to normal style, and then click the Bullet List button on the toolbar. That item drops out of the list, becoming just a plain bit of text. The remainder of the list remains unaffected, and the parts above and below that former list item will each comprise a separate list.

▶ OTHER BULLETS

You can use more than just the one default bullet. If you right-click the list and select Paragraph/List Properties from the popup menu, you can choose from a drop-down list called Bullet Style. The options are a solid circle, an open circle, or a solid square for the bullet.

▶ NONTEXTUAL CONTENT

While most of the content of lists is text, you can also use other things such as horizontal rules or even images and tables. The latter two will not line up as neatly as text or lines, because they are higher than a line of text. You can also insert targets in lists. Perhaps the most interesting use of unusual content, though, is links. You can insert a link for each list item to build a quick hyperlink menu.

CROSS-REFERENCE

See Chapter 15 for more information on hyperlink menus.

FIND IT ONLINE

c|net has some good table tips at **http://builder.cnet. com/Authoring/Htmltips/ss02i.html**.

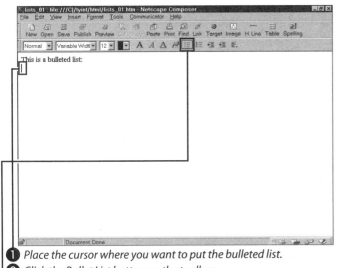

1 *Place the cursor where you want to put the bulleted list.*

2 *Click the Bullet List button on the toolbar.*

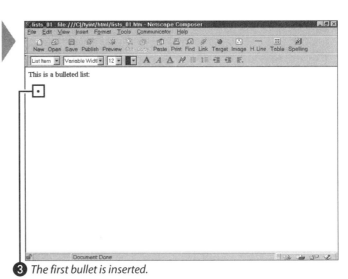

3 *The first bullet is inserted.*

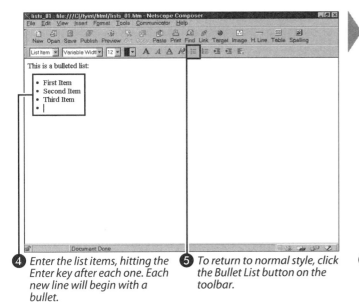

4 *Enter the list items, hitting the Enter key after each one. Each new line will begin with a bullet.*

5 *To return to normal style, click the Bullet List button on the toolbar.*

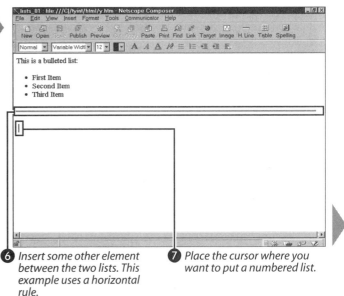

6 *Insert some other element between the two lists. This example uses a horizontal rule.*

7 *Place the cursor where you want to put a numbered list.*

Creating Lists
Continued

To insert a numbered list, you follow the exact same procedure as you did to insert a bulleted list, except that you start off by clicking the Numbered List button on the toolbar, as shown in the figure on the upper left. Remember that numbered lists are best used for material that needs to appear in a certain order, like a list of steps to take to accomplish a task, a "top ten" list, or instructions in a recipe. If you're using a numbered list but find that the items really don't need to appear in that order, you may be better off using a bulleted list instead.

The last kind of list, the description list, is not nearly as common as the other two, but it does bear mentioning. If you're constructing a glossary or dictionary, then you'll want to use the Description List approach. This means that you put in two paragraphs, the first of which is the term being defined (called the *Description Title*), and the second of which is the definition itself (called the *Description Text*). This time, no list button appears on the toolbar, but you use the Paragraph Styles button instead. Place the cursor in the paragraph holding the term, click the Paragraph Styles button and select Desc. Title from the drop-down menu, as shown in the figure on the upper right. For the definition itself, select Desc. Text instead. The results of all these types of lists as viewed in a Web browser are shown in the figure on the lower right.

TAKE NOTE

▶ ENDLESS LISTS

It's no coincidence that a horizontal rule separates the two lists in the figure on the upper left. If you don't put some other element between two lists, then the first list takes on the characteristics of the second one. In other words, if you have a bulleted list, and then immediately put in a numbered list, the bulleted list becomes a numbered list.

▶ NUMBERING SCHEMES

You don't have to settle for 1, 2, 3 as a numbering scheme in your numbered lists. If you right-click the list and select Paragraph/List Properties from the popup menu, you get a drop-down list called Number Style. The options include Roman numerals or alphabetical headings (upper or lower case). You can also choose which number the list starts with (the default is 1). In the case of letters, you'll have to figure out the starting number by counting through the alphabet (the default 1 means A, 2 is B, 3 is C, and so forth). The actual numbers aren't shown in the Composer screen, but are represented by symbols (see the figure on the upper left) like the hash mark for numbers. Roman numerals are represented by "X" for upper case and "x" for lower case; alphabetical headings have "A" for upper case and "a" for lower case. The actual numbers, Roman numerals, or letters are displayed in Navigator. Click the Preview button to view them.

CROSS-REFERENCE

See Chapter 13 for information on horizontal rules.

FIND IT ONLINE

Try the Web Developer's Virtual Library table page at http://WDVL.com/Authoring/HTML/Tables/.

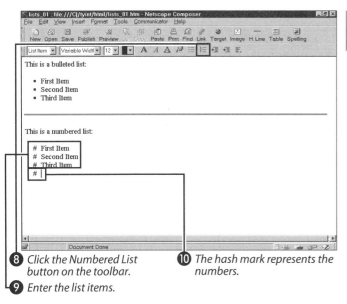

⑧ Click the Numbered List button on the toolbar.

⑨ Enter the list items.

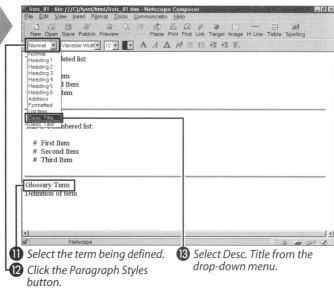

⑩ The hash mark represents the numbers.

⑪ Select the term being defined.

⑫ Click the Paragraph Styles button.

⑬ Select Desc. Title from the drop-down menu.

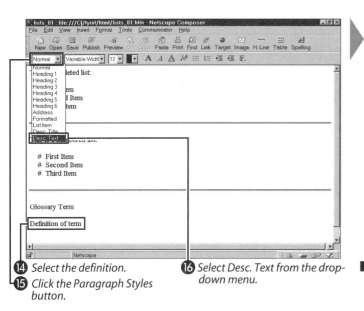

⑭ Select the definition.

⑮ Click the Paragraph Styles button.

⑯ Select Desc. Text from the drop-down menu.

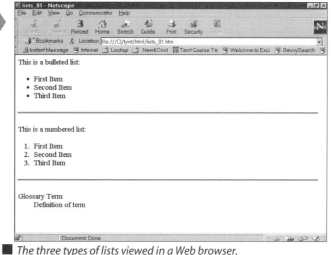

■ The three types of lists viewed in a Web browser.

Personal Workbook

Q&A

1 What is *cell span*?

_____

_____

_____

_____

2 How do you insert a new row?

_____

_____

_____

_____

3 What are the two options in setting cell or table width?

_____

_____

4 What is a *description list* used for?

_____

_____

5 How do table backgrounds differ from Web page backgrounds?

_____

_____

_____

6 How do Web browsers display cells with no content?

_____

_____

7 How many optional bullets exist?

_____

_____

8 What happens when text is larger than the cell that contains it?

_____

_____

_____

_____

ANSWERS: PAGE 386

EXTRA PRACTICE

1 Make a table and then insert and delete rows and cells in it.

2 Try putting one table inside another.

3 Make up some bulleted and numbered lists and then experiment with different bullet and numbering options.

4 Set a background color for a table and then set a background image for a cell within it.

5 Set a background image for a table and then insert an image into one of its cells.

6 Change the cell span for three different cells in a table.

REAL-WORLD APPLICATIONS

✔ You have data in a spreadsheet that you'd like to put in a table on your Web page. See if your spreadsheet supports exporting to HTML format.

✔ You have a table that requires both side and top labels. You might consider using cell spanning to set up top and side cells of different sizes from the rest of the table to accommodate the labels.

✔ You'd like to take advantage of the structure of a table without it being obvious that you're using one. You can achieve this by varying the cell size and setting the border width to zero.

✔ You want to line up dollar amounts, but no decimal alignment exists. Try using right alignment to achieve the same effect.

Visual Quiz

What does this box mean? What goes in it? Where can it be placed?

_____

_____

_____

_____

_____

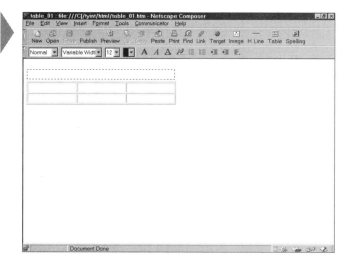

Personal Workbook
Answers

Chapter 1

see page 4

1 **What does *HTML* stand for?**

A: *Hypertext Markup Language.* HTML is itself actually a subset of SGML, the *Standard Generalized Markup Language.*

2 **What is a *home page*?**

A: The page your Web browser starts at. Also, *home page* can mean your own personal Web page, whether it's the one your browser starts at or not.

3 **What are the three kinds of hyperlinks?**

A: Text, image, and image map.

4 **What does *session history* mean?**

A: A list of all the pages you've visited in your current session of Web surfing. In Navigator, this listing disappears every time you shut down the program. In Internet Explorer, the listing is kept for the current session and the past month's sessions.

5 **What does *URL* stand for?**

A: Uniform Resource Locator.

6 **What is the difference between *bookmarks* and *favorites*?**

A: The only difference is the fact that *bookmarks* is the name Netscape gives to sites whose location you've noted and Microsoft calls them *favorites*.

7 **What is a collection of Web pages called?**

A: A *Web site*.

8 **What are the two most popular Web browsers?**

A: Netscape Navigator and Microsoft Internet Explorer.

Visual Quiz

Q: **The item on the right side of the screen is a shameless plug. What is the one on the left side? How do you display it? How do you hide it?**

A: The history list. You display it by clicking the History button in the toolbar. It can be shut down either by clicking the History button again or by clicking the X in the upper right-hand corner of the history list.

Personal Workbook Answers

Chapter 2

see page 22

1 **How do you print a table of a Web page's links in Internet Explorer?**

A: Select the *Print table of links* option in the Print Options dialog box.

2 **How do you get text from a Web page into a word processor?**

A: Copy and paste.

3 **What happens if you save a Web page as plain text?**

A: The Web browser strips out all the HTML coding as it saves the file. This means that, if you open the file as a Web page, it won't display properly.

4 **What is a *frameset*?**

A: The main Web page that acts as the container for frames.

5 **How do you view an image separately from its Web page?**

A: In Navigator, right-click the image and then select View Image from the popup menu. The image will appear all by itself. In Internet Explorer, you first need to right-click the image and then select Properties from the resulting popup menu. Highlight the URL that appears in the Properties dialog box, and then use the Ctrl+C key combination to copy the URL. Close the Properties dialog box and paste the URL into the Address bar near the top of the browser, and then hit the Enter key.

6 **What is *shareware*?**

A: Software you try before you buy. Small software companies often use this technique to market their software, relying on people to register their use of their programs.

7 **Why do you need plug-ins?**

A: To extend the functionality of Web browsers.

8 **What is a *certificate authority*?**

A: Organizations that exist for the sole purpose of verifying the actual identity of people and organizations online. VeriSign is the premier online certificate authority.

Visual Quiz

Q: **What is the dialog box in the figure? How do you call it up? What do the options do? Which ones are necessary for normal usage?**

A: It's the print options dialog box in Internet Explorer. It's called up with the File ➪ Print menu option. In addition to the usual print options, which are all you need for normal usage, it has special options for printing framed pages and linked pages.

Chapter 3

see page 44

1 **What is a *spider*?**

A: A program that searches the Web.

2 **What is a *Web index*?**

A: A Web site that categorizes other Web pages and offers links to them — as opposed to a pure *search engine*, which adds every term on the page to its database.

3 **How do you find a term on a Web page you're viewing?**

A: By using the local find command in your Web browser. In Internet Explorer, select Edit ➪ Find (on this page) from the menu. In Navigator, choose Edit ➪ Find in page. In both browsers, you can use the Ctrl+F key combination instead. This brings up the Find dialog box, which is identical in both browsers, except that

PERSONAL WORKBOOK ANSWERS

Internet Explorer has one more checkbox option — *Match whole word only*. Type your search terms (called *keywords*) in the box labeled *Find what*.

④ What is a *keyword*?

A: A single search term used in a search engine or the local Find command.

⑤ What is the difference between the Search buttons in Navigator and Internet Explorer?

A: In Navigator, the Search button has a picture of a flash-light on it; in Internet Explorer, it has a picture of a mag-nifying glass over a globe.

⑥ Who was George Boole?

A: A 19th-century British mathematician.

⑦ What are the three Boolean operators?

A: AND, OR, and NOT.

⑧ What does "Yahoo" stand for?

A: Yet Another Hierarchical Officious Oracle.

Visual Quiz

Q: How would you get a Web page that looked exactly like this one?

A: Click the Search button in Netscape Navigator and select AltaVista as your search engine on the Net Search page.

Chapter 4

see page 58

① What is a *hover color*?

A: A Microsoft Internet Explorer–specific setting that changes the color of a link when your mouse pointer is over it.

② Why should you refrain from using custom colors?

A: They don't necessarily show up well in other people's Web browsers. The proper display of custom colors depends upon a high-end graphics card.

③ What are *dynamic fonts*?

A: Fonts that are downloaded at the time you view a Web page so you can see it the way its designers intended.

④ How do you speed up download time?

A: By setting your Web browser to not download image files. You can also elect to disable Java and JavaScript, as well as cutting out all multimedia files.

⑤ How do you add a custom link button?

A: In Navigator, point at a link on a Web page, press the left mouse button and, without releasing it, drag the pointer to the Personal Toolbar. Then release the mouse button and you've got a new toolbar button. If you want to add a button linked to the currently displayed page, just do the same procedure, but drag the Location icon to the toolbar instead.
In Internet Explorer, click a link from a Web page and drag it to the Links bar, and then drop it there. To add the currently displayed page to the Links bar, drag the Explorer icon from the Address bar.
With either browser, the result is a customized entry in the appropriate toolbar.

⑥ How do you move a toolbar?

A: In either Navigator or Internet Explorer, just drag the toolbars into the position you want them and drop them there. The other toolbars move out of the way to make room for them, dropping down if you're moving a toolbar up or moving up if you're moving a toolbar down. You can also put two toolbars on the exact same level, although some of the buttons may be invisible in such a case.

7 **What is a secure Web site?**

A: A remote computer that exchanges information with your Web browser that is encrypted so it can't be read in transit by third parties. Secure servers are commonly used for purposes of Internet commerce, and are largely found at commercial Web sites.

8 **Why do browsers use disk caches?**

A: So they don't have to reload every page every time you visit it. Caches actually include all sorts of files you have accessed, such as image files.

Visual Quiz

Q: **What is this? How do you get to it? What do you do there?**

A: It's the Netscape Navigator Bookmarks editing screen. Click the Bookmark icon and then select Edit Bookmarks from the popup menu to get there. You can delete bookmarks at this window, including those for custom toolbar icons.

Chapter 5

see page 90

1 **What is the @ symbol in an e-mail address?**

A: A symbol meaning "at." Thus, yourname@yourisp.com tells someone who you are and where you can be found online.

2 **What is the difference between a *client* and a *server*?**

A: *Clients* ask for the service and *servers* provide it.

3 **What is one way to send e-mail to more than one person?**

A: Distribution lists, carbon copy, or blind carbon copy.

4 **What does *bcc* stand for?**

A: Blind carbon copy.

5 **When should you use your spelling checker?**

A: In formal contexts such as business communications. The basic rule here is, if the message is important, take the time to run the spelling checker.

6 **What is *netiquette*?**

A: Internet etiquette, the evolving set of customs for getting along on the Internet. No official set of rules define what netiquette is, but its essence is that, if you wouldn't like it done to you, don't do it to someone else.

7 **What is an *emoticon*?**

A: An icon to show emotion in e-mail, newsgroups, and chat rooms. The most common emoticon is the smiley face, used to denote a grin. :-)

8 **What does *SMTP* mean?**

A: Simple Mail Transfer Protocol.

Visual Quiz

Q: **What does this checkmark next to a person's name tell you about the message?**

A: That it has already been read.

Chapter 6

see page 124

1 **What kind of files can be attached to an e-mail message?**

A: Any kind.

2 **What is *sig* short for?**

A: Signature file.

3 **How long should a sig be?**

A: About four to seven lines.

Personal Workbook Answers

4 **How do you put an e-mail address from an address book into a message?**

A: Double-click the name in the address book.

5 **Who needs to know the password for an encrypted message?**

A: The sender and recipient.

6 **What are *filtering rules*?**

A: Rules that govern the treatment of incoming e-mail messages.

7 **Where do deleted messages go?**

A: Into a special folder called the Deleted Messages folder.

8 **What is a *mailing list*?**

A: E-mail addresses for groups of people who share common interests. Subscribers send messages to a common address where the mailing list software automatically relays a copy of each message to every subscriber. Replies to the messages go to either the whole list or the sender of the message, depending on settings.

Visual Quiz

Q: **What do these two buttons do? What is the difference between them?**

A: They're both Print buttons, and they both do the same thing.

Chapter 7

see page 156

1 **How is the Usenet newsgroup system organized?**

A: Into categories and subcategories that help describe their content and purpose. For instance, computer science issues are discussed under the comp.sci hierarchy of newsgroups.

2 **What is a *news server*?**

A: The computer and/or program that provides newsgroups.

3 **What is a *news reader*?**

A: The program that receives newsgroups from the news server.

4 **What does *alt* mean?**

A: Anarchists, Lunatics, and Terrorists.

5 **What is a *FAQ*?**

A: A list of *Frequently Asked Questions*. FAQs are often provided for newsgroups, mailing lists, or any other type of group.

6 **Name one of the newsgroups for newbies.**

A: Newbie newsgroups include alt.newbie, alt.newbies, news.announce.newusers, and news.newusers.questions.

7 **What is a *message header*?**

A: Basic information such as the title and size of a message, identity of the sender, and the message date and time.

8 **How do you go online?**

A: Click the Online button.

Visual Quiz

Q: **What does this symbol mean?**

A: That the message has been read.

Personal Workbook Answers

Chapter 8

see page 168

❶ What does *IRC* stand for?

A: Internet Relay Chat.

❷ What is a *chat server*?

A: The computer and/or program that provides chat services.

❸ How do you add new chat servers?

A: Type in a new server in the Chat Connection dialog box. The addresses of other chat servers are available from a number of sources.

❹ What is a *host*?

A: The leader of a chat room.

❺ What is a *chat log*? How do you create one?

A: A *chat log* is the ability to save a chat to disk line by line as it progresses. The save feature in Microsoft Chat only saves what has already been said. If you want to save more of the conversation later, you'll have to repeat the save operation.

❻ How many basic characters come with Microsoft Chat? How many backgrounds?

A: Twelve characters, three backgrounds.

❼ What is the difference between *kicking* and *banning*?

A: A person who is *kicked* (temporarily kicked out) can return to the chat room at another time. Someone who is *banned* cannot return to the chat room.

❽ How do you create a new chat room?

A: Use the Create Room button; click the Enter Room button and enter a room name that doesn't exist; or create a chat room when you first log on to the chat server, and specify the name of a nonexistent chat room in the Connect dialog box when it asks you which one you want to enter.

Visual Quiz

Q: What is this character's name? How do you find out?

A: The name is Xeno. You find out by clicking the character names on the Character tab in either the Chat Connection or Microsoft Chat Options dialog boxes.

Chapter 9

see page 188

❶ What is the difference between an ordinary Internet site and an online community?

A: If a site is designed to foster a feeling of belonging, rather than just visiting — a home on the vast network of networks — then it succeeds as a community.

❷ What is one advantage of free e-mail, other than the cost?

A: Other than the fact that you don't have to pay for it, having an e-mail address at an online community offers you a high degree of stability. If you move, change jobs, leave school, change your Internet Service Provider, or do anything else that otherwise might affect your e-mail address, your address at the online community still remains the same and you won't miss out on any mail.

❸ Name two online communities.

A: America Online, CompuServe, Parent Soup, Tripod, GeoCities.

❹ What is an *online neighborhood*?

A: A segment of an online community with shared interests.

Personal Workbook Answers

⑤ How do online communities support themselves financially?

A: Usually through advertising.

⑥ What is the structure of a GeoCities Web page address?

A: The URL of a GeoCities home page is composed of the GeoCities main URL plus the neighborhood you choose, plus the area within the neighborhood, plus the "house number" you select within the area.

⑦ What type of e-mail servers does GeoCities use?

A: POP and SMTP.

⑧ Can you use Microsoft Chat in GeoCities chat rooms?

A: No.

Visual Quiz

Q: What do these choices mean? What other Web page are they duplicated on?

A: They tell File Manager which files in your directory to list. The options are exactly duplicated in the GeoCities File Manager itself.

Chapter 10

see page 206

① What are the three items of special equipment you need for Internet telephony?

A: A sound card, a microphone, and speakers.

② In what way can two of the three Internet telephony items be combined?

A: In a telephony headset.

③ What is the minimum modem speed required by FreeTel?

A: At least 14.4 Kbps.

④ What are the two ways to find names in the directory?

A: Scrolling or searching.

⑤ What does the Intro do?

A: It tells the person you're calling something about yourself.

⑥ How do you set the Intro to remain for multiple calls?

A: Check the *Keep intro* checkbox.

⑦ How do you adjust the microphone and speaker settings?

A: On the left side of your screen are some special controls. Adjust the microphone volume with the lowest slider in the top panel. Adjust the VOX setting with the top slider in the top panel. Adjust the speaker volume down with the top control in the bottom panel.

⑧ How do you call an unlisted FreeTel user?

A: You have to know the person's name. Type the name that he or she uses into the edit box on the left side of the screen and click the Dial button.

Visual Quiz

Q: What is different about this screen compared to the normal one? What button did you push to get here?

A: The screen is in testing mode — a new button labeled Talk appears above the directory window and, farther to the right, you'll see the words Full Duplex (or Half Duplex, depending on your sound card). Lastly, the word Testing appears at the extreme right. You clicked the TestMic button to get here.

PERSONAL WORKBOOK ANSWERS

Chapter 11

see page 224

1 What are your three basic options when creating a new page?

A: The New Page command, templates, or the Page Wizard.

2 What is a *template*?

A: A file that holds basic Web page structure over which you type specific information.

3 Why shouldn't you save a page created with the Page Wizard from Navigator?

A: Because Navigator won't save the associated files.

4 What does *FTP* stand for?

A: File Transfer Protocol.

5 What is the advantage of using Notepad for your HTML editor?

A: It saves unformatted files.

6 What does *publishing* mean in Composer?

A: Uploading your Web pages and associated files to your Web server.

7 What icon does a Web page use for a missing image file?

A: An image with a folded corner and a question mark in the center.

8 Do you have to use an image editor with Composer?

A: No.

Visual Quiz

Q: How do you get to this dialog box? What are your two main options from here?

A: You click the New button and then, in the New Page dialog box, you click the From Template button. From here, you can click the Choose File button to get a local template or click the Netscape Templates button to go online and get your choice of prepared templates.

Chapter 12

see page 254

1 How do you print HTML source code?

A: Select Edit ⇨ HTML Source from the menu. This launches your HTML editor with the HTML source code for the Web page already loaded. To print the file, just select File ⇨ Print from the editor's menu. You first have to chose an HTML editor to use this function.

2 What is *metadata*?

A: Data that doesn't show up on the visible Web page.

3 What's the best way to get document information in Composer?

A: With the Document Info plug-in.

4 How do you access plug-ins in Composer?

A: Via the Tools menu.

5 What Composer bug causes a Web search?

A: Using Composer to view the page source and hitting the Ctrl+P key combination. This mounts a Web search using the Excite search engine.

6 What are *keywords* used for?

A: To describe your pages' content so Web search programs used by Web search engines can properly index your Web site.

Personal Workbook Answers

7 **How do you enter terms in your personal dictionary?**

A: Either click the Learn button during a spelling check or click the Edit Dictionary button and manually add to it by typing new terms in the New Word box and then clicking the Add button.

8 **What is the source for a frame composed of?**

A: A Web page.

Visual Quiz

Q: What is this screen? How do you get there? What are your options?

A: It's the personal dictionary for the spell checker. You get there by clicking the Edit Dictionary button. You can manually add terms to it, replace terms in it, or delete terms from it.

Chapter 13

see page 270

1 **Why does the left-align button exist?**

A: To realign paragraphs that are either centered or right-aligned.

2 **What three font faces are common to most computers?**

A: Times New Roman, Arial, and Courier New on PCs; Times Roman, Helvetica, and Courier on Macintosh computers.

3 **How do you make a default setting for Web page colors and background images?**

A: Change the color settings for text and for hypertext links or the background color and background images in the Page Properties dialog box. To make the color choices the default for any future Web page you create

in Composer, click the checkbox labeled *Save these settings for new pages*.

4 **What is the difference between a *horizontal line* and a *horizontal rule*?**

A: None. It's just a matter of phrasing. Composer has a Horizontal Line button, but the HTML source code that it generates uses the HR element.

5 **What is a *character code*?**

A: The assignment of a number for the referencing of special characters.

6 **What is a *character entity reference*?**

A: The assignment of natural language codes for special characters.

7 **What HTML element is used for indenting?**

A: The BLOCKQUOTE element.

8 **Why is the underlining of text frowned upon?**

A: Because it makes the text look like a hyperlink.

Visual Quiz

Q: What is this menu? What would this particular menu choice do to the selected text?

A: It's the Paragraph Styles drop-down menu. It makes the text italic and sets it off from surrounding text by adding a space between it and the preceding lines.

Chapter 14

see page 298

1 **What was the original meaning of *clip art*?**

A: Drawings cut from prepared art books.

384

Personal Workbook Answers

② **What does *JPEG* stand for? Why is it sometimes called *JPG*?**

A: *Joint Photographic Experts Group.* JPEG is often abbreviated to JPG because of the old Windows 3.*x* and DOS three-character limit on file extensions.

③ **Does a JPEG file have the property of transparency?**

A: No.

④ **What is a *Web ring*?**

A: A group of Web sites that deal with a common topic and are connected together. Web rings tie sites together using previous, next, and random jumps.

⑤ **What is a major difference between the GIF87 and GIF89 formats?**

A: Transparency or animation.

⑥ **What happens to the file size of an image when you resize the image in Composer?**

A: Nothing.

⑦ **What is *alternate text*?**

A: Text that appears on a Web page in place of an image while the image is being loaded.

⑧ **What determines the color of a border in HTML?**

A: The text color.

Visual Quiz

Q: **What is this button for? How is it different from the one to its right? How do you get to this dialog box?**

A: It aligns text next to an image exactly between the top and bottom of it. The other button still centers the text, but the descenders drop below the line. You get here by right-clicking the image and selecting Image Properties from the popup menu.

Chapter 15

see page 332

① **What is the difference between a *relative URL* and an *absolute URL*?**

A: A relative URL doesn't have the address of the Web site prefixed to it. An absolute URL includes everything necessary to find the Web address from anywhere.

② **What does the *href* attribute do?**

A: Gives the Web address for a link.

③ **What kind of links does drag and drop work for?**

A: Text links.

④ **What methods does Composer provide for modifying the words in text links?**

A: None.

⑤ **What are the three methods for removing links?**

A: Right-click a text link and then select the Remove Link menu option. Alternatively, use the Remove Link button in the Link dialog box, or select Edit ➪ Remove Link from the main menu. Only the Remove Link menu option alerts you to the fact that all links will be removed.

⑥ **What is a *fragment URL*?**

A: Also known as a *target*, it's an address within a Web page appended to the URL of that page. Targets on local Web pages can be referenced alone by relative URLs, but remote Web pages not on the current site need to be referenced with an absolute URL.

⑦ **What HTML element do links and targets both use?**

A: The A (anchor) element.

PERSONAL WORKBOOK ANSWERS

⑧ How does the Table of Contents plug-in set up a link menu?

A: By putting targets before each of the headings in a Web document, and then creating a set of links that point to those targets.

Visual Quiz

Q: What is this dialog box? How do you get to it? Why is the link text already filled in? What is special about the Remove Link button?

A: It's the Link Properties dialog box. You get there by right-clicking a text link, and then selecting Link Properties from the popup menu. The text is already filled in because this is an existing text link. The reason it's special is because if you select text that has more than one link in it and then tell Composer to remove the link, it's the only link removal option that asks you which one you want to remove.

Chapter 16

see page 354

❶ What is *cell span*?

A: The ability of a cell to cover more than one column or row. Cell span is commonly used to either create special headings in a table or for Web page design purposes that don't include borders on the table.

❷ How do you insert a new row?

A: Place the cursor in the row before the one you want to add, and then right-click it and select Insert ⇨ Row from the popup menu. The new row is added instantly.

❸ What are the two options in setting cell or table width?

A: Percentage of the containing object or absolute pixel measure.

④ What is a *description list* used for?

A: Dictionary-style definitions.

⑤ How do table backgrounds differ from Web page backgrounds?

A: Other than appearing in a table, there is no difference.

⑥ How do Web browsers display cells with no content?

A: They don't.

⑦ How many optional bullets exist?

A: Three.

⑧ What happens when text is larger than the cell that contains it?

A: The cell expands vertically to accommodate the text unless the nonbreaking text option is used, in which case the cell expands horizontally to accommodate the text.

Visual Quiz

Q: What does this mean? What goes in it? Where can it be placed?

A: It defines the caption area for a table. The text for a caption goes in it, and it can be placed either above or below a table.

Index

Symbols & Numbers

A

Index

Index

Index

INDEX

G

H

Index

Index

INDEX

Index

Continued

Index

Index

Index

Y

Z

my2cents.idgbooks.com

Register This Book — And Win!

Visit **http://my2cents.idgbooks.com** to register this book and we'll automatically enter you in our fantastic monthly prize giveaway. It's also your opportunity to give us feedback: let us know what you thought of this book and how you would like to see other topics covered.

Discover IDG Books Online!

The IDG Books Online Web site is your online resource for tackling technology — at home and at the office. Frequently updated, the IDG Books Online Web site features exclusive software, insider information, online books, and live events!

10 Productive & Career-Enhancing Things You Can Do at www.idgbooks.com

- Nab source code for your own programming projects.

- Download software.

- Read Web exclusives: special articles and book excerpts by IDG Books Worldwide authors.

- Take advantage of resources to help you advance your career as a Novell or Microsoft professional.

- Buy IDG Books Worldwide titles or find a convenient bookstore that carries them.

- Register your book and win a prize.

- Chat live online with authors.

- Sign up for regular e-mail updates about our latest books.

- Suggest a book you'd like to read or write.

- Give us your 2¢ about our books and about our Web site.

You say you're not on the Web yet? It's easy to get started with IDG Books' *Discover the Internet,* available at local retailers everywhere.